# Wild Women in the Whirlwind

**edited by**
**Joanne M. Braxton and**
**Andrée Nicola McLaughlin**

# Wild Women in the Whirlwind
## Afra-American Culture and the Contemporary Literary Renaissance

**RUTGERS UNIVERSITY PRESS**
New Brunswick, New Jersey

Second paperback printing, December 1990

Frontispiece: Joanne Battiste, *Ain't I a Woman?* (1989). Reproduced courtesy of the artist.

*Joanne M. Braxton and Andrée Nicola McLaughlin gratefully acknowledge permission to reprint from the following:*

Gwendolyn Brooks for excerpts from "Second Sermon on the Warpland," in *Blacks* (Chicago: The David Company, 1987).

South End Press and the *Massachusetts Review* for "The Difficult Miracle of Black Poetry in America or Something Like a Sonnet for Phillis Wheatley" by June Jordan. This piece, part of the collection *On Call: Political Essays* (Boston: South End, 1985), was also published in the *Massachusetts Review* 27, no. 2 (Summer 1986).

Temple University Press for "A Poet's Retreat: The Diaries of Charlotte Forten Grimké (1837–1914)" by Joanne M. Braxton from her *Black Women Writing Autobiography: A Tradition Within a Tradition* (Philadelphia: Temple University Press, 1989).

Rutgers, The State University for "'Up the Country . . .' and Still Singing the Blues: Sippie Wallace" by Daphne Duval Harrison from her *Black Pearls: Blues Queens of the 1920s* (New Brunswick, N.J.: Rutgers University Press, 1988).

Indiana State University for "The Sexual Mountain and Black Women Writers" by Calvin Hernton, *Black Literature Forum* 18, no. 4 (Winter 1984).

*Massachusetts Review* for excerpts from "Harriet Jacobs: Incidents in the Life of a Slave Girl" by Joanne M. Braxton, *Massachusetts Review* 27, no. 2 (Summer 1986).

Harcourt Brace Jovanovich for the quotation from *Horses Make the Landscape More Beautiful,* by Alice Walker (1984).

*Phylon—The Atlanta University Review of Race and Culture* for "African Tradition in Toni Morrison's *Sula*" by Vashti Crutcher Lewis, *Phylon* 48, no. 1 (March 1987).

Toni Cade Bambara and Sonia Sanchez for "Voices Beyond the Veil: An Interview of Toni Cade Bambara and Sonia Sanchez" by Zala Chandler.

Audre Lorde for interviews and poems and Garth St. Omer for interviews in "Audre Lorde and Matrilineal Diaspora: 'moving history beyond nightmare into structures for the future . . .'" by Chinosole.

Library of Congress Cataloging-in-Publication Data

Wild women in the whirlwind: Afra-American culture & the contemporary
literary renaissance / Joanne M. Braxton and Andrée Nicola McLaughlin.
    p.  cm.
    Bibliography: p.
    Includes index.
    ISBN 0-8135-1441-X (cloth)   ISBN 0-8135-1442-8 (pbk.)
    1. American literature—Afro-American authors—History and
criticism.   2. American literature—Women authors—History and
criticism.   3. American literature—20th century—History and
criticism.   4. Afro-American women—Intellectual life.   5. Women and
literature—United States.   6. Afro-American women in literature.
I. Braxton, Joanne M.   II. McLaughlin, Andrée Nicola, 1948–
PS153.N5W47   1989                      89-30380
810.'.9'9287—dc19                         CIP

For my mother, Mary Ellen Weems Braxton, and for the memory of my father, Harry McHenry Braxton, Sr.

Joanne M. Braxton

For the memory of my parents, Willie Mae Newman McLaughlin and Joseph Lee McLaughlin.

Also for the community of Winbrook Apartments (the projects), The Hill, and The Valley in White Plains, New York, which nurtured me from birth to womanhood.

Andrée Nicola McLaughlin

# Contents

**Part III**  ***Visions and Re-visions***

# Audre Lorde

## Foreword

It's not that we haven't always been here, since there was a here. It is that the letters of our names have been scrambled when they were not totally erased, and our fingerprints upon the handles of history have been called the random brushings of birds.

An academic at Tuskegee discovers twenty-five to thirty Black writers from the American South who have never been mentioned in any bibliography. Most of these unheard artists are women. Black. Invisible words.

So often we have printed our visions upon our children, our nieces and our nephews. Maybelle's young'uns from down the street after supper who drank lemonade and listened to our stories as the fireflies reported in corners of the wooden rockered porches. The kerosene lamps. The later conversations after they were in bed which were not whispered on purpose because we knew what youngsters hear when they think we do not intend them to hear always stays longer in their imaginations.

But our words have been there. And they have been, in Cheryl Clarke's words, "a necessary bread." That bread has been too often uneaten because it came cloaked in other people's prejudgments— that nothing we said or did had any resonance at all. But Black women have survived. And our words have survived. So that the children of those Black women who never drank peaceful lemonade, or lay at night protected, were wide open to the sound of crickets embroidering the story of how Maybelle's sister's second girl Leota— you couldn't do nothing with her but she sure had spunk—came down from college after Christmas and next thing you know she had Dee-Dee's three youngest lined up on the sofa jumping up and down, giving them each quarters to yell "Down with capitalism!" So that those children will also have access to varied pieces of their Black woman's weaponry.

And the children of the children who never saw a firefly nor dreamed a moon, or who cowered in earth dugouts in the outback bush while their mothers tried to lead the government agents away from kidnapping them to servant school, those daughters of Black women who grew up in the Magnolia Projects and Algiers Green to the sound of grinding gears and elevated trains and the siren screams at midnight sometimes human sometimes not and whose lives, laced with roaches, were bruised and seeking. These daughters' daughters did survive, and how is our blessing, our vision, and our world. Black women's words are testament that we were there, bridges through one another's realities, tough and tender. Intricate and nourishing. And no matter where we find ourselves to be, we can plot each other's words like roadmaps toward a future.

The first Black woman to command a spaceship, or head the United Nations, needs to know that in 1955 a Black woman named Rosa Parks refused to give up her seat in a bus in Montgomery, Alabama, and sparked what is known as the Civil Rights Movement. She also needs to know that 101 years before, in 1854, a Black woman named Elizabeth Jennings had also refused to give up her front seat in a trolley in New York City and began a trial that resulted in the desegregation of all public transportation in New York City. She also needs to know that was the same year that Charlotte Forten, young and Black in Massachusetts, wrote in her diary, "I wonder that every colored person is not a misanthrope," and "I am hated and oppressed because God gave me a *dark skin.*" In their struggles and their achievements, Black women who follow us need to know that other Black women have fought and survived the same Black woman-hatred, and that we wished to share, with passion and with beauty, the questions as well as the strengths that we learned throughout those struggles. And not all our songs are mourning.

Just as I, a young Black woman writer in the 1950s, needed to know (and unfortunately did not) that Angelina Weld Grimké existed, and that she was not only a Black woman playwright and poet but also a woman who loved women, so also even now there is growing a group of Black women writers who need to know that, among other possibilities, it is possible to be a Black lesbian feminist literary critic like Barbara Smith and "live to tell the story." And they will know because books like this one exist, providing a spectrum of Black women's words and lives.

It is so important that *Wild Women in the Whirlwind* is edited by Black women, literary women who share our legacies of power and fight. For most of all, Black women who are our inheritors will need to know why so many of these facts about their Black woman's history have been so hard to come by. They will need to know that hatred destroys by silence, by trivialization, by the pretense that nothing we have to say is worth anything simply because we are saying it. And of course there is the other side of that erasure so cleverly practiced against Black women and our words by all those establishments that presume hierarchy over us: the arrogant assumption that anyone else knows better than we do which of our words should survive.

This book stands as a bulwark against those fallacies.

# Acknowledgments

Many people contributed to the birth of *Wild Women in the Whirlwind*. Elaine Showalter was a source of inspiration at the 1984 NEH Summer Seminar in Women's Literature and Culture at Rutgers University, where Andrée Nicola McLaughlin and I met; during that summer, the idea for what would become *Wild Women* was born. Leslie Mitchner, our editor at Rutgers University Press, has worked patiently over a period of five years to help bring this work to fruition.

I am indebted to my co-editor and the other contributors and to Hazel Carby, Paula Giddings, Gloria Hull, Gerda Lerner, and Peggy McIntosh for their intellectual stimulation and moral support. Temple University Press was gracious enough to permit me to reprint "A Poet's Retreat: The Diaries of Charlotte Forten Grimké" from *Black Women Writing Autobiography: A Tradition Within a Tradition*. Among my colleagues at the College of William and Mary, I would like to thank Meryl Altman, Susan Donaldson, Ann Reed, and members of the faculty women's studies seminar for their timely input and Bonnie Chandler and William Smyth for their help with manuscript preparation.

No words can adequately express my appreciation to Julia Brazelton, my friend, colleague, and my first-line of defense; to my mother, Mary Ellen Weems Braxton; or to my constant companion and protector, Ling Kor's Little Kiwi. Each has sustained, strengthened, and nurtured me in ways that have contributed directly to my ability to complete this book.

J.M.B.

This book is the product of many people's efforts. Thanks are due to Abdus-Saboor ibn Yusif and Jo-Ann Makeda McLaughlin, my brother and sister, who lent assistance in all ways possible; to Gloria I. Joseph and Acklyn R. Lynch, mentors who have most inspired and directed my intellectual inquiries in human cultures, women's studies, and the arts for nearly two decades; to Celia Alvarez, Carolyn Carelock, Zala Chandler, Don Quinn Kelley, and Bob Moore, my friends, comrades, and colleagues who provided critical input, editorial assistance, and personal support from the inception of this project to its completion; to Chris Bernier and Gail Lewis of London, Gwyned Simpson of New York City, and Rudo Gaidzanwa at the

University of Zimbabwe whose insightful comments on reading sections of *Wild Women in the Whirlwind* in manuscript served to improve it; also to Faith Childs who generously gave professional advice.

And I owe much gratitude to the indomitable international network of Black women activists, theorists, and artists with whom there were discussions germane to my research for the book: In Aboriginal Island (Australia), Uma; in Angola, Filomena Amador Da Silva Rocha; in Aotearoa (New Zealand), Sue Culling, Titewhai Harawira, Marie Laufiso, and Nerissa TePatu; in Brazil, Sueli Carneiro; in Canada, Beryle M. Jones, Makeda Silvera, and Esmeralda Thornhill; in Colombia, Berta Ines Perea Diaz; in Great Britain, Rosieta Burton, Vashti Penny Cunin, Noreen Howard, Liliane Landor, Rose-Marie McDonald, Heidi Mirza, Chenzira J. Mutasa, Jasminder Kaur Parmar, Nazreen Subhan, and Lindewe Tsele; in Surinam, Cornelly Fitzjames and Nadia Raveles; in Uganda, Maxine Ankrah; in the United States, Iona Anderson, Toni Cade Bambara, Safiya Bandele, Johnnetta B. Cole, Diadre, Maua Flowers, Lourdes Garcia, Miriam Jimenez-Roman, Shelby Lewis, Audre Lorde, Charshee McIntyre, Rosemari Mealy, Vicki Meminger, Imani Rashid, Gwendolyn Rogers, Loretta Ross, Maya Sharpe, Barbara Smith, Nkenge Toure, Sandy Watson, and Dessima Williams; in Venezuela, Irene Ugueto; in West Germany, Katharina Oguntoye; and in Zimbabwe, Sekai Holland.

Thanks also to scholars Delridge Hunter, Roberto Marquez, James Turner, and Preston Wilcox in the United States for directing me to or sharing relevant print resources, and to Jagdesh Gundara of the University of London Institute of Education, Centre for Multicultural Education, for providing occasion and facilities for my cross-cultural studies. In addition, I wish to acknowledge Elaine Showalter at Princeton University and faculty participants in her 1984 "Women's Writing and Women's Culture" seminar for their early encouragement, and Mason Cooley at City University of New York and faculty participants in his 1987–88 "Writing Workshop" as well as my colleagues in the Humanities Division at Medgar Evers College, especially Steve Cannon and Phyllis Jackson, for their technical advice.

On behalf of both co-editors, I extend expressions of appreciation to Linda Yaa Asantewa Johnson, Marilyn Nance, Paula Vogel, and Clara Williams for helping to identify appropriate photos or the photographers of the same for use herein, and to photographer Dawoud

Bey for his professional services. A special thanks goes to Keisha Watson, my research assistant and a budding "wild woman" in her own right, and to the McLaughlin-Mayo-Wimbush and Shipman-Newman-Creech clans who have been there when it counts. Finally, much appreciation is due to Rutgers University Press director Kenneth Arnold for his initial receptiveness to the concept of a work treating contemporary Black women's literary renaissance; to senior editor Leslie Mitchner for her standing commitment to the publication of *Wild Women in the Whirlwind*; and to my co-editor Joanne M. Braxton for sharing this experience.

A. N. McL.

# Wild Women in the Whirlwind

# Joanne M. Braxton

# Afra-American Culture and the Contemporary Literary Renaissance

As a poet and a scholar, I feel fortunate to have witnessed the literary rebirth of black women writers during the last twenty years and to have been a part of that coming of age in some small way; it has been a wonderful time of opportunity, a great time to be a Black woman. It is no small thing to come of age with a renaissance, to mature with the consummate flowering of a long and vital continuum. I was nineteen years old when I met June Jordan and Alice Walker in my days as a student poet at Sarah Lawrence College. I profited from Jordan's weekly critiques of my work and the lessons she taught me about "the responsibility that love implies." Walker, who had just published her volume *Once,* and who was a recent alumna of our institution, commanded the respect and loyal admiration of all the Black women students; I was thrilled when she returned my correspondence, writing of the forsythia that bloomed in her yard in Jackson, Mississippi, while snow still covered the ground in Bronxville. She was gracious and generous and kind, even though (as she told me later) she was somewhat intimidated by my "militant" exterior. I remember that Alice's daughter Rebecca, who was then a small (but articulate) child, slept in my arms while her mother gave the convocation address to my senior class, the class of '72. Imagine what teaching this address (available in Walker's *In Search of Our Mothers' Gardens*) does for me now! And I was not alone, for the things I feel I share with other sister souls of that time and place. We, collectively, were on the verge of something. We could not see the immensity of the thing before us, but we could feel it, and we knew it was there, as surely as we knew our own names.

Today, it would seem, Black women writers have arrived. But it would be a grave mistake to read the works of an Alice Walker, a June Jordan, a Toni Morrison, a Gayl Jones, or a Toni Cade Bambara in isolation and out of context without considering the road they have taken, for, as I have argued elsewhere, Black women writers are grounded in a chosen kinship with their literary antecedents, stretching back through the Black Arts Movement of the 1960s to the so-called Harlem Renaissance and back even further to the novelists, poets, and slave narrators of the eighteenth and nineteenth centuries.[1] This flowering has its roots in the struggle for freedom, literacy, and equality as well as the Black woman's struggle for self-definition and personal respect.

The current rebirth is the most extensive written exploration of that realm of shared language, reference, and allusion within the Veil of our Blackness and our femaleness, and yet, even before the foremothers of today's writers gave conscious written form to their artistic expression, they had established their oral traditions in the Americas through material and verbal lore. By passing along cherished recipes to subsequent generations, by testifyin', by telling the story of their religious conversions, or by singing the spirituals or the blues, Black women helped to revise and extend this oral tradition. Denied access to literacy, these creative foremothers nevertheless maintained an underground railway for the survival of the spirit. Parallel to this unwritten tradition ran the eighteenth and nineteenth century written tradition of Lucy Terry, Phillis Wheatley, Harriet E. Wilson, Harriet A. Jacobs, Frances Ellen Watkins Harper, and many others. Black women of letters like Zora Neale Hurston, Jessie Fauset, Nella Larsen, and Georgia Douglas Johnson later emerged as some of the principals in the Harlem Renaissance and other literary movements of the twenties and thirties. Thus, the current flowering of Black women's writing must be viewed as part of a cultural continuum and an evolving consciousness, a consciousness that will continue to evolve and unfold. This distinctively Black and feminine awareness derives from what I suggest we call the Afra-American experience.[2]

For most of us, those who wait anxiously for the next volume from our favorite Black woman writer, today's renaissance is welcome indeed, though some male writers and critics express alarm over the images of Black men presented in works by Black women as well as what they feel is inequitable treatment by the publishing establishment. I appreciate the sensitivity and indeed the insecurity that some Black men feel, but the hostile tone taken by a few of the most influential is almost intolerable. Because when we disagree, we must disagree in love. We are still in a survival situation in America, and we should never forget that fact. What we are witnessing, in fact, is a swinging of the pendulum, for as Maya Angelou has often pointedly said, "Nature abhors an imbalance." Writing in the *Village Voice,* critic Thulani Davis asserts that "Black male writers of several generations have been repeatedly described by critics as being involved in 'father/son' conflict: you guessed it, the son rebels against the father. Richard Wright and Ralph Ellison, the daddies of them all, apparently had no daughters." Not only that, but it also seems that Margaret Walker and Ann Petry had no sons. Again, Thulani Davis asks us to "imagine": "Imagine a John Coltrane who had heard only one '78' by Charlie Parker, one LP by Billie Holiday. Imagine a Cecil Taylor who did not grow up with the sounds of Art Tatum and Duke Ellington, and you have some idea how amazing it is that we have writers like Lorraine Hansberry and Toni Morrison."[3] The emergence of the Black woman writer as what Maya Angelou might call a "formidable character" or what June Jordan might call a "difficult miracle" is cause for celebration today. For too long, the voices and creativity of Black women have been suppressed. If indeed an imbalance exists, nature will take care of it with another swing of the pendulum, hopefully sooner rather than later, and eventually we will all get together for a long-overdue family reunion.

A host of anthologies and numerous works of Black feminist literary criticism and critical theory have contributed to the definition of the current renaissance in Black women's writing. Contemporary Black women writers like Toni Morrison, Alice Walker, and Toni Cade Bambara have won recognition for their literary achievements in awards ranging from the American Academy and Institute of Arts and Letters Award, the National Book Critics Circle Award, the American Book Award, and the Lillian Smith Award to the Zora Neale Hurston Award, the Langston Hughes Medallion, the National Book Award, and the Pulitzer Prize. Perhaps the most encouraging sign of the times, however, was the appearance, in 1988, of the thirty-volume Schomburg Library of Nineteenth-Century Black Women Writers, published by Oxford University Press. This series, edited by

Henry Louis Gates, brought together a bouquet of distinguished scholars including Hazel Carby, Mary Helen Washington, Gloria T. Hull, Valerie Smith, and William Andrews, each of whom wrote an introduction to one of the individual volumes which included the works of Phillis Wheatley, Ann Plato, Amanda Smith, Frances Ellen Watkins Harper, Pauline Hopkins, Alice Dunbar-Nelson, and others. Writing in the *New York Times Book Review,* Eric Sundquist argues that the *Schomburg Library* "will dramatically change the landscape of Afro-American literature and American cultural history. . . . What the *Schomburg Library* . . . demonstrates is that black men *and black women* have never hesitated to grasp the pen and write their own powerful story of freedom."[4] Writing in *The Women's Review of Books,* Marilyn Mobley goes even further: "The *Schomburg Library* corrects the erroneous assumption that black women were not writing; it also corrects the assumption that they were not reading. The whole notion of intertextuality within and outside of this canon deserves further study. How did writers who did not read one another's work nevertheless read similar cultural codes in similar ways, and seem to echo one another?" She goes on to remind us "that the work of revising not only the canon, but our interpretations of it, is far from complete."[5]

*Wild Women in the Whirlwind: Afra-American Culture and the Contemporary Literary Renaissance* is part of the continuing process of reading, rereading, and revising that has established the validity of Black women writing in America as a tradition within a tradition. This anthology is an exploration of the ways in which Black women writers interpret their experience as they read the metaphors and symbols of the dominant and oftentimes oppressive culture that they rise within and against; it is also an analysis of codes and symbols which may be understood only within the Veil of Blackness and femaleness. In this sense, the current volume is an exploration of intertextuality, not only within Black female literary tradition but also within the Black and female experience which has given rise to this tradition.

*Wild Women in the Whirlwind* was conceived during the summer of 1984 at the NEH "Women in Literature" seminar which was directed by Elaine Showalter at Rutgers University in New Brunswick, New Jersey, and which social theorist Andrée Nicola McLaughlin and I attended along with ten other scholars committed to the inclusion of women's voices in the canon of American literature. Andrée and I have different scholarly perspectives, and, therefore, the building of this book has been a learning experience for us both. Although we originally viewed this volume as one to be devoted to Black feminist literary scholarship, our focus gradually broadened to include a consideration of the cultural and political imperatives that have contributed to the current renaissance in Black women's writing. Ultimately, I believe, the volume profits from our sometimes difficult collaboration, for the finished product is polished, yet rich in its diversity. It fills several gaps in contemporary black feminist scholarship without being confined to any narrow genre, and it is politically honest, dealing with issues of race, class, ethnicity, gender, and sexual preference as well as more traditional literary concerns. We are particularly indebted to Audre Lorde who insisted that this book not go to press without an essay specifically treating the image of the Black lesbian in literature, and we feel that Barbara Smith's fine essay on this topic represents a major contribution to Black and feminist scholarship.

The volume itself is divided into three sections, "Foremothers," "Redefining the Veil," and "Visions and Re-visions." The word *foremother* usually means female ancestor, one who has preceded and who has gone on, but by definition, foremother can also mean one who has gone in front, someone who has been a leader, someone who has stood at the foreground of cultural experience. These women have inhabited both the public and private sphere as workers and nurturers. Some, like Phillis Wheatley, Ann Plato, Frances Ellen Watkins Harper, Anna Julia Cooper, and Ida B. Wells wrote books and gave lectures and poetry readings; others who might not have been literate in the usual sense expressed themselves orally, in song, or in forms of material culture including quilting and furniture making. They believed in God, and they believed that God was on their side. They were our mothers and grandmothers; they were "ordinary women of courage."

For us, these women remain sources of consciousness and personal strength: models of independence, self-reliance, perseverance, and self-determination. Contemporary Black women writers are linked to those who went before first and foremost by the "mother tongue." In the words of Temma Kaplan (writing in the *Barnard Occasional Papers*): "Often in the most oppressive situations, it is the memories of the mothers handed down through the daughters that keeps a community together. The mother tongue is not just the words or even the array of symbols available to a people to resist its tormentors. The mother tongue *is* the oral tradition. And through the oral tradition, women acting as mothers create political possibilities for new generations."[6] The "mother tongue" and the collective spirit of Americans of African descent gave birth to authentic products of culture and consciousness including spirituals and shouts, work songs, and the blues. In "Black Women and Music: A Historical Legacy of Struggle," Angela Y. Davis examines the world view and social outlook of Afra-American musicians. As she writes of the power of "Nommo," the "magic power of the word," in shaping song and experience, Davis's essay speaks not only to the work of Ma Rainey and Bessie Smith, but to the anonymous multitudes whose singing was primarily a private form of artistic expression. Davis looks at the ways blueswomen revised certain concepts of ideal womanhood and served as spokeswomen for themselves and their communities.

In "The Difficult Miracle of Black Poetry in America or Something Like a Sonnet for Phillis Wheatley," June Jordan reflects on the importance of the emergence of the woman who was, in the words of H. L. Gates, "the progenitor of the black literary tradition . . . all subsequent black writers have evolved in a matrilinear line of descent . . . each, consciously or unconsciously, has extended or revised a canon whose foundation was the poetry of a black woman."[7] Jordan, one of the foremost poets in America today, acknowledges this descent in a lively prose-poem of praise for Wheatley's miraculous achievement as a black woman publishing in the eighteenth century and lauds the persistence of black poetry in America: "Like the trees of winter / like the snow which has no power / makes very little sound / but comes and collects itself / edible light on the black trees / The tall black trees of winter / lifting up a poetry of snow / so that we may be astounded / by the poems of black / trees inside a cold environment." In "Establishing the Identity of the Author of *Our Nig,*" Henry Louis Gates and David Curtis outline their search for documentation of the life and writing of Harriet E. Wilson, author of the earliest known novel by a Black American woman. Gloria I. Joseph removes Sojourner Truth from historical ambiguity, elaborating on her Afrocentric world view in "Sojourner Truth: Archetypal

Black Feminist." Continuing in the pursuit of "difficult miracles," my own "A Poet's Retreat: The Diaries of Charlotte Forten Grimké (1837–1914)" examines the problems facing a Black literary woman of the nineteenth century as she sought a resolution between her talent and the private sphere to which Black women were publicly consigned. Robert Fehrenbach's study of Angelina Weld Grimké's *Rachel* establishes the importance of Grimké's play as one of the first attempts to portray realistic black images onstage.

"'Up the Country'. . . . and Still Singing the Blues: Sippie Wallace," by Daphne Harrison, and "This Little Light of Mine: Dramatizing the Life of Fannie Lou Hamer," by Billie Jean Young, celebrate two foremothers who were leaders and spokespersons for their communities. "The blues is life . . . the blues as art . . . is life," writes Harrison of Sippie Wallace who at the end of her life spent her time creating spirituals, not blues. In "This Little Light," Young discusses drama as a vehicle for public myth making and inspiration, as audiences strive to emulate the spiritual strength of Fannie Lou Hamer, civil rights activist and leader of the Mississippi Freedom Democratic Party. Young records a segment of a conversation she had with Mrs. Hamer's husband following her death in 1977, a conversation which captures much of the vitality of "This Little Light": "'If you'd known she was gonna be a helluva woman like that, Pap, would you have been scared to marry her?' He looked at me, grinned a gold-toothed grin: 'Damn straight, baby.'" The spirit of Fannie Lou Hamer exemplifies the foremother speaking in the "mother tongue" to create political possibilities for future generations, connecting the living with the dead and the as yet unborn.

"Redefining the Veil" explores the immediate interior of what Andrée Nicola McLaughlin calls the "multiple consciousness" of Black women who possess not "two warring ideals in one dark body" but many. Ever aware of the Veil's ubiquitous presence, the Black woman writer seeks to transform it and thus attain authentic self-consciousness, for the Veil, like human consciousness, is neither immutable nor static. In "Black Women, Identity and the Quest for Humanhood and Wholeness: Wild Women in the Whirlwind," McLaughlin discusses Black women's adoption of new socio-political identities. In McLaughlin's words, "The value of comparative examination of Black women's literature and experiences is discerning similarities and differences in premises, material or spiritual, which shape human consciousness and inform social movements. Disseminating these theoretical perspectives and realities born of diverse ethics and histories aids understanding of ourselves and others for a better world." She theorizes that Black women use culture and political-class movements for self empowerment. Régine Altagrâce Latortue's "In Search of Women's Voices: The Woman Novelist in Haiti" adds another cross-cultural perspective to the volume and explores the little-known tradition of Haitian women writers. Comparing depictions of Haitian women in the selected works of male and female Haitian novelists, Latortue reveals disparate perspectives on gender and color contradictions within the world created by these works. In "The Sexual Mountain and Black Women Writers," Calvin Hernton perceptively analyzes ways in which Black women writers and scholars have employed a vision based on difference to redefine their relationships to American society and to the world community as a whole. Barbara Smith's "The Truth That Never Hurts: Black Lesbians in the Fiction of the 1980s" examines yet another aspect of the Veil of Black and female self-awareness and literary tradition. Smith's essay updates her now famous *Toward a Black Feminist Criticism* (1977). "Perhaps most urgently," she writes, "I wanted to illuminate the existence of Black Lesbian writers and to show how homophobia insured that we were even more likely to be ignored or attacked than Black women writers generally." Smith invites us to embrace a new consciousness of Black and female gender preference as she puts forth "a vision for Black Lesbians surviving whole." Joanne V. Gabbin's "A Laying On of Hands" examines images of healing in contemporary writing by Black American women. Nellie Y. McKay's lucid "The Autobiographies of Zora Neale Hurston and Gwendolyn Brooks: Alternate Versions of the Black Female Self" explores the autobiographies of Brooks and Hurston as they step "outside the boundaries of conventional patterns in Black autobiography." McKay argues that Hurston and Brooks "created alternate versions of the Black female self that go well beyond refuting the negative stereotypes of Black women in much of American literature." Barbara Omolade's "The Silence and the Song: Toward a Black Woman's History through a Language of Her Own" explores a dilemma of the Black female intellectual in the white male-dominated academy and proposes the Afra-American writer as a model for a new definition of both the self and the Veil.

The third and final section, "Visions and Re-visions," celebrates the hard-won but authentic self-awareness achieved by Afra-Americans who have broken through the Veil to see things, in the terminology of poet Adrienne Rich, "newly." This authentic Black and female self transcends artificial boundaries to place the Black woman at the center of human experience, art, and consciousness, instead of at the periphery. It unites the once warring and fragmented souls of single selves into one harmonious whole, one dark and female self.

To revise is to see "newly," to create, in the words of Audre Lorde, "structures for the future." Essays in this section examine the visions of Black women who are shaping a future that is at once inclusive and particular. Three essays in this section explore the uses of cultural memory in contemporary works of fiction and autobiography by Black American women. My "Ancestral Presence: The Outraged Mother Figure in Contemporary Afra-American Writing" analyzes the archetypal image of the outraged mother and argues that even when memory is clearly fiction, it permits people to bear witness and leave testaments for future generations. Vashti Crutcher Lewis's "African Tradition in Toni Morrison's *Sula*" examines the African aesthetic at work in Morrison's fiction. In "'Somebody Forgot to Tell Somebody Something': African-American Women's Historical Novels," Barbara Christian observes the differences between slave narratives and the contemporary historical fiction by Black women writers which spring from the oral history of slavery and those who survived it. In "Voices Beyond the Veil," Zala Chandler interviews Toni Cade Bambara and Sonia Sanchez, both of whom speak to the necessity of Black people remaining connected with our history, our selves, each other, and, most important, our future. In "Spirituality in the Novels of Alice Walker," Rudolph P. Byrd discusses Walker's works as models for healing and transformation—models that "enrich, enlarge and bolster our spirits." Chinosole's "Audre Lorde and Matrilineal Diaspora" examines the links among Black women worldwide which enable them "to experience distinct but related cultures while retaining a special sense of home as the locus of self-definition and power." Chinosole celebrates Lorde's vision of a "matrilineal diaspora" as viewed in selected works and as a model for the future. Finally, Gale P. Jackson's "A Selected Bibliography of English-Language Works by Black Women of the Americas" provides a teaching tool invaluable for classroom use.

*Wild Women in the Whirlwind* brings together a diverse group of scholars—Black, white, male, and female—who explore cultural, political, and literary imperatives which have shaped the Black woman's consciousness and which define the Afra-American aesthetic. The volume takes many forms as it reflects the chosen kinship and intertextual relation of the participating artists and scholars and their antecedents as well as their contemporaries. (We have extended the kinship network to claim each other with the family kiss.) Ultimately, *Wild Women* reflects the vitality and diversity of the renaissance it addresses, looking back to the past to posit models for survival in the future as well as to a vision of future wholeness. It is in this framework that the essence and import of this rebirth can best be understood.

## Notes

1     See Joanne M. Braxton, "Introduction," *Black Women Writing Autobiography: A Tradition Within a Tradition* (Philadelphia: Temple University Press, 1989).

2     "Harriet Jacobs' *Incidents in the Life of a Slave Girl:* The Redefinition of the Slave Narrative Genre," *Massachusetts Review* 27 (Summer 1986), 379–387. Here I argue that black women "have been as invisible to the dominant culture as rain," and that "we have been knowers but we have not been known." I further assert that study "of all such texts and testimonies by women will allow us to fill out an understanding of that culture and experience which I have designated as Afra-American, and help us to correct and expand existing analyses based too exclusively on male models of experience and writing."

3     Thulani Davis, "Family Plots: Black Women Writers Reclaim Their Past," *Voice Literary Supplement* (March 1987), 4–5.

4     Eric Sundquist, "A Great American Flowering," *New York Times Book Review,* July 3, 1988.

5     Marilyn E. Mobley, "When and Where They Entered," *Women's Review of Books* 5, nos. 10 and 11 (Summer 1989).

6     Temma Kaplan, "Introduction," *The Barnard Occasional Papers on Women's Issues* 3, no. 2 (Summer 1988), 2–3.

7     Henry Louis Gates, "Foreword: In Her Own Write," Schomburg Library of Nineteenth-Century Black Women Writers (New York: Oxford University Press, 1988), x.

# Andrée Nicola McLaughlin

# A Renaissance of the Spirit: Black Women Remaking the Universe

Who would have believed that the "Kidnapped African" would be the architect of a literary renaissance in a foreign land?[1] Who would have expected that thrice within a margin of one hundred years after slavery's abolition, the descendants of slaves—for whose forebears reading and writing were against the law—would produce some of the most widely read writers in the modern world? Who could have known that, following in the steps of the Harlem Renaissance and the Black Arts Movement, the "daughters of the captivity" would become leading spokespersons of their own causes with international constituencies? The literary upsurge by Black women in the second half of the twentieth century unveils a renaissance of the spirit inspired by those who have refused to surrender. Those who have resisted their oppression. Those who have undertaken to remake the universe to own their future.

That a unique renaissance of literary dimensions is upon us asserts itself in the sheer volume of works produced in the last two decades by Black women in Africa, Europe, the Pacific, and the Americas.[2] Certainly, Amerafrican women, Black women in the Americas, who are writing represent only a part of a much larger phenomenon that is taking place. The fictional works of Ama Ata Aidoo (Ghana), Barbara Burford (U.K.), Buchi Emecheta (Nigeria-U.K.), Bessie Head (South Africa), Jamaica Kincaid (Antigua), Toni Morrison (U.S.A.), Flora Nwapa (Nigeria), Grace Ogot (Kenya), Miriam Tlali (South Africa), and Alice Walker (U.S.A.) have made a forceful entry on the world stage, enjoying extensive readerships.

The impressive development of Black women's literature reaches beyond the Anglophone sphere. The emergence of Black female

Francophone writers, for example, has been no less dramatic. Contemporary Haitian novelists Marie Chauvet, Nadine Magloire, and Marie-Thérèse Colimon are representative of this trend, and "African female novelists Mariama Bâ (*Une Si Longue Lettre,* 1980; *Un Chant Ecarlate,* 1984), Aminata Sow Fall (*Le Revenant,* 1976; *La Grève des Battu,* 1979; *L'Appel des Arènes,* 1982), and Nafissatou Diallo (*De Tilène au Plateau: Une Enfance Dakaroise,* 1975) are among those noted for their accurate and penetrating portrayals of the woman."[3]

Although the novel figures most prominently as the genre in which Black women are being distributed and promoted today, poetry remains the most popular—reflected in both the quantity of women writing verse and the high value of orature in Black culture. The international standing of poets/oral artists Barbara Chase-Riboud (U.S.A.-France), Lorna Goodison (Jamaica), Audre Lorde (U.S.A.), Nancy Morejón (Cuba), Marlene Nourbese Philip (Trinidad and Tobago-Canada), Sonia Sanchez (U.S.A.), and Bobbi Sykes (Australia) exemplifies the status poetry commands, while the unprecedented publication, in Britain during 1987, of two anthologies of Black women's creative writings, *Blackwomantalk Poetry* and *Watchers and Seekers,* incisively illustrates a predilection for poetry. This is further demonstrated by the principal role countless women poets (known as *griotes* in West Africa) retain in the Afro-Latin American and African folkloric traditions such as those of Afro-Uruguayans and Nigeria's Hausa. The longevity and strength of parallel traditions of oral literature in Aboriginal culture, particularly storytelling and songmaking, render poetry a "natural process" of literary expression, according to senior Aborigine poet Kath Walker.[4]

Black women are producing, in addition to novels and poetry, political essays, drama, short stories, and personal narratives to an extent never before witnessed. Anthologies such as *Farbe Bekennen* (Germany, 1986), *Charting the Journey: Writings by Black and Third World Women* (U.K., 1987), and *Home Girls: A Black Feminist Anthology* (U.S.A., 1983) emanate from Black women's amplified literary representation.

Personal testimonies of Black women's experiences in work and in life have been culled in Makeda Silvera's *Silenced* (Canada, 1983), Awa Thiam's *Black Sisters Speak Out: Feminism and Oppression in Black Africa* (France, 1978), and Beverley Bryan, Stella Dadzie, and

Suzanne Scafe's *Heart of the Race: Black Women's Lives in Britain* (U.K., 1985). Black organizations of women, namely the Zimbabwe Women's Bureau and Jamaica's Sistren Theatre Collective, have done the same in *We Carry a Heavy Load: Rural Women in Zimbabwe Speak Out* (1981), and *Lionheart Gal: Life Stories of Jamaican Women* (1986), respectively.

Working in the autobiographical genre, again Black women have made their presence felt. Maya Angelou has created an art of autobiography through her well-received serial narratives. Likewise, the autobiographies of political activists and artists such as Angela Davis (*Angela Davis: An Autobiography*, 1974), Enelia Paz Gómez (*Black in Colombia*, 1985), Ellen Kuzwayo (*Call Me Woman*, 1985), Miriam Makeba (*Makeba: My Story*, 1987), Winnie Mandela (*Part of My Soul Went with Him*, 1985), Assata Shakur (*Assata: An Autobiography*, 1987), and Tina Turner (*I, Tina*, 1986) have found broad audiences.

Black women are also well known for their compelling drama. They include such playwrights as Efua Sutherland (Ghana), Zulu Sofola (Nigeria), Rebeka Njau (Kenya), Alice Childress (U.S.A.), Fatima Dike (South Africa), Ntozake Shange (U.S.A.), and Eva Johnson, the first Black woman playwright in Australia, with her widely acclaimed *Tjindarella*. Among anthologies we find Margaret B. Wilkerson's (U.S.A.) *9 Plays by Black Women*, 1988, which brings together the works of both early and contemporary African-American women playwrights, as well as the popular new plays of Sistren Theatre Collective, an independent Jamaican theater company of much repute, which are now being compiled and edited by Rhonda Cobham.

Commanding critical attention on several continents are the plays and short stories of the versatile Ama Ata Aidoo (Ghana). In the United States, J. California Cooper continues to distinguish herself as one of the most prolific and talented young Black women short story writers and playwrights, and the short stories of Beryl Gilroy (Guyana-U.K.), also a novelist and autobiographer, can be heard on British radio. African-Americans Sharon Bell Mathis, Mildred D. Taylor, and Brenda Wilkinson have made their mark in children's fiction as have Jamaica's Jean D'Costa and Opal Palmer Aidisa. Achieving recognition for her literature, award-winning Octavia Butler (U.S.A.) is still uniquely situated as one of only a few Black writers of science fiction.

Seminal nonfiction works penned by Black women include the socio-economic treatise of Uganda's Christine Obbo (*African Women: Their Struggle for Economic Independence*, 1980) and the socio-political exposé of Aborigine Cheryl Buchanan (*We Have Bugger All!: The Kulaluk Story*, 1974); historical studies by Jamaican writers Lucille Mathurin Mair (*The Rebel Women in the British West Indies During Slavery*, 1975) and Sylvia Wynter (*Jamaica's National Heroes: A Historical Argument*, 1971) as well as Surinam's Astrid MacLeod (*Hoe duur was de Suiler?*, 1987) and African-American Paula Giddings (*When and Where I Enter: The Impact of Black Women on Race and Sex in America*, 1984); and anthropological works edited and authored by Nigerian-born Ifi Amadiume (*Afrikan Matriarchal Foundations*, 1987), African-American Beverly Lindsay (*Comparative Perspectives of Third World Women*, 1980), and Sierra Leone's Filomena Chioma Steady (*The Black Woman Cross-Culturally*, 1981).

Other groundbreaking enterprises are the efforts in biography, a genre in which more Black women are writing in recent years. Teresa Martínez Arce de Varela (*Mi Cristo Negro*, 1983), poet, novelist, and the first and preeminent recorder of Afro-Colombian life and culture, has authored the *Biografía de Diego Luis Cordoba*, 1987. Some notable biographical endeavors in the United States include Alexis DeVeaux's *Don't Explain: A Song of Billie Holiday*, 1980, Gloria Hull's *Give Us This Day: The Diary of Alice Dunbar-Nelson*, 1984; and *Color, Sex, and Poetry*, 1987; and Margaret Walker Alexander's treatment of Richard Wright's life, *Richard Wright: Daemonic Genius*, 1988.

## Comparative Tendencies in Black Women's Literature

Black women are writing prolifically in diverse genres in European languages, indigenous languages, dialects, and in combinations thereof. This does not suggest that their literary expression is internationally or even regionally uniform in its development and manifestations, nor in the purview of day-to-day experiences it brings to bear. The first work of any type by Afro-German women, for instance, was published as recently as 1986, a major feat in a society for which the existence of Black Germans is reminiscent of eras of national shame—the Nazi reign and German colonialism.[5] Also appearing in the 1980s has been Zimbabwean women's English literature of a political nature which, unlike their Shona and Ndebele literature, could only get published after Independence.[6] In another stream, we find anthologies in Britain written by and about Black women which include writings by women of African and of Asian descent.

The political essay, a genre in which Black women are working in increasing numbers, offers room for some comparison of their literary works internationally. Outside Western societies, one meets with, for example, entire works authored by women's collectives and organizations: Latin American and Caribbean Women's Collective (*Slaves of Slaves: The Challenge of Latin American Women,* 1980); Organization of Angolan Women (*Angolan Women Building the Future: From National Liberation to Women's Emancipation,* 1984); and Vukani Makhosikazi Collective (*South African Women on the Move,* 1985). In places like Britain and the United States, however, single-author collections of political essays are more likely to be the case, such as those by Wilmette Brown (*Black Women and the Peace Movement,* 1983), Angela Davis (*Women, Race, and Class,* 1981; *Women, Culture, and Politics,* 1989), Bell Hooks (*Ain't I A Woman,* 1981; *From Margin to Center,* 1984), June Jordan (*Civil Wars,* 1981; *On Call: Political Essays,* 1985), and Audre Lorde (*The Cancer Journals,* 1980; *Sister Outsider,* 1984; *A Burst of Light,* 1988).

Of course Black women's written expression has been and continues to be stifled by harsh degrees of exploitation, conflict, and oppression. The conditions of writers in Surinam, Uganda, and the Dominican Republic are exemplary of writers in many "Third World" nations where neocolonialism impedes emergence of viable industries or social institutions with capacity for publishing and distribution. Novelist, poet, and playwright Astrid Roemer (Surinam-the Netherlands) attests that, in general, "money and connections" are required to publish.[7] Under these circumstances, the publication of Black women's literature usually conforms to existing patterns of dependency on former colonial powers and other Western nations.

Social biases and socio-economic underdevelopment in racially hierarchical societies prove almost intractable impediments to writing itself and to the accessibility of literature by or about, for instance, Afro-Peruvian, Afro-French Guianese, and Afro-Brazilian women. While the literary flowering, particularly of the historical novel and the testimonio, among Latin American women receives a universally warm welcome, Afro-Latin women's voices are vaguely heard. Brazil's Carolina Maria de Jesus provides first-hand insight from her diary, *Child of the Dark,* when she writes, "I wonder if God knows the favelas exist and that the favelados are hungry? . . . Here in the favelas almost everyone has a difficult fight to live. But, I am the only one who writes of what suffering is. I do this for the good of the others."[8]

The literary voices of Afro-Latin American women have, nevertheless, breasted the tides of hardship and invisibility. These writers have prevailed in the face of social condemnation for inveighing against subjugation and writing in traditionally male-dominated genres. Carolina Maria de Jesus prefigured the impulse of a Black political and cultural reawakening in today's Brazil; Colombia's seventy-five-year-old Teresa Martínez Arce de Varela now amasses and publishes her own writings for which many others have claimed credit in the past. Notwithstanding the common plight of poverty for Brazil's slum-confined Black majority and for eight million Afro-Colombians, their situation affords distinct stories of survival— within a professed "racial democracy" and under an unpretentiously color conscious state, respectively.

For Afro-Caribbean women writers of French expression, skin color and the social transitions implicit in foreign control and de-colonization are thematic preoccupations. Isolation typically besets female characters in works by women novelists of Haiti, Martinique's Marie-Flore Pélage, or Guadeloupe's Maryse Condé, Michele Lacrosil, and Miriam Warner-Vieyra. Belonging to a tradition in modernity that defines a human being as "male, white, privileged, and power-ful," the Black woman grapples with what Don Quinn Kelley terms "the dilemma of 'existential loneliness'": "[While] life is both urgent and immediate because choice is possible and death is inevitable and final . . . , loneliness . . . stems from her lack of affirmative options."[9] Characterized as a literature of "confinement and alienation,"[10] this body of autobiographical fiction also represents a discourse of reflec-tion. The writers of these novels, along with Guadeloupe's Simone Schwarz-Bart, vest Black women with responsibility for adapting tra-ditional values to negotiate the contradictions of societal flux.

Themes of conflict, identity, and change similarly predominate in the literature of the Pacific's Black women, members of cultural groups which trace their origins to India, Indonesia, Hawaii, and other areas of Asia and the Pacific as well as Africa. Their writings confront the varying cataclysmic effects of Western rule on their societies, including the trauma of unparalleled nuclear weapons testing and buildup, within an expanse of more than thirty thousand islands. A concern for stabilizing island cultures is reflected in the titles, sardonic or plain-spoken, of Fijian Jo Nacola's collection of plays, *I Native No More* (1976); Papua New Guinean Nora Vagi Brash's radio dramas, *The High Cost of Living Differently* (1976) and *Which Way, Big Man?* (1977); of Solomon Islander Jully Sipolo's poetry, *Civilized Girl* (1981); and Aborigines Monica Clare's prose, *Karobran: The Story of an Aboriginal Girl* (1978), Sally Morgan's autobiography and biography, *My Place* (1987), and Faith Bandler's historical study, *Turning the Tide* (1989). Black women writers of these and other works are participants in a "conscious drive" by Pacific Islanders currently to develop new written literatures; by and large, they argue for hastier decolonization and relief from Eurocentrism.[11]

The writings of Black women in South Africa can best be appreciated as a literature of rebellion. The novels and short stories of Miriam Tlali, for example, challenge colonialism and its trappings. Calling her female characters "combative," realistically depicted as "mothers and militants at the same time," Tlali contends Black women "know what it means to combine political militancy with ironing shirts and washing socks."[12] The publication of an uncensored version of *Muriel at Metropolitan* (1975) and Tlali's refusal to compromise the content or title of her second novel, *Amandla* (1980), dramatize the social conflict underlying South Africa's existing ban on these and her later books; Tlali won't conform to minority rule.

The writing of Mozambique's Lina Magaia evokes a radically different experience, a nation's post-independence struggle to survive devastation. Her highly acclaimed *Dumba Nengue: Run for Your Life, Peasant Tales of Tragedy in Mozambique* (1988) discloses the unspeakable crimes committed by South African-funded "bandits" against unarmed civilians. To be certain, these accounts of ongoing atrocities are a triumph in the face of campaigns to crush the Mozambican people and the truth about their reality. Translation enterprises commensurate with the development of Black women's literature would broaden access to valuable works on the order of Magaia's collection, first published in Portuguese. A new tradition of Black women writing on various continents already beckons a multilingual dialogue.

## A Renaissance's Position of Influence

The scope and impact of an intercontinental Black women's literary renaissance can be measured by several protracted activities. First is the voluminous scholarship defining the imperatives of Black women's literary endeavors and offering evidence of a growing cadre of Black women literary critics. The novels of Trinidad and Tobago's Merle Hodge (*Crick Crack, Monkey,* 1970), Jamaica's Erna Brodber (*Jan and Louisa Will Soon Come Home,* 1980), and Belize's Zee Edgell (*Beka Lamb,* 1982) are among the subjects of a developing feminist criticism of Anglophone Caribbean women's literature in studies by Yakini Kemp, Evelyn O'Callaghan, and others. Additionally, the scholarship of Bridget Jones, Régine Latortue, Ineke Phaf, Karen Smyley Wallace, and Betty Wilson is shaping a woman-defined literary theory of Francophone Caribbean women's writings; these critics have built on Maryse Condé's pivotal *La parole des femmes: essais sur des romancieres des Antilles de langue française* (*A Woman's World: Essays on Black Women Novelists of the Caribbean of French Expression,* 1979). Critical activity concerning contemporary Afro-Latin American women writers is also transpiring, albeit with considerably less intensity. Some works that explore the currents of Amerafrican women's literature in the Caribbean and in Latin America include: *Caribbean Fiction and Poetry* (1970), edited by Marjorie Engber; *Creole Drum: An Anthology of Creole Literature* (1975), edited by Jan Voorhoeve and Ursy Lichtveld; Richard L. Jackson's *Black Writers in Latin America* (1979); Ian Smart's *Central American Writers of West Indian Origin: A New Hispanic Literature* (1984); and *Out of the Kumbla: Caribbean Women and Literature* (1989), edited by Carole Boyce Davies and Elaine Savory Fido. Directories of criticism are provided in Richard L. Jackson's *The Afro-Spanish American Author: An Annotated Bibliography of Criticism* (1980), and Daryl Cumber Dance's *Fifty Caribbean Writers: A Bio-Bibliographical and Critical Sourcebook* (1986).

A proliferation of anthologies and critical studies imparts the present force of the literary tradition of contemporary Amerafrican women in the United States. Works of note include: *Keeping the Faith: Writings by Contemporary Black American Women* (1974), edited by Pat Crutchfield Exum; *Black-Eyed Susans* (1975), *Midnight Birds* (1980), and *Invented Lives* (1987), edited by Mary Helen Washington; *Frances, Zora, and Lorraine: Essays and Interviews on Black Women and Writing* (1979), edited by Juliette Bowles; Barbara Christian's *Black Women Novelists: The Development of a Tradition, 1892–1976* (1980) and *Black Feminist Criticism: Perspectives on Black Women Writers* (1985); *Black Sister: Poetry by Black American Women, 1746–1980* (1981), edited by Erlene Stetson; *But Some of Us Are Brave* (1982), edited by Gloria T. Hull, Patricia Bell Scott, and Barbara Smith; *Confirmation: An Anthology of African American Women* (1983), edited by Amiri Baraka and Amina Baraka; *Black Women Writers at Work* (1983), edited by Claudia Tate; *Black Women Writers (1950–1980): A Critical Evaluation*, edited by Mari Evans (1984); *Conjuring: Black Women, Fiction, and Literary Tradition* (1985), edited by Marjorie Pryse and Hortense J. Spillers; Susan Willis's *Specifying: Black Women Writing the American Experience* (1987); Hazel V. Carby's *Reconstructing Womanhood: The Experience of the Afro-American Woman Novelist* (1987); Calvin Hernton's *The Sexual Mountain and Black Women Writers* (1987); Elizabeth Brown-Guillory's *Their Place on Stage: Black Women Playwrights in America* (1988); the multivolume Schomburg Library of Nineteenth-Century Black Women Writers (1988), edited by Henry Louis Gates, Jr.; and Ann Allen Shockley's *Afro-American Woman Writers, 1746–1933* (1989). Also, national journals, *Black Scholar* (March/April 1986) and *SAGE: A Scholarly Journal on Black Women* (Spring 1985), have published special issues on Black women writers. Three anthologies were on the cutting edge of this critical trend: *The Black Woman: An Anthology* (1970), edited by Toni Cade Bambara; *Night Comes Softly: An Anthology of Black Female Voices* (1970), edited by Nikki Giovanni; and *This Bridge Called My Back: Writings by Radical Women of Color* (1981), edited by Cherríe Moraga and Gloria Anzaldúa.

Anthologies and journals lend optimal entry into a budding tradition of written literatures by Black women in the Pacific, including their oral poetry and narratives in translation. They encompass such works as: *Some Modern Poetry from the Solomon Islands* (1975), edited by Albert Wendt; *MANA Annual of Creative Writing*, No. 3 (1977), edited by Marjorie Crocombe; *Voices of Independence: New Black Writing from Papua New Guinea* (1980), edited by Ulli Beier; *Lali: A Pacific Anthology* (1980), edited by Albert Wendt; and *Some Modern Poetry from Vanuatu* (1981), edited by the South Pacific Creative Arts Society. Each of these anthologies provides a critical survey of Pacific literary tendencies as does *Solomons* (1985), an anthology of the journal *Pacific Moana Quarterly*, edited by Julian Maka'a. *MANA Review, Identity,* and *Kovave* are other important journals of language and literature in which Black women's writings are presented and critiqued, and valuable bibliographic guides to Pacific works can be found in, for example, *Asian/Pacific Literature in English: Bibliographies* (1978), edited by Robert E. McDowell and Judith H. McDowell and *Silence and Invisibility: A Study of the Literatures of the Pacific, Australia, and New Zealand* (1986) by Norman Simms. The *Writers from the South Pacific* (1989), a bio-bibliographical critical collection also by Simms, promises to be the most extensive study of contemporary Pacific writers to date.

Early treatments of African women writers by African critics Omolara Ogundipe-Leslie, Micere Mugo, and Yinka Shoga have been extended by the publication of major works of criticism such as: *The East African Experience: Essays on English and Swahili Literature* (1980) edited by Ulla Schild; Lloyd Brown's *Women Writers in Black Africa* (1981); Ursula Barnett's *A Vision of Order: A Study of Black South African Literature in English, 1914–1980* (1983); Oladele Taiwo's *Female Novelists in Modern Africa* (1984); Rudo B. Gaidzanwa's *Images of Women in Zimbabwean Literature* (1985); *Ngambika* (1986) edited by Carol Boyce Davies and Anne Adams Graves; and *Women in African Literature Today* (1987), edited by Eldred Durosimi Jones. *Sturdy Black Bridges* (1979), edited by Roseann P. Bell, Bettye J. Parker, and Beverly Guy-Sheftall, retains the distinction, however, of treating Black women's writing (in Africa, the Caribbean, and the United States) as a literary crescendo of intercontinental proportion. In addition, African and Caribbean women writers are among the foci of an anthology of criticism on Third World women writers, *Unheard Words,* 1985 (first issued as *Ongehoorde Woorden,* 1984), edited by Mineke Schipper.

A series of recent conferences on Black women's writings constitute a second type of activity that indicates the interest and energy sparked by Black women's literary endeavors. The "Black Women Writers and the Diaspora Conference" at Michigan State University in 1985 convened some five hundred people, including Black women writers and critics from Africa, the Caribbean, and the United States. The year following, in St. Croix, Virgin Islands, a grassroots women's organization, Sojourner Sisters, assembled nineteen women writers of various nationalities for the first international "Caribbean Women's Conference: The Historical and Cultural Ties That Bind." An "International Conference on Women Writers of the English-Speaking Caribbean" convened in Wellesley, Massachusetts, in 1988. This forum brought together Black women writers living in Canada, the United Kingdom, Guyana, France, the United States, and the Caribbean. While these were key gatherings held in the Americas, there have been similar meetings on other continents: a 1982 conference on African women and literature in Mainz, West Germany; a 1985 conference focus on "Women Writers" at the International Book Fair in Harare, Zimbabwe; and a 1986 Black women writers conference in Amsterdam, Holland. Significantly, each of these assemblies addressed the materialization of Black women's literature within an international context.

Perhaps one perennial testimony to this literary renaissance will be the vehicles Black women have developed to ensure that their voices are sustained. They have established their own publishing enterprises: Blackwomantalk in Britain; Sister Vision in Canada; SERITI sa SECHABA in South Africa; and Kitchen Table: Women of Color Press in the United States. Publications undertaken by Black women, including *Afrekete* (West Germany), *NETWORK: A Pan-African Women's Forum* (Zimbabwe), *SAGE: A Scholarly Journal on Black Women* (U.S.A.), and *Gen* and *African Woman* (U.K.), also exemplify efforts of this vein. Similarly inspired by Black women's affirmation in literature and in other realms of human activity, Sonia Sanchez first introduced, at the University of Pittsburgh in 1969, a course, "The Black Woman," which has served as a catalyst for subsequent university courses. Black women's studies in academe—from Nigeria and Ghana to Zambia and the Sudan as well as in Canada, the United States, and the Caribbean—along with Black women's organizations form the principal avenues for the study of Black women's literature. This discipline of study, in the manner of the literary renaissance itself, has incited the production of more imposing writings in addition to having unleashed a demand for Black women's written expression of earlier periods. The momentum to advance and preserve Black women's works remains constant with the offering of the first graduate course on women writers ("Caribbean Women

Novelists") at the University of the West Indies (in St. Augustine, Trinidad and Tobago) in 1986–1987, designed and taught by now-ambassador to the United Nations, Marjorie Thorpe.

## Geopolitics and Women's Literature

The intercontinental boom in literature by Black women should be examined in a geopolitical context to fully appreciate its import. For it both represents and simultaneously occurs with a worldwide burgeoning of literature by women of different cultures. This vantage point enhances assessment of *WAHINE KAITUHI: Women Writers of Aotearoa* (1985), which introduces a distinct generation of culturally Polynesian, yet politically Black, Maori women writers: Patricia Grace, the first Maori woman to be published; "hard-hitting" political essayist Donna Awatere; esteemed novelist and short story writer Keri Hulme; and many more. Miriama Evans writes that, in the Pacific, "Maori women as a group have claimed a slither of space in mainstream New Zealand literary tradition only since the 1970s."[13] Furthermore, in tandem with those by African-Americans, writings by Asian Pacific, Middle Eastern, Amerindian, and Latina women writers in the United States are flourishing without precedent—typified by works of Mitsuye Yamada, Azizah al-Hibri, Paula Gunn Allen, and Nicholasa Mohr, respectively.

The power of the Latina literary tradition becomes evident by a spate of recent anthologies of literature and criticism, among them *Cuentos: Short Stories by Latinas* (1983) edited by Alma Gómez, Cherríe Moraga, and Mariana Romo-Carmona; *Woman of Her Word: Hispanic Women Write,* edited by Evangelina Vigil (1983); *Compañeras: Latina Lesbians* (1988), edited by Juanita Ramos; and *Breaking Boundaries: Latina Writing and Critical Readings* (1989), edited by Asunción Horno-Delgado, Eliana Ortega, Nina M. Scott, and Nancy Saporta Sternbach. In like fashion, the growth in literature by women of continental Latin America has been cause for important critical examinations of, for example, writings or testimonio by Chile's Isabel Allende, Bolivia's Domitila Barrios de Chungara, Nicaragua's Gioconda Belli, and El Salvador's Claribel Alegría. Aspects of this tradition are made available by a variety of works, including some in

English: *Woman Who Has Sprouted Wings: Poems by Contemporary Latin American Women Poets* (1988), edited by Mary Crow; *The Defiant Muse: Hispanic Feminist Poems from the Middle Ages to the Present, A Bilingual Anthology* (1986), edited by Angel Flores and Kate Flores; and Naomi Lindstrom's *Woman's Voice in Latin American Literature* (1989).

Corresponding observations can be made regarding the wealth of literature being produced by women in the Eastern Hemisphere which has also come into strong focus in the last two to three decades. Bringing some of the diverse currents of content and style of North African, Middle Eastern, and Asian women's writings are such anthologies as: *Women of the Fertile Crescent: Modern Poetry by Arab Women* (1978), edited and translated by Kamal Boullata; *The 1002nd Night: A Selection of Short Stories Written by Egyptian Women* (1975), edited by Yusuf as-Saruni; *Seven Contemporary Chinese Women Writers* (1982), edited by Gladys Yang; and soon-to-be-released *Manushi: Voices of Indian Women's Liberation*, edited by Madhu Kishwar and Ruth Vanita and *Contemporary Prose by Saudi Women*, edited by Aman Mahmoud Attieh. The more recent development of international anthologies and collections, most pronounced in the undertakings of European and North American women, speaks to the breadth of women's literary endeavors.

Where does the growth in writings by Black women in the Americas converge with and diverge from the maturation of women's literary expression in so many different parts of the world? Commenting on the belated development of Black women's literature, *Black Scholar* noted: "On the one hand, a white, male-dominated publishing industry hadn't seen fit to publish the works of black women writers; on the other hand, even among the black intelligentsia, only the male articulation of the black experience had been viewed as worthy of literary expression."[14] An analogous argument, by extension, applies to the publication of literature by the majority of the world's women who have shared the experiences of colonial, primarily European, and patriarchal domination. With the colonial era in regression, however, shifts in power relations have ushered in a new period in which a variety of societies and groups have created publishing outlets. More significantly, women are involved in independent publishing on a much greater scale than before, and, to a degree, occupy senior-level editorial positions within the mainstream industry.

Independent presses, such as Sheba Feminist Publishers in London, Orlanda Frauenverlag in Berlin, Three Continents Press in Washington, D.C. and Alice Walker's Wild Trees Press, have made immeasurable differences for Black women writers. Trade unions, like the South African Congress of Trade Unions (SACTU), and international organs, such as the African Training and Resource Center for Women (ATRCW) in Addis Ababa, have similarly been instrumental in publishing works by and about women. In Japan, an informal network of Japanese women has facilitated the translation and publication of literature by Black women of various countries for more than ten years. Women's International Resource Exchange (WIRE), a nonprofit women's collective in the United States, also continues a decade-long commitment to reprint and distribute information and analyses about Third World women in English and Spanish. Notably, women publishing women account for the abundance of women in print today.

The most salient factor in the blossoming of women's literature is a new social consciousness, a feminine consciousness underlying the reality of more women deciding to write *and* to write more—irrespective of being published. Symbolizing one cultural expression of this awareness, literary efflorescence progresses in synchrony with a proliferation of women's creative enterprises in the visual arts, music, and dance, and with the vast expansion of women's organizations in politics, education, health, and other areas.

The unique origins and development of feminine awareness distinguish the particularity of its representations among women. For example, Joanne M. Braxton, speaking of women of African descent in the United States, attributes their consciousness to an "Afra-American experience." When we look at women of this experiential background, we find a vibrant African-American feminist movement sparking much of the contemporary intellectual and artistic activity. To the extent that the literary traditions of all women address notions of women's, ethnic, and national cultures, the particular experiences of women within these cultures determine the texture and strength of their literary voices.

## The Renaissance as a Literary Movement

Consistent with previous renaissances in history that have marked a new age, the intercontinental Black women's literary renaissance parallels other social movements. It has been largely informed by the Black consciousness, or nationalist, movement and the women's movement. Moreover, an awareness of the struggles by oppressed peoples globally for democratic, national, and human rights has shaped Black women's political culture fundamentally.

Black feminine consciousness, having its counterpart among women from every region the world over, is the basis of an expanding challenge to the postulates of domination in all its forms. It protests and takes to task the economic and cultural superstructures that exploit earth's life by pollution, militarism, human oppression, and other means. This awareness, at its root, is anti-imperialist and antipatriarchal, most recently rekindled in the era of the Vietnam War, the incarceration of Angela Davis, the independence movements in Africa, Asia, and Latin America, the many struggles for human rights by diverse oppressed groups; and energized by the United Nations Decade for Women (1976–1985) and by national liberation victories from Zimbabwe to Vanuatu.

The social consciousness of Black women conveys that there is no possibility of straddling the tempest of life:

> . . . but know the whirlwind is our commonwealth.
> Not the easy [woman], who rides above them all,
> not the jumbo brigand,
> not the pet bird of poets, that sweetest sonnet,
> shall straddle the whirlwind.
> Nevertheless, live.[15]

Resisting in the "whirlwind," Black women are responding to: full-scale (military) conflicts that involve over 20 percent of the world, killing more women and children than combatants; economic domination in which "women and girls are half of the world's population, do two-thirds of the world's work hours, receive a tenth of the world's income, and own less than a hundredth of the world's property";[16]

social attitudes and institutions that encourage racist, sexist, and sectarian violence; the derogation of their identity through the suppression and vilification of their cultures, languages, and histories; and the plight of their offspring who have been made disproportionate victims of the world economic order, narcotics, environmental contamination, and war.

A human condition has impelled a consciousness large enough for the times. Evolving within the matrix of a universal quest for self-determination and autonomy, Black feminine consciousness extols "community"—independent of any single ideology.[17] This age, which brings the pursuit of human rights center stage, proffers motion "to define and medicate the whirlwind."[18]

Linking arms with other communities which feel the imperative for qualitative change, Black women are redesignating the parameters of resistance. In the context of personal and political transformation, they are building on the historical confluences of reform and revolt to gain power over their lives. The Black women's movement seeks to create new political frameworks that can rebalance the economic, cultural, and ecological orders upon which the material, spiritual, and physical well-being of humanity and, ultimately, the survival of the planet depends. Implicit in this vision is the value of the self and the potential of all individuals: "Any fundamental change must begin with the concept of the individual as the maker of history, responsible for creating [her] social environment, convinced of [her] actions as historically significant, and therefore of how [she] thinks, feels, and judges and the positions [she] takes on social issues as not only personally but socially relevant."[19]

The reordering of political systems necessitates changing human consciousness and human behavior. Hence, Black women writers bear witness against domination based on nationality, race, gender, class, ethnicity, sexuality, and other indexes of difference. They refute, most basically, the values and societal standards which cast human existence in terms that are fallacious and destructive.

Creating a new reality rooted in diversity and equality, women of the intercontinental Black women's literary renaissance are redefining themselves as well as language and forms of expression within frameworks of cultural continuity. A mission of this magnitude requires that sisters-in-praxis invoke those who have not surrendered.

Those who have resisted their oppression. Those who have undertaken to remake the universe to own their future. These are the
nameless and famous "Foremothers," women of valor, who left us
models of resourcefulness and perseverance. . . . The masses and
our leaders who, "Redefining the Veil" in the course of saying "No!"
to oppression, render new possibilities and point us in new directions. . . . The ancestors whose understanding of the unity of the
universe, their holistic world-views, provide us with "Visions and
Re-visions" for transformation.

In forging new conditions for the existence of oppressed peoples,
their cultures and Earth, Wild Women find the truest expression of
their humanity and yield a renaissance of the spirit. These *Wild
Women in the Whirlwind,* who sing the blues *and* sing about freedom
and justice, dance a new destiny for us all:

> determined women
>    a'go on ploddin'
> seeing the rainbow of liberty
> smelling the flowers of freedom
> riding the clouds of justice
> sailing the waves toward home
> **wild women**
>    **in the whirlwind**
> determined women
>    go on! [20]

# Notes

1     Herbert Harris, Jr., "Kidnapped African," *The Informer* [Houston,
Tex.], August 6, 1983, p. 2. Harris uses the phrases "Kidnapped African"
and "daughters of captivity."

2     Throughout this work all references to "the Americas" encompass the Caribbean.

3     Karen Smyley Wallace, "Women and Alienation: Analysis of the
Works of Two Francophone African Novelists," in *Ngambika: Studies of
Women in African Literature,* ed. Carole Boyce Davies and Anne Adams
Graves (Trenton, N.J.: Africa World Press, Inc., 1986), p. 63.

4    L. E. Scott, "Writers from a Dying Race: Black Poets in Australia," *The Black Scholar, Journal of Black Studies and Research* 11, no. 3 (January/February 1980), 72.

5    Katharina Oguntoye, "Naming Our Condition: The Afro-German Movement," paper presented at the 1988 Cross-Cultural Black Women's Studies Summer Institute, House of the Lord Church, Brooklyn, New York, July 19, 1988, p. 3. Oguntoye and May Opitz are co-editors of *Farbe Bekennen,* the first published work of any type by Afro-German women. The Black presence in Germany is largely an outcome of two periods. First, the Second Reich or new German Empire obtained colonies in Africa, Asia, and the Pacific; all were eventually surrendered under the terms of the Treaty of Versailles after Germany's defeat in World War I. Secondly, after World War II and the fall of Germany's Third Reich, African and Asian troops that Britain and France had recruited from their own colonies were part of the occupying forces. Many of these troops made West Germany their home as did many United States troops which, then and now, have included African-Americans. In her paper, Oguntoye suggests that a normative national posture of denial as it concerns these eras has served to suppress the Black voice.

6    Rudo B. Gaidzanwa, *Images of Women in Zimbabwean Literature* (Harare: The College Press [Pvt] Ltd., 1985), p. 7.

7    Ineke Phaf, Interview with Astrid Roemer (Surinam) in "Women and Literature in the Caribbean," in *Unheard Words: Women and Literature in Africa, the Arab World, Asia, the Caribbean and Latin America,* ed. Mineke Schipper, trans. Barbara Potter Fasting (London: Allison & Busby Limited, 1985), p. 201.

8    Carolina Maria de Jesus, *Child of the Dark,* trans. David St. Clair (New York: E. P. Dutton & Co., Inc. 1962), pp. 55, 43.

9    Don Quinn Kelley, "Winter Poems: Existential Loneliness and Africana Consciousness" (Copyrighted Research, 1986), pp. 5, 8. A treatise.

10    Betty Wilson, trans., Introduction to *Juletane* by Myriam Warner-Vieyra (London: Heinemann Educational Books Ltd., 1987), p. vii. Wilson uses the phrase "confinement and alienation" to characterize Black women's literature of the Francophone Caribbean as a whole; however, she is not categorical and draws distinctions among writers.

11    See Sam L. Alasia, Introduction to *Solomons: A Portrait of Traditional and Contemporary Culture in Solomon Islands,* ed. Julian Maka'a (Hamilton: Outrigger Publishers, 1985) and Albert Wendt, Introduction to *Lali: A Pacific Anthology* (Auckland: Longman Paul, Ltd., 1980) for full discussions of cultural and political imperatives in contemporary Pacific literature.

12     Mineke Schipper, Interview with Miriam Tlali (South Africa) in "Women and Literature in Africa" in *Unheard Words,* p. 65.

13     Miriama Evans, "Maori Women's Writing," in *Wahine Kaituhi: Women Writers of Aotearoa (New Zealand),* ed. Spiral (Wellington: Spiral, 1985), p. 59.

14     "Black Women Writers and the Diaspora," Editorial, *The Black Scholar, Journal of Black Studies and Research* 17, no. 2 (March/April 1986), p. i.

15     Gwendolyn Brooks, from "Second Sermon on the Warpland," in *In the Mecca* (New York: Harper & Row, 1964); *Blacks* (Chicago: The David Company, 1987), p. 454.

16     "Women at Work," 1/1978, International Labor Office, Geneva, editorial.

17     Celia Alvarez and Andrée Nicola McLaughlin, "Women, Culture and Consciousness," *Dialogues,* Cross-Cultural Black Women's Studies Audio Productions, 1986.

18     Brooks, "Second Sermon," p. 455.

19     Grace Lee Boggs, "The Black Revolution in America," in *The Black Woman: An Anthology,* ed. Toni Cade (New York: The New American Library, Inc., 1970), p. 221.

20     Andrée Nicola McLaughlin, from "Determined Women A'Go On Ploddin'," *Woman of Power,* "Woman As Warrior" [Cambridge, Mass.], no. 3 (Winter/Spring 1986), 96.

# *Part I*

---

# Foremothers

Fannie Lou Hamer addresses supporters of the Mississippi Freedom Democratic Party outside the Capitol in Washington, D.C., on September 17, 1965, following the defeat of the party's challenge to the 1964 election of five white Mississippians to the U.S. House of Representatives. A year earlier, she had led an unsuccessful effort to seat MFDP members as the official Mississippi delegation to the Democratic Party's national convention, on the grounds that African-Americans were excluded from Mississippi's election process. In the wake of these two rejections, Mrs. Hamer declared, "We'll come back year after year until we are allowed our rights as citizens." Photo: AP/Wide World Photos

# Angela Y. Davis

# Black Women and Music:
# A Historical Legacy of Struggle

T hroughout the history of the African presence in America, song and dance have informed the collective consciousness of the Black community in vital and enduring ways. Music has long permeated the daily life of most African-Americans; it has played a central role in the normal socialization process; and during moments characterized by intense movements for social change, it has helped to shape the necessary political consciousness. Any attempt, therefore, to understand in depth the evolution of women's consciousness within the Black community requires a serious examination of the music which has influenced them—particularly that which they themselves have created.

Social consciousness does not occur spontaneously. As Marx and Engels pointed out, it arises on the basis of concrete conditions of human life in society. "It is not the consciousness of men [and women!—AYD] that determines their being, but, on the contrary, their social being that determines their consciousness."[1] If it is true that music in general reflects social consciousness and that African-American music is an especially formative element of Black people's consciousness in America, the roots of the music in our concrete historical conditions must be acknowledged. For Black women in particular, music has simultaneously expressed and shaped our collective consciousness.

African-American women who have had the most enduring impact on popular culture have been deeply rooted in the ethnic musical traditions of our community, traditions forged originally on the continent of Africa, then reshaped and honed by the conditions of slavery, the Reconstruction years, and the two world wars. And indeed, precisely because Black music resides on a cultural continuum which has remained closest to the ethnic and socio-historical heritage of African-Americans, it has been our central aesthetic expression, influencing all the remaining arts. Black music, writes James Cone,

> unites the joy and the sorrow, the love and the hate and the despair of black people and it moves the people toward the direction of total liberation. It shapes and defines black being and creates cultural structures for black expression. Black music is unifying because it confronts the individual with the truth of black existence and affirms that black being is possible only in a communal context.[2]

In this essay I will first examine some of the critical moments in the history of Black music before the "Classic Blues" era, initiated by Gertrude "Ma" Rainey, emerged. My emphasis will be on the roles women played in shaping that history. I then will explore the musical contributions of Rainey, a seminal female figure in the Black music tradition, while analyzing and evaluating her catalytic role in awakening collective social consciousness about the African-American predicament. This analysis will attempt to single out some of the specific ways her music gave expression to the emotional dimensions of Black women's lives during the first decades of this century—their consciousness of self, their grasp of the dynamics of male-female bonds as well as female-centered relationships, and the link between these processes and the objective factors conditioning Black women's lives.

W.E.B. Du Bois wrote that Black music is "the most beautiful expression of human experience born this side of the seas . . . It remains as the singular spiritual heritage of the nation and the greatest gift of the Negro people."[3] During the period of slavery, music alone escaped the devastating cultural genocide wrought by the slaveocracy on the lives of Africans who were involuntarily and forcibly transported from their homeland to the shores of North America. While Black people were denied the right to speak in their native tongues, to engage in their traditional religious practices, to build their traditional families and communities, they were able to sing as they toiled in the fields and as they practiced their newfound Christian religion. Through the vehicle of song, they were able to preserve their ethnic heritage, even as they were generations removed from their original homeland and perhaps even unaware that their songs bore witness to and affirmed their African cultural roots. If they were permitted to sing, it was only because the slaveocracy's ethnocentric naiveté prevented them from comprehending the social function of African music, or indeed of music in general. Interpreting the slave songs as amusement or, at best, as a phenomenon facilitating work or the Christian religious indoctrination they hoped would result in the collective internalization of social inferiority on the part of the slaves, the slaveholders either acquiesced in or actively encouraged the slaves to sing their work songs and their spirituals.

Traditional West African music was never merely amusement or entertainment; it was always functional and was a central ingredient of every facet of community life. Always inextricably linked to economic activity, communal interrelationships, and spiritual pursuits, all of which were themselves interrelated, music as an aesthetic abstraction from the activities of daily life was unknown to the African ancestors of slaves in the United States. Ernest Borneman has enumerated eight different kinds of song which functioned in a basic way to regulate the community's cultural patterns. Among these are the songs associated with young men whose purpose was to influence young women: "songs of courtship, songs of challenge, songs of scorn."[4] One can't help but speculate that the author's failure to acknowledge the possibility that young women also sang songs to influence the men is an omission that must be attributed to the influence of sexism on his scholarship, for the societies to which he makes reference had distinct female courtship customs. Borneman further enumerates mothers' educational and calming songs: play songs, game songs, and lullabies. Again he discusses the songs older men used in the preparation of boys for manhood, but fails to recognize the corresponding songs used for the passage from girlhood to womanhood. Among the remaining types of songs he acknowledges are those "used by workers to make their tasks easier: work songs to stress the rhythm of labor, group songs to synchronize collectively executed work, team songs sung by one team to challenge and satirize the other."[5] West African music was functional in the deeper sense that it was more than an external tool, utilized to facilitate a given human activity. Rather it was always considered to be a part of the activity itself. Thus music was not employed as an aesthetic instrumentality, external to work but facilitating its execution; rather work songs were inseparable from the very activity of work itself. Janheinz Jahn has referred to the West African philosophical concept of *Nommo*—"the magic power of the word"—as being the very basis of music. According to the world-view of West African culture—if such a generalization is permitted—the life force is actualized by the power of the word. "According to African philosophy man has, by the force of his word, dominion over 'things.' He can change them, make them work for him and command them."[6]

Song is the practice of *Nommo*. As an African proverb affirms, "the spirit cannot descend without song." This song is not rigorously differentiated from everyday speech as came to be the case with European music, for most West African languages incorporate several of the basic structural elements of music: pitch, timbre, and timing.[7] A word uttered at a certain pitch may have a different meaning from the same word spoken at another pitch. The same dynamic applies to timbre and timing.

A further factor differentiating African from European music is the structural emphasis on rhythm as opposed to the emphasis on melody and harmony in European music. Rhythm's central role derives from its part in the process of *naming,* of imbuing things with the life force, in short, of humanizing the environment. There is a striking parallel to be drawn between the West African notion of *Nommo* and Karl Marx's definition of labor as "the living, shaping fire."[8] It can be argued, in fact, that the process of "naming" is something of a spiritual transmutation of the labor process—an ideological expression of what human labor can accomplish in society.

Throughout the history of Black music in the United States, *Nommo* was destined to remain the very essence of Black music making. African-American women musicians would rely on the power of *Nommo,* which would permit them to incorporate in their music and to impart to others by means of their music a collective consciousness and a very specific communal yearning for freedom. *Nommo* would moreover assist them in shaping through song an expression of the special meaning of Black womanhood, its realities, its limitations, its socio-historical legacy, and its collective potential with respect to the forging of a new society, based on economic, racial, and sexual equality.

Once Africans were forcibly planted in North America, they began to practice music-making in conjunction with the economic activity imposed on them by the conditions of slavery. The work songs they sang were "more than simply a means to ease hard physical labor."[9] They provided opportunities for commentary on the oppressiveness of slave work.

> Well, captain, captain, you mus' be blin'
> Look at you watch! See ain't it quittin' time?
> Well captain, captain, how can it be?
> Whistles keep a-blowin' you keep a-working me.[10]

The slaves sang in the old African tradition, but injected a new content into their music, a content that quite specifically reflected the conditions of their oppression and their desire to transform their collective predicament. But there were often references to the African past.

> The Negro work song became another example of the Negro's attempt to make the agonies of slavery bearable by integrating them with the images of his African past. There was no getting away from the miseries of planation labor, so the work was infused with the songs of better days and soon the songs were to influence the music of the slaves and their descendants.[11]

Aside from lullabies sung by slave women to white babies (and indeed those sung to their own as well) and possibly other songs related to specifically female domestic tasks, one discovers few gender distinctions in the great body of work songs of the slaves. This is not surprising, since there was a distinct lack of a sexual division of labor in the chattel slave system. Economically, the women were called upon to perform the same tasks as the men and while sexual abuse and the violation of women's reproductive rights, for example, constituted a special form of oppression for women, the overall predicament was not qualitatively differentiated from that of their brothers, fathers, sons, and husbands. Like the work songs, the spirituals place little or no emphasis on the specificity of women's experiences within their commentary on the collective experience of oppression. The historical and spiritual transcendance of the religious slave songs did not, however, establish a male supremacist vision of the slave experience. On the contrary, the aesthetic community forged by means of the spiritual was one which was based in the concrete participation of the individual slaves, men and women alike.

> The spirituals are historical songs which speak about the rupture of black lives; they tell us about a people in the land of bondage and what they did to hold themselves together and to fight back. We are told that the people of Israel could not sing the Lord's song in a strange land. But, for Blacks, their *being* depended upon a song. Through song they built new structures for existence in an alien land. The spirituals enabled blacks to retain a measure of African identity, while living in the midst of African slavery, providing both the substance and the rhythm to cope with human servitude.[12]

The incorporation of concrete historical conditions related to the slaves' desire to live free, human lives, into religious songs which, on their face, transcended concrete historical realities, can be clearly illustrated by the songs employed by the woman who became the most prominent conductor on the Underground Railroad—Harriet Tubman. In his 1942 article entitled "General Tubman, Composer of Spirituals," Earl Conrad argued that Harriet Tubman made abundant use of spirituals to facilitate the process of leading masses of people to their freedom. Although "Old Chariot" may have had an obvious eschatological meaning, its worldly dimension involved a public proclamation of the preparations under way for the trek northwards. Harriet herself, in fact, was also known as "Old Chariot"—a name that rhymed with her own.[13]

> When the old chariot comes,
> I'm going to leave you.
> I'm bound for the promised land.
> I'm going to leave you.

Conrad gives an account of one of Harriet Tubman's trips during which she was compelled to leave a party of fugitive slaves in order to find food for them:

She dared not go back to them til night, for fear of being watched. . . . They listen eagerly for the words she sings, for by them they are to be warned of danger or informed of safety. Nearer and nearer comes the unseen singer, and the words are wafted to their ears.

> Hail, oh hail, ye happy spirits,
> Death no more shall make you fear,
> Grief nor sorrow, pain nor anguish
> Shall no more distress you there.
>
> Around him are ten thousand angels,
> Around him are ten thousand angels.
> They are always hovering around you
> Till you reach the heavenly land.
>
> Jesus, Jesus will go with you;
> He will led you to his throne;
> He who died has gone before you
> Trod the winepress all alone.
>
> He whose thunders shake creation;
> He who bids the planets roll;
> He who rides upon the tempest
> And his sceptre sways the whole.
>
> Dark and thorny is the desert
> Where the pilgrim makes his ways.
> Yet beyond this vale of sorrow
> Lies the field of endless days.

This spiritual served as a sign that the slaves should listen for a further song-signal. If she sang this one a second time, they knew that they could leave their hiding places, but if she sang a verse of "Go Down Moses," this was an indication that there was danger and they should remain hidden.[14] Other verses of "Go Down Moses" were used to summon together those who would be accompanying Harriet Tubman on the long journey to freedom, and "Wade in the Water" warned the fugitive slaves that bloodhounds were on their track and if they walked in the shallow waters of rivers and streams, the dogs would lose their scent.[15]

Tubman's spirituals were functional not only in the sense that they provided concrete information about the struggle for liberation, they also were functional in the sense that they assisted in the forging of a collective social consciousness—indeed of both an aesthetic and a socio-historical community of individuals who had a very basic need to be free. Collective consciousness of freedom does not automatically accompany oppression. That consciousness must be actively created. For Black people in the United States during the era of slavery, the spiritual played a fundamental role in communicating the ingredients of that collective consciousness to masses of slaves. Freedom was named—literally and metaphorically—in accordance with the West African tradition of *Nommo*.

> Oh Freedom, oh Freedom!
> Oh Freedom, I love thee!
> And before I'll be a slave,
> I'll be buried in my grave,
> And go home to my Lord and be free.

Another outstanding Black woman of the slave era also used song to make her point about freedom. Sojourner Truth used religious hymns to convey her message of freedom and she even composed her own verses, such as the following ones, which were sung at an abolitionist meeting.

> I am pleading for my people,
> A poor downtrodden race,
> Who dwell in freedom's boasted land,
> With no abiding place.
>
> I am pleading that my people,
> May have their rights restored;
> For they have long been toiling,
> And yet have no reward.
>
> They are forced the crops to culture,
> But not for them they yield,
> Although both late and early
> They labor in the field.

Whilst I bear upon my body
The scars of many a gash,
I am pleading for my people
Who groan beneath the lash.[16]

W. E. B. Du Bois described the coming of freedom for Black slaves in the South as the rising of a new song:

> There was joy in the South. It rose like perfume—like a prayer. Men stood quivering. Slim dark girls, wild and beautiful with wrinkled hair, wept silently; young women, black, tawny, white and golden, lifted shivering hands and old and broken mothers, black and gray, raised great voices and shouted to God across the fields, and up the rocks and the mountains.
>
> A great song arose, the loveliest thing born this side the seas. It was a new song. It did not come from Africa, though the dark throb and beat of that Ancient of Days was in it and through it. It did not come from white America—never from so pale and hard and thin a thing, however deep these vulgar tones had driven. Not the Indies nor the hot South, the cold East or heavy West made that music. It was a new song and its deep and plaintive beauty, its great cadences and wild appeal wailed, throbbed and thundered on the world's ears with a message seldom voiced by man. It swelled and blossomed like incense, improvised and born anew out of an age long past, and weaving into its texture the old and new melodies in word and thought.[17]

However, the new-found freedom was to present a whole host of new problems for the former slaves, indeed, entirely new modes of oppression emanating from a transitional socio-economic system which had left slavery behind and would rapidly move in the direction of industrial capitalism. A new song was indeed eventually consolidated, but it was not the song of freedom, corresponding to the goal so passionately sought in the spirituals of slavery times. It was a song called the blues, which enumerated, again in the West African tradition of *Nommo,* the new troubles Black people faced in a world that still refused to accept them as equals, a society that thrived on the systematic exploitation and discrimination meted out to the former slaves. The blues also incorporated a new consciousness about private love relationships, which had been denied to Black people, except in a rudimentary way, as long as they were slaves. In many ways, in fact, interpersonal relationships functioned as metaphors for the freedom they sought: trouble in the relationship was trouble in the overall social universe. The happiness they sought in their relationships indicated by the expression of a need for "a good woman" or for "a man who won't treat me mean" symbolized their search for a life which would be free of the countless brutal realities encountered in postslavery America. If there was a hidden meaning behind the religious language of the spirituals, there was also a hidden meaning behind the sexual language of the blues. As the spirituals consolidated a collective social consciousness of the need to fight for freedom under slavery, the blues also forged a communal consciousness, one that was based on the communication and sharing of African-Americans' individual suffering and the expression of the possibility of prevailing over the most intransigent problems.

Gertrude "Ma" Rainey was called the "Mother of the Blues" because she was the first widely known black entertainer who used blues as the basis of her repertoire. The first blues singers, who were predominantly male, were not formal entertainers, but rather individuals who engaged in the same economic activity as their peers, but who were most capable of incorporating the group's personal as well as social experiences into song. Ma Rainey, on the other hand, performed in circuses, tent shows, minstrel and medicine shows, singing all the same about the Black predicament and establishing the basis in song for the sharing of experiences and the forging of a community capable of persevering through private tribulations and even of articulating new hopes and aspirations. Ma Rainey's most essential social accomplishment was to keep poor Black people grounded in the Southern tradition of unity and struggle, even when they had migrated to the North and Midwest in search of economic security. As Sandra Lieb has pointed out,

> For her audience, whether listening to her records in a small Mississippi town or watching her perform in Chicago, she was a reminder, a witness, an affirmation of Southern black culture as positive, resilient, and life-affirming, even as great numbers of people were being uprooted and displaced from that culture by migration to the North.[18]

The most vivid account of Ma Rainey's impact on her audience is contained in a poem by Sterling Brown. He describes the audience as consisting of people who had come from all around on mules and on trains, from the river settlements, from lumber camps and from "blackbottom cornrows." He continues, in the third and fourth verses:

Ma Rainey,
Sing yo' song:
Now you's back
Whah you belong.
Git way inside us,
Keep us strong . . .
Sing us 'bout de hard luck
'Roun' our do';
Sing us 'bout de lonesome road
We mus' go . . .

I talked to a fellow, an' the fellow say,
"She jes' catch hold of us, somekindaway.
She sang 'Backwater Blues' one day . . .
An' de folks, dey natchally bowed dey heads an' cried,
Bowed dey heavy heads, shet dey moufs up tight an' cried,
An' Ma lef' de stage, an' followed some de folks outside,"
Dere wasn't much more de fellow say;
She jes' gets hold of us dataway.[19]

The vast majority of Ma Rainey's blues revolve around problems emanating from personal relationships. However, the meaning of sexual love for the former slaves and their descendants was far more central than it might have been if their lives had offered more options for creative expression. Because of the objective limitations imposed by the economic circumstances surrounding them—Black people in the South during that period were by and large sharecroppers or tenant farmers and those in the North who found work were miserably exploited and always risked being the first fired—their only immediate hopes for happiness resided in the possibility of establishing a love relationship that would provide them with personal fulfillment.

Moreover, the language of sexual love in Ma Rainey's blues meta-phorically reveals and expresses a range of economic, social, and psychological difficulties which Black people suffered during the post–Civil War era. And the desire to find a good man symbolizes the desperate desire to create a life free of poverty, discrimination, and all the other material causes of the blues. It is most often the case that Ma Rainey's songs do not explicitly point to the causes of Black people's misery; they are generally referred to simply as the "blues." And indeed, in the West African tradition of *Nommo,* she often sim-ply names the blues. Consider the text of "Blues Oh Blues":

> Oh blues, oh blues, oh blues, oh blues, blues, oh blues.
> I'm so blue, so blue, I don't know what to do.
> Oh blues, oh blues, oh blues.

> I'm going away, I'm going to stay; I'm going away, I'm
>     going to stay
> I'm going away, oh mama's going to stay.
> I'm going to find the man I love some sweeet day.

> Oh blues, oh blues, oh blues, oh blues, blues, oh blues.
> I'm so blue, so blue, oh mama don't know what to do.
> Oh blues, I'm blue, oh blues.[20]

In this song, Rainey calls the name of the blues over twenty times, thus conjuring up all the various causes of her miserable predica-ment and at the same time using the power of the word to magically assert control over circumstances otherwise far beyond her reach. This magical, aesthetic assertion of control over the blues is an im-plicit expression of the real need to transform the objective condi-tions that are at the root of these blues: a camouflaged dream of a new social order. This is the powerful utopian function of the blues. The language in which this dream is expressed is the language of sexual love, thus "I'm going to find the man I love some sweet day." If Ma Rainey's audience was as deeply moved as Sterling Brown's poem indicates, they must have sensed the deeper meaning of her words.

A characteristic dynamic of Ma Rainey's music is the public com-munication of private troubles. This dynamic contains an implicit recognition of the social nature of Black people's individual situations and at the same time it allows for the development of a collective social consciousness within the Black population. The consciousness of the social character of Black people's suffering is the precondition for the creation of a political protest movement—and, indeed, by the 1920s, such movements had begun to crystallize.

"Bad Luck Blues" begins by alerting the audience of the singer's intention to publicize her own situation: "Hey, people, listen while I spread my news (*Repeat*) / I want to tell you people all about my bad luck blues." She continues by asking the audience to acknowledge the commonality of her problem and theirs, for implied in the question of the second stanza is that they have certainly experienced something similar to the episode which has caused her to be afflicted with the blues.

> Did you ever wake up just at the break of day,
> Did you ever break up just at the wake of day,
> With your arm around the pillow just where your daddy
>     used to lay?

While her words refer to a concrete situation—the loss of a love partner—the deeper meaning of this language has to do with need or desire in general. Certainly every Black person who listened to Ma Rainey sing was in need of something critically important in her or his life. Sharing and communicating need was a central feature of the blues, and the process of developing an awareness of the collective nature of the experience of need was very much related to the ability of the African-American people to survive when all odds were against them.

During the historical era leading up to the 1920s, the Jim Crow system of segregation was consolidated, Black people were systematically disfranchised, and the Ku Klux Klan and other terrorist groups were responsible for untold thousands of lynchings. The economic predicament of Black people in the South caused many to travel northwards in search of jobs, and there they discovered that racism was often just as devastating as in the South. During the summer months of 1919, there were so many bloody riots directed against African-American people, that this season came to be known as the Red Summer of 1919. Certainly Ma Rainey's fans perceived the deeper meaning of songs like "Bad Luck Blues." A few of Ma Rainey's songs directly attacked the issue of Black people's economic misery, and some of them, such as "Ma and Pa's Poorhouse Blues," use humor to soften the cutting edge of oppression. This blues was recorded together with "Papa" Charlie Jackson and is introduced by a dialogue between them about the hard times they are both experiencing. The dialogue concludes:

> *Ma:* Charlie, you know I'm broke?
> *Charlie:* Ma, don't you know I'm broke too? What we gonna do?
> *Ma:* Let's both go to the poorhouse together.
> *Charlie:* All right, let's go together.

At the end of this blues, they both sing: "We better go to the poorhouse, try to live anyhow." The comic dimension of this particular song, unambiguously conveyed by the duo's performance, reveals and simultaneously encourages the African-American community's resilience and its powers of perseverance. Its message is clear: unity is the community's saving grace.

In other songs, Ma Rainey calls upon Black people who have traveled North to look back to their Southern homeland for consolation and inspiration. "South Bound Blues" specifically evokes the situation of a woman who has accompanied her man to the North, only to have him leave her in that alien world:

> Yes I'm mad, my heart's sad,
> The man I love treated me so bad;
> He brought me out of my home town,
> Took me to New York and threw me down.

> Without a cent to pay my rent,
> I'm left alone, without a home;
> I told him I would leave him and my time ain't long.
> My folks done sent the money, and I'm Dixie bound.

Her decision to return home gives her the strength to consider the eventuality of challenging the man who is responsible for her troubles: "I told him I'd see him, honey, some of these days, / And

I'm going to tell him 'bout his low down dirty ways." The last verse is celebratory and optimistic:

> Done bought my ticket, Lord, and my trunk is packed,
> Going back to Georgia, folks, I sure ain't coming back.
> My train is in the station, I done sent my folks the news,
> You can tell the world I've got those Southbound blues.

The message of this song clearly indicates that African-American culture rooted in the Southern experience is the source of Black people's creative energy and of their ability to survive as a people. As in most of Ma Rainey's songs, the focal point is an interpersonal relationship, and the man in the relationship is evoked in an accusatory fashion. However, the adversities attributed to male behavior within a love relationship can also be interpreted as the material hindrances of racism. What is needed to survive these difficulties is the inspiration that comes from knowing that Black people in the South have survived the Middle Passage from Africa and at least two centuries of slavery, as well as the horrendous racism in the aftermath of slavery. The actual return by train to Georgia described in "South Bound Blues" is also a spiritual identification with the Black ethos of the South. That ethos incorporates the cumulative struggles Black people have collectively waged over the centuries, struggles that alone have insured our survival.

"South Bound Blues" also evokes the special problems encountered by Black women—since its protagonist is a woman who finds herself betrayed and mistreated by a man whom she has accompanied to an alien and hostile world. The spiritual identification encouraged with the Black culture of the South is with a culture that necessarily produced a standard of womanhood based on self-reliance and independence. In other words, "South Bound Blues" also appeals to women to summon up within themselves the courage and independence of their foremothers.

Several of Ma Rainey's songs are direct exhortations to Black women to develop a spirit of self-reliance that directly contradicts the ideological notion of womanhood prevalent in the larger society. "Trust No Man" advises women not to depend absolutely on their men if they do not wish to be deceived.

> I want all you women to listen to me,
> Don't trust no man no further than your eyes can see;
> I trusted mine with my best friend,
> But that was the bad part in the end.

> Trust no man, trust no man, no further than your eyes
>     can see.
> I said, trust no man, no further than your eyes can see.

> He'll tell you that he loves you and swear it's true,
> The very next minute, he's going to trifle on you;
> Ah—trust no man, no further than your eyes can see.

While on its face, this song might appear to be utterly, though perhaps only temporarily, antimale, its deeper meaning might have less to do with the proclamation of Black men's negative traits than with the need for Black women to develop economic and psychological independence. W. E. B. Du Bois's essay, "The Damnation of Women" describes the development of economic independence among Black women during the postslavery era and argues that African-American women's experiences demonstrated to the larger society that women could not be imprisoned in the home and that they could not be required "on pain of death to be nurses and housekeepers."[21] "Trust No Man" implies that women should not be compelled to be appendages to men, blindly following their lead, but rather should carry forth the historical legacy of independence forged throughout the history of Black women's presence in North America.

Another song that directly addresses women, "Prove It On Me Blues" has most frequently been interpreted simply as a bold affirmation of lesbianism. Of course Ma Rainey's emotional and sexual ties with women have been documented and it has been speculated that she and Bessie Smith engaged at one time in relations with each other. On the surface, "Prove It On Me Blues" is a flaunting song about women-identified emotional and sexual relations, but it is also about the affirmative emotional links between Black women, whatever their sexual identification might be.

> I went out last night with a crowd of my friends,
> They must have been women, 'cause I don't like no men.

Wear my clothes just like a fan,
Talk to the gals just like any old man;
'Cause they say I do it, ain't nobody caught me,
Sure got to prove it on me.

Certainly close emotional relationships between Black women—as family members, as workers, or as political activists—have been an important source of female independence. These relationships have so often been denied by those who would portray Black women as chronically competitive personalities, especially where men are concerned.

Gertrude "Ma" Rainey made an inestimable contribution both to the musical culture of the Black community and to the development of a collective social consciousness related to the specificity of the African-American predicament. Until very recently, her cultural value had been virtually ignored. Derrick Stewart-Baxter's *Ma Rainey and the Classic Blues Singers* was the only book-length study devoted to the blueswomen of Ma Rainey's era, and only a few pages in that short book were actually dedicated to Ma Rainey herself. In 1981, Sandra Lieb published her pioneering book, *Mother of the Blues: A Study of Ma Rainey*. Her book is an extremely valuable scholarly contribution, although it does not explore the entire spectrum of meaning in Ma Rainey's songs. A further study should evaluate the texts of Ma Rainey's blues, relating them to the general socio-historical context in which they were created and performed, which includes not only the objective conditions of her time, but also the music's cultural continuum, a continuum that reaches back to Harriet Tubman's spirituals, to slave women's work songs, and indeed to the original West African musical tradition of *Nommo*. Only then will we be in a position to accurately evaluate the part played by Ma Rainey's music in the forging of Black social consciousness and ultimately in the creation of a vital mass movement for Black equality.

Bessie Smith's music, much of it recorded simultaneously with Ma Rainey's—and, indeed, some of it prior to her elder's first recordings—was created in the same tradition as that of the "Mother of the Blues." The women's blues tradition also directly influenced the work of Billie Holiday. While it is not possible here to examine the body of these two women's work, an appropriate conclusion of this essay might be the texts of the most revealing political songs of these two artists. For Bessie Smith, it is "Poor Man's Blues":

> Mr. rich man, rich man, open up your heart and mind
>      (*Repeat*)
> Give the poor man a chance, help stop these hard, hard times.
>
> While you're living in your mansion, you don't know
>      what hard times mean (*Repeat*)
> Poor working man's wife is starving, your wife is living
>      like a queen.
>
> Please listen to my pleadin', 'cause I can't stand these hard
>      times long (*Repeat*)
> They'll make an honest man do things that you know is
>      wrong.
>
> Now the war is over; poor man must live the same as you
>      (*Repeat*)
> If it wasn't for the poor man, mister rich man, what would
>      you do?

For Billie Holiday, it is, of course, "Strange Fruit":

> Southern trees bear a strange fruit
> Blood on the leaves, blood on the root
> Black bodies swinging in the Southern breeze
> Strange fruit hanging from the poplar trees
> Pastoral scene of the gallant South
> The bulging eyes and the twisted mouth
> Scent of magnolia sweet and fresh
> Then the sudden smell of burning flesh
> Here is a fruit for the crows to pluck
> For the rain to gather, for the wind to suck
> For the sun to rot, for the tree to drop
> Here is a strange and bitter crop.

# Notes

1     Karl Marx and Frederick Engels, *Marx and Engels on Literature and Art* (Moscow: Progress Publishers, 1976), p. 41.

2     James Cone, *The Spirituals and the Blues* (New York: The Seabury Press, 1972), p. 5.

3     W.E.B. Du Bois, *The Souls of Black Folk* (New York: New American Library, 1969), p. 265.

4     Ernest Borneman, "The Roots of Jazz," in *Jazz,* ed. Nat Hentoff and Albert J. McCarthy (New York: Da Capo Press, 1975), p. 3.

5     Ibid., p. 4.

6     Janheinz Jahn, *Muntu, The New African Culture* (New York: Grove Press, 1961), p. 135.

7     Borneman, "Roots," p. 6.

8     Karl Marx, *Grundrisse der Kritik der Politischen Oekonomie* (Berlin: Dietz Verlag, 1953), p. 266.

9     Giles Oakley, *The Devil's Music, A History of the Blues* (New York: Harcourt Brace Jovanovich, 1976), p. 39.

10     Ibid., p. 39.

11     Borneman, "Roots," p. 14.

12     Cone, *Spirituals and the Blues,* pp. 32–33.

13     Earl Conrad, "General Tubman, Composer of Spirituals: An Amazing Figure in American Folk Music," *The Etude* (May 1942), p. 305.

14     Ibid., p. 305.

15     John Lovell, Jr., *Black Song: The Forge and the Flame* (New York: The Macmillan Company, 1972), p. 196.

16     Jacqueline Bernard, *Journey Toward Freedom, The Story of Sojourner Truth* (New York: W. W. Norton and Company, 1967), pp. 149–150.

17     W.E.B. Du Bois, *Black Reconstruction in America* (New York: Meridian Books, 1964), p. 124.

18.     Sandra Lieb, *Mother of the Blues: A Study of Ma Rainey* (Amherst: The University of Massachusetts Press, 1981), p. 79.

19     Ibid., pp. 14–15.

20     This text and the remaining texts of Ma Rainey's, Bessie Smith's, and Billie Holiday's songs are based on my own transcriptions.

21     W.E.B. Du Bois, *Darkwater, Voices from Within the Veil* (New York: Harcourt, Brace and Howe, 1920), p. 18.

# June Jordan

# The Difficult Miracle of Black Poetry in America or Something Like a Sonnet for Phillis Wheatley

I t was not natural. And she was the first. Come from a country of many tongues tortured by rupture, by theft, by travel like mismatched clothing packed down into the cargo hold of evil ships sailing, irreversibly, into slavery; come to a country where, to be docile and dumb, to be big and breeding, easily, to be turkey/horse/cow to be cook/carpenter/plow to be 5'6" 140 lbs. in good condition and answering to the name of Tom or Mary; to be bed bait; to be legally spread legs for rape by the master/the master's son/the master's overseer/the master's visiting nephew; to be nothing human nothing family nothing from nowhere nothing that screams nothing that weeps nothing that dreams nothing that keeps anything/anyone deep in your heart; to live forcibly illiterate forcibly itinerant; to live eyes lowered head bowed; to be worked without rest to be worked without pay to be worked without thanks to be worked day up to nightfall; to be 3/5ths of a human being at best: to be this valuable, this hated thing among strangers who purchased your life and then cursed it unceasingly: to be a slave: to be a slave: come to this country a slave and how should you sing? After the flogging the lynch rope the general terror and weariness what should you know of a lyrical life? How could you, belonging to no one, but property to those despising the smiles of your soul, how could you dare to create yourself: A poet?

A poet can read. A poet can write.

A poet is African in Africa, or Irish in Ireland, or French on the Left Bank of Paris, or white in Wisconsin. A poet writes in her own language. A poet writes of her own people, her own history, her own vision, her own room, her own house where she sits at her own table quietly placing one word after another word until she builds a line and a movement and an image and a meaning that somersaults all of these into the singing, the absolutely individual voice of the poet: At liberty. A poet is somebody free. A poet is someone at home.

How should there be Black poets in America?

It was not natural. And she was the first. In 1761, so far back before the revolution that produced these United States, so far back before the concept of freedom disturbed the insolent crimes of this continent, in 1761, when seven-year-old Phillis stood, as she must, when she stood nearly naked, as small as a seven-year-old, by herself, standing on land at last, at last, after the long, annihilating horrors of the middle Passage. Phillis, standing on the auctioneer's rude platform: Phillis For Sale:

Was it a nice day?

Does it matter? Should she muse on the sky or remember the sea? Until then Phillis had been somebody's child. Now she was about to become somebody's slave.

Suzannah and John Wheatley finished their breakfast and ordered the carriage brought 'round. They would ride to the auction. This would be an important outing. They planned to buy yet another human being to help with the happiness of their comfortable life in Boston. You don't buy a human being, you don't purchase a slave, without thinking ahead. So they had planned this excursion. They were dressed for the occasion, and excited, probably. And experienced, certainly. The Wheatleys already owned several slaves. They had done this before; the transaction would not startle or confound or embarrass or appall either one of them.

Was it a nice day?

When the Wheatleys arrived at the auction they greeted their neighbors, they enjoyed this business of mingling with other townsfolk politely shifting about the platform, politely adjusting positions for gain of a better view of the bodies for sale. The Wheatleys were good people. They were kind people. They were openminded and thoughtful. They looked at the bodies for sale. They looked and they looked. This one could be useful for that. That one might be useful for this. But then they looked at that child, that black child standing nearly naked, by herself. Seven or eight years old, at the most, and frail. Now that was a different proposal! Not a strong body, not a grown set of shoulders, not a promising wide set of hips, but a little body, a delicate body, a young, surely terrified face! John Wheatley agreed to the whim of his wife, Suzannah. He put in his bid. He put down his cash. He called out the numbers. He competed success- fully. He had a good time. He got what he wanted. He purchased yet another slave. He bought that Black girl standing on the platform, nearly naked. He gave this new slave to his wife and Suzannah Wheatley was delighted. She and her husband went home. They rode there by carriage. They took that new slave with them. An old slave commanded the horses that pulled the carriage that carried the Wheatleys home, along with the new slave, that little girl they named Phillis.

Why did they give her that name?

Was it a nice day?

Does it matter?

It was not natural. And she was the first: Phillis Miracle: Phillis Miracle Wheatley: The first Black human being to be published in America. She was the second female to be published in America.

And the miracle begins in Africa. It was there that a bitterly anony- mous man and a woman conjoined to create this genius, this lost child of such prodigious aptitude and such beguiling attributes that she very soon interposed the reality of her particular, dear life be- tween the Wheatley's notions about slaves and the predictable out- come of such usual blasphemies against Black human beings.

Seven-year-old Phillis changed the slaveholding Wheatleys. She altered their minds. She entered their hearts. She made them see her and when they truly saw her, Phillis, darkly amazing them with the sweetness of her spirit and the alacrity of her forbidden, strange in- telligence, they, in their own way, loved her as a prodigy, as a girl mysterious but godly.

Sixteen months after her entry into the Wheatley household Phillis was talking the language of her owners. Phillis was fluently reading the Scriptures. At eight and a half years of age, this Black child, or "Afric's Muse," as she would later describe herself, was fully literate in the language of this slaveholding land. She was competent and eagerly asking for more: more books, more and more information. And Suzannah Wheatley loved this child of her whimsical good luck. It pleased her to teach and to train and to tutor this Black girl, this Black darling of God. And so Phillis delved into kitchen studies commensurate, finally, to a classical education available to young white men at Harvard.

She was nine years old.

What did she read? What did she memorize? What did the Wheatleys give to this African child? Of course, it was white, all of it: White. It was English, most of it, from England. It was written, all of it, by white men taking their pleasure, their walks, their pipes, their pens and their paper, rather seriously, while somebody else cleaned the house, washed the clothes, cooked the food, watched the children: Probably not slaves, but possibly a servant, or, commonly, a wife: It was written, this white man's literature of England, while somebody else did the other things that have to be done. And that was the literature absorbed by the slave, Phillis Wheatley. That was the writing, the thoughts, the nostalgia, the lust, the conceits, the ambitions, the mannerisms, the games, the illusions, the discoveries, the filth and the flowers that filled up the mind of the African child.

At fourteen, Phillis published her first poem, "To the University of Cambridge": Not a brief limerick or desultory, teenager's verse, but thirty-two lines of blank verse telling those fellows what for and whereas, according to their own strict Christian codes of behavior. It is in that poem that Phillis describes the miracle of her own Black poetry in America:

> While an intrinsic ardor bids me write
> the muse doth promise to assist my pen

She says that her poetry results from "an intrinsic ardor," not to dismiss the extraordinary kindness of the Wheatleys, and not to diminish the wealth of white men's literature with which she found herself quite saturated, but it was none of these extrinsic factors that compelled the labors of her poetry. It was she who created herself a poet, notwithstanding and in despite of everything around her.

Two years later, Phillis Wheatley, at the age of sixteen, had composed three additional, noteworthy poems. This is one of them, "On Being Brought from Africa to America":

> Twas mercy brought me from my Pagan land,
> Taught my benighted soul to understand

> That there's a God, that there's a Savior too:
> Once I redemption neither sought nor knew
> Some view our sable race with scornful eye,
> "Their color is a diabolic die."
> Remember, *Christians,* Negroes, black as Cain,
> May be refin'd, and join the angelic train.

Where did Phillis get these ideas?

It's simple enough to track the nonsense about herself "benighted": *benighted* means surrounded and preyed upon by darkness. That clearly reverses what had happened to that African child, surrounded by and captured by the greed of white men. Nor should we find puzzling her depiction of Africa as "Pagan" versus somewhere "refined." Even her bizarre interpretation of slavery's theft of Black life as a merciful rescue should not bewilder anyone. These are regular kinds of iniquitous nonsense found in white literature, the literature that Phillis Wheatley assimilated, with no choice in the matter.

But here, in this surprising poem, this first Black poet presents us with something wholly her own, something entirely new: It is her matter-of-fact assertion that "once I redemption neither sought nor knew," as in: Once I existed beyond and without these terms under consideration. *Once I existed on other than your terms.* And, she says, *but* since we are talking with your talk about good and evil/redemption and damnation, let me tell you something you had better understand. I am Black as Cain *and* I may very well be an angel of the Lord: Take care not to offend the Lord!

Where did that thought come to Phillis Wheatley?

Was it a nice day?

Does it matter?

Following her "intrinsic ardor," and attuned to the core of her own person, this girl, the first Black poet in America, had dared to redefine herself from house slave to, possibly, an angel of the Almighty.

And she was making herself at home.

And, depending on whether you estimated that nearly naked Black girl on the auction block to be seven or eight years old, in 1761, by the time she was eighteen or nineteen, she had published her first book of poetry, *Poems on Various Subjects Religious and Moral.* It was published in London, in 1773, and the American edi-

tion appeared, years later, in 1786. Here are some examples from the
poems of Phillis Wheatley:

from "On the Death of Rev. Dr. Sewell":

> Come let us all behold with wishful eyes
> The saint ascending to his native skies.

from "On the Death of the Rev. Mr. George Whitefield":

> Take him, ye Africans, he longs for you,
> *Impartial Savior* is his title due,
> Washed in the fountain of redeeming blood
> You shall be sons and kings, and priest to God.

Here is an especially graceful and musical couplet:

> But, see the softly stealing tears apace.
> Pursue each other down the mourner's face;

This is an especially awful, virtually absurd set of lines by Ms.
Wheatley:

> Go, Thebons! great nations will obey,
> And pious tribute to her altars pay:
> With rights divine, the goddess be implor'd,
> Nor be her sacred offspring nor ador'd.
> Thus Manto spoke. The Thebon maids obey,
> And pious tribute to the goddess pay.

Awful, yes. Virtually absurd, well, yes, except consider what it
took for that young African to undertake such a persona, such values, and mythologies a million million miles remote from her own
ancestry, and her own darkly formulating race! Consider what might
meet her laborings, as a poet, should she, instead, invent a vernacular precise to Senegal, precise to slavery, and therefore accurate to
the secret wishings of her lost and secret heart?

If she, this genius teenager, should, instead of writing verse to comfort a white man upon the death of his wife, or a white woman upon the death of her husband, or verse commemorating weirdly fabled white characters bereft of children diabolically dispersed, if she, instead, composed a poetry to speak her pain, to say her grief, to find her parents, or to stir her people into insurrection, what would we now know about God's darling girl, that Phillis?

Who would publish that poetry, then?

But Phillis Miracle, she managed, nonetheless, to write, sometimes, towards the personal truth of her experience.

For example, we find in a monumental poem entitled "Thoughts on the Works of Providence," these five provocative lines, confirming every suspicion that most of the published Phillis Wheatley represents a meager portion of her concerns and inclinations:

> As reason's pow'rs by day our God disclose,
> So we may trace him in the night's repose.
> Say what is sleep? and dreams how passing strange!
> When action ceases, and ideas range
> Licentious and unbounded o'er the plains.

And, concluding this long work, there are these lines:

> Infinite *love* whene'er we turn our eyes
> Appears: this ev'ry creature's wants supplies,
> This most is heard in Nature's constant voice,
> This makes the morn, and this the eve rejoice,
> This bids the fost'ring rains and dews descend
> To nourish all, to serve on gen'ral end,
> The good of man: Yet man ungrateful pays
> But little homage, and but little praise.

Now and again and again these surviving works of the genius Phillis Wheatley veer, incisive and unmistakable, completely away from the verse of good girl Phillis ever compassionate upon the death of someone else's beloved, pious Phillis modestly enraptured by the glorious trials of virtue on the road to Christ, arcane Phillis intent upon an "Ode to Neptune," or patriotic Phillis penning an encomium to General George Washington ("Thee, first in peace and honor"). Then do we find that "Ethiop" as she once called herself, that "Africa's muse," knowledgeable, but succinct, on "dreams how passing strange! When action ceases, ideas range / licentious and unbounded o'er the plains."

Phillis Licentious Wheatley?

Phillis Miracle Wheatley in contemplation of love and want of love?

Was it a nice day?

It was not natural. And she was the first.

Repeatedly singing for liberty, singing against the tyrannical, repeatedly avid in her trusting support of the American Revolution (how could men want freedom enough to die for it but then want slavery enough to die for that), repeatedly lifting witness to the righteous and the kindly factors of her days, she was no ordinary teenage poet, male or female, Black or white. Indeed, the insistently concrete content of her tribute to the revolutionaries who would forge America, an independent nation state, indeed the specific daily substance of her poetry establishes Phillis Wheatley as the first decidedly American poet on this continent, Black or white, male or female.

Nor did she only love the ones who purchased her, a slave, those ones who loved her, yes, but with astonishment. Her lifelong friend was a young Black woman, Obour Tanner, who lived in Newport, Rhode Island, and one of her few poems dedicated to a living person, but neither morbid nor ethereal, was written to the young Black visual artist, Sapio Moorhead, himself a slave. It is he who crafted the portrait of Phillis that serves as her frontispiece profile in her book of poems. Here are the opening lines from her poem, "To S. M., A Young African Painter, On Seeing His Works":

> To show the lab'ring bosom's deep intent,
> And thought in living characters to paint.
> When first thy pencil did those beauties give,
> And breathing figures learnt from thee to live,
> How did those prospects give my soul delight,
> A new creation rushing on my sight?
> Still, wondrous youth! each noble path pursue,
> On deathless glories fix thine ardent view:
> Still may the painter's and the poet's fire
> To aid thy pencil, and thy verse conspire!

And many the charms of each seraphic theme
Conduct thy footsteps to immortal fame!

Remember that the poet so generously addressing the "wondrous youth" is certainly no older than eighteen, herself! And this, years before the American Revolution, and how many many years before the 1960s! This is the first Black poet of America addressing her Brother Artist not as so-and-so's Boy, but as "Sapio Moorhead, A Young African Painter."

Where did Phillis Miracle acquire this consciousness?

Was it a nice day?

It was not natural. And she was the first.

But did she, we may persevere, critical from the ease of the 1980s, did she love, did she need freedom?

In a poem typically titled at such length and in such deferential rectitude as to discourage most readers from scanning the poem that follows, in the poem titled, "To the Right Honorable William, Earl of Dartmouth, His Majesty's Principal Secretary of State for North America, etc."; Phillis Miracle has written these irresistible, authentic, felt lines:

No more America in mournful strain
Of wrongs, and grievance unredress'd complain,
No longer shalt Thou dread the iron chain,
Which wanton tyranny with lawless head
Had made, and with it meant t' enslave the land
Should you, my Lord, while you peruse my song,
Wonder from whence my love of Freedom sprung,
Whence flow these wishes for the common food,
By feeling hearts alone best understood,
I, young in life, by seeming cruel of fate
Was snatch'd from Afric's fancy'd happy seat.
What pangs excruciating most molest
What sorrows labour in my parent's breast?
Steel'd was that soul and by no misery mov'd
That from a father seized his babe belov'd
Such, such my case. And can I then but pray
Others may never feel tyrannic sway?

So did the darling girl of God compose her thoughts, prior to 1772.
And then.

And then her poetry, these poems, were published in London.

And then, during Phillis's twenty-first year, Suzannah Wheatley, the white woman slaveholder who had been changed into the white mother, the white mentor, the white protectorate of Phillis, died.

Without that white indulgence, that white love, without that white sponsorship, what happened to the young African daughter, the young African poet?

No one knows for sure.

With the death of Mrs. Wheatley, Phillis came of age, a Black slave in America.

Where did she live?

How did she eat?

No one knows for sure.

But four years later she met and married a Black man, John Peters. Mr. Peters apparently thought well of himself, and of his people. He comported himself with dignity, studied law, argued for the liberation of Black people, and earned the everyday dislike of whitefolks. His wife bore him three children; all of them died.

His wife continued to be Phillis Miracle.

His wife continued to obey the "intrinsic ardor" of her calling and she never ceased the practice of her poetry.

She hoped, in fact, to publish a second volume of her verse.

This would be the poetry of Phillis the lover of John, Phillis the woman, Phillis the wife of a Black man pragmatically premature in his defiant self-respect, Phillis giving birth to three children, Phillis the mother, who must bury the three children she delivered into American life.

None of these poems was ever published.

This would have been the poetry of someone who has chosen herself, free, and brave to be free in a land of slavery.

When she was thirty-one years old, in 1784, Phillis Wheatley, the first Black poet in America, she died.

Her husband, John Peters, advertised and begged that the manuscript of her poems she had given to someone, please be returned.

But no one returned them.

And I believe we would not have seen them, anyway. I believe no one would have published the poetry of Black Phillis Wheatley, that grown woman who stayed with her chosen Black man. I believe that the death of Suzannah Wheatley, coincident with the African poet's twenty-first birthday, signalled, decisively, the end of her status as a child, as a dependent. From there we would hear from an independent Black woman poet in America.

Can you imagine that, in 1775?

Can you imagine that, today?

America has long been tolerant of Black children, compared to its reception of independent Black men and Black women.

She died in 1784.

Was it a nice day?

It was not natural. And she was the first.

As the final judge for this year's [1986] Loft McKnight Awards in creative writing, awards distributed in Minneapolis, Minnesota, I read through sixteen manuscripts of rather fine poetry.

These are the terms, the lexical items, that I encountered there:

> Rock, moon, star, roses, chimney, Prague, elms,
> lilac, railroad tracks, lake, lilies, snow geese,
> crow, mountain, arrow feathers, ear of corn, marsh
> sandstone, rabbitbush, gulley, pumpkins, eagle,
> tundra, dwarf willow, dipper bird, brown creek,
> lizards, sycamores, glacier, canteen, skate eggs,
> birch, spruce, pumphandle

Is there anything about that listing odd? I didn't suppose so. These are the terms, the lexical items accurate to the specific white Minnesota daily life of those white poets.

And so I did not reject these poems, I did not despise them saying, "How is this possible: Sixteen different manuscripts of poetry written in 1985 and not one of them uses the terms of my own Black life! Not one of them writes about the police murder of Eleanor Bumpurs or the Bernard Goetz shooting of four Black boys or apartheid in South Africa, or unemployment, or famine in Ethiopia, or rape, or fire escapes, or cruise missiles in the New York harbor, or medicare, or alleyways, or napalm, or $4 an hour and no time off for lunch.

I did not and I would not presume to impose my urgencies upon white poets writing in America. But the miracle of Black poetry in

America, the *difficult* miracle of Black poetry in America, is that we have been rejected and we are frequently dismissed as "political" or "topical" or "sloganeering" and "crude" and "insignificant" because, like Phillis Wheatley, we have persisted for freedom. We will write against South Africa and we will seldom pen a poem about wild geese flying over Prague, or grizzlies at the rain barrel under the dwarf willow trees. We will write, published or not, however we may, like Phillis Wheatley, of the terror and the hungering and the quandaries of our African lives on this North American soil. And as long as we study white literature, as long as we assimilate the English language and its implicit, English values, as long as we allude and defer to gods we "neither sought nor knew," as long as we, Black poets in America, remain the children of slavery, as long as we do not come of age and attempt, then, to speak the truth of our difficult maturity in an alien place, then we will be beloved, and sheltered, and published, and praised.

But not otherwise. And yet we persist.

And it was not natural. And she was the first.

This is the difficult miracle of Black poetry in America: that we persist, published or not, and loved or unloved: we persist.

And this is: "Something Like a Sonnet for Phillis Miracle Wheatley":

> Girl from the realm of birds florid and fleet
> flying full feather in far or near weather
> Who fell to a dollar lust coffled like meat
> Captured by avarice and hate spit together
> Trembling asthmatic alone on the slave bloc
> built by a savagery travelling by carrriage
> Viewed like a species of flaw in the livestock
> A child without safety of mother or marriage
>
> Chosen by whimsy but born to surprise
> They taught you to read but you learned how to write
> Begging the universe into your eyes:
> They dressed you in light but you dreamed
> with the night.

From Africa singing of justice and grace,
Your early verse sweetens the fame of our Race.

And because we Black people in North America persist in an irony profound, Black poetry persists in this way:

> Like the trees of winter and
> like the snow which has no power
> makes very little sound
> but comes and collects itself
> edible light on the black trees
> The tall black trees of winter
> lifting up a poetry of snow
> so that we may be astounded
> by the poems of black
> trees inside a cold environment.

# Gloria I. Joseph

# Sojourner Truth: Archetypal Black Feminist

W ho was this woman called Sojourner Truth? Isabella Baumfree was her given name, her surname being a Dutch nickname applied to her father. It is said that Sojourner Truth was born in 1797, but her birth was not accurately recorded. The vital statistics of Black people were customarily left unrecorded because of then-prevailing attitudes: "Negras aren't thoroughbreds and one doesn't make a fuss over registering a litter of mutts." It is known that Sojourner was born in the latter part of the eighteenth century in New York State's Ulster County; she died November 26, 1883, and was buried in Oak Hill Cemetery in Battle Creek, Michigan.

Sojourner Truth has been described as abolitionist, lecturer, women's rights activist, freedom fighter, domestic servant, evangelist, author, social worker, and a concerned and militant champion for the rights of her Black brothers and sisters. To list these occupations and roles, however, does not do justice to Sojourner's superordinate experiences, her uncanny wit, or her intellectual genius. As an archetypal Black feminist, Sojourner was a revolutionary whose life reflected the integrity and commitment to oppose any force that sought to deny Black people and other oppressed groups their basic human rights and dignity. Fighting personal and institutional bias during the period in which she lived, she charted a new way of existing on the shores of North America.

Sojourner was a prototype of generations of Black women to follow who would possess a strong sense of self as a Black person and a female. Her antiracist and antisexist consciousness opposed the oppression and the exploitation of the many for the few. During the antebellum history of the United States, she emerged as a precursor of Black women activists involved in the struggle to overcome racism, classism, and heterosexism, as well as sexism in the New World. In her life span, she used her experiences and those of other Black women as a barometer for articulating and taking measures for social change, and as a gauge for assessing the viability of proposed social tactics or policy reforms. Many Black women, also of the belief that gender and patriarchy were as central as race and class to understanding historical phenomena, would in her wake express her revolutionary ideas and emulate her deeds.

On the basis of her deeds and accomplishments, her name should be as well known as Susan B. Anthony, Elizabeth Cady Stanton, and Jane Addams. Among famous Black personages in history, her name should be side by side with W. E. B. Du Bois, Frederick Douglass, and Harriet Tubman. Her witticisms and adages are equal to those of Will Rogers and Benjamin Franklin, and her acts of courage comparable to those of Joan of Arc and Marie Curie. Instead, she remains one of the Black women whose histories have not adequately been treated. When her name is recognized in academic arenas, it is most often associated with her "Ain't I a Woman" speech, her peculiar grammar, and her heroic acts. Rarely is there any mention of the philosophical constructs and revolutionary concepts underlying her words and deeds.

A frightening example of the way in which Sojourner is misknown was made clear to me in one of my classes while teaching at Cornell University in the activist Sixties. I asked the class, which to my pleasure had a large number of Black students, "Who was Sojourner Truth?" A female student, with a look of pride and some arrogance, boldly explained to the class that "Sojourner Truth was a Black woman who white people thought was a man, and at a conference when a white man teased her calling her a man, she opened her dress and exposed her breasts to prove she was a woman." I was utterly astonished and kept my amazement under control as I explained that Sojourner's greatness did not lie in the fact that she was not a transvestite!

Nearly twenty years since that incident, too little of substance has been written about the profoundness and progressive-mindedness of this incredible woman. The experiences of Sojourner Truth have been recorded with a superwoman motif: a Black oddity with mysterious powers and great physical strength. Few historians have described her as a person of great mental and spiritual depth—a woman who earned worldwide fame for her stance on slavery, temperance, penal reform, and women's rights. There is a twenty-two-cent commemorative stamp honoring her in the Black Heritage Series; several women's organizations and publications are named after her; and about a half dozen authors have written books about her. Although honored in this way, why is the recognition so paltry given the magnitude of her greatness?

The current Women's Movement has brought Sojourner to the attention of feminists, but she is usually included as an "also ran," while the greatness and exploits of the pre– and post–Civil War white feminists and abolitionists are often extolled. Many of her feats remain unheralded. For example, relatively well known is the heroic behavior of Rosa Parks, a Black seamstress who—when she refused to give up her seat to a white man on a segregated bus in Montgomery, Alabama—sparked the Civil Rights Movement in 1955 with Black people's successful bus boycott. Virtually unknown is the fact that Sojourner was responsible for integrating a local transportation system. In the early 1860s, Sojourner protested Black people's restriction to Jim Crow cars. Her complaints led to congressional action banning segregated cars in the District of Columbia.

Passing the law itself did not mean that it would be followed, so Sojourner battled repeatedly with conductors who did not want to enforce the law. She confronted and combatted streetcar drivers and conductors and infuriated passengers, but she persevered. When drivers ignored her signal that indicated she wanted to board, she would cry out in her inimitable voice, "I WANT TO RIDE!"

And ride she did. On one occasion, she encountered a conductor who tried to shove her from the streetcar. In the fracas Sojourner suffered a dislocated shoulder. She took her case to court, won, and the conductor lost his job. Sojourner's comment after the tremendous victory was, "Before the trial was ended, the inside of the cars looked like pepper and salt."[1] This was one of many performances that attest to the vigilance with which Sojourner adhered to her principles, her courage in confronting injustice, and her wisdom in selecting appropriate actions. Almost a century apart, Rosa Parks and Sojourner Truth fought similar battles—battles they waged on behalf of themselves and, simultaneously, in the interests of the larger Black community.

Perhaps the relative dearth of critical studies about Sojourner Truth can be attributed to the claim that she was not a literate woman. Sojourner did not leave behind numerous treatise and books, or reams of scholarly writings and oratory. Yet, as Angela Davis noted of Harriet Tubman in 1971, Sojourner Truth's place in the Western intellectual tradition is not commensurate with her role and "has been consistently and grossly minimized."[2] Surely, Sojourner's legacy was as much her revolutionary philosophy as her activism—as an unflinching advocate of the human rights of the oppressed, especially Black people and all women.

There are, in the last decade, some writings that have begun to contextualize Sojourner in proper historical perspective as both an activist *and* a theorist in the *Black* and Women's liberation struggles of her day. They include Beverly Guy-Sheftall's "Remembering Sojourner Truth: On Black Feminism," *Catalyst;* Bettina Aptheker's *Women's Legacy: Essays on Race, Sex, and Class;* Victoria Ortiz's *Sojourner Truth: A Self-Made Woman,* a well-researched young adult book; and Raya Dunayevskaya's considerable works which consistently acknowledge Sojourner as a woman of both "revolutionary force" and "revolutionary reason."

Historical accounts of Sojourner's life commonly cite that Sojourner was deeply religious and that her beliefs had a great bearing on the way in which she lived her life. Her piety is invariably placed within the context of Western, patriarchal, organized religion and not within the African culture with which she and many other of her contemporary Black brethren were closely identified. But if Sojourner's religious experience was in any way typical of the millions of African people in the Americas, it can be reasonably assumed that her beliefs were informed by a combination of the African world view and the Judeo-Christian ethic.[3]

To examine the life of Sojourner within the framework of African cosmology and epistemology provides a deeper understanding of her activism, her thinking, and the legacy she left for Black feminists. In addition to her life setting forth the parameters of activism exercised by Black women today, her radical ideas remain a part of Black people's collective consciousness. Her words and deeds were wholly consistent with an Afrocentric perspective that African-American women activists assert in these times, distinguishing themselves as *Black* feminists.

The African world-view provides insight into the manner in which Sojourner lived her life—a style that has been interpreted as fearless, peculiar, extraordinary, and unique. African cosmology grows out of a fundamental belief in an indivisible and inexhaustible relationship among God, mankind, and the cosmos.[4] From the Afrocentric perspective, the material and spiritual world are inseparable—a view which informed all aspects of the social, political, educational, moral, and psychological dimensions of African community life. The quality of "fearlessness" associated with Sojourner could very well have been based upon her unequivocal dedication to structuring her reality to maximize the possibility of the most positive, earthly experience. Since (the African) reality is at once both spiritual and material, all is interrelated, interdependent, interconnected, and integrated. In this way of looking at things, everything becomes "spirit manifest." There is no "pie in the sky" separate from a hellish material existence.

Characterization of Sojourner as "extraordinary," "peculiar," and "unique" might also be traceable to her African world-view. In many traditional African societies, women were socially and economically independent and held in high esteem; aspects of egalitarian social organization were carried to and retained in the Americas by African people. Debunking the Western claim that women's autonomy was "foreign to the cultural heritages of Third World peoples," Eleanor Leacock wrote in the 1980s that, even today, "women anthropologists . . . are finding many attitudes and practices that indicate women's former status and persisting importance."[5] Undoubtedly, the prejudices of the times in which Sojourner lived did not validate her on any level—as a Black person, woman, slave, or domestic servant. To speak or act independently in the face of such prevalent biases would have provoked a range of reactions. Thus, for Sojourner, validation of her sense of mission and her importance as an African woman would have found only one source—the African world-view.

The oneness of reality and the principle of women's autonomy inherent in the Afrocentric world-view were constantly demonstrable in Sojourner's words and deeds. This is why she expressed incredulity and impatience when she confronted the passivity of feminists in the Women's Movement. Basically in agreement with the women's rights activists of her time, among them Lucy Stone, Lucretia Mott, Frances Gage as well as Susan B. Anthony and Elizabeth Cady Stanton, Sojourner Truth had a different outlook concerning direct action. For example, in 1850 at a women's conference, Sojourner had pointedly informed her counterparts, "Sisters, I aren't clear what you be after. If women want any rights more than they got, why don't they just take them and not be talking about it?"[6] Without fear of ostracism, Sojourner's passionate commitment to the need and urgency for social action reflected a blanket assumption that militancy was right. After all, by the logic of the Afrocentric perspective, the spirit is manifest in what one does and does not do.

The uncompromising stand Sojourner took in the face of the proposed Fourteenth Amendment to the United States Constitution vividly exemplifies her fearlessness, her staunch devotion to a qualitative experience in the "here and now." The Amendment, which gave Black males the vote but omitted any reference to women, outraged white suffragettes who felt betrayed. Previously in 1848 at the historic Seneca Falls Convention, Frederick Douglass had delivered an eloquent plea on behalf of women's right to vote. But by 1867, after the Civil War, it was Sojourner who stood alone for the all-but-forgotten Black women. Frederick Douglass and Frances Watkins, both Black activists, and Wendall Phillips and Abby Keely Foster, white long-time supporters of the Women's Movement, uniformly argued that the Black male slave's suffering entitled him to prior consideration.

The political perspicacity of Sojourner was obvious as she spoke to the issue of enfranchisement in her deep, sonorous voice: "My friends, I come from another field—the country of the slave. They have got their liberty—so much good luck to have slavery partly destroyed, not entirely. I want it root and branch destroyed. Then we will all be free indeed. I have a right as much as a man." She continued, "There is a great deal of stir about colored men getting their rights but not a word about the colored women's theirs, you see, the colored man will be masters over the women, and it will be just as bad as it was before. So I am for keeping the thing going while things are stirring, because if we wait 'till it is still, it will take a great while to get it going again."[7]

Sojourner was doggedly vigilant in not accepting anything short of full recognition of Black women's equality. Importantly, her reasoning is the genesis of parallel activity among twentieth-century Black feminists who have extended the Civil Rights and Black Power struggles of the fifties and sixties into an African-American feminist movement, "keeping the thing going while things are stirring."

Sojourner's words over a century ago imparted a consciousness of what contemporary African-American feminists have termed "the simultaneity of oppression." Speaking as a Black person and a woman, Sojourner identified patriarchal domination as another form of oppression. In her essay, "The Black Dimension in Women's Revolution," Raya Dunayevskaya aptly poses the question, "Have we even today, as we inveigh against 'male domination,' compared that to Sojourner's separation from Frederick Douglass after the Civil War for being 'short-minded' because he did not wish to burden the struggle for the passage of the Fourteenth Amendment by demanding also the right of women to vote?"[8] Sojourner Truth's concept of "short-minded" was a new language of thought for those who would impose a limitation to freedom.

Like David Walker's *Appeal to the Colored Citizens of the World* in 1829, Sojourner's appeal was pregnant with recognition that the suffering of any group or individual was wrong. Sojourner stood, in effect, fiercely committed to the logic of the Afrocentric world-view: any form of bondage is antithetical to God, a spiritual essence, consciousness, or energy that underlies the totality of creation. Suffering by God's creations assails God.

Although some might argue that Sojourner's views were typical of the feminist consciousness of her associates, it merits mention that Sojourner did not identify with the feminists of her period, only their common political objectives. Her ridicule of their class frivolity often provoked criticism from those who thought her behavior inappropriate for a woman. Imagine the nineteenth-century women's rights activists seated in the audience as Sojourner demanded, "What kind of reformers are you, with goose-wings on your heads, as if you were going to fly, and dressed in such ridiculous fashion, talking about reform and women's rights. It appears to me, you had better reform yourselves first."[9]

Another essential component of Afrocentric thought is sacrifice.[10] It is not conceived of as giving up or relinquishing something, as in the Western concept, but rather as a redistribution of necessary energy—a redistribution of the life force that permeates all living things and that is the power behind all living things.

In the African world-view, an unwillingness or failure to redistribute energy for the betterment of the world is no more than ungodly and requires active "reform." Sojourner's forceful honesty caused many of her white feminist associates to react with feigned and true horror. A present-day parallel is that of white feminists who are intimidated when Black feminists challenge stinginess or preoccupation with academic chatter and glamour in the face of the blight of apartheid and other human catastrophes.

The principle of sacrifice was key to how Sojourner made her place in the world. The problems she faced as a Black woman in the 1800s are distinctly the same as the ones Black women face today. Now as in yesteryear, an inordinate number of Black women live in poverty and raise children single-handedly, on scandalously pitiful incomes, while corporate America's living standards are shamefully opulent. Her observations of the condition of the poor in New York during the mid-1840s sound as if she were assessing the society in 1989: "Truly, here the rich rob the poor and the poor rob each other."[11]

Sojourner's work with the freed slaves after the Civil War provided her with the opportunity to understand more fully how the lives of her people were used for the enrichment of others. She detailed with painstaking accuracy how the vast and manifold contributions that Black people had made to the development of the United States had yet to be acknowledged or rewarded. "We have been a source of wealth to this republic," she proclaimed. "Our nerves and sinews, our tears and blood, have been sacrifices on the altar of this nation's avarice. Our unpaid labor has been a stepping stone to its financial success. Some of its dividends must surely be ours."[12] How often is Sojourner Truth's name associated with this revolutionary concept of reparations, a theme which has been extolled by numerous Black Power advocates?

From the Afrocentric perspective, Sojourner's work among those who lived in misery and poverty in Freedman's Village in Virginia should not be equated with sacrifice of her life to work among the "wretched of the earth." The underlying aim of the Afrocentric conceptual system is to achieve everlasting peace and happiness. Her work, therefore, represented an attempt to achieve a perpetual state of bliss for humankind through a redistribution of energy to create a life force. In terms of the African cosmology, what happens to one affects all. Modern expressions of this type of thinking were Black women's activism and credo which focused upon stemming the mysterious murders of Black children in Atlanta, Georgia: "Atlanta is all of us!" African cosmology is also evident in women of color's statement "Tawana is everybody's child," referring to the racist and sexist victimization of a young Black girl that captured national attention.[13] To sacrifice means to struggle since there can be no optimal existence while anyone suffers.

Sojourner's involvement with diverse groups in a variety of settings and often under trying conditions conformed to the African world-view. The route to perennial happiness and peace is cooperation with your fellow human beings to create or sustain a life force. Interpersonal relationships are accorded highest value in the Afrocentric conceptual system in contrast to the Western belief system in which the highest value of existence is the acquisition of material objects. Sojourner's cooperation with even hostile elements was fraught with a mindfulness of her intrinsic value and what constituted Godliness. "Take . . . how she handled the hypocritical ministers [white Abolitionists] who were taunting her, when she asked, 'Don't you believe in Jesus?' And when they said they did, how she told them, 'Well, Jesus is the son of God and Mary. Man had nothing to do with it.'"[14]

From the Afrocentric perspective, Sojourner's remarks were more than statements of Christian religious fact. If there is an "indivisible and inexhaustible relationship among God, mankind and the cosmos," then the clergy's blatant contempt for her divorced them from any affinity to Jesus. By the African world-view, all creations are valued manifestations of God. This world-view and her place within it gave her full license to respond without trepidation.

"I can't read, but I can read people," a characteristic Sojourner quote, could very well have been the postscript for her encounter with the Christian clergy. It would have been an appropriate statement in light of African epistemology. According to Linda Myers, "In the Afro-centric vein we assume self-knowledge is the basis of all knowledge, and one knows through symbolic imagery and rhythm. To the extent that we have assumed that self-knowledge is the basis of all knowledge and we are knowing more and more about this one essential essence, then how this essence is manifesting, how it's appearing, becomes extraordinarily critical."[15] Placing Sojourner within her African heritage, the declaration that she could "read people" represented an expressed confidence in her ability to identify the spiritual essence of others based upon her knowledge of self.

Sojourner is tied to Black feminists of today not only by a condition, but also by a collective consciousness based on a way of knowing that is distinctly African. Explaining the process of knowing that underlies African cosmology, Myers states:

> Everything in experience becomes a symbol or symbolic of infinite spirit-symbolic imagery. Whatever is coming into experience, into five-sense awareness, is automatically processed. It is processed not just by the count-and-measure-data, but also by the extrasensory acknowledgement that this is indeed spirit manifesting. In addition to knowing through this symbolic imagery, we also have to add rhythm. This is extra-ordinarily critical because everything that comes into experience is not "real." It is necessary to make a determination based upon the rhythm, based upon the nature of the inter-relatedness, the relationship of this appearing to what we already know is true.[16]

Sojourner's power as an African-American woman hinged on her extrasensory processing of "infinite spirit-symbolic imagery" using rhythm and judging the imagery's interrelatedness to determine the truth of the imagery. Grounded in African epistemology and cosmology, this is the same power Black feminists are reasserting by reclaiming their African roots. They repossess the strength of the personal within the realm of a world-view which links the spiritual dimension with the political dimension of their lives.

The bountiful accomplishments of Sojourner Truth deserve in-depth analysis if for no other reason than their continuing social relevance. Immediately after the official abolition of slavery, Sojourner was on the frontlines for civil rights, women's rights, and Black Power, including the desegregation of public transportation, voting rights, and reparations—battles that have continued into the second half of the twentieth century.

Western ethnocentric intellectualism and cultural imperialism are prime reasons for scholars being blind to Sojourner's magnitude. Among history scholars, it has not been a popular tradition to conduct research on Black slave women. Western scholars have also dismissed her Black culture and her Black experiences. Certainly too many academicians are content to ignore the retention of Africanisms by Black slaves and their descendants in the New World. Add to this that the society is threatened by the radical ideas Sojourner articulated which still have meaning to the dispossessed African-American masses in the United States. It takes courage, energy, and intellectual rigor plus access to the publishing world to restore Sojourner to her rightful place in the annals of history.

The late Raya Dunayevskaya has been one of a handful of white scholars to criticize the feminist historical analysis of the women's rights movement:

> All underestimate the Black dimension which inspired the white, middle-class, educated women to strike out on their own. Sojourner Truth and sometimes also Harriet Tubman are dutifully mentioned, condescendingly, admitting their bravery—and of course their suffering as slaves—but never as Reason which drove the educated to face reality: that the Black women were the orators, generals, yes, thinkers.[17]

That Sojourner was not only brave but also an orator, general, and a *thinker* challenges all feminists, especially Black feminists, to set about the critical, historical contextualization of Sojourner Truth. Dunayevskaya appropriately has stated that "there is no such thing as women's history that is not the actual history of humanity's struggle toward freedom"; she simultaneously has called upon feminists to learn "the language of thought, Black thought."[18] Appreciation of an African-centered consciousness is essential to unearthing the contributions and legacy of Sojourner Truth.

Sojourner Truth must be seen in the contexts of an Afrocentric world-view and of her revolutionary intellect. Although in an alien land, she was heir to an African reality in which the material and spiritual worlds are one—spirit manifest. Her God was one of positive action, and she invoked this God in all of her revolutionary activity. Consistent with the distribution of energy that is necessary to achieve the underlying goals of the African world-view, everlasting peace and happiness, Sojourner sacrificed for the various struggles of African-Americans, women, and the poor. Despite criticisms, taunting, and attempts at subordination by members of the many communities with whom she worked, she would not compromise her principles. Her militant ideas were born of the scope of her life experiences, and self-knowledge was the core of her power. Sojourner is an archetypal personage, a forerunner and model for contemporary Black feminists as they struggle for freedom and justice in her image.

## Notes

1      Victoria Ortiz, *Sojourner Truth: A Self-Made Woman* (New York: Lippincott Company, 1974), p. 81.

2      Angela Y. Davis, "Relections on the Black Woman's Role in the Community of Slaves," *The Black Scholar* 3 (December 1971), 9.

3      See Robert Farris Thompson, *Flash of the Spirit* (New York: Vintage Books, 1984).

4      For a discussion of the literature, see Charlyn Harper, "How to Think Black: Toni Cade Bambara's *The Salt Eaters*," *Black Studies,* No. 6 (1983–1984), 35.

5      Eleanor Burke Leacock, *Myths of Male Dominance: Collected Articles on Women Cross-Culturally* (New York: Monthly Review Press, 1981), pp. 314–315.

6      Ortiz, *Sojourner Truth,* pp. 82–83.

7      Jeanne Deroin and Pauline Roland, *Sojourner Truth: Keeping the Thing Going While Things Are Stirring,* reprint from An American Women's Movement, pp. 129–130.

8      Raya Dunayevskaya, "The Black Dimension in Women's Liberation," in *Women's Liberation and the Dialectics of Revolution* (Atlantic Highlands, N.J.: Humanities Press International, Inc., 1985), pp. 49–50.

9      Ortiz, *Sojourner Truth,* p. 138.

10      Harper, "How to Think Black," 38.

11      Ortiz, *Sojourner Truth,* p. 119.

12      Ibid. p. 121.

13      Quoted from a statement by Dr. Andrée Nicola McLaughlin, June 21, 1988, Women of Color press conference at Bethany Baptist Church Brooklyn in support of Tawana Brawley and her family.

14      Dunayevskaya, "Black Dimension," p. 185.

15      For a full discussion of the literature, see Dr. Linda James Myers, "How to Think Black: Toni Cade Bambara's *The Salt Eaters,*" *Black Studies,* No. 5 (1983–1984), 40.

16      Ibid., p. 41.

17      Dunayevskaya, "Black Dimension," p. 80.

18      Ibid.

# David Ames Curtis and Henry Louis Gates, Jr.

## Establishing the Identity of the Author of *Our Nig*

I picked up a copy of *Our Nig* while browsing at the University Place Bookshop in New York City, in May 1981. The full title of this novel is *Our Nig; Or, Sketches from the Life of a Free Black, In a Two-Story White House, North. Showing that Slavery's Shadows Fall Even There. By "Our Nig."* I was curious about this title: I am an avid collector of images of Blacks in literature and art, and I had not before encountered the use of "nigger" in a title published before the end of the Civil War. I assumed that *Our Nig* was a book full of happy, shiny "darkies," strumming banjos out in the field. Since I did not especially relish the notion of entering this fabricated, racist world, I put *Our Nig* on the shelf where it sat for about one year.

In May 1982, I read it. Immediately, I was convinced that *Our Nig* was a creation of a Black novelist. There were several reasons for this, which I shall not belabor here. However, no reason was of more importance to my hypothesis than the most obvious one: Mrs. H. E. Wilson *claimed* to be Black. There was little to be gained by "passing" for Black in 1859, neither within the publishing world nor without it. "Claim," perhaps, is too strong a term, for the author of *Our Nig* does not make a case for her racial identity; rather, she presumes its self-evidence, and treats the matter accordingly. While some white authors, such as Mattie Griffiths, had adopted a Black persona in their novels, few had pretended to be Black. No Black author became wealthy from writing a book, although Frederick Douglass, among others, fared rather well as a writer. Presenting her race as Black, and not bothering to demonstrate or "establish" it, H. E. Wilson, it seemed to me, was quite probably a Black woman. An interracial marriage, rendered with some balance, and a depiction of a dishonest Black "fugitive slave," also were remarkably uncommon aspects of the sentimental novel. If the author were Black, then this Mrs. Wilson would be the first Black, male or female, to publish a novel in the United States. But how could I establish the race and authorship of "Mrs. H. E. Wilson"? This essay recounts that curious tale.

H. L. Gates

The text entitled *Our Nig* is as extraordinarily structured as it is compelling. From Mrs. Wilson's succinct and straightforward "Preface" to the last of three appended letters, there unravels in 140 pages a tale of oppressions suffered, endured, comprehended, and, finally, transformed into literature. The nature of these oppressions varies from the lot of a white woman (the protagonist's mother in the text) ostracized from her society because of an interracial marriage, to the virulent Northern racism experienced by a black woman, called Frado, who suffers physical beatings and verbal negation of her humanity. Along the way, the text details the hypocrisy of "professed abolitionists who didn't want slaves at the South, nor niggers in their own houses, North," and of Frado's husband—who masqueraded as a fugitive slave—as well as Frado's plight as an indentured domestic servant. That Mrs. Wilson was able to gain control over her circumstances sufficiently to write about the oppression she experienced and the double standards she perceived is remarkable, especially since she informs the reader that she has "purposely omitted what would most provoke shame in our good anti-slavery friends at home."

Mrs. Wilson wrote her fictionalized autobiography primarily for the purpose of raising money to support her child, not for the "advancement of literature," the advancement of the race, nor for the "benefit of posterity," and quite assuredly not for the interest of today's literary critics. Consequently, the details of her life are frustratingly sparse, even with the appended biographical letters as a guide. That she determined not to include those events that would most embarrass Northerners proved to be even more frustrating to the attempt to reconstruct her life.

The "Preface" to *Our Nig*, signed by "H. E. W.," consists of a one-page apology for "this attempt of [a] sister to be erudite." It includes an explanation of Mrs. Wilson's "experiment . . . [to] aid me in maintaining myself and my child without extinguishing this feeble life" and an appeal to "my colored brethren universally for patronage." Anticipating strong criticisms for her very explicit indictment of Northern white racism in the midst of severe agitation against chattel slavery, she tries to assure her readers that "my mistress was

wholly imbued with *southern* principles." Mrs. Wilson ends by calling on her fellow blacks to "rally around me a faithful band of supporters and defenders."

Early on we were able to locate some evidence concerning Mrs.
Wilson and her work. A copy of the copyright, registered at the District Court of Massachusetts and bearing the name of "Mrs. H. E.
Wilson," was obtained by Alexandra Gleysteen at the Library of Congress. Lacking even a first name for Mrs. Wilson at this point, but
knowing that the book had been registered with the District Court,
whose central building is located in Boston, we checked the *Boston
Directory* and located a Harriet Wilson (no middle initial), living in
Boston from 1855 to 1863. To ascertain her race, we examined the
1860 federal census for Massachusetts. A painstaking name-by-name
search, undertaken by Donna Dennis, turned up a Harriet Wilson,
"52" years old and a "widow," born in Fredericksburg, Virginia. This
Mrs. Wilson lived with a Daniel and Susan Jacobs. All three persons
were listed as "B[lack]." A quick recheck of the *Boston Directory* confirmed that the Jacobses were living in the same house as Mrs. Wilson
for the year 1860—and for that year only.

Also, a "Harriet Wilson, dressmaker," was listed in the *Boston Directory* for the year 1856 only. It was not clear whether this was a
different Harriet Wilson, or the business address for the "Harriet
Wilson, widow." In either case, this single-year entry was especially
encouraging since internal evidence from both the novel and the appended letters indicated that both Mrs. Wilson and her autobiographical protagonist, Frado, were quite adept at the art of dressmaking.

Our next step was to undertake an analysis of Mrs. Wilson's "Preface" and the appended letters along with the plot of *Our Nig*. We
then systematically compared these two accounts, one fictional, the
other possessing a prima facie validity. Accordingly, we broke down
the plot structure of *Our Nig* into 160 units; any clues concerning
characters, periods of time, types of work engaged in, and so on were
recorded in order, following exactly the unfolding of the plot. Similarly, the three appended letters, possibly all written under pseu-
donyms ("Allida," "Margaretta Thorn," and "C. D. S."), provided
additional clues, and these we analyzed into distinct bits of information and recorded in chronological order. All three of these letters
supported many of the plot functions of *Our Nig*. The longest and

most detailed of the three, written by Allida, described "Alfrado's" novel as "an Autobiography."

We soon ran into difficulties, however, as we began to search for evidence concerning other aspects of Mrs. Wilson's life. The city directory for Worcester, Massachusetts, yielded no information about our author for the period in which we believed her a resident of "W——, Massachusetts," based on information provided in "Allida's" appended letter. Other Massachusetts city directories for W—— towns were not available, although we were able to narrow, tentatively, the list of possible W—— towns by identifying the south central part of Massachusetts as the area where the straw hat sewing industry flourished in the 1840s and 1850s. Westborough, Ware, Walpole, and Worcester seemed to be the most likely possibilities; yet, we have not been able to establish positively any details of Mrs. Wilson's life during this period.

False leads were generated simply by our speculations, which were almost all that we had to pursue. The letter signed "C. D. S." is addressed from "Milford," and we assumed that this was another Massachusetts city. This seemed to be a reasonable hypothesis, but proved to be completely wrong.

It was soon clear that informed speculation would not be sufficient to establish the identity of the author of *Our Nig*. Still focusing on the Massachusetts ties Mrs. Wilson was reported to have had, we called the Suffolk County Probate Court in Boston and got the information that a Harriet Wilson (still no middle initial) had died in Boston in 1870 and that her "daughter and only surviving next of kin" had filed a Petition for Administration of the Estate on January 31, 1870, as this Mrs. Wilson, "widow," had died intestate.

Through an examination of the *Boston Directory, A. M'Elroy's Philadelphia Directory,* federal census records, and vital statistic records for the states of Massachusetts and Pennsylvania, we were able to piece together the identities, residences, and vital histories of a "Harriet Wilson, widow," her daughter, her grandchildren, and those persons who acted as sureties in the administration of her will. All of this data concerning this middle-aged black woman, born in a slave state, did not overlap with any elements of the fictional narrative of a young, northern mulatto indentured servant nor with the biographical details about the author provided in the appended letters.

It was only when we left Boston and Massachusetts, and continued our research in New Hampshire, that we began to establish definite information concerning the life of Harriet E. Wilson. A major breakthrough occurred at the New Hampshire Bureau of Vital Records in Concord. While pursuing one of our more unlikely dead-end leads, a volunteer genealogical aide at the Bureau, Mrs. Eugene W. Leach, searched quietly through the death records of *all* Wilsons in New Hampshire, on her own initiative. When she got to the "G" Wilsons she announced that she had found the death record for a George M. Wilson, who died of the "Fever" on February 15, 1860, at the age of "7 years, eight months." His race was listed as "Black" and he was said to be the son of Harriet E. (!) Wilson and Thomas Wilson. The respective "birthplaces" of the child's parents were Milford and Virginia, and George M. Wilson was reported to have been born in Goffstown, the town where the Hillsborough County Farm was located.

Since we knew from the novel and from the appended letters that both the fictional character Frado and the real Mrs. Wilson gave birth to their only child on such a County Farm, this death record was our most significant discovery to that time. This breakthrough, however, was immediately followed by frustration. There still was no birth or death record for Mrs. Wilson at the Bureau. Even with the first name for her husband, it was not possible to locate a marriage record for this couple.

The death of George M. Wilson was confirmed by a check of the February 29, 1860, *Farmer's Cabinet.* This local newspaper, published in the adjoining town of Amherst, New Hampshire, included the information that the full name of Mrs. Wilson's son was "George Mason Wilson," and that he was the "only son of H. E. Wilson." The date of death is "February 13, 1860"—a slight discrepancy—and the paper confirms that his death occurred in Milford, New Hampshire.

Our next breakthrough occurred during a visit to the Milford Town Clerk's office. Nancy Schooley, Helen Draper, and Wilfred Leduc entered into the excitement of the research and soon found the marriage record for Thomas Wilson and a Harriet Adams. We still do not know why this record was entered at Milford but never found its way to the Bureau in Concord. No race was listed on the report, and the only recorded information included the date of the marriage (October 6, 1851), a designation of where each came from (again, Virginia and Milford), and the name of the minister who "returned" this marriage record to the Town Clerk in April of the following year (Rev. E. N. Hidden).

It was then that we encountered the first two of what would become five fires. Rev. David L. Clarke, the present pastor of the First Congregational Church of Milford, New Hampshire, informed us that Reverend Ephraim Nelson Hidden was the fifth pastor of the church, so we can assume that this marriage took place in Milford; but, he also informed us, the church marriage records for that period had been destroyed by a fire. We also discovered that the records for the Hillsborough County Farm for the period Mrs. Wilson and her son were staying there were also destroyed by a fire. (The institution that was a County Farm over a century ago is now a County Nursing Home also located in Goffstown.)

Armed with the new information concerning Mrs. Wilson's son, her maiden name, and her residence in Milford and Goffstown, another census search at the Federal Archives Research Center in Waltham, Massachusetts, proved the most successful of all the research concerning the identity of Mrs. Harriet E. Adams Wilson. The 1850 federal census for Milford, New Hampshire, includes only one black woman, a Harriet Adams. This "22"-year-old "B[lack]" woman was living with the family of Samuel Boyles. This piece of information not only extended the known period of Harriet E. Adams Wilson's life by one year but also confirmed that a black Harriet Adams was living in Milford, New Hampshire, probably before our author moved to W——, Massachusetts, and before Thomas Wilson and Harriet Adams moved (back?) to Milford to marry. Most importantly, however, we obtained from this census the probable date of Mrs. Wilson's birth (ca. 1827–1828), with the additional information that she was born in "New Hampshire," thus reinforcing the death record report that the "birthplace" of George Mason Wilson's mother was "Milford." As the attached "Plot Summary and Biography" reveals, the chronological correlation between the fictionalized autobiography and the known events of Mrs. Wilson's biography overlap almost perfectly.

From these old records unfolds a tale of tragedy and irony. Mrs. Harriet E. Adams Wilson, her health and working abilities ruined for life by the cruel treatment of her northern white mistress, decided to render her story into an autobiographical, sentimental novel, a dubiously saleable commodity at that time. Trying desperately to sustain herself and her son—both of whom were abandoned by her free black husband, who had masqueraded as a fugitive slave "lecturer"—she wrote from intimate experience a bold indictment of northern white racism and of hypocritical abolitionists of both races, apparently hoping that liberal white northerners and her "colored brethren" might "rally around" her and purchase her book. Instead, within six months of the publication of *Our Nig,* her only son, fostered to a family in Milford, New Hampshire, died of the fever; and her other child, the book *Our Nig,* the offspring produced by her creative labor of literary daring, died of neglect, unpurchased, unreviewed, unread, and lost to the world for nearly a century and a quarter. If Mrs. Wilson could not prevent, by her literary efforts, the "extinguishing" of her son's "feeble life," then, ironically, her son's death ultimately made possible the positive identification of his mother as the first Afro-American woman novelist.

At the time of this most significant and exciting discovery, Harriet Wilson returned to the shadows. No more information has been discovered concerning her life, and the much more tedious and mundane task of determining where she was *not* had to be commenced. The following list of leads pursued, which did not yield any results, we present in outline form, conforming to the style of the "Plot Summary and Biography" and the "Chronology" published in the Random House edition of *Our Nig,* to facilitate easy cross-referencing. By publishing this record of unsuccessful research efforts, we seek to spare other scholars from repeating research that we have already completed. We hope, rather, that someone will follow other leads and clues so that as many aspects as possible of Mrs. Wilson's life can be discovered and retrieved.

### Birth of Harriet Wilson

I. No birth record for Harriet Adams has been found, after a search at the New Hampshire Bureau of Vital Records; Milford, New Hampshire, Town Clerk's records; and the Amherst, New Hampshire, Town Clerk's office.

II. The Amherst, New Hampshire, *Farmer's Cabinet* did not list birth announcements in its columns.

III. The records of the Milford, New Hampshire, First Congregational Church records were destroyed by fire.

## Early Life of Harriet Wilson

IV.   Carter G. Woodson's *Free Negro Heads of Families in the United States in 1830* does not list any Adams families living in New Hampshire in 1830.

V.    A search of the 1840 federal census for Hillsborough County, New Hampshire, showed that no black woman named Harriet Adams was listed.

## The W——, Massachusetts, Period

VI.   With over two dozen Walker families listed in the 1850 federal census as living in W——, Massachusetts, towns, it is impossible to determine which "Mrs. Walker" (p. 135 of the Appendix) sheltered Harriet Adams.

VII.  A search of the *Worcester City Directory* did not produce any results. No directories for Westborough, Ware, or Walpole were located.

VIII. The Milford, New Hampshire, First Congregational Church's marriage records were destroyed in a fire.

## Birth of George Mason Wilson

IX.   A search at the New Hampshire Bureau of Vital Records produced no record of the birth of George Mason Wilson in Goffstown or anywhere else in New Hampshire.

X.    The Amherst, New Hampshire, *Farmer's Cabinet* did not list birth records in its columns.

XI.   The 1852 vital records of Goffstown, New Hampshire, were destroyed in a fire.

XII.  A search of the church records of the Goffstown, New Hampshire, First Congregational Church yielded no birth record for George Mason Wilson.

XIII. The Hillsborough County Farm's records were also burned in a fire.

## New Hampshire Period after the Birth of George Mason Wilson

XIV.  A search of the tax records of Milford, New Hampshire, the federal census for Milford, and Ramsdell's *The History of Milford* yielded no families by the name of Thorn nor any person with the initials "C. D. S." although we did find two persons listed in these sources with the initials "C. S." (Catherine Shannahan and Charles Shepard).

## Second Massachusetts Period

XV.     The business section of the *Boston Directory* does not list a Harriet Wilson as a dressmaker, milliner, or hairdresser.

XVI.    Business licenses were not in use in Boston until 1907.

## Publication of *Our Nig*

XVII.   No records of the printer of *Our Nig,* Rand & Avery, could be located.

## Death of George Mason Wilson

XVIII.  The church records of the Milford, New Hampshire, First Congregational Church were burned.

## Period after the Death of Mrs. Wilson's Son

XIX.    No blacks fitting the description of Harriet E. Adams Wilson appear in the 1860 census for Hillsborough County.

XX.     There is no name index for the 1855 or 1865 Massachusetts census nor for the 1860 federal census, so it would be extraordinarily difficult at this time to check whether or not Mrs. Harriet E. Wilson was residing in Massachusetts after she moved from New Hampshire. This shall be possible, however, once the Accelerated Indexing Systems project, sponsored by the Church of Latter Day Saints, has completed its indexing of the 1860 United States Census. This work is now in progress.

Having thus reached a temporary standstill in our research into Mrs. Wilson's life and history, we await the publication of the index to the 1860 federal census. Meanwhile, we return to her fictionalized "Autobiography" to speculate upon her fate after the death of her son. The ultimate chapter, in which she abandons the mask of fiction and appeals directly to the reader in her own voice for sympathy and support, contains the following statement: "She passed into the various towns of the State she lived in, then into Massachusetts" (p. 129).

We finish, as we began, with questions as to the whereabouts of this bold but forgotten author. Is "Harriet Wilson, widow," or, more likely, "Harriet Wilson, dressmaker," our obscure one-time writer? Do these two entries designate the same or different persons? Was there another black woman living in Massachusetts at that time, who was the Harriet Wilson we have been seeking, or did she die between February 15, 1860 (the date of George Wilson's death record) and the summer of 1860, when the federal census was undertaken? Finally, as we have cautioned ourselves all along, we recognize again that nineteenth-century census data, and other vital statistics, were notoriously inaccurate, often based upon hearsay, and sometimes themselves purely fictional. We look forward, therefore, with hope and anticipation, but not complete assurance, that additional biographical details of Harriet E. Adams Wilson's life will be brought to light and confirmed.

Plot Summary of *Our Nig*          Biography of Harriet E.
                                            (Adams) Wilson

CHAPTER I

1   Mag Smith was "early deprived of parental guardianship, far removed from relatives." (p. 5)

2   As she "merged into womanhood," (p. 5) as an orphan, she was seduced and abandoned. (p. 6)

3   Mag left her "few friends," sought "asylum among strangers," and gave birth to a child who died within a number of weeks. (p. 6)

4   She "removed [herself] from the village" except when seen "returning her work to her employer." (p. 8)

5   "Thus she lived [in her hut] for years." (p. 8)

6   "A kind-hearted African" supplied her with fuel in exchange for her "mending or making garments." (p. 9)

7   The fictional town is called "Singleton." (p. 10)

8   The "African" "Jim" hits on the idea of marrying Mag. (p. 10)

9   The     "next     Saturday"

(p. 11), "he prevailed; they married" (p. 12), despite the "sermon on the evils of amalgamation." (p. 13)

## CHAPTER II

10   "A comfortable winter she passed after her marriage." (p. 14)

Birth of Harriet E. Wilson

ca. 1828

11   Within "time," they have "two pretty mulattos." (p. 14)

I   Born in Milford? New Hampshire, ca. 1828

12   Within a "few years" (p. 14), "he became the victim of consumption" and died. (p. 15)

13   "She was now expelled from companionship with white people." (p. 15)

14   She returned to her "hovel" accompanied by Jim's business partner, Seth Shipley. (pp. 15–16)

Early Life of Harriet E. Wilson

ca. 1834

15   Seth and Mag resolve to give away their "beautiful mulatto" six-year-old child, Alfrado, to the Bellmonts. (p. 17)

II   Mrs. Wilson "was taken from home so young," according to Margaretta Thorn.

16   "One bright summer morning" (p. 20), the family departs leaving Frado at the Bellmont's "large, old fashioned, two-story white house." (p. 21)

## CHAPTER III

17   The Bellmonts debate whether to keep the abandoned Frado, or send her to the "County Home." (p. 24–6)

18   Frado is kept and put to work: feeding the hens; driving the

cows; bringing in wood chips; dish-washing, etc. (p. 29)

19   Not doing her work exactly as commanded would be punished "by a whipping." (p. 29)

20   "Thus passed a year . . . Her labors were multiplied."

ca. 1835

21   At age seven, she was "indispensable." (p. 30)

22   On "opening day" at school, Frado is taunted by the other children as a "nigger." (p. 31)

23   Between terms of school, she was given more duties, including hay raking and guarding the grazing herd. (p. 39)

24   Frado is not allowed to shield her skin from the sun, since Mrs. Bellmont wants to make sure she is darker than daughter Mary Bellmont. (p. 39)

ca. 1837

CHAPTER IV

25   Now nine years old, Mrs. Bellmont decided that Frado should quit school. "She felt that her time and person belonged solely to her." (p. 41)

26   At the end of the Spring, "absent son" James Bellmont comes to visit. (p. 42)

CHAPTER V

27   "James' visit concluded." (p. 52)

28   Frado hopes that he will take her away with him after his planned marriage. (p. 52)

29   She receives "additional burdens," including milking the cows, and tending the flocks of sheep (p. 52) and harnessing the horse. (p. 53) In short, to "do the work of a boy."

30   James marries Susan, a "Baltimorean lady of wealthy parentage." (p. 55)

CHAPTER VI

31   "James had now been married a number of years." Mrs. Bellmont visits him in Baltimore, installing Mary as housekeeper in her absence. (p. 62)

ca. 1842

32   Now fourteen, Frado must "do all the washing, ironing, baking, and the common et cetera of household duties." (p. 63)

33   Mr. and Mrs. Bellmont return after "long . . . weeks," with the news that James has not sent for her. (p. 65)

34   James arrives in the early Spring, seeking "restorative northern air." He is sick and "feeble." (p. 67)

35   Frado's health continues to decline from being overworked, and from having no shoes to wear until after the first frost. (pp. 65–6)

CHAPTER VII

36   "Month after month passed away," without an improvement in Frado's condition. (p. 73)

CHAPTER VIII

37    Another son of the Bellmont's—Lewis, who is a partner
in business with James—arrives.
Seeing James's declining health, he
decides to return to Baltimore with
his sister Mary accompanying him.
(pp. 78–79)

38    Mrs. Bellmont, doubting
that blacks have souls, prevents
Frado from reading the Bible.
Frado, however, continues to do
so in her own room. (pp. 86–87)

39    Mrs. Bellmont claims that
Frado "can't be spared" by letting
her go to church any more." (p. 89)

40    Mr. and Mrs. Bellmont argue about the learning abilities of
Frado and blacks in general. Also
her monetary value and services
are discussed. (pp. 89–90)

CHAPTER IX

41    "Frado was becoming seriously ill." (p. 94)

42    Frado "resolved to persevere" in prayer, despite Mrs. Bellmont's statement that "'prayer was
for whites, not for blacks.'" (p. 94)

CHAPTER X

43    Frado astonishes Mrs. Bellmont and prevents a beating by
threatening not to work for her
any longer if she is hit again. Frado
"stood like one who feels the stirring of free and independent
thoughts." (p. 105)

44    "Thus passed a year"
(p. 105) where Frado received "the

usual amount of scoldings, but fewer whippings." (pp. 105–106)

45    Daughter Mary Bellmont dies in Baltimore. (p. 106)

CHAPTER XI

46    "Frado had merged into womanhood." (p. 115) She spends her free time with her school books.

ca. 1846

47    With the "approaching Spring," Frado is free to leave and resolves to do so. Despite "delicate health," and pleas from Mrs. B. that she stay and be "grateful" for her situation, she leaves. (pp. 116–117)

48    "Frado was engaged to work for a family a mile distant." (p. 117)

49    Frado was given "a present of a silver half dollar" from Mrs. B. Frado was "alone in the world" with "one decent dress," a Bible from Susan, and a lame leg from a fall during the past year. (p. 117)

50    During a "pleasant" "first summer," Frado earned enough money to buy a small wardrobe. She also "prepared her own garments." (p. 117)

51    Mrs. Moore, her employer, was a "kind friend" (p. 117), but Frado's "failing health" hindered her work. (p. 118)

52    She moved to the house of a clergyman, and "her engagement with Mrs. Moore finished in the fall." (p. 118)

53    By "winter she entirely gave

III    "Never enjoyed any degree of comfortable health since she was eighteen years of age," according to Margaretta Thorn.

up work" as she was "thoroughly sick." (p. 118)

54    Frado again hopes she will die from her illness. She is removed to the Bellmont's farm, in a drafty out-building.

55    Frado "became reckless of her faith" (p. 119), but "slowly improved" her health under the care of Aunt Abby. (pp. 120–121)

56    Frado returns to Mrs. Moore's house, but again her work proves to be too much for her. (p. 121)

ca. 1847

57    Mrs. B. refuses to take her back.

58    "Two maidens, (old,)" take Frado in for public charity, for two years (p. 122).

ca. 1849

59    A greedy Mrs. Hoggs takes her in.

60    When Frado learns to be "very expert with a needle" (p. 122) while recovering from her illness, Mrs. Hoggs reports her to the authorities as an "imposter." (p. 123)

61    "This brought on a severe illness of two weeks, when Mrs. Moore again sought her." (p. 123)

62    Mrs. Moore's husband deserts her and their four children. (p. 123)

63    Frado is pronounced ill again, and is allowed back on public charity at the Moore's house.

64    "Here she remained till sufficiently restored to sew again." (p. 124)

August 24, 1850

65    She moved to Massachusetts to sew straw bonnets. A "plain, poor, simple woman, who could see merit beneath a dark skin" (p. 124), heard her sorry story and took her in.

66    She soon became "expert with the needle" and "soon equalled her instructress." (p. 124)

67    Frado begins reading history and other "useful books." (p. 124) She continued her Christian experience.

IV    According to the 1850 federal census for Milford, New Hampshire, Harriet Adams was a 22-year-old black woman born in New Hampshire, and living with the family of Samuel Boyles.

The W——, Massachusetts Period

V    "Allida" reports that Harriet Wilson was brought to W——, Massachusetts by an "itinerant" colored lecturer.

VI    W——, Massachusetts was an "ancient town" with a straw hat industry.

VII    According to "Allida," Harriet E. Wilson:

A    Became an "inmate" of Mrs. Walker's household in W——, Massachusetts.

B    Began immediately as a "straw-sewer."

C    Soon her "constitution was greatly impaired."

D    Became at that point Mrs. Walker's domestic help.

VIII    The W——, Massachusetts, town is thought to be Westborough, Ware, Walpole, or Worcester.

IX    "Allida" reports that "months passed." And then in the "early Spring of 1842,"

A    The "lecturer" returns, this time with a fugitive slave.

B    The fugitive slave had been a house servant.

C    "Suffice it to say," she says in a vague and discreetly Vic-

CHAPTER XII

68    A fugitive slave arrives, and proposes marriage to Frado. (p. 126)

69    They move back to Singleton and marry there. (p. 127)

torian tone, "an acquaintance was formed, which, in due time, resulted in marriage."

D    "In a few days, she left W——, . . . and took up her abode in New Hampshire."

X    Given that "Allida" attests in 1859 to knowing Mrs. Wilson only about eight years (i.e., ca. 1851– 1852), this date (of "1842") could not be a correct one from first hand knowledge. Most likely, this date is rather a typographical error for 1851 or 1852, considering that Thomas Wilson married Harriet Adams in fall 1851 (this marriage being reported in the spring of 1852).

Marriage of Thomas Wilson and
Harriet Adams

October 6, 1851

XI    Thomas Wilson is reported to have married a Harriet Adams on October 6, 1851 in Milford, New Hampshire.

A    Thomas Wilson's residence is listed as "Virginia."

B    Harriet Adams's residence is listed as "Millford."

C    The marriage record was "returned by Rev. E. N. Hidden" in April of the following year.

D    The 1850 federal census lists Rev. Ephraim N. Hidden as a Cong[regational] Clerg[yperson].

70    Her new husband, Samuel, would leave frequently to "lecture," often for weeks. (p. 127)

71    Samuel runs away to sea. (p. 127)

72    It turns out he was not a fugitive slave, after all. (p.128)

(May or June 1852)

73    Left alone, she becomes ill, accepts public charity again, and gives birth to a child. (p. 128)

Birth of George Mason Wilson

XII    George Mason Wilson was born in late May or early June of 1852.

    A    His race is listed as "Black" on his death record.

    B    His parents were Thomas and Harriet Wilson, of Virginia and Milford, New Hampshire, respectively.

XIII    The birth occurred in Goffstown, New Hampshire—where the Hillsborough County Farm was located at the time.

XIV    "Allida" reports that "for a while" things went well for the new couple. But then the husband ran away to sea. "Days passed; weeks passed," and then Mrs. Wilson felt she had to go to the "County House," where she gave birth to her child.

New Hampshire Period after Birth of George Mason Wilson

XV    "Allida" reports that "then" the husband returned. The family moves to "some town in New Hampshire, where, for a time, he supported her and his little son decently well."

74    "The long absent Samuel unexpectedly returned, and rescued her from charity." (p.128)

75    Again "after a long desertion . . . , he had become a victim of yellow fever, in New Orleans." (p.128)

XVI    "But again he left her as before," and this time for good, reports "Allida."

76    "She left ["her babe"] in charge of Mrs. Capon, and procured an agency, hoping to recruit her health, and gain an easier livelihood for herself and child." (p. 129)

XVII    Margaretta Thorn reports that the son was put on the "County Farm" while Mrs. Wilson was "in her sickness" and not able to "pay his board every week."

XVIII    "At length," Ms. Thorn reports, "a kindly gentleman and Lady took her little boy into their own family." Mrs. Wilson had taken him "from *that* place [the "County Farm"] and now he has a home."

XIX    Mrs. Wilson, says Ms. Thorn, "wishes to educate her son." Ms. Thorn reports that as of her writing (1859), the child is accepted, well-adjusted, and shows promise.

1855?

77    She "passed into the various towns of the State she lived in, then into Massachusetts." (p. 129)

Second Massachusetts Period

XX    The 1855 *Boston Directory* lists a Harriet Wilson as a "widow, house, 7 Robinson Alley."

XXI    The next year, 1856, a Harriet Wilson, "widow," is living in a "house, 4 Webster ave."

XXII    Also, a Harriet Wilson, "dressmaker," has a business(?) address at 19 Joy Street.

XXIII    Harriet Wilson is listed as a "widow" living in a "house, 4 Webster ave." from 1856 to 1863. After that year, she disappears from the *Boston Directory*.

78    She had various encounters with "Kidnappers," "Professed abolitionists" who "mistreated" her, "who didn't want slaves at the South, nor niggers in their own houses, North." (p. 129)

79    "A friend . . . provided her with a valuable recipe, from which she might herself manufacture a useful article for her maintenance." (p. 129)

XXIV    Allida reports that "the heart of a stranger was moved with compassion, and bestowed a recipe upon her for restoring gray hair to its former color. She availed

80 "To the present time," she is employed in this type of manufacture. (pp. 129–130)

herself of this great help, and has been quite successful; but her health is again failing" and she has decided to write her "autobiography" as "another method of procuring her bread." No dates or places are given in this section of "Allida's" account of Mrs. Wilson's life after her husband left her.

August 18, 1859
Publication of *Our Nig*

XXV    *Our Nig* was copyrighted on August 18, 1859.

XXVI    This novel was published by Mrs. Wilson on September 5, 1859.

XXVII    A copy was deposited at that time "by Mrs. H. E. Wilson, in the Clerk's office of the District Court of the District of Massachusetts."

XXVIII    The novel *Our Nig* was printed for the author by George C. Rand & Avery printing company of Boston, Massachusetts. Rand & Avery were not known as regular publishers of novels.

Death of George Mason Wilson
February 13 or 15, 1860

XXIX    George Mason Wilson, aged "7 years, 8 months," died in Milford, New Hampshire, on February 13 or 15, 1860.

A    His race is listed as "Black."

B    His parents were Thomas and Harriet E. Wilson.

C    He died of the "fever."

D    He was the "only son of H. E. Wilson."

XXX    Mrs. Wilson's son, for whom she wrote *Our Nig,* hoping to realize enough money to be able to provide for him, died within six months after this book was published.

Period after the Death of Mrs. Wilson's Son

XXXI     Mrs. Wilson was not living with the Boyles family according to the 1860 federal census for Milford, New Hampshire.

XXXII     In the last chapter of the novel, the author, speaking in her own voice as she pleads for support for herself in her present destitute condition, tells how "Alfrado" "passed into the various towns of the State she lived in, then into Massachusetts."

XXXIII     No other information has been found concerning Mrs. Wilson for the period after the death of her son, except for the information contained in the *Boston Directories* for 1855–1863.

81     While "still an invalid," she remains religious and determined to "elevate" herself. (p. 130)

82     "Only a few years have elapsed since Mr. and Mrs. B. passed into another world." Mrs. B.'s death was "unspeakable." She died at Lewis's home. (p. 130)

83     "Only a few months since, Aunt Abby entered heaven." (p. 130)

84     "Jack and his wife rest in heaven." (p. 130)

85     "Susan and her child are yet with the living." (p. 130)

86     Jane "has never regretted her exchange of lovers." (pp. 130–131)

87     "Frado has passed from their memories," but she remembers them still. (p. 131)

# Joanne M. Braxton

---

# A Poet's Retreat: The Diaries
# of Charlotte Forten Grimké
# (1837–1914)

> To be burned in case of my death immediately.
> He who dares read what here is written.
> Woe be unto him.
>> Unpublished pencil inscription,
>> Diary 2 (January 1, 1857–
>> January 27, 1858)

> In the earnest path of duty
>   With the high hopes and hearts sincere,
> We, to useful lives aspiring
>   Daily meet to labor here.

> No vain dreams of earthly glory
>   Urge us onward to explore
> Far-extending realms of knowledge
>   With their rich and varied store;

> But with hope of aiding others,
>   Gladly we perform our part;
> Nor forget, the mind, while storing,
>   We must educate the heart,—
>> "Poem" (1856)

harlotte Forten Grimké, a turn-of-the-century Black woman poet, scholar, teacher, and translator, is remembered chiefly for a version of four of her five manuscript diaries edited by Ray Allen Billington and published as *The Journal of Charlotte L. Forten, 1854–1862* (1953).[1] As a young Black woman poet reading *The Journal of Charlotte L. Forten* in the early 1970s, I was put off by the diarist's romantic language, as well as her class pretensions, and I resisted all identification with her.

Years later, when I read Dr. Anna Julia Cooper's typed manuscripts of all five diaries, I began to see them as a series of interrelated texts sustaining progression and development.[2] Restoring Billington's editorial omissions presented a more rounded view of the diarist's day-to-day life, beyond her commentary on matters of political and historical significance; I began to view the published edition of the diaries as a mutilated text. Yet even when I read the typed copy with omissions restored, Forten seemed aloof and distant; she refused to speak with me.

In the hope of improving my relationship with the subject of my interest, I began to read what Forten read: Shakespeare, Blake, Keats, Wordsworth, Lydia Maria Child, Emerson, the Brownings, and the Brontës. And I read what she wrote: her "Life on the Sea Islands," her "Personal Recollections of Whittier," and a handful of unpublished essays as well as the dozen or so poems published during her lifetime, and *Madame Therese, or the Volunteers of '92,* a novel by Emilie Erckmann and Alexander Chartrian, which she translated from the French for Scribners.[3]

When I returned to the Moorland-Spingarn Collection to read the original handwritten manuscript diaries for possible omissions, Charlotte began to smile on me. And when I held the slender, leather-bound volumes, each covered with a graceful marbled paper, and when I read the delicate, faded black ink handwriting, I could feel the tension of pen against paper, and I could hear a voice. It was, unmistakably, the voice of a poet, struggling to be heard—the voice of Charlotte Forten Grimké.

The first and second diaries cover the dates from May 24, 1854, to December 31, 1856, and from January 1, 1857, to January 27, 1858.

These diaries, which Charlotte Forten kept between the ages of seventeen and twenty-one, describe her life as a schoolgirl in Salem, a young abolitionist, and an aspiring poet and writer. The third and fourth diaries cover the span from January 1858 to February 1863 and from February 1863 to May 1864, respectively. Here, she records her continuing personal development and her participation in the historic "Port Royal Experiment" on the South Carolina Sea Islands during the Civil War. She begins her fifth diary in November 1885, and makes her final entry in July 1892, twenty-two years before her death in 1914. The final diary remained unpublished until 1988, when it was included in a new collection of Forten's work edited by Brenda Stevenson.[4] This diary presents an intimate view of Forten's thirty-five-year marriage to the Reverend Francis J. Grimké, a distinguished black Presbyterian minister, who was also the nephew of white feminist abolitionists Sarah Grimké and Angelina Grimké Weld via their brother Henry Grimké and a slave woman, Nancy Weston (Billington, *Journal,* 29).

Taken together, the five manuscript diaries show an intelligent Black and female cultural sensibility struggling to balance political, intellectual, and emotional conflicts, and to forge a public voice. Although intended as a private one, the diarist's autobiographical act relates to the development of a public voice in the move to objectify and take control of experience through the writer's craft; in the pages of her diaries, she gains distance between herself as subject and object. This essay examines Charlotte Forten Grimké's use of the diary as a tool for the development of her political and artistic consciousness and as a means of self-evaluation; for her, the diaries also represent a retreat from potentially shattering encounters with racism and a vehicle for the development of a Black and female poetic identity, a place of restoration and self-healing.

The product of an environment that was both abolitionist and feminist in nature, Charlotte Forten grew up in the Philadelphia home of her paternal grandfather, James Forten, a wealthy and respected free black who advocated abolition and women's rights. The daughter of Mary Wood and Robert Bridges Forten, she was named for her grandmother, Charlotte Forten, Sr., who lived to be one hundred years old.[5] In 1837, the year Charlotte was born, her aunts Sarah and Margaretta Forten, both active in the Philadelphia Female

Anti-Slavery Society, organized a national convention of Black women abolitionists (Billington, *Journal,* 13). The Fortens were cultured and well-educated, yet, like other free Blacks in the "City of Brotherly Love," they found themselves excluded from museums, stores, ice cream parlors, and restaurants. Predictably, the Fortens chose a private tutor over a segregated public school education for Charlotte. Stifled by years of living primarily in her grandfather's house and by being shut out from much of the typical social routine in which other girls participated, Charlotte Forten grew into an intensely introspective adolescent, continually examining and reexamining her intellectual and literary development. Thus she grew up separated from the dominant culture by race, and from much of the Black community by economic and educational privilege or by class and culture.

In 1854, Robert Bridges Forten responded to his daughter's developing isolation by sending her to the Higginson Grammar School in Salem, Massachusetts, where she lived with the Charles Lenox Remond family. Significantly, she began her first diary (May 24, 1854– December 31, 1856) with the advent of her stay in Salem, marking the initial separation from her home and Philadelphia. But even in "free" Massachusetts, Charlotte felt the sting of white racism: "I wonder that every colored person is not a misanthrope. Surely, we have everything to make us hate mankind. I have met girls in the classroom—they have been thoroughly kind and cordial to me, —perhaps the next day met them in the street—they feared to recognize me; these I can but regard now with scorn and contempt" (*Diary* 1; Wednesday, 12 September 1854). When encounters such as these threatened her sense of self, Charlotte, looking back on them from her own perspective and laying claim to her experience, sought refuge in the language and the pages of her private diary. Here, she confronted the dominant white culture in small, homeopathic doses, analyzing, and gaining psychological distance. On July 17, 1854, she entered, "I am hated and oppressed because God gave me a *dark skin.* How did this cruel, this absurd prejudice ever come to exist? When I think of it, a feeling of indignation rises in my soul too deep for utterance" (*Diary* 1; 17 July 1854). For young Charlotte Forten, the diary becomes a private (and therefore defensible) "territory" of the mind and a retreat from the racism and sexism of the dominant culture.

The first and second diaries also demonstrate the young poet's quest for literary models. In Salem, she read voraciously and attended an impressive number of readings, lectures, and anti-slavery fairs. Caught in the 1850s surge of politics and romanticism, she found Hawthorne's gothic tales "thrilling" and enjoyed walks by the sea and in the moonlight. On Christmas Day 1858, she came away from Emerson's lecture "On Beauty" "much pleased" (*Diary* 3; 25 December 1858). Quaker poet John Greenleaf Whittier, a special friend, sought her out for nature walks and for talks on farming and spiritual development. Among her favorite writers were Blake, Keats, Wordsworth, Emerson, the Brontës, and Lydia Maria Child. Charlotte Forten apparently accepted Mrs. Child's promotion of "a love of reading as an unspeakable blessing for the American female."[6] Engaged in the quest for literacy and self-respect, Forten found books a means of knowing a world from which she felt excluded, a route to transcendence of her perceived cultural isolation: "And hence are *books* to us a treasure and a blessing unspeakable. And they are doubly this when one is shut out of society as I am, and has not opportunities of studying those living, breathing, *human* books, which are, I doubt not, after all, the most profoundly interesting and useful study" (*Diary* 3; 1 January 1860). Charlotte Forten, as a young abolitionist, read and reread in 1854 Elizabeth Barrett Browning's powerful feminist-abolitionist polemic, "The Fugitive Slave at Pilgrim's Point," as "most suitable to my feelings and the times." On May 30, 1854, she added this commentary to the diary: "how earnestly and touching does the writer portray the bitter anguish of the poor fugitive as she thinks over all the wrongs and sufferings that she has endured, and of the sin the tyrants have driven her but which they alone must answer for!" (*Diary* 1; 30 May 1854). Hence, the young Black writer identified both with the literary sensibility of the white author of the poem and with the feminine heroism of its narrator, an outraged mother who rebels against her rapist master, murdering the child she has borne by him.

Naturally, Charlotte Forten's heroes and heroines included the fugitive slaves themselves, whose experiences were beginning to come to light not only through polemical poetry and fiction, but through first-hand narratives, and the camera. One entry in her second diary describes her reactions on being shown "a daguerreotype of a young slave girl who escaped in a box. . . ." She continues: "My heart was full as I gazed at it; full of admiration for the heroic girl, who risked all for freedom; full of bitter indignation that in this boasted land of liberty such a thing *could occur*. Were she of any other nation her heroinism would receive all due honor from these Americans, *but as it is,* there is not even a single spot in this broad land, where her rights can be protected, —not one" (*Diary* 2; 5 July 1857). Perhaps there is a sense in which the girl in the box can be viewed as a metaphor for her own experience of separateness from and isolation within the dominant culture, for although she herself was free, Charlotte Forten recognized the interrelatedness of her oppression with the bondage of the slave woman.

Determined to live a full and expansive life, to *live out* herself, she responds to a feeling of restlessness which portends the rise of modernism in Black women's writing. "I wonder," she wrote in her second manuscript diary on January 2, 1858, "why it is that I have this strange feeling of not *living out myself*. My existence seems not nearly full or expansive enough—This longing for—something, I know not what?" (*Diary* 3; 2 January 1858). What she seeks, without her conscious knowledge, is, in the words of critic Margaret Homans, "a return to her proper origins," the place where her identity (and her own subjective voice) reside.[7] Like other Black women writing autobiography in nineteenth-century America, Charlotte Forten discusses family, society, her profession and her duty to her race; she also writes of her longing for an image of her deceased mother. "How I love to hear of her," she wrote. "What a pleasure it would be if I had an image of her, my own dear mother!" (*Diary* 2; 15 April 1858). Lacking such a portrait, she set out to paint her own, and she would create her images with words.

Charlotte Forten's poetry, noted for "its quiet simplicity and controlled tension" might well qualify her as a "literary lady." Although she published no more than a handful of poems, some of these received critical acclaim. Praising her "The Angel's Visit" (1860), William Wells Brown wrote, "for style and poetic diction, it is not surpassed by anything in the English language. Were she white, America would recognize her as one of its brightest gems."[8] Although minor in the dominant tradition, Charlotte Forten's poetry possesses rich descriptive imagery, intense lyricism, and sheer dramatic power.

Given the choice of a public voice and a private one, Charlotte

Forten, in a different time, and in a culture where she did not bear the dual stigma of race and gender difference, might have blossomed as a poet. In her third and fourth diaries (January 1858 to February 1863 and February 1863 to May 1864, respectively), she gains the desired distance between self as subject and object, making a clearer distinction between the public and the private voice. During these years, she published more actively than at any other period, placing "Two Voices" (1858), "The Wind Among the Poplars," "The Slave Girl's Prayer," and "The Angel's Visit" (c. 1860) in the *National Anti-Slavery Standard* and *The Liberator*.[9] In "The Angel's Visit," the poet's angel-mother/muse returns to plant the kiss of tradition and restore a childhood sense of wholeness threatened by the "cruel wrongs" that might destroy the motherless child who drifts from her roots:

> A sudden flood of rosy light
>     Filled all the dusky wood,
> And, clad in shining robes of white,
>     My angel mother stood.
>
> She gently drew me to her side,
>     She pressed her lips to mine,
> And softly said, "Grieve not, my child"
>     A mother's love is thine.
>
> I know the cruel wrongs that crush
>     The young and ardent heart;
> But falter not; keep bravely on,
>     and nobly bear thy part. (Brown 475-476)

In this public creative act, the motherless speaker of the poem claims the identity of both poet and daughter, still attempting to come to terms with the vocation of poethood, as well as her experience of race and gender difference. In "The Angel's Visit," the speaker of the poem recovers the "material origins" of her "feminine creativity" and creates a vehicle for the potential realization of her black and female poetic identity.

That Charlotte Forten never realized her literary goals may be attributed, in part, to what Margaret Homans has called a pressure "to conform to certain ideas of ideal womanhood, none of which included a poet's vocation."[10] To add that racial conflicts intensified

Forten's confusion may be redundant, for as Claudia Tate has written, "Nowhere in America is the social terrain more rugged than where a social minority and a 'weaker' gender intersect."[11]

Providing a testing ground for the development of Charlotte Forten's poetic identity and her public voice, diaries three and four also narrate her participation in the "Port Royal Experiment" during the Civil War. Forten's attraction to this experiment—designed to prove the fitness of former slaves for freedom—may be explained, in part, by her strong sense of duty to her race. Early in 1862, U.S. General Rufus Saxton, commander of the military district composed of Port Royal and the South Carolina Sea Islands, wrote to the War Department to request instructors to teach former slaves. Charlotte Forten answered the call immediately, but was turned away, ostensibly because she was a woman.[12] Despite her disappointment, she showed her determination to go to Port Royal. Refused in Boston, she applied to the Philadelphia Port Royal Relief Association, where she was again discouraged because of the dangers to a woman working in a war zone. However, John Greenleaf Whittier interceded, and on May 27, 1862, Charlotte Forten, as an accredited agent of the Philadelphia Port Royal Relief Association, sailed from New York aboard the steamship *United States.*[13]

In terms of her inner life, the experiment, viewed romantically as part of her duty to her race (and her transcendental, or higher, purpose), promised a partial solution to her predicament of isolation, a reconciling of intellect and a sense of Christian duty with the so-called cult of true womanhood. An inscription written in pencil inside the front cover of diary four confirms this interpretation. Speaking of her experience as a teacher of former slaves at Port Royal, she comments, "This is what the women of this country need—healthful and not too fatiguing outdoor work in which are blended the usefulness and beauty I have never seen in women." Forten speaks of her labor as "healthful"; it might also be viewed as *health-building* in that it offered her opportunities to work for the sublime balance between usefulness and beauty.

The Port Royal diaries modify the impulse toward self-sufficiency with the Christian ideal of duty and service, as revealed in this reflective entry, made on Charlotte Forten's twenty-fifth birthday: "The accomplishments, the society, the delights of travel which I have dreamed of and longed for all my life, I am now convinced can never be mine. If I can go to Port Royal, I will try to forget all these desires. I will pray that God in his goodness will make me noble enough to find my happiness in doing my duty" (*Diary* 3; 17 August 1862). Always something of a self-apologist, she makes use of the apology as a type of literary strategy, for she does not wish to appear presumptuous or self-serving. Moreover, doing one's Christian duty absolves a woman of the need to conform to the cult of true womanhood and opens up new avenues of identity. Many entries in diaries three and four have a lyrical, poetic quality. She describes her romantic vision of the voyage to Port Royal in an entry written on white letter paper and headed by the title "At Sea—1862":

> Oh, how beautiful those great waves were as they broke upon the sides of the vessel, into foam and spray, pure and white as new fallen snow. People talk of the monotony of the sea. I have not found it monotonous for a moment, since I have been well. To me there is "infinite variety," constant enjoyment about it. . . . One of the most beautiful sights I have yet seen is the phosphorescence in the water at night—the long line of light in the wake of the steamer, and the stars, and sometimes balls of fire that rise so magically out of the water. It is most strange and beautiful.
>
> (*Diary* 3; 12 October 1862)[14]

Here, once again, the diary becomes a testing ground for the development of a poetic identity, as Charlotte Forten explores her experience in language.

Simultaneously, she continues her use of the diary as a tool of personal restoration and self-healing. An entry made on her arrival at Port Royal provides an example of this use. She has "overheard" a conversation between two white Union officers, a conversation that she has judged to be deliberately calculated to disturb her: "The word 'nigger' was plentifully used, whereupon I set them down as *not* gentlemen. Then they talked a great deal about rebel attacks and yellow fever, and other alarming things. We saw through them at once" (*Diary* 3; 28 October 1862). Maintaining an admirable detachment, she finds refuge in the pages of her diary, balancing her encounter with these racists with a lyrical description of the singing Black boatmen who rowed her from St. Helena to Port Royal:

The row was delightful. It was just at sunset—a grand Southern sunset; and the glamorous clouds of crimson and gold were reflected in the waters below, which were as smooth and calm as a mirror. Then as we glided along, the rich sonorous tones of the boatmen broke upon the evening stillness. The singing impressed me very much. It was so sweet and strange and somber.

(*Diary* 3; 28 October 1862)

Transforming and transcending, she brings the values of romantic poetry to her text as she comments on the power of Black spirituals to "lift [her] out of [her]self."[15] A parallel between the diarist's romantic mode of self-expression and the "transcendental present" of the slave spiritual emerges here, and Charlotte Forten responds to both oral and literary traditions as she seeks her own voice: "The singing was very beautiful. I sat there in a kind of trance and listened to it, and while I listened looked through the open windows into the grove of oaks with their moss drapery. 'Ah wild that my tongue c'ld utter the thoughts that arise in me!'" (*Diary* 3: 2 November 1862). Yet, despite a sensitivity to Black communication styles and the language of feeling, she remained an outsider. From the viewpoint of her own standard English voice, the lyrical orality of the slave spiritual was still foreign to the New England–educated diarist; she stood outside the veil of the Black folk experience.

Although she generally reserved her diary entries as a record of the growth of her own mind, she did send an excerpt to John Greenleaf Whittier "for private perusal." Whittier submitted "Life on the Sea Islands" to the *Atlantic Monthly* where it was published in two segments in May and June 1864.[16] The published article, subtly different from the form of the private journal entries, displays more thematic and topical development than the strictly chronological diaries. Likewise, this account shows more detailed analysis and seems more publicly autobiographical, giving focused attention to her role as a teacher of former slaves. Significantly, she refers to her young scholars as "my children," seeking a public persona that would redeem her in the eyes of the "cult of true womanhood."

By the time she comes to the end of her fourth and final Port Royal diary, the entries have become less frequent; however, they display the thematic and topical development that distinguishes diary four from the earlier diaries. Thus, strictly speaking, diary four adheres more closely to the form of what is properly called a journal than any of the earlier diary texts where organization is chronological and based on early entries which lack formal continuity. Oddly, diary four omits the diarist's reaction to her father's death in April 1864. (Robert Forten died in Philadelphia after contracting typhoid fever in Maryland where he was recruiting black troops for the Union Army; Billington, *Journal,* 14).[17] Although the completion of the fourth diary coincides roughly with her father's death, she makes no comment about it—a very curious omission indeed. After her father's death, she returned to Philadelphia, where she remained for seven years before moving to Washington, D.C.

An interruption of twenty-two years ensues between the fourth and fifth diaries. During most of these years, Charlotte Forten attempted to support herself as a writer of children's stories and as a translator of novels, from French and German to English. It was a point of honor with her to support herself solely by her own literary efforts. In these years, Whittier played an active role as her mentor and protector, but requests for help of various kinds eventually exhausted him. After one of her continuing bouts with illness, Whittier wrote: "I am pained to hear of Charlotte Forten's illness. I wish the poor girl could be better situated—the wife of some good, true man who could appreciate her as she deserves."[18]

In 1878 she married such a man. Having moved to Washington, D.C., Forten taught for a year at the Sumner School and later worked as a clerk in the U.S. Treasury Department; she also joined the Fifteenth Street Presbyterian Church and married its pastor, Rev. Francis James Grimké. Called the "black Puritan," Rev. Grimké upheld ideals of Black womanhood as well as Black manhood, exposing the sexual double standard of the South and attacking it in his sermons.[19] As the son of a slave woman sired by a white master, he was well qualified to do so.

Despite the fact that Charlotte Forten was nearly thirteen years older than her husband, the two were drawn together by the magnetism of like minds: both Francis Grimké and Charlotte Forten were isolated by the tensions of race and intellect; both faced the "crisis of confidence," as defined by Ann Douglas in *The Feminization of American Culture,* which confronted American ministers and literary women of the mid-nineteenth century. According to Douglas, both literary women and ministers shared a feminizing "impulse toward articulation and change," but they were "confined to the kitchen and the pulpit," and "forbidden to compete in the markets of the masculine world." As a reaction, Douglas argues, these ministers and literary women often stressed illness "as a way . . . to dramatize their anxiety that their culture found them useless and wished them no good." They also used their illnesses "as a means of getting attention, of obtaining psychological and emotional power even while apparently acknowledging the biological correlatives of their social and political unimportance."[20] Perhaps this parallel development explains, in part, Forten's life-long invalidism as well as the continual ill health of her beloved husband Francis; in this sense, her experience reflects that of other literary women of nineteenth-century America who chose to marry ministers.

During the years of her marriage, Charlotte Forten Grimké continued to write poetry, but although her craft improved, her perspective changed substantially with age. Gone is the rebellion and conflict of the early poems, replaced by a tone of reflection and contemplation, as seen in her poem "Wordsworth," stylistically reminiscent of that poet's "The Prelude":

> In youth's fair dawn, when the soul, still untired,
> Longs for life's conflicts, and seeks restlessly
> Food for its cravings in the stirring songs,
> The thrilling strains of more impassioned bards;
> Or, eager for fresh joys, culls with delight
> The flowers that bloom in fancy's fair realm—
> We may not prize the mild and steadfast ray
> That streams from thy pure soul in tranquil song
> But, in our riper years, when through the heat
> And burden of the day we struggle on,
> Breasting the stream upon whose shores we dreamed.

No longer the dreaming youth, the poet has entered "the riper years," "breasting the stream" of the dominant tradition, meeting, opposing, and balancing against it at the crest. She has grown, in her own words: "Weary of all the turmoil and the din / Which drowns the finer voices of the soul;" and weary of her struggle against the tide. Seeking now "the finer voices of the soul" she turns to the hiero-

phant in his temple, speaking in a neutral voice but embracing symbolic polarities she avoided in her earlier poems.

> We turn to thee, true priest of Nature's fane,
> And find the rest our fainting spirits need,—
> The calm, more ardent singers cannot give;
> As in the glare intense of tropic days,
> Gladly we turn from the sun's radiant beams
> And grateful hail fair Luna's tender light.[21]

Associating the sun with the active "masculine" principle and the
glaring heat of the struggle, the poet seeks a retreat into a "feminine"
radiance symbolized by "fair Luna's tender light." She retreated into
the inner solaces of a marriage that would be, for her, a source of
renewal and rejuvenation.

Together, the Grimkés braced each other, finding in their marriage a retreat from the anxieties of constant confrontation with the
dominant culture. Here she found the balance, the communion she
had achieved earlier only in the pages of her diary. Charlotte Forten
Grimké found love, not the glaring love of subordination and domination that passes with the day, but a radiant, tender, and enduring
one—a higher marriage.

Although she maintained diary five in a bound notebook of one
hundred forty pages, she apparently used only forty-three. Pages
forty-four to one hundred are empty, and unfortunately, pages one
and two have been lost. Had they not been, they might have furnished insight into the reasons that Forten returned to diary keeping. We may speculate that she found life with Rev. Grimké in "The
High Ranks of Afro-America" to be another adventure, or that she
may have been influenced by watching Rev. Grimké keep his own
diaries.[22] On the other hand, it is possible that she returned to diary
keeping to objectify her many personal losses and the separations
from her husband occasioned by her ill health. Although the diary
includes the dates from January 1885 to July 1892, there are fewer
and fewer entries as her health worsens. Most of the entries occur
between 1885 and 1889. There are no entries for 1890 or 1891 and
only one for 1892.

The fifth and final diary has a very different character from that of
the first four. This diary represents the work of a mature woman who

has become a chronic invalid but who has also found personal happiness in her marriage with Rev. Francis Grimké—a noble man who apparently possessed all of the gentleness and kindness of his slave mother and none of the faults of his white master/father. In this diary, Forten writes of her 1885 move to Florida and her desire "to accomplish something" in "missionary labor" as well as "direct church work . . . among the lower classes" (*Diary* 5; 29 November 1885). The Grimkés clearly saw themselves as part of a Black elite setting an example.

Although they held themselves a bit above the less fortunate people in the small town in which they lived, the Grimkés were warmly received into the new parish. One evening while they were still at the boarding house, they were asked to come to church and were then escorted to their new home. They found the cottage "beautifully lighted" with a "sitting room and bedroom very comfortably furnished . . . besides a handsome writing table for F's study, and a kitchen table, plates, and other useful articles." Their home, the classic "dog-trot" of Southern architecture, had been built with "a hall through the center, —a style," Forten remarked, "I have always liked, —a study and a bedroom on one side, sitting room and kitchen on the other. Our pictures and books make the place very homelike" (*Diary* 5; 15 November 1885). But there was no study for Forten and no desk either. The idealized view she presents of her marriage in diary five may be justifiable, but the critic must ask why she never found fulfillment in her own work. Perhaps the answer lies in the social restrictions placed on her as a minister's wife, or in her reluctance to assume a public voice.

Greatest among the losses sustained by the Grimkés (including Whittier's deteriorating health and the death of family members and other friends from the old abolitionist network), was the death of their only child, a daughter, Theodora Cornelia, who died less than a year after she was born.[23] On December 19, 1885, the diarist made this reflective entry:

We have been married seven years today, —they would have been seven happy years had it not been for that one great sorrow! Oh my darling, what unspeakable happiness it would have been to have her with us to-day. She would be nearly six years old, our precious New Year's gift, how lovely and companionable I know she would have been. But I must not mourn. Father, it was Thy will. It *must* be for the best. I must wait. (*Diary* 5; 19 December 1885)

Already cut off from her primary link to Black woman's culture through the early death of her mother, Forten is further separated from that feminine tradition because the loss of her daughter denies her the possibility of acting out the role of mother. Her reflections centered on the idea that Theodora would have been "lovely and companionable," a creature balanced in beauty and intellect, another potential source of identity for the mother herself. When she writes, "I must wait," Forten, already nearing the end of her biological generativity and still childless, probably does not mean that she must wait for another child. Rather, she must wait *on the Lord* for an understanding of the inherent ironies of her life. She continues to use her diary for restoration and self-healing, as a tool for readjusting her psychic balance.

During the Grimkés's many separations, the diary was still Charlotte's best companion and at times her only confidant. During the spring and summer of 1887, she found it necessary to go North "for her health," spending May in Washington and June and July at Newport. "Beautiful, beautiful Newport!" she would write in July 1887, "In spite of illness I enjoy the sea and the rocks." She added: "If my dear, dear F. were only here to share the happiness with me" (*Diary* 5; July 1887). The next entry, for October 1887, begins, "Back home with my dearest F. How glad I am to see him and find him well. I hope we shall not be separated again" (*Diary* 5; October 1887).

In several entries, she notes that she was "too unwell" to attend evening service. In fact, her illness prevented her from maintaining her diary with any regularity. "I having been able to write only at long intervals in my journal. My head and eyes are so bad that I can't use them much of the time" (*Diary* 5; October 1887). In April 1888, she suffered in the Florida heat, complaining of mosquitoes and fleas. "If one could only spend six months here, and the remainder of the year at the North! Sometimes I become dismayed at my almost continual ill health. It unfits me for work, and there is so much to be done here" (*Diary* 5; April 1888).

Although a physician examined her in Newport in July 1888, "he could find no organic disease, —only weakness" (*Diary* 5; July 1888). This brings us back to Ann Douglas's discussion of the "cultural uses of sickness for the nineteenth century minister and lady" (92). Certainly, it could be argued that the invalid used her ill health to dramatize her anxiety over a culture that found her useless (as the very appellation *invalid* implies). Rev. Francis Grimké was affected to a lesser degree; he developed a competent public voice in his highly articulate sermons. His wife, on the other hand, became more and more retiring, publishing less and less, and making fewer entries in her diaries as her headaches increased and her vision dimmed.

There are few entries for 1889, the year Rev. Grimké resumed ministry of the Fifteenth Street Presbyterian Church in Washington, and none for 1890 or 1891. In 1892, his wife would make only one entry, in Ler, Massachusetts, during the month of July. "The last three years have been full of work and of changes, but on the whole, happy ones," she wrote. "The greatest drawback has been constant ill health, which seemed to culminate this summer, and I was obliged to leave [W]ashington with its intense heat, sewer gas, and malaria, before it was time for Frank to. I was sorry to leave him, but hope he will join me next week" (*Diary* 5; July 1892). This entry, typical of those made during the years of her declining health, proved to be her last. She died of a cerebral embolism in Washington, D.C., on July 23, 1914, twenty-two years after her last entry.[24]

On his wife's death, Rev. Francis Grimké wrote a testament of praise for the years of their marriage. "Not only my love for her, but my highest respect for her remained to the very last," he wrote shakily. "I have always felt that I was very fortunate in being thrown into such close and intimate company with so rare and beautiful a spirit." In thirty-five years of marriage, he wrote, he had never been able to detect anything "little, mean, contemptible, or unbecoming about her." He found his wife "an unusual woman, not only of great strength and character, but also sweet of temper, gentle, loving, full of the milk of human kindness."[25]

Poet Angelina Weld Grimké, daughter of Francis Grimké's brother Archibald, would remember her "Aunt Lottie" with a poem "To Keep the Memory of Charlotte Forten Grimké." The Grimké poem attempts to place her aunt's "gentle spirit" in the stream of eternity:

> Where has she gone? And who is to say?
> But this we know: her gentle spirit moves
> And is where beauty never wanes,

Perchance by other streams, mid other groves;
And to us here, ah! She remains
A lovely memory
Until eternity.
She came, she loved, and then she went away.
(*Crisis*, 9 January 1915)

Wherever she has gone, Charlotte Forten Grimké did not die without leaving her mark on a tradition of Black women's writing. Her private autobiographical act portends the rise of literary forms less restrictive than most nineteenth-century narratives by Black American women, and the diaries themselves offer untold insight into one Black woman's search for a poetic identity and a public voice. In her own words:

Knowing this, toil we unwearied.
With true hearts and purpose high;—
We would win a wreath immortal.
Whose bright flowers ne'er fade and die.[26]

## Notes

1     See Ray Allen Billington, ed., *The Journal of Charlotte L. Forten* (New York: Dryden Press, 1953). Billington omits the fifth and final diary as well as large sections of the first three diaries describing "the weather, family affairs, and other matters of purely local interest." This amounts to about one-third of Forten's five original handwritten texts. This edition is hereafter cited in the text as Billington, *Journal,* followed by page number. *The Journals of Charlotte Forten Grimke,* ed. Brenda Stevenson, is a more complete version of Forten's work that has recently been published in the Schomburg Library of Nineteenth-Century Black Women Writers (New York: Oxford University Press, 1988).

2     All five of the original manuscript diaries, along with the typewritten copies transcribed by Dr. Anna Julia Cooper, can be found in the Grimké Family Papers at the Moorland-Spingarn Research Center, Howard University, Washington, D.C. The author gratefully acknowledges permission to quote from this source.

3     Forten's published works include poetry, articles, and autobiography. See also: "Interesting Letter from Charlotte L. Forten," *Liberator* 19

(12 December 1862), 7; "Life on the Sea Islands," *Atlantic Monthly* 13 (May–June 1864); "Personal Recollections of Whittier," *New England Magazine* 8 (June 1893); and *Madame Therese: or the Volunteers of '92.*

The most complete bibliographies of Forten's work are found in Joan R. Sherman's "Afro-American Women of the Nineteenth Century: A Guide to Research and the Bio-Bibliographies of the Poets," in *But Some of Us Are Brave*, ed. Gloria T. Hull, Patricia Bell Scott, and Barbara Smith (New York: Feminist Press, 1977) and in Erlene Stetson, *Black Sister: Poetry by Black American Women, 1746–1980* (Bloomington: Indiana University Press, 1981).

4       *The Journals of Charlotte Forten Grimké*, ed. Stevenson, includes the fifth and until recently unpublished diary.

5       Dorothy Sterling, *We Are Your Sisters: Black Women in the Nineteenth Century* (New York: Norton, 1984), 119–120.

6       Lydia Maria Child, quoted in Ann Douglas, *The Feminization of American Culture* (New York: Alfred A. Knopf, 1977), 62.

7       Margaret Homans, *Women Writers and Poetic Identity* (Princeton: Princeton University Press, 1977), 17.

8       William Wells Brown, quoted in Rita Joan Sherman, *Invisible Poets* (Urbana: University of Illinois Press, 1974), 95.

9       Sherman, "Afro-American Women," 254.

10       Homans, *Women Writers,* 5.

11       Claudia Tate, *Black Women Writers at Work* (New York: Crossroad Press, 1983), 1.

12       *Diary* 3; 14 September 1862: "I got little satisfaction from the B[oston] Com[mission]," Forten wrote. "They were not sending women at present, etc."

13       Charlotte Forten and John Greenleaf Whittier visited each other frequently during the 1850s and 1860s, and maintained an active correspondence through the 1870s. Forten was one of many women writers Whittier assisted in the mid-nineteenth century; he edited her work, helped her find jobs, and acted as her unofficial literary agent, making contacts with publishers and occasionally receiving funds on her behalf.

14       An undated note handwritten on the stationery of Dr. Anna Julia Cooper and found in the Rev. Francis Grimké Papers reads, in part: "Nobody wants to take a pig in a poke. Here are two 'samples'—may they help 'sell' the job. The 'At Sea—1862' is not in the notebooks, and it has not been typed." Thus it would appear that "At Sea—1862," an entry written in Forten's hand on white letter paper, was not included in the original notebook manuscript. Dr. Cooper apparently made the decision to add this entry to the typewritten fair copy text in an attempt to help sell the manuscript to potential publishers. Dr. Cooper's letter carries no date. See the Grimké Family Papers, Moorland-Spingarn Research Center.

15    For a discussion of the "transcendent present" in slave spirituals, see James A. Cone, *The Spirituals and the Blues* (New York: Seabury, 1972), 92–97.

16    See John Greenleaf Whittier, editor's note to Charlotte L. Forten's "Life on the Sea Islands," in *Atlantic Monthly* (May 1864).

17    See also *The Liberator,* 13 May 1864, for the obituary of Robert Bridges Forten.

18    Whittier, in *Letters of John Greenleaf Whittier,* ed. John B. Picard (Cambridge: Harvard, Belknap Press), 8:278, No. 1198. When Forten married Francis S. Grimké in 1878, Whittier sent a wedding gift of fifty dollars.

19    Grimké's sermons, Grimké Family Papers, the Moorland-Spingarn Research Center.

20    Douglas, *Feminization,* 92.

21    Charlotte Forten Grimké, "Wordsworth," undated. Anna Julia Cooper Papers, Moorland-Spingarn Research Center.

22    Francis J. Grimké's notebook diaries are located in the Grimké Family Papers, Moorland-Spingarn Research Center.

23    Rayford W. Logan and Michael R. Winston, eds., *Dictionary of American Negro Biography* (New York: Norton, 1982), 233.

24    Ibid.

25    Undated typed copy of Rev. F. J. Grimké's testimonial to the memory of his wife, CFG, on the occasion of her death. The Grimké papers, Moorland-Spingarn Research Center.

26    Angelina Weld Grimké, "To Keep the Memory of Charlotte Forten Grimke," *The Liberator* 23, 24 August 1856.

# Robert J. Fehrenbach

# An Early Twentieth-Century Problem Play of Life in Black America: Angelina Grimké's *Rachel* (1916)

At the turn of this century, the Afro-American had been subject for well over a hundred years to the distortion of Black American images in the literature and drama written by whites. Sterling Brown describes this American stereotype in *Negro Poetry and Drama* as "the comic Negro, addicted to the use of big words, to gaudy finery, to brawling with the razor, and to raiding chicken roosts."[1] Serious treatments of the Negro by whites either sentimentalized the race or focused on the problem-riddled near-white Negro involved in an unlikely romantic miscegenation plot. In the American drama of the early 1900s, these distortions were maintained. In addition, direct attacks were made upon blacks by the likes of Thomas Dixon in his novels, *The Leopard's Spots* (1902) and *The Clansman* (1905), the second of which was dramatized and produced at the Amsterdam Theatre in New York the year of its publication and later made into the movie, *The Birth of a Nation* (1914). The Afro-American clearly had cause to defend the race from white friends and foes alike, to tell the Black side of the story, and to present the race more realistically in literature and drama, the very instruments by which it had so long been demeaned. Not surprisingly, therefore, the March 1915 issue of *Crisis*, the organ of the

National Association for the Advancement of Colored People, carried the following announcement:

> The Drama Committee of the N.A.A.C.P., authorized by the national body for the purpose of studying ways and means of utilizing the stage in the service of our cause, has been at work for several weeks. The committee is anxious to have race plays submitted for examination.[2]

Already aware of the need for such a drama, a thirty-five-year-old Black woman, Angelina Grimké, had written the first drafts of a play titled, "Blessed Are the Barren." The full name of this playwright, Angelina Weld Grimké, reveals her ties to the famous abolitionist and feminist, Angelina Grimké Weld, the great-aunt after whom she was named. Born in 1880 of a racially mixed marriage, Grimké was reared by her father Archibald Grimké, prominent Black attorney, newspaper editor, and author, after he and her mother, Sarah Stanley, were separated and divorced. As Gloria T. Hull writes in *Color, Sex, and Poetry: Three Women Writers of the Harlem Renaissance,* Grimké was brought up in a "liberal, aristocratic society of old Boston" and was educated at some of the finest private schools at which she was "probably the only black student."[3] Indeed, as Hull summarily characterizes her, Grimké was among those Black women of the late nineteenth and early twentieth centuries "whose family trees had more white than black roots" (p. 109). Yet from this woman of such a socially favored and advantaged life comes a scathing indictment of a white racist society. For Grimké's play depicts an educated and highly sensitive Black woman, Janet Loving, who, after hearing of the lynching of her father and half-brother in the South and after experiencing first-hand the more subtle cruelty of racism in the North, vows never to marry and never to bring children into a racist world where they are destined for humiliation and suffering.[4]

Her play, in the hands of staff members of the NAACP around the first of the year, 1915, was forwarded in January or February to John Garrett Underhill, the white New York critic, playwright, producer, and member of the Board of Directors of the NAACP. Throughout the spring and summer of 1915, Underhill corresponded with Grimké, making suggestions and reading her revisions of the play. On March 3 and 4, 1916, a Black troupe, the National Guy Players, under the auspices of the NAACP Drama Committee, performed the play at the Miner Normal School, a teacher's college for Afro-Americans in Washington, D.C. Janet Loving was now Rachel Loving and the play was titled *Rachel,* doubtless after the sensitive and long-barren Biblical figure.

There is no question about the purpose of the play or of the Washington production. The announcement on the program read: "This is the first attempt to use the stage for race propaganda in order to enlighten the American people relative to the lamentable condition of the millions of Colored citizens in this free republic." Approximately a year later, on April 25, 1917, the play was restaged at the experimental, community theater The Neighborhood Playhouse, on New York's lower East Side. The New York performance, which retained most of the Washington actors in the lead roles, was arranged with the aid of Underhill and again was presented under the auspices of the NAACP. One month later, May 24, 1917, at the urging of Maud Cuney-Hare, the prominent musician, writer, and daughter of the Black leader, Norris Wright Cuney, the play was again performed, this time in Cambridge, Massachusetts, at Brattle Hall, the auditorium of the Cambridge Social Union. The performance, given by amateur actors, was sponsored by a local church, St. Bartholomew's. Like the first, the second and third productions were in the non-professional theater and were mounted for propaganda purposes. American theatrical history was probably less on the minds of those involved with the three productions than was the cause of social justice the play was designed to serve. But whatever the intentions of Grimké and the NAACP, for the first time a play written by an Afro-American that dealt with the real problems facing American Blacks in contemporary, white, racist society was performed by entirely Black companies.

As drama, *Rachel,* received virtually no critical attention for over fifty years after the initial reaction to its publication in 1920.[5] Recently, however, that inattention has been countered by several informative treatments of the play. In his 1974 anthology of plays by Black Americans, James V. Hatch included with the text of *Rachel* prefatory comments that are instructive if necessarily brief; in 1978, Jeanne-Marie A. Miller offered a perceptive reading of the play in a short survey of Grimké's work; and in 1979, Carolyn Amonitti

Stubb's unpublished dissertation on Grimké contained a section on *Rachel* that emphasized its propagandistic character. Hull's 1987 comments on *Rachel* as part of an examination of Grimké's complete writings, published and unpublished, constitute the most recent treatment of the play, with a special focus on its autobiographical character.[6] The place of *Rachel* in American theatrical history, however—especially Black theatrical history—has been given little attention. This inattention is unfortunate, for an examination of the dramatic form of the work together with an analysis of the play within its historical context shows that *Rachel,* despite its imperfections, shares much with more recent, more widely praised, and more popularly known Black dramas. Moreover, such a study reveals that *Rachel,* allowing for the differences between the societies, the theaters, as well as the audiences of 1916 and the last quarter of the twentieth century, is an effective dramatic treatment of the life of Blacks in white America; it attests both to white America's persistent refusal to recognize the problems of a racist society and to the American theater's resistance to admit those problems to its stage.

Not surprisingly, this early play—a dramatic and theatrical first—is flawed. The general thesis of this realistic treatment of racist America, however, was to be repeatedly expressed and improved upon as the American theater and its society matured and became more receptive to that subject, and as Black playwrights were admitted to the stage and, through longevity, found their voice. That voice, the reader today must remember, includes not only Amiri Baraka, Theodore Ward, and Ed Bullins of the sixties and seventies, but Willis Richardson of the twenties, Langston Hughes of the thirties, and Lorraine Hansberry of the fifties.

Set in a "northern city" sometime during the first decade of the twentieth century, the play's first act opens in a small apartment with eighteen-year-old Rachel Loving, full of "life, health, joy, [and] youth" giddily apologizing to her mother for arriving home late: she had been detained by a new neighbor, Jimmy, the "darlingest little brown boy you ever saw." The presence of John Strong, a Black college graduate who is forced to work as a waiter, flusters the young woman as he arrives to pick up sewing his mother had left with Mrs. Loving, a seamstress. After Strong leaves, Rachel, still excited over Jimmy, tells her mother that she believes "the loveliest thing of all the lovely things in the world is just being a mother."

Mrs. Loving seems preoccupied and disturbed, and Rachel and Tom, her brother who has just arrived home from school, try to cheer her. But nothing—including bringing in Jimmy—helps, and the two younger Lovings find themselves talking about being called "nigger" by acquaintances and schoolmates. Finally Mrs. Loving reminds them that ten years ago that very day, October 16, Rachel and Tom's father and their half-brother, George, had died; up to now she had kept the manner of their deaths from the children. She then reveals that they had been lynched. The father, owner of a small "negro paper" in the South where they lived at the time, had denounced in his newspaper a lynching of an innocent Black man by a white mob which then, in turn, lynched him and George, but not before Mr. Loving had shot four of the mob in his and George's defense. Tom reacts to Mrs. Loving's story with pride and expresses anger at the "devils with white skin." Rachel expresses shock and horror at the news and sadly reflects that the South is full of little Jimmys who will be brought up only to suffer—and perhaps die—like young George. Knowledge of this cruel injustice causes the formerly happy Rachel to denounce bitterly "this white Christian nation" and to wonder as well about the nature of God's justice which permits such things to happen.

Act two opens four years later in the same apartment with Jimmy now adopted by Rachel, his parents having died nearly three years before. There is happiness in the household, but trouble lies beneath the surface. Tom, now an electrical engineer, can find no job. John Strong, who has become a close friend of the family, tells how he fears that in spite of his college degree he has reached his occupational limit as a headwaiter. He apparently is resigned to his status and urges Tom to give up his search for a position as an electrical engineer and to become a waiter also. Contributing to this somber atmosphere is the date October 16, the anniversary of the lynching of Mr. Loving and George.

After John and Tom leave, Mrs. Lane, a Black woman searching for an apartment in the neighborhood, arrives at the Loving apartment with her daughter, Ethel, an unattractive and pitifully frightened child. Mrs. Lane recounts the cruel treatment of Ethel both by white pupils and by her teacher at her school in another neighborhood. The treatment has taken its psychological toll on the child, and Mrs. Lane is looking for another place to live so her daughter can attend a school where she will not be tormented and called "nigger." While Rachel assures her that the school in their neighborhood has no such racial problems, the dour Mrs. Lane advises Rachel not to marry: life is so difficult for Negroes in this society that one should not bring any Black children into the world. Struck by this incident and by this woman's advice, Rachel does not react happily to a gift of flowers which arrives from John shortly after Mrs. Lane and Ethel leave. The sense of futility and unhappiness grows for Rachel as Jimmy arrives to report that he has been called "nigger" and hit with a stone on his way home from school. Later, Rachel's private reaction reveals a woman angry about the past, despairing about the present, and pessimistic about the future.

A week following, when Act Three opens, the playful activity of Jimmy is only a frail veneer of happiness on the Loving family's sober mood. Rachel tells Jimmy a bedtime fairy tale about a pair of little boys who were living an unhappy life but found happiness in the mythical Land of Laughter having avoided the Land of Riches, the Land of Power, and the Land of Sacrifice. Mrs. Loving and Tom, in a conversation about Rachel while she is putting Jimmy to bed, reveal that they are both worried about Rachel who in the last few days has been anxious and depressed. Tom then departs to begin his job as a waiter, having given up any hope of finding something better, Rachel leaves to visit a sick neighbor child, and John arrives to hear Mrs. Loving's expression of concern about Rachel who apparently had fainted the day Jimmy was attacked at school. After regaining consciousness she stayed in bed for days and hardly spoke to anyone, including Jimmy. Later, Strong asks her to marry him, and at first she accepts—tense and fearful. But when Jimmy's call from out of a nightmare reminds her of his maltreatment, of his and all the suffering of the Blacks—Mrs. Loving, Tom, John, Mrs. Lane and Ethel, Mr. Loving and George—she rejects Strong, marriage, and bringing Black children into the world. She sends Strong away, and in despair she returns to comfort the crying Jimmy.

The contemporary critical reaction to this somber play is interesting and instructive; it allows us, who know a Black Theater against which Grimké's play seems to pale in form if not in message, to judge the drama and to sense its impact by contemporary standards. In praising the Washington production, a review in the *Washington*

*Evening Star* cites *Rachel* for expressing the "point of view of the people on the colored side of the color line," for depicting forcefully the "Wrongs suffered by the colored race as a result of . . . 'the white man's blight of prejudice.'" Ralph Graves in the *Washington Post,* March 19, 1916, notes that "race prejudice," the subject of *Rachel,* "has not been clouded by the introduction of any hint of the problem of miscegenation." He senses in the play "the same note of pessimism" found in the French dramatist, Eugène Brieux. However tame the subject and the treatment may seem to theater-goers today, Montgomery Gregory of the Department of Dramatics at Howard University and later director of the Howard Players, wrote Grimké on March 5, following the Washington production: "I want to express to you my sincere appreciation of your artistic achievement in laying bare the real *soul* of our race and in depicting with cruel accuracy its daily agonies. You have dared to reveal the *truth.*"

After reading the draft sent him in 1915, Underhill thought it the best first play he had ever read in spite of its many faults. He believed the 1917 New York production a "capable and skillful performance of a capable and skilfully written play . . . successful and highly creditable to all concerned." Maud Cuney-Hare, writing to Grimké immediately after seeing the May, 1917, Cambridge production, testified to the daily suffering of a Black, even a socially prominent Black, in white America in her comment on the drama's realism: "To me, the conditions are not one bit over-drawn. Because I have been so close to it all this winter and have returned home so heart-sick over it all, the play was very real." She wrote that at least fifty whites had been in the audience and quoted a Cambridge friend who "wished a larger white audience could [have seen] the play." She rather optimistically continued: "But those present could not help but catch the story and the seed will grow."

When the play was published four years later, Grimké's contemporaries again commented on the drama. Jessie Fauset, the black writer, novelist, and sometime literary editor of *Crisis,* noted its naturalistic flavor. Forcing a comparison, but nonetheless noting one of the play's dominant characteristics, she says that *Rachel* reminded her of Ibsen, "for the action progresses from one depth of sad dreariness to another."[7] Interestingly, in a letter about the play, written to Ralph Graves four years earlier, Grimké admitted to having read a good deal of Ibsen as well as two naturalistic dramatists: Strindberg and Hauptmann. Writing in *The Nation,* Walter F. White, black novelist and man of letters, provided this balanced view: "The book is a scathing indictment of American race prejudice. . . . [Grimké's] language at times is a bit stilted and she does not always make her characters talk like normal human beings." White says, however, that the "faults of style were far less obvious" in the production at The Neighborhood Playhouse in New York. "Miss Grimké has done a striking piece of work in portraying the burden of color in America."[8]

What is most surprising about the reception to Grimké's play is the attention it received from the white press all over the United States. Designed in great part to awaken white America to its destruction of the Negro, *Rachel* makes no attempt to placate the whites or to justify their attitudes. The drama gives them no excuse, no way out. Yet the white press not only accepted these charges about white racist America, it revealed a sympathetic understanding of the condition of the Black American. The following are representative comments made in the press across the country following the play's publication:

> This play is rooted in a hot sense of injustice and hurt. It is a drama of defeat. [It shows] the futility of individual effort on the part of the colored people, since no amount of effort is able to overcome the arrogance of the white race.
>
> *Washington Post,* December 5, 1920

> It aims to present in a dramatic way the wrongs which innocent men, women, and even children are compelled to suffer through the stupidity and brutality of whites.
>
> *Catholic World,* December 1920

And from the former capital of the Confederacy,

> In this three-act play the "black man's burden" is vividly portrayed in a way that brings out all of the pathos and tragedy connected with it.
>
> *Richmond Times-Dispatch,* September 5, 1920

One other contemporary comment is of interest. In a letter dated December 6, 1921, H. G. Wells writes to Grimké, paternalistically but sympathetically:

Many thanks for your play—a most moving one that has stirred me profoundly. I have long felt the intensity of the tragedy of the educated coloured people. Some day I hope I may find a way to help your folk.

Many of these comments express as much hope for future plays by Black Americans for Black audiences as they express satisfaction with *Rachel.* For no Black playwright before Grimké had presented the everyday horrors of the twentieth-century Negro American: the discrimination, the cruelty, and, indeed, the murder of body and spirit, to which the Black American was subject. As Sterling Brown has said of the drama of Negro life up to this time in theatrical history: "Problems such as segregation, exploitation and other denials of democracy, all uncomfortable theatre fare, were shelved, whereas the perplexities of a handful of fair mulattoes were misconceived and exaggerated beyond recognition."[9] For a Black American to see or to read for the first time a drama that attempted to deal honestly with the real problems of Negro life in the United States must have been exciting and encouraging. Perhaps the unhappy history of the Black person's role in American drama up to that time explains why the critics chose to emphasize the strengths rather than the weaknesses of this first racial problem play.

Weaknesses there are. Many were noted by Underhill in his correspondence in 1915 with Grimké when the play was in its early drafts. The major faults of the final form are its sentimentality, the several static, typed characters, and the artificial and stilted dialogue. Despite these flaws, and despite the limited achievement of the play, the playwright's talents—as Underhill also observed when he first read the play—cannot be denied.

Without question, the play suffers from sentimentality, a judgment dependent more, perhaps, on recent standards of taste than those prevalent in 1916. Hatch observes: "*Rachel* is in the Louisa May Alcott tradition. Miss Grimké is writing with true feeling, but the four wars since the writing make her tender feelings seem Victorian and precious" (p. 138). A number of characters and incidents—as well as dialogue—contribute to the sentimental nature of much of the play. There is much kissing, hugging, and weeping. Mrs. Loving is never called anything but "Ma dear" by Rachel, and cute children, talking a kind of baby talk, abound, causing Hatch to suggest that they would be a "director's nightmare" (p. 138). Most of the sentimentality, however, is associated with the highly emotional young woman who is the title character.

In Rachel, Grimké wanted to create an extremely sensitive young woman, one who could be affected both by gentleness and beauty and by cruelty and ugliness. This sensitivity in her character does not fundamentally change in the play. As a child Rachel had been subjected to the same name calling and tormenting that Jimmy, her adopted son, later experiences (p. 94). But with the bright comfortable optimism of childhood, still apparent in the eighteen-year-old girl of the first act, Rachel had been able to suppress her early experiences. Now, however, with her loved ones suffering and with racial prejudice growing instead of abating (from Tom, denied professional employment because of his race: "Every year, we [Blacks] are having a harder time of it" [p. 49]; and from Mrs. Lane: "Every year things are getting worse" [p. 57]), Rachel, no longer a child, fears that happiness for Blacks is no less a dream than is the Land of Laughter in the fairy tale she tells Jimmy at the beginning of the third act (pp. 69–73). Thus arises the major conflict in the play: Rachel must either continue her Pollyanna view of life in spite of abundant contradictory evidence, or despair under the weight of the "burden of race" in a racist society. Responding as fully to the horror of racism as she did to human kindness, she becomes bitter and dour. "If you see things as they are," she says, "you're either pessimistic or morbid" (p. 51).

Though she tries she is, according to Tom, unable to adjust to racism as John Strong, her would-be husband and the more practical of the two, apparently can. Practicality is hardly her dominant characteristic; she is the sensitive innocent crushed by the weight of reality. Her response is negative and ultimately destructive.[10] The emotional extremes of Rachel's character are excessive, and one feels embarrassed and uncomfortable by their display. This emotionalism, this sentimental character, however, clearly derives from Grimké's desire to present a person capable of being first a happy, hopeful girl, and then a cynical, bitter, and hopeless young woman and to point the finger at the cause for that dramatic change.

The other characters undergo less change; indeed, some of their names type them as static characters. Mrs. Loving is the stable, long-suffering mother, strong and tender, loved and loving. Tom is the angry but proud young man, who gives into realities but not without a fight and not without a lingering bitterness. John Strong is the pragmatist; he gives into the injustice with resignation and little anger. One has mixed feelings about Strong; he seems too easily resigned to his condition, but Grimké makes clear that Strong's surrender to the realities of a racist society is the result of an earlier struggle of some length. The strength in this man, reflected in his name, seems to be less in his ability to carry on the struggle against discrimination and more in his ability to carry on in life for those he loves—his mother and Rachel—with some success in spite of that discrimination which causes others to despair. Mrs. Lane and her daughter, Ethel, are the very pictures of such despair: she, the woman broken, and Ethel, the child shattered by a racist society. Among these examples provided by the characters, Rachel, the too-sensitive woman, chooses despair, and out of love for others unborn refuses to be responsible for bringing a child into the world to suffer a Black person's fate in white America.

The contrasting structure Grimké has given the play complements Rachel's character change and serves the playwright's thesis well. Time is needed to give verisimilitude to Rachel's dramatic disintegration; thus the playwright chooses the three-act form. Each act focuses on one particular demonstration of racial prejudice, each of which is juxtaposed with a potential happiness which is destroyed by the racism. Act one contrasts a young high school graduate's excited hope for her and her brother's futures with the discovery that her father and half-brother had been lynched. Rachel's new knowledge turns her earlier hope into fear and melancholy. Act two also opens optimistically: Tom is now an electrical engineer and Rachel is a mother, having adopted Jimmy. These happy circumstances are contrasted in the act with Tom's inability to find employment because he is Black and Rachel's inability to protect Jimmy from being hounded and called "nigger" by white schoolchildren. At the opening of the third act, happiness is present again, but it is only as substantial as the mythical Land of Laughter in the fairy tale which Rachel tells Jimmy. Totally crushed and depressed at the end of the act as she was happy, even giddy, four years earlier, Rachel is momentarily tempted by John Strong's happy proposal of marriage. But faced with bringing children into the world to be called "nigger," to be refused an opportunity to provide a living for themselves and their families, and to be afraid for their very lives because they are

Black, she rejects marriage and motherhood, thereby refusing to create life to have it destroyed.

The quality of Grimké's dialogue is uneven. The endearments and cute children's talk have already been cited as contributing a sentimentality the play could have well done without. Often associated with this sentimental style, indeed contributing to it, is the artificial language Grimké sometimes makes her characters speak. Reflecting on the suffering of children shortly after learning of Jimmy's problems at school, Rachel says: "And, suddenly, some day, from out of the black, the blight shall descend, and shall still forever—the laughter on those little lips, and in those little hearts" (p. 62). And Tom, near the end of the play, in a conversation with his mother about the change that has come over Rachel: "I don't know, Ma, but I feel, as you do; something terrible and sudden has hurt her soul; and, poor little thing, she's trying bravely to readjust herself to life again" (p. 79).

Similarly, the speeches of the characters occasionally are unnatural and preachy. Tom's long attack upon the Southern whites, quoted here only in part, is stilted speechifying, however earnest:

> And, in the South today, there are white men. . . . They have everything; they're well-dressed, well-fed, well-housed; they're prosperous in business; they're important politically; they're pillars in the church. I know all this is true—I've inquired. Their children (our ages, some of them) are growing up around them; and they are having a square deal handed out to them—college, position, wealth, and best of all, freedom, without galling restrictions, to work out their own salvations. With ability, they may become—anything; and all this will be true of their children's children after them. (A pause). Look at us— and look at them. We are destined to failure—they, to success. Their children shall grow up in hope; ours, in despair. Our hands are clean;—theirs are red with blood of a noble man—and a boy. They're nothing but low, cowardly, bestial murderers. The scum of the earth shall succeed. (p. 42)

Sometimes Grimké provides the characters with statements which strain the reader's belief. Mrs. Loving, in telling of the night the whites lynched her husband and her son, describes seventeen-year-old George as he was being dragged through the house: "He never made an outcry. His last words to me were: 'Ma, I am glad to go with Father.' I could only nod to him" (p. 25). And worse yet, though a dozen men broke down the Lovings's front door and their bedroom door, and though Mr. Loving shot four of the abductors in the bedroom before he and George were overpowered and dragged down the hall, Mrs. Loving can say to Rachel and Tom: "While they were dragging them down the steps, I crept into the room where you were. You were both asleep. Rachel, I remember was smiling" (p. 25).

On occasion, Grimké would have done well to prune her work. Some of the speeches are overlong; they either dwell on points long after they are made or wander, touching upon matters only peripherally related to the speaker's subject. An example: even allowing for Rachel's youthful garrulity (Mr. Loving calls her a "chatter-box") and for the importance her love of children has for the plot of the play, the following statement by the young woman tends to ramble:

And, Ma dear, if I believed that I should grow up and not be a mother, I'd pray to die now. I've thought about it a lot, Ma dear, and once I dreamed, and a voice said to me—oh! it was so real—"Rachel, you are to be a mother to little children." Wasn't that beautiful? Ever since I have known how Mary felt at the "Annunciation." (*Almost in a whisper*) God spoke to me through some one, and I believe. And it has explained so much to me. I know now why I just can't resist any child. I have to love it—it calls me—it—draws me. I want to take care of it, wash it, dress it, live for it. I want the feel of its little warm body against me, its breath on my neck, its hands against my face. (*Pauses thoughtfully for a few moments*). Ma dear, here's something I don't understand: I love the little black and brown babies best of all. There is something about them that—clutches—at my heart. Why—why— should they be—oh! pathetic? I don't understand. It's dim. More than the other babies, I feel that I must protect them. They're in danger, but from what? I don't know. I've tried so hard to understand, but I can't. (*Her face radiant and beautiful*). Ma dear, I think their white teeth and the clear whites of their big black eyes and their dimples everywhere—are—are—(*Breaks off*). And, Ma dear, because I love them best, I pray God every night to give me, when I grow up, little black and brown babies—to protect and guard. (*Wistfully*). Now, Ma dear, don't you see why you must never laugh at me again? Dear, dear, Ma dear? (pp. 12–13)

Yet more often than not, especially for a first drama, the dialogue works. For example, the tension and anxiety felt by Rachel in the presence of John Strong—first as an eighteen-year-old school girl alone with an older, attractive, and attentive man and later as a woman sorely tempted by his offer of marriage but determined to remain unmarried and barren—is conveyed naturally in the dialogue. Also, the language and tone of Tom's speeches are appropriately varied as he plays a variety of roles: the optimistic school boy who has made the football team, the good-natured Latin student mockingly speaking in Latinate English, the angry son who learns of his father's lynching, the indulgent, playful uncle to Jimmy, and the shamed and bitter young man going off to a waiter's job, are all successfully conveyed.

By far the greatest challenge to Grimké in writing dialogue, however, is to show in Rachel's speeches the character's disintegration from a happy, giddy young schoolgirl of eighteen into an ill-ridden, embittered woman of twenty-two, prematurely aged by tribulations. Rachel's early chattering and bubbling talkativeness has already been cited. In contrast to these, and among the most powerful sections of the play, are Rachel's increasingly bitter thrashings out at injustices, at ugly racial prejudice, and at the God who allows these inhumanities to exist.

In Act one, after hearing of her father's and half-brother's lynchings, Rachel begins immediately to think of the Southern Black children, born and yet unborn, who will someday be lynched by white, Christian Southerners: "They will laugh and play and sing and be happy and grow up, perhaps, and be ambitious—just for *that?* . . . How horrible! Why—it would be more merciful—to strangle the little things at birth . . . Why it—makes—you doubt—God!" (pp. 27–28). At the end of Act two, after having witnessed the psychological annihilation of the ostracized Ethel Lane, after having heard Jimmy tell of his treatment at the hands of white boys, and after having seen her brother rejected in his profession because of his race, Rachel says:

> First, it's little, black Ethel—and then it's Jimmy. Tomorrow, it will be some other little child. The blight—sooner or later strikes all . . . the blight shall descend, and shall still forever—the laughter in those little lips, and in those little hearts . . . Why, God, you are making a mock of me; you were laughing at me. I didn't believe God could laugh at our sufferings, but He can. We are accursed, accursed! We have nothing, absolutely nothing. (pp. 62–63)

Then, vowing never to have children, she says, comparing her mercy to God's cruelty: "You can laugh, Oh God! Well so can I . . . But I can be kinder than You . . . If I kill, You Mighty God, I kill at once—I do not torture" (p. 63).

And, finally in the last act, in her rejection of Strong's offer of marriage and children, the haggard and despairing Rachel cries:

> I am twenty-two—and I'm old, you're thirty-two—and you're old; Tom's twenty-three—and he is old. Ma dear's sixty—and she said once she is much older than that. She is. We are all blighted; we are all accursed—all of us, everywhere, we whose skins are dark—our lives blasted by the white man's prejudice . . . And my little Jimmy—seven years old, that's all—is blighted too. In a year or two, at best, he will be made old by suffering . . . If it nearly kills me to hear my Jimmy crying, do you think I could stand it, when my own child, flesh of my flesh, blood of my blood—learned the same reason for weeping? Do you? (pp. 93–94)

Perhaps the effectiveness of these and similar passages is reduced by their excesses, by their length. Yet the passion, the anger, the hurt of a distraught and damaged human being cannot be missed.

The attitudes of Afro-Americans about their role in American society, a predominantly white society, have varied over the years, and the prevailing attitudes in different generations have not always been the same. Many living in the second half of the twentieth century and used to the dramatic statements of Baraka, Bullins, Ward, and others of similar talents will not be pleased by Grimké's play, some because Rachel gives up, others because she idealistically wants to live in a world uncolored by prejudice. By their actions and statements, the Loving family reveals an implicit desire to be accepted by white society on that society's terms. Peacefully integrated schooling is sought, the importance of correct standard English grammar is emphasized, education (including learning Latin) is urged as a way to gain equal treatment, proper manners are gently drummed into children, and everyone must be clean and neat. That these gestures are futile in their quest for admission into the larger society around them only baffles or angers the Lovings. They never give any sign of altering the quest itself. Today, many Blacks would say that Grimké's error was not in choosing the wrong means but in choosing the wrong ends for her characters.

But these same critics of Grimké's ends cannot help but notice similarities between the observations and ideas she expressed over three generations ago and those more philosophically compatible Black dramatists have made during the last generation. Grimké covers the whole social spectrum in her play and she finds every significant American institution wanting. Blacks are discriminated against in employment, in schools—by student and teacher alike—in "white Christian" churches, and of course, in theaters. The personal world is as bad for Grimké's characters as the institutional society. Whites either call them deprecating names ("nigger") or ignore them. Rachel observes that white people are kinder to their animals than they are sensitive to their Black fellow human beings.

The results of this maltreatment on Grimké's characters are varied: some, notably the children, are psychologically impaired (Ethel is literally terrified, Jimmy has nightmares); others' sense of self-respect is destroyed (Mrs. Lane: "My husband and I are poor, and we're ugly and we're black"). Some live their lives with sad resignation and try to make the most of a limited life (Strong); others live with shame combined with bitter resentment (Tom); still others lose all personal hope and despair of the future for them and their people (Rachel). Through it all, the whites are depicted believing their injustice just and themselves followers of Christ.

It is an outrageous picture Grimké paints, variations of which have been seen frequently on the stage in recent years. If Grimké's depiction differs from that presented in the recent Black Theatre and is found wanting by the reader today because of, by comparison, its acquiescent nature, the knowledge that Grimké's expression was its first expression on the American stage—a stage inhospitable to the play's thesis and racially restricted itself—should temper that unfavorable reaction.

Indeed, when *Rachel* was performed in the spring of 1916 in Washington, no professional Black theatrical company and virtually no audience for plays of Negro life existed. The first play written by an Afro-American to be presented professionally by Black Americans in New York was not to be seen until 1923; that year the Ethiopian

Art Players mounted at the Frazee Theatre *The Chip Woman's Fortune* by Willis Richardson who, it is important to note, attributed the origins of his interest in drama to seeing the 1916 production of *Rachel.*[11] The first Broadway production of a play by a Black, *Appearances* by Garland Anderson, did not come until two years later in 1925, and commercially successful plays depicting the life of Black Americans were still years away. But even in August, 1916, W. E. B. Du Bois saw the significance of *Rachel.* Du Bois wrote that there "will undoubtedly be the slow growth of a new folk drama built around the actual experience of Negro American life. Already there are beginnings here and there, but especially in Washington, where [was] produced Angelina Grimké's strong play, 'Rachel.'"[12] Not surprisingly, others focused on the established professional theater of that time for signs of a serious Black presence on the stage. The three one-act plays of Negro life by Ridgley Torrence, the white playwright, performed by the Hapgood Players, Black Americans all, at the Garden Theatre in New York in the spring of 1917 brought from James Weldon Johnson:

> April 5, 1917 is the date of the most important single event in the entire history of the Negro in the American theatre; for it marks the beginning of a new era. On that date . . . the stereotyped traditions regarding the Negro's histrionic limitations were smashed. It was the first time anywhere in the United States for Negro actors in the dramatic theatre to command the serious attention of the critics and of the general press and public.[13]

However important the joint effort by Torrence and the Hapgood players was to the history of the Black actor in the American theater, and however important it was to establishing that an audience existed in America for plays dealing with authentic Negro life, it was Grimké's play, not Torrence's, that first depicted the real life and character of the Black American on the American stage, where before there had existed only a distorted Black figment of a white imagination. It was the voice of a Black woman in 1916 that first brought to the American theater the life of the Black American as only the Black American can know it.

# Notes

1     Sterling Brown, *Negro Poetry and Drama* (Washington, D.C.: The Associates in Negro Folk Education, 1937), p. 106.

2     *Crisis* 9 (1915), 215.

3     Gloria T. Hull, *Color, Sex, and Poetry: Three Women Writers of the Harlem Renaissance* (Bloomington: Indiana University Press, 1987), pp. 109, 115.

4     The typescript of this play is among Miss Grimké's collected papers in the Moorland Room, Founders Library, Howard University, Washington, D.C. Unless otherwise stated, all references in this essay are to letters, newspaper articles, and memorabilia found in those papers. Often no dates or pagination are on these materials. I am grateful to the staff of the Moorland Room for the many courtesies extended me during the preparation of this essay.

5     *Rachel: A Play in Three Acts* (Boston: The Cornhill Co., 1920). The play was photographically reprinted in 1969 by the McGrath Publishing Company, College Park, Maryland, and also appears in the anthology, James V. Hatch, ed., *Black Theater, U.S.A.: Forty-five Plays by Black Americans, 1847–1974* (New York: The Free Press, 1974), pp. 137–172. All references to the play in this article are to the McGrath reprint.

6     Jeanne-Marie A. Miller, "Angelina Weld Grimké: Playwright and Poet, *CLA Journal* 21 (1978), 513–524; Carolyn Amonitti Stubbs, "Angelina Weld Grimke: Washington Poet and Playwright," *DAI* 39 (1979), 4941A–42A; for Hull's book and Hatch's anthology, see notes 3 and 5 respectively.

7     *Crisis* 21 (1920), 64.

8     *The Nation* 114 (1922), 101–102.

9     *Negro Poetry and Drama*, p. 113.

10     Noting this reaction, Hilda Josephine Lawson, in "The Negro in American Drama," *Bulletin of Bibliography* 17 (1940), 28, says that the play argues ridiculously for race suicide. Grimke makes clear in a letter (an undated and unaddressed copy of which is among her papers) that the play was addressed less to blacks than it was directed toward whites. Her purpose was not to provide an answer for blacks seeking a solution to racial discrimination—certainly not race suicide in any case—but rather to cause whites to see the destructive power of that discrimination.

11     *Crisis* 34 (1927), 158.

12     *Crisis* 12 (1916), 169.

13     (New York: A. A. Knopf, 1930), p. 175.

# Daphne Duval Harrison

# "Up the Country . . ." and Still Singing the Blues: Sippie Wallace

He left home one morning just 'bout the dawn of day,
Now he [was] gone one morning just 'bout the dawn of day.
Some old long tall woman stole my man away.

So many days Lawd, I stole away and cried,
So many days Lawd, I stole away and cried,
Didn't have no blues but I just wasn't satisfied.
Shorty George is *the* only man I choose . . .

Texas-style blues singing and piano playing was introduced to an expanded audience when Okeh Records released Sippie Wallace's rendition of "Shorty George" in October 1923. For the first time, many blues lovers would hear the shouting wail that typified Wallace's vocal style and for which she had become known as the "Texas Nightingale" in her native state.

We cannot draw direct causal links from Wallace's childhood experiences at the turn of the century to the achievements of peak years as an artist from 1923 to 1927. Yet the events and encounters beginning within her family and neighborhood greatly influenced her public and private life and they continued to pervade her blues writing and performance until her death in 1986. Hers is a clear case of "the blues is life . . . the blues is art . . . is life." When Wallace said, "I sings the blues to comfort me on," she confirmed that the blues is an integral part of her life. When she declared that singing the blues "is my job," she acknowledged the blues as a source of livelihood. Her comment about trying to keep her blues compositions from sounding "churchy" indicates her recognition of the blues as a distinct art. The blues is an existential art form that provides a creative outlet and a catharsis for Wallace and her audience.[1]

Wallace's music-making is so bound up with her living that one cannot readily discern where the performer enters and the elderly matron exits or vice versa. In private conversations one would hear a confirmation of the values expressed on stage or in public. The charm and twinkling wit on stage were also manifested in the little pranks she played on her "children" and friends at home. Consequently, while her relationship with the music and lyrics evolved in the performance, her commentary on stage, in media settings, or in private conversation reveals an internal consistency that is often lacking in many performances. In contrast, Helen Humes, former singer with Count Basie's band, could sing a blues as well as or better than some of Wallace's contemporaries, but she emphatically stated that the blues was just another type of music to her no different than the ballads or pop tunes.[2] She did not identify with the blues as a source of personal expression or emotional outlet as Wallace did. Wallace's life story reveals some of the forces that shaped her as a person and performer—close family ties, low economic status, strong religious feelings, love of music.

• • •

Beulah Belle Thomas was born to George and Fanny Thomas on 1 November 1898 in Houston, Texas, a frontier town with a growing black population at the turn of the century. Cotton was still king on the large plantations that employed many of the blacks who migrated there from Louisiana and Mississippi.[3] Blacks were still heavily influenced by plantation rhythms—backbreaking work from sun-to-sun, Monday to Saturday, large gatherings for Saturday night frolics, and church all day Sunday. Those who worked in towns and cities were laborers or domestics, and among these were the Thomases, who had thirteen children. Wallace was the fourth child of the religious, hardworking couple who neither indulged in nor approved of the Saturday night "wang dangs" that spawned such blues notables as "Ragtime" Henry Thomas and "Blind Lemon" Jefferson. Though the elder Thomases did not live to see it, two of their sons, George Jr. and Hersal, and one of their daughters, Beulah, rose to stardom on the vaudeville circuit.

Beulah, nicknamed Sippie by her siblings, spent her preteen years singing and playing at the family church, Shiloh Baptist. It was there that she earned a certificate for singing from a Sunday school teacher. Although she had very little formal education beyond elementary school, her older brother George and sister Lillie encouraged her musical career. Under George's tutelage she began to learn the popular music her mother disdained. Wallace described how she began writing her own blues lyrics, too, with his coaching.

> You see, my brother wrote music, you know, and I used to always hang around him all the time. And my brother never did have no words and I used to hear the words, get the words from different women, you know, girls come around singing. I get the words, I put them down on a piece of paper, and I carry them in a room and learn them. And then by listening, then I learn how to put them together.[4]

Wallace's parents, like most good Baptists, would not countenance the "devil's music" in their home and punished their children if they were caught listening to it or playing it. They believed, as did the mass of black working-class people, that the only music fit to sing came from hymnals and church songbooks. The nonreligious or antireligious themes that emerged in slave seculars and eventually evolved into the work songs and the blues of southern blacks were regarded, therefore, as "devil's music."[5] According to James Cone, however, the blues reflect the same existential tensions as spirituals in black people's search for truth in the reality of the black experience. He contends that it is a mistake to attempt to interpret black life without the commentary of both blues and spirituals since they "flow from the same bedrock of experience."[6] Perhaps Wallace (and her peers) intuitively realized this, because she and her brothers defied their parents' strict interpretation of what was vulgar and what was acceptable.

By the time she was in her teens, she had succumbed to the catchy rhythms of her brother's piano playing and joined him in his creative efforts. When George Jr. went to New Orleans to pursue his musical career in 1912, fifteen-year-old Sippie soon followed. In New Orleans she met and married Frank Seals. This was a mistake, caused by her youth and her inexperience with men:

> I've been the biggest fool in the world. I believe everything everybody said was true, you know. Just like if you'd say "I love you." Well, I got a little enough sense to believe that you love me. I ain't got no better

sense than that. And mostly—and then when I first, you know, when I first married, I thought that you get a husband wasn't nobody going to have him but you. But that's the wrongest thing and it's the wrongest way to teach a child, 'cause can't no woman have a man by herself. Girl, you going to have help. I don't care how good you are, you going to have help. Then you couldn't have no husband by yourself, nohow.

So, my brother, me and him wrote "Adam and Eve Had the Blues." I got all mine [ideas], got them from the Bible . . . this is true facts. . . .

And Eve is the cause of all of us having the blues, child. Even little dogs have the blues, even little birds have the blues, even little bees, even everything has it. Everything been having trouble.[7]

"Adam and Eve Blues" probably evolved differently from the way that Wallace recalled it, but her recollection of the process by which her personal experience evolved into song is true to life. Her blues links religious and secular ideas and reaffirms the belief that the blues is a universal experience.

> When Adam and Eve was in the Garden of Eden
> They didn't know till the good Lord walked out.
> Eve turned around and soon she found out,
> Yes, what it was all about.
> Eve called her husband and she got close to her spouse.
> She said, "Here's some fruit, eat it, will make us fine."
> She said, "Eat some fruit, the good Lord is gone."
> Adam said, "Yeah, it won't take long."[8]

The broken marriage affected Wallace profoundly enough for her to pay tribute to her mother's admonitions about "keeping company" in the first blues she wrote, "Caldonia." It is interesting to see how Wallace used the noun, "mama," in this rendition sung at her home in 1975.

> Oh Caldonia, you treat your mama mean.
> Oh Caldonia, you treat your mama mean.
> You don't trust her like she's no human being.

In the first stanza, "mama" refers to herself as she decries the inhumane treatment of a lover. However, the second stanza takes a curious turn as "mama's" advice about men is recalled. In stanza three the traditional "muddy waters" line is used as a lead into the third line, which reiterates the theme of family and spouse abuse, common to many blues.

> And if you had listened to what your mama said,
> And if you had listened to what your mama said,
> You would not been here having those blues today.

> You drink muddy water and you sleep in a hollow log.
> You drink muddy water and you sleep in a hollow log.
> And you treat all your family just like a dog.

She employed another traditional blues line, "I looked up on the mountains," for the transition from the general statement about the family to focus on the infidelity of her lover. The shift from remorse to anguish replays the admonition of her mother and acknowledges that "no woman have a man by herself."

> I looked up on the mountain, looked far as I could see,
> I looked up on the mountain, looked far as I could see,
> The woman had my daddy, Lord, and the blues had me.

> You can take my baby, but you sure can't keep him long.
> You can take my baby, but you sure can't keep him long.
> I got a new way of loving, you better believe you women can't
>     catch on."

The optimism of the last stanza is typical of many blues in its affirmation of the belief in one's ability to alter the chain of events affecting one's life. In this example, Wallace resorts to a boastful assertion of her sexual prowess as the tool for turning the tide. In so doing she cleverly accomplishes two goals in "Caldonia"—atonement for disobeying her mother, and resolution of her feelings of abandonment.

Sixty years later Wallace reminisced that "Mama didn't want me to go with boys . . . [but] I was a fool, anybody was all right with me. Just as long as it was a boy. Mama never let me receive company." [10]

Both parents had died by the time Wallace returned home around 1918 to live with her siblings. The stagestruck young woman could not forget her experiences in New Orleans's Storyville district where brother George's friends included King Oliver and the soon-to-be famous Louis Armstrong. Disappointment in love was overshadowed by the burning desire to dance and sing in one of the tent shows that visited Houston on the Theater Owner's Booking Association circuit.

The teeming crowds of black folk would gather on both sides of Houston's streets to watch the parade and hear the lively orchestras play the latest ragtime and marching tunes. Wallace figured that with her talent, she might get a chance to play or sing for one of the showpeople, so she and other budding musicians waited around all day hoping to be noticed. For many of these aspirants, the only jobs available were temporary—to help raise the tent, hawk tickets, or pass out handbills—and Sippie's first break was not any better. Wallace began her roadshow career as a maid and stage assistant to a Madame Dante, a snakedancer with Phillip's Reptile Show. As she described one of her experiences she could barely contain the laughter that bubbled inside.

> I was scared when I started waiting on her. See, my church name is Beulah and when the tent show came around the block from my house the show was so good they kept it there. So I used to play the blues down there because I knowed a girl who worked there. So when they got me to earn work on an opening chorus, you know, where you dance, I couldn't dance so Madame Dante asked me to be her maid. I used to light her incense. I would do like this [she demonstrated a wiggle and hand movement] and back up, then light it. Then, she'd just do a butterfly dance and I'd go out there and get a great big snake named Cary. He was very long and big. So when Madame was all loosened up she'd motion for me to bring the cane basket with the snake, you know. And I was just as scared as I can be and I had that thing just like this here when one time out in the middle of the stage that old snake come sticking his head up and I let it fall. [She laughs heartily.] It was jumping all out that thing. Child, I let that thing go and I flew. I never will forget that.[11]

By mentioning her lack of dancing talent and her willingness to work as a maid, Wallace underscored two things: jobs on stage were scarce but much sought after, and domestic labor was a mainstay for black women, even in show business.[12] There was no bitterness in that compromise for Wallace because it brought her close to her goal of becoming a performer. As Madame Dante's maid she began her travels around Texas, from Houston to Dallas to Galveston to Waco and all the little towns in between.

Wallace soon gained a reputation as the "Texas Nightingale" as she sang with small bands for picnics, dances, and holiday celebrations. From these she went with tent shows around Texas as a singer, not a maid.

Her first recordings revealed a seasoned performer who had learned her craft well. She owed much to her brother George, who was by this time a respected composer and music publisher in Chicago. He was on the recording staff of the W. W. Kimball Company's music roll division and director of his own orchestra when Wallace, Hociel Thomas (a niece who was also an aspiring blues singer), and Hersal Thomas, her baby brother, arrived to join him. He played a significant part in getting the trio going.

Hersal Thomas was a superb pianist who often accompanied his sister when she performed, although he was only thirteen or fourteen years old. His musical gifts included composition also, and his name was listed on sheet-music credits as well as on recordings. Sippie and George renewed their songwriting partnership to produce the popular "Shorty George" and "Underworld Blues." The musically talented Thomases, George, Sippie, and Hersal, quickly became famous in the recording field. George's "Muscle Shoals Blues" was a best-seller in 1922 but it did not match the popularity of Wallace's first recordings on the Okeh label, "Shorty George" and "Up the Country Blues." The Windy City had a new star. Her first recording purportedly sold 100,000 copies—quite a feat for a newcomer in a young field.

In just a few months, Wallace's portrait was featured in the ads for her recordings hailing the "Texas Nightingale" as one of General Phonograph Corporation's new race stars. The dignified portrait was often accompanied by "exceptionally high-type dialect, especially prepared to appeal to the colored race," according to a trade magazine for the phonograph industry.[13] Examples of that so-called "high-type dialect" appeared in a series of monthly full-page ads featuring each of the Okeh recording artists, Wallace among them.[14] General Phonograph was unabashadly pursuing the dollars from the "colored population" through the *Chicago Defender*. Employing dialect in that manner would be considered objectionable by most consumers

today, but back then the ads were successful in selling Wallace's recordings. Fortunately, they did not use the obscene caricatures found
in some ads.

Wallace's blues style is a mix of Southwestern rolling bass honky-
tonk and Chicago shouting moan, a seductive brew that fit her per-
sonality. She had a strong, smooth voice and good articulation that
pushed the words straight forward (a quality that blues pianist
Sammy Price considers imperative to good singing).[15] Her ability to
shift moods within a song adds a dimension that is missing in singers
such as Victoria Spivey and Mamie Smith. An unorthodox sense of
timing and accentuation of words give her lyrics punch and tension.
In the first verse of "Shorty George," for example, the third line has
more weight because she drags out "tell" and "I" for emphasis and
authenticity.

> I wrote a letter *and* mailed it by air,
> I wrote a letter and I mailed it in the air,
> You can *tell* by that, *I* got a man somewhere.[16]

The plaintive swoop in the last verse is a device Wallace used to
wrench tears from the most ordinary melody. Her slide down a fourth
on "Shorty" and up a fourth on "only man" gives a twist that ends
that song with a dynamic surge of melodic emotion ("Shorty George
is *the* ONLY MAN I choose").

"Shorty George" remains a Wallace classic after sixty years because of her distinctive phrasing, punctuated by those mournful
slides and shifting moods. Eddie Heywood's stride piano set a loping
pace to allow the vocal a full range of flexibility. When Wallace sang
"Shorty George" in the 1980s, although age forced her to sing in a
lower octave, she still used a singing shout that grabbed the listener
and made him or her want to join in the call.

The contrast in mood of the second side of her inaugural recording, "Up the Country Blues," demonstrated that she could convey a
broad spectrum of mood and feeling. No pleas here for "Shorty
George." Instead we hear a wronged woman who does not stand by
weeping and wringing her hands, but who ushers the mistreating
two-timer out of her house and out of her life. The listener is convinced that her singing conveys her own manner of dealing with
hurt and anger. Any woman who has been betrayed by a "sweet

daddy" who spent her money while steadily two-timing her can identify with Wallace's answer to this dilemma.

In "Special Delivery Blues," with Louis Armstrong on cornet and
Hersal on piano, Wallace portrays the scorned woman who is unwill-
ing to accept the finality of rejection by her lover. The mellow rolling
piano in the introduction is ably contrasted by Louis Armstrong's
crisp staccato notes. Hersal's use of tremolo chord progressions,
which follow Wallace's ascending melodic line, builds each line to an
intensity, which is relieved by Armstrong's brief broken phrases. She
slides up a fourth on the last word of the first line in each stanza,
imitating the piano roll, dragging out every ounce of melancholy
from each word. The last line of each stanza releases the tension with
an upbeat tempo and syncopated chord progressions.

He said, "I'm leaving you, Baby. It almost breaks my hear-ar-art,"
He said, "I'm leaving you, Baby. It almost breaks my heart.
But remember sometimes that *the* best of friends must part.
• • •
Hey, Mr. Mailman, Did you bring me any ne-e-ews?
Mr. Mailman, Did you bring me any news?
'Cause if you didn't it will give me those "Special Delivery Blues."[17]

Wallace's vocal signature was stamped on many blues like these.
Whether she was pleading with or lambasting her man, she employed the ascending melisma and the intervallic leaps to emphasize
meaning and mood and to achieve a powerful effect.

Many of the ideas for her blues came out of her personal concerns.
She repeatedly commented that she would just be "thinking it over
in my mind, child, and it would just come to me to make a song
about what was troubling me." The joy and satisfaction that grew out
of the creative interaction she shared with her brothers is reflected in
her exuberant renditions of "Shorty George" and "Up the Country
Blues." But other occasions and relationships inspired her to write in
a different mood. Among them were "Can Anybody Take Sweet
Mama's Place?" and "He's the Cause of Me Being Blue" with Clarence
Williams.

A very attractive, buxom young woman, Wallace had already re-
married by the time she joined her brother in Chicago. Her second
husband was Matthew Wallace, a dapper Houstonian whom she

adored. Their union had to bear the strains of big city living and all of its temptations—unattached women, drinking, and gambling. For a while Matthew played a major role in the further development of his wife's career, serving as her manager and, on occasion, as master of ceremonies, and as co-author of a couple of her blues. As was typical for stage acts, he used dramatic gimmicks to introduce his wife, such as this one:

> The curtain would open and you wouldn't see nothing but this big record player, . . . you know, a Victrola. Then Matt, he would come out and open the door, don't you know, and then I would step out singing while Hersal was playing the piano. It was beautiful, child, you should of seen it.[18]

Unfortunately, Matt's penchant for gambling interfered with his effectiveness and eventually led to financial problems for the couple. Perhaps this is one of the reasons why Wallace said "A Gambler's Dream," written by Hersal, was one of her favorite blues. She remarked that every time she sang it she thought about her mother's admonitions. Ironically, it was her niece, Hociel, and not Sippie, who recorded it for Okeh in 1925.[19]

Her recording about gambling was "Jack of Diamonds Blues," which was issued in March 1926 along with "Special Delivery Blues." "Jack of Diamonds," written by Matt Wallace and Hersal Thomas and featuring Armstrong and Thomas, does not have her usual emotional impact or dynamic vocal flexibility. The tale is one of strife brought about by gambling fever and the strain it puts on a relationship.

> Jack of Diamonds, you appear to be my friend,
> Jack of Diamonds, you appear to be my friend,
> Gambling is going to be our end.

The use of a metaphor, Jack of Diamonds, rather than a name, conceals the gambler's real identity but reveals the deceptive behavior that soon becomes destructive.

> You stole all my money and cut up all my clothes,
> You stole all my money and cut up all my clothes,
> And you come home broke and tried to put me out of doors.

The frustration of trying unsuccessfully to please turns to resignation, and the blues ends by acknowledging the cruelty of her lover.

There is nothing in this world I've found that pleases you.

I love Jack of Diamonds but he was a cruel man,
I love Jack of Diamonds but he was a cruel man,
He would play dice and cards and his game was old coon can.[20]

The promotion of Wallace as a recording artist in 1923 and 1924 enhanced her stage career as well. Soon she was a regular headliner on the TOBA circuit. Her life was busy with travel to the big cities on the route—Chicago, Oklahoma City, Dallas, Galveston, and her hometown, Houston. Always a lover of beautiful, fancy stage costumes, Wallace would wear feathers and sequined gowns, low-cut to emphasize her full-bosomed figure. Her pecan brown round face was accented by full lips and big, soft brown eyes, which were most expressive as she sang. And when she sang she could drain the listener emotionally, pleading to "Sweet Daddy"; lashing out at the "mistreater"; or teasing like an accomplished vamp. In between engagements she could be found in Okeh's studios in New York or Chicago. Wallace counted among her close friends blues singer Sara Martin and the comedy team, Butterbeans and Susie, all of whom were on the Okeh label at one time, and who served time on the TOBA. She entertained these and other show biz friends with fine dinners, and was the guest of many other friends as she traveled.

Meanwhile, Detroit had replaced Chicago as home base for her, Matt, Hociel, and Hersal. Both Hersal and Hociel had cut their own recordings by 1925, so the Thomases were a musical family of quite some note. They settled into an area on Detroit's Eastside, which was densely populated by blacks, Russian Jews, and Italians. Matt worked as a laborer when he could find work.[21]

The deaths of the three siblings who had been instrumental in the development of her career came unexpectedly during her peak years on stage. In 1925 she was summoned to the bedside of her dying older sister, Lillie, who had taught her how to sing as a child. Then, in June 1926, Hersal succumbed at sixteen to food poisoning. And in 1928, George Thomas's songwriting and publishing career ended suddenly when he was run down by a streetcar in Chicago, bringing an end to the brilliant trio's collaborations.[22]

In their years together, the talented brothers and sister had produced some solid winners in the blues field. "Bedroom Blues" was
one of Wallace's best. Its theme is abandonment.

> I was thinking 'bout my sweet daddy, I mean all night long,
> I was thinking 'bout my sweet daddy, I mean all night long,
> 'Cause he left me here in this old lonesome home.

She is denied the relief of free-flowing tears to assuage her loneliness.

> Lawd, I tried to cry, but my tears refused to fall.
> Lawd, I tried to cry, but my tears refused to fall.
> I was all alone, no one to love at all.[23]

Wallace's initiative and push for a stage and recording career derived not only from her desire to make it big but also from the fact
that singing and playing were her only tools for making a living. Fortunately, she could better her existence while expressing herself
creatively. Her vivid, matter-of-fact style was an outgrowth of life on
the rugged road from poverty to prosperity. Still, her early religious
training tempered her behavior and served her well as she struggled
with career, family, and marital strife. She observed and disapproved
of the sometimes irrational outbursts by Bessie Smith, Mamie Smith,
and Spivey when they drank too heavily and created scenes at parties, but she acknowledged that she loved a good time, too. When
asked if the hard conditions of stage life may have caused many of
the performers to drink heavily, Wallace gave a forthright answer
that revealed her early upbringing.

> People just get besides theirselves, you know. They get an inch and
> take a foot. Because they made some heroes some people can make a
> "pure D ass" out of themselves, you know, hurt their own self. . . . I
> drank beer but I didn't act like a fool; I was not a party girl. I was a
> theatrical woman and loved it, but I knew how to act, you know.[24]

"Knowing how to carry yourself" was important to the Texas warbler
who believed that proper manners gained respect from others. She
and most of her peers valued their personal integrity and did not sell
out in order to achieve their goals. Helen Humes used exactly the

same phrase when she spoke about her years on stage: "I didn't have that [people talking about her], because . . . I knew how to carry myself in the right way."[25] Black mothers at all socioeconomic levels hammered that principle into their daughters as a means of developing self-respect and protecting their reputations. Wallace's mother was no different. Understanding this is critical to understanding the black woman blues singer, not just as a folk figure, but as an artist whose professional and personal standards dictated choice of material and manner of presentation.

Wallace could play the piano as well as sing so she was hired by local musicians for socials and club dates, a practice she continued in Detroit long after her blues recording career had ended in 1929. I queried Wallace about the attitudes of the men with whom she performed toward the women singers and pianists, because I wondered if they respected them and valued them as professional colleagues. She admitted that she was not readily accepted as a leader of a group, but she told the following story to illustrate that the deciding factors were getting bookings and being able to pay the players.

> It was my job. And then I asked them how much they charged, you know, and finally after I got them their first two jobs then they got to be my orchestra. And that time they wasn't getting but five dollars a man. It was that time when I first started "St. Louis Blues" and "Barrelhouse Man" and all. And they didn't want any kind of junky piece, you know, they didn't have no special song.[26]

Linda Dahl's discussion of the careers of Lil Hardin, Lovie Austin, and other women pianists confirms that the main ingredient for getting with a band and staying was ability.[27]

Although she was exploited by record producers, scouts, and songwriters, as were her blues-singing sisters, Wallace did not consider herself a victim. Perhaps her close relationship and collaboration with her brothers diminished any effect of male domination while nurturing the excitement and exhilaration of creating and making music with them on record and on stage. Unfortunately, she, like others, had no control over her written and recorded work in terms of royalty agreements.

Once she was recognized as a "hot" item on disc, she was pursued by the black male songwriters who depended on talent like hers to sell their songs. She was not naive about the exploitation of her talents or the cutthroat nature of the business. She knew she could get royalties for her compositions but she accepted the practice of being paid a flat fee for a recording. One might expect Wallace, since her brother was in the publishing business, would insist on royalties. On the other hand, she might have felt that the money was staying "in the family," since his livelihood was derived from the recording company's profits. Underlying all of her discussions about her appearances and recordings was a tacit trust and acceptance of the terms made by the "head people," as illustrated in the following remarks:

> When I sing in concerts now I just get a salary, no share in the gate receipts—that goes to the head people. When I make records they give me a contract but when I first started they was only paying one hundred dollars a record. Only unless you owned the song could you get royalty every few months. But if you didn't, somebody would pay you fifty dollars for singing and then the company would pay me fifty dollars to record it.[28]

Her acceptance of male control was not atypical behavior for a woman raised in a home that upheld traditional views of men and women. For Wallace the bold move was in her break away from her religion's sanction against women performing blues on stage. Although she did not exercise the option to assert herself in the management of her career as did some of her illustrious counterparts, such as Alberta Hunter, Edith Wilson, Ida Cox, and Victoria Spivey, she used her talent wisely and well.

Okeh boldly advertised Wallace as the "Texas Nightingale . . . one of the leading stars of the Race . . . with her high C blues wailing," an appropriate assessment of the talents and vocal style that led them to press at least forty-one sides while she was under contract between 1923 and 1927.[29] Eddie Heywood, Clarence Williams, Perry Bradford, Hersal Thomas, and Danny Wilson were pianists on various sides which also featured rising instrumentalists Louis Armstrong, Buddy Christian on banjo, and Sidney Bechet on clarinet.

An unexplained recording hiatus of two years was ended when she was put under contract in 1929 by RCA Victor Records. There, she made four sides but only two were issued, the popular "I'm a Mighty Tight Woman" and "You Gonna Need My Help." The 1926

Okeh recording of "Mighty Tight" had Cicero Thomas on cornet and
Hersal on piano, but in 1929 Wallace accompanied herself on piano
backed by Natty Dominique, cornet; Honoré Dutrey, trombone; and
Johnny Dodds on clarinet. "Mighty Tight Woman," one of the few
erotic blues recorded by Wallace, demonstrated her superb vocal
phrasing and her pianistic abilities (and I wish they had been recorded more often). The delightful mixture of naive sweetness and
vampish sensuality captures the spirit of the streetwise black woman,
confident and independent, yet absurdly expecting real love.

I come to you, sweet man, falling on my knees,
I come to you, pretty papa, falling on my knees,
I ask, if you ain't got nobody, kind daddy, take me please.

This blues illustrates the dynamics of black male-female relationships, as seen in the woman's feigned submissiveness followed by a
brash display of sexual arrogance in the second and third stanzas:

'Cause I'm a mighty tight woman, I'm a real tight woman, I'm a
    jack-of-all trades.
I can be your sweet woman, also be yo' slave.
I can do things so good, till you will not [see yo' head].

If you're a married man, you ain't got no business here,
'Cause when you're out with me, I might make yo' wife shed tears,
'Cause I'm a mighty tight woman, and there is nothing that I fear.[30]

The final stanza shifts the mood from that of an abject groveling
woman to one who is in total command.

The hint of morality that surfaces in the final verse points out the
ambiguities that pervaded the mores of the black community. Wallace's inclusion of this particular blues in her repertoire reflects that
same ambivalence. Her home training taught her to exercise restraint
in her public behavior, yet this blues typifies the contradictions of
externally imposed restraint versus internally driven passions and
desires. A clue may lie in her interpretation of this song. In the recorded version, the voice is coyly sincere. Although it was one of the
last records Wallace cut in the "blues decade," "Mighty Tight Woman"
has not only remained a favorite of old-timers but has also become a
hit with the present generation of blues lovers.

Wallace produced some noteworthy sides during her Okeh years, using subject matter that ranged from jealousy, mistreatment, and vengeance to skin color and natural disaster, all treated with equal verve and vigor. The twinkle of her eyes belied the vocal threats of physical revenge by a jilted lover. The mournful wail drew sympathetic sighs from understanding listeners who identified with the tragedy of love gone cold.

Sippie Wallace's career suffered the same decline as that of her peers when the record industry faltered during the Depression. She had not developed versatility of style and repertoire as Wilson or Hunter did, so she could not gain employment as a comedienne or sultry chanteuse. Hers was a raw country-style talent well-suited to belting the blues but not to sweet mellow ballads, and Detroit was a blues city not a Cotton Club town. She lacked the training and experience to change, and sorely missed the guidance of her brother, George, at this critical point in her career. Without him she had no songwriting partner to inspire her and to put her musical ideas on paper. Chicago and New York songwriters who could get work were no longer writing blues but rather the fast-paced show or revue tunes.

Wallace's stage bookings dwindled and finally petered out. By 1932 she had slipped into obscurity along with many of her other singing sisters. Her husband, family, and church became the focal points of her life. In the 1940s she became the guardian of Hociel's orphaned daughters. Her installation as a nurse in her church brought her joy and satisfaction, as did her work with the choir.

It was to church music that she turned her songwriting and piano-playing abilities for the next three decades. Her return to the roots of her musical tree nurtured her creativity. Conversations about "her" church and "her" choir sparkled with ardor.

> I hear a good number at church and I play. Here I got a little old choir. My choir—I write any kind of song I want and let them sing, you know. Now this is something I tried but they won't learn them. They want to learn. They want to learn, but they can't. Now your key is important, too. When I got my certificate for singing our teacher said, "Learn your key and anybody can play for you if you know your key." And so all I got to do is say play me so and so in G or play me such a number in F or in B or something like that. Like when I sang "Pre-

cious Lord," now that was in G, I mean. F. See? [Plays.] Now I got to play it in the anthem. Now here's the anthem part. Ain't it good? Now here's "The Lord Is My Shepherd." Ain't that pretty? Uh-huh.[31]

During the session in 1975 Sippie played and sang several religious songs she had written for her choir, interlacing the songs with comments. She introduced each one by saying, "Now here's something I like."

I said the good Lord wasn't able to give me rest after all my labor.
All your tears you'll turn to smiles up to haven after a while.
When I sit down at his knees I know my journey will be complete.
I need rest, rest on my journey, Lord, and never tire.
I need rest, I need rest, rest for my journey, Lord, and never tire, oh after a while.
I need rest, rest for my journey, Lord, after a while, after a while.[32]

She explained her feelings about the church and her music, the spirituals and blues, in the following manner:

I shout sometime, it feels so good. Because I mostly do blues for jobs. But for my heart it's at church. That's why I make it to church all the time. Everytime I go I always ask can I sing the spirtuals.[33]

Wallace, the blues singer, might have remained obscure for the rest of her life except for an occasional club date in Detroit. For more than twenty years, she issued just two recordings. In 1945 Mercury Records released the great "Bedroom Blues." Backed by Albert Ammons, piano, and his Rhythm Kings (which included Artie Starks, clarinet; Lonnie Johnson, guitar; and John Lindsay, bass), she proved, without a doubt, that her voice and style had not diminished over the years. Although the recording was excellent, the blues audience had already shifted its attention to the Chicago and Memphis sound. Bebop, swing, rhythm and blues were all struggling for the attention of the listening public, so her record did not sell and she slipped back into obscurity. The next recording on Detroit's Fine Arts label, in 1959, suffered the same anonymity but it must have convinced her friend, Spivey, to keep urging her to come out of "retirement" and try the folk-blues festival circuit that was sweeping the

country.[34] As a result, Wallace went to Europe in 1966 and capti-
vated a new, younger generation of blues enthusiasts.

The Storyville recording of her Copenhagen performance demonstrated that the second coming of Sippie Wallace was long overdue.
With Roosevelt Sykes and Little Brother Montgomery sharing the
piano, she presented new renditions of her old classics, "Trouble
Everywhere I Roam," "Shorty George," "Special Delivery Blues," and
"I'm a Mighty Tight Woman," and introduced "Women Be Wise,
Don't Advertise Your Man." One reviewer wrote: "Visiting Europe in
1966, Sippie Wallace astonished by the breadth of her singing and a
delivery recalling Bessie Smith."[35] He commented that the remakes
with Montgomery and Sykes in Denmark were of "exceptional merit."

Bathed by the spotlight of Lincoln Center's Avery Fisher Hall,
Wallace at eighty could still evoke some of the deepest emotions as
she sang the blues. The pathos that came through her voice could be
matched only by the expression on her face; and any listener, whether
a novice or longtime blues lover, could identify with those feelings as
she closed her eyes and sang. What was left of the once vibrant,
strong, steady voice was a husky talking-singing sound, but the loss
of vocal flexibility was made up for by the expressiveness she put
into each word, each phrase. The famous plaintive slide could still be
heard, although in a much lower register. There was no mistaking
that what she sang about she had experienced, yet she still had a
ready smile and that good-natured sense of humor that often made
herself the butt of a joke. No one could doubt that Wallace understood the deepest meaning of the blues. Wallace's career spanned
more than sixty years, yet there was a freshness every time she sang.
Though the fingers trembled and missed some notes when she attempted to accompany herself, she dauntlessly continued—delivering a soul-touching "Precious Lord Take My Hand" or a rousing
"Women Be Wise."

When this generously built woman, who looked like the typical
huggable grandmother, welcomed visitors into her modest home in a
quiet Detroit neighborhood, a broad, gap-toothed grin spread over
her face. She needed no prodding to sit down at the piano and sing
whatever was requested, and before you knew it your soul was
touched by the warmth of Wallace's gospel or blues songs. You em-
pathized strongly with her sorrow, exuberance, or humor as she sang

one song after another, many of them her own compositions. Everyone who knew Beulah "Sippie" Thomas Wallace loved her. Jolly and candid when chatting with new acquaintances as with old friends, she was serious about her music twenty-four hours a day. She was charming, flippant, wise, and sometimes naive, but always sincere and honest. Her warmth, her sincerity, and deep religious sense came through when she was singing the blues, for she cared deeply about communicating with her listeners and wanted to share her feelings with every one of them.

Her religious and family values still had a great influence on her attitude toward the blues and the propriety of her stage career when she was in her eighties.

> I wanted to be a blues singer, because another girl wanted to be a blues singer. I wanted to be a blues singer like she was. But I don't know why, because I always was in church.[36]

Over and over, she expressed concern about violating church doctrine when she talked about continuing to sing the blues professionally while serving as pianist for her church in Detroit. The clearcut decisiveness of her youth had been replaced by a sense of guilt. The essence of her ambivalence came through when she remarked that she was trying to stop playing and singing the blues but that everybody wanted her to keep on. When asked why she wished to stop, she replied, "Because I play for the church, you know." She felt that if she performed in other places besides the church someone from her congregation might hear her and she wouldn't want people to get the wrong impression. She felt that playing for the church and still singing the blues was wrong, unless it was someone's job; then it was all right, but she was still uncomfortable because her pastor or some church member might not like the idea. She settled the matter by saying, "Suppose this wasn't nothing but a job, you see, you try to make good of everything you do."[37] Wallace could not stop singing the blues and live.

Without skipping a beat, and sure that she had dealt with the issue satisfactorily, she stopped talking, turned to her piano, and moaned through one of the dozens of songs she had penned in recent years.

Yesterday, I saw you leave,
I laughed and sang,
I wouldn't grieve.
But after my laughter came tears.

I told my friends,
I didn't care,
I laughed about the whole affair.
But after my laughter came tears.

My pride kept me from showing you,
That I was blue.
Oh, but by myself,
Don't nobody know what I've gone through.

My lips don't feel,
My heart's in pain.
I made believe, but never again,
'Cause after my laughter came tears.

With a heavy sigh she said, "Lord, that singing worry me so, when my husband died, girl. I've been a lonesome soul." She finally admitted that she not only sang the blues because it was a job but because it "helped to comfort me on." Wallace quickly began talking about the new songs she was writing and how everything she wrote "end up in church. I end up 'churchy' sure as you walk."[38] This disturbed her because she believed that there must be some distinction between what she composed as a blues and what she composed as a church song. She used a simple device: "to keep it from ending up like a church song I got to play it fast, not slow, like it should go."[39] It is often difficult to distinguish between the music of the church and the blues, because both come from a well of deep personal feelings— one toward a spiritual being, the other toward a human being.[40] Wallace and many other blues singers such as her contemporaries Spivey, Cox, and Martin and, more recently, Sister Rosetta Tharpe, Aretha Franklin, and Mavis Staples, demonstrated that the boundary between the two fluctuates.

A small notepad filled with her ideas for new hymns and blues was always close at hand, evidence of Wallace's continuing creativity. The ups and downs in her stage career did not diminish her capacity and desire to produce new music. The church and its rich musical heritage continued to provide the inspiration for her creative output over the thirty or so years that she was absent from the stage.

Wallace's retirement from her position as church musician in 1980, along with a resurgence of singing engagements, assuaged her internal conflict about the blues and the church. And although crippling arthritis hampered her piano-playing, and a minor stroke had left her speech slightly slurred, neither of these handicaps diminished her performances. She was sought after as a performer in clubs in the Detroit area, and at major blues concerts in Washington, New York, and Boston. Her appearance on NBC-TV's "Today" show in 1983 demonstrated that she was enjoying every minute of her rejuvenated career. Detroit honored her with a special Sippie Wallace Day that featured a blues concert. She was cherished as a local treasure, and she and other outstanding Michigan women were inducted into the Michigan Hall of Fame with a lavish dinner and ceremony in October 1983. She appeared on local and national television, grand as ever in her wide-brimmed hats with ostrich plumes, singing the blues with a joy that she could barely contain. Her delivery still had vigor and style, and her audiences, though fifty to sixty years younger than she, responded with cheers, laughter, and prolonged applause. Her program freely mixed the blues and church songs as the spirit moved her. In recent recordings, there is that same depth of feeling and her inimitable phrasing, spiced with a combination of zest and flirtation. Her last album was nominated for a 1983 Grammy award. "A Mighty Tight Woman" is no longer a museum piece but a hearty manifesto of female assertiveness.

The Texas Nightingale continued to perform until shortly before her death. To the astonishment of many, she accepted an engagement to appear at blues concerts in Germany and Denmark in the spring of 1986, just six months prior to her passing. She was widely acclaimed for those performances, which were videotaped and recorded.[41]

In numerous ways, Wallace was the archetypal woman blues singer—gusty, yet tender; bereft, but not downtrodden; disappointed, yet hopeful; long on talent, short on funds; legendary, but not widely acclaimed; exploited, but not resentful; independent, yet vulnerable. Her life story is not resplendent with dramatic events that capture the imagination—a bronze Cinderella whom Prince Charming rescued from drudgery and cruelty. Instead, it might be considered quite pedestrian except for her musical talent; it did not save her from toil and grief but did enable her to communicate her feelings about life's triumphs and disasters.

Her music is a wonderful admixture that reflects her personal and artistic perspectives. By dint of extremely hard work, often under stressful conditions, she coped with life and retained a sense of her personal integrity. She sat on stage, regal in a beaded chiffon dress, large hat, and lace gloves, and created her personal picture of the world by utilizing her lusty vocal talents and keen insights. She sang for her living, that was her job; and she believed that when she sang she provided her listeners with information about her life that might help them to come to grips with their own lives.

Sippie Wallace died on her eighty-eighth birthday, November 1, 1986.

## Notes

1    See James Cone's *The Spirituals and the Blues: An Interpretation* (New York: Seabury Press, 1972), discussion on the existential nature of the blues.

2    Helen Humes, interview with the author, New York, March 1975.

3    Alwyn Barr, *Black Texans: A History of Negroes in Texas, 1528–1971* (Austin: Jenkins Publishing Co., 1973), 169–170.

4    Sippie Thomas Wallace, interview with the author, Detroit, 24 January 1975.

5    Leroi Jones, *Blues People* (New York: Wm. Morrow, 1963), 235.

6    Cone, *Spirituals,* 111–112.

7    Wallace interview.

8    Ibid.

9    Performed by Wallace during interview, 1975. The original recording was issued by Okeh, May 1924.

10    Wallace interview.

11    Ibid.

12    Alberta Hunter's first job after she arrived in Chicago was as a potato peeler. Billie Holiday recalled her days as a domestic working along-

side her mother. Ethel Waters, Mamie Smith, Sara Martin, and Chippie Hill each returned to jobs as waitresses and maids when times were bad. The "Kitchen Mechanic Blues" was a satirical portrait of black domestics.

13    *Talking Machine World* 21 (15 May 1925), 116.

14    See the *Chicago Defender,* 21 February 1925, pt. 1, 12, for an example of the ads used.

15    Sammy Price, interview with the author, New York, 1977.

16    "Shorty George Blues," Okeh, 1923.

17    "Special Delivery Blues," Okeh 8238, March 1926.

18    Sippie Wallace, interview with the author, Detroit, October 1976.

19    John Godrich and R. M. W. Dixon, *Blues and Gospel Records* (London: Storyville Publications, 1969), 654.

20    "Jack of Diamonds Blues," Okeh 8328, March 1926. The circumstances of Wallace's marriage and her comments regarding the "Gambling Blues" lead me to the conclusion that perhaps her memory was clouded and she confused that blues with "Jack of Diamonds."

21    Demographics obtained from *Polk's Detroit Directory,* 1923–1924 edition, 35.

22    Announcements in the *Chicago Defender,* 12 June 1926 and 12 August 1929, confirm Mrs. Wallace's accounts of these deaths.

23    "Bedroom Blues," Okeh 8439, November 1926.

24    Wallace interview, 1976.

25    Humes interview.

26    Wallace interview, 1975.

27    Linda Dahl, *Stormy Weather: The Music and Lives of a Century of Jazz-Women* (New York: Pantheon Books, 1984) 22–29.

28    Wallace interview, 1976.

29    Godrich and Dixon, *Blues and Gospel Records.*

30    "Mighty Tight Woman," RCA Victor BVE 48870-2, February 1929, reissued on RCA Victor LP 534, 1966.

31    Wallace interview, 1975.

32    Ibid.

33    Ibid.

34    Len Kunstadt, "The Comeback of Sippie Wallace," *Record Research* 88 (January 1968), 3.

35    Brian McCarthy, *Jazz on Record, 1897–1942* (Essex, England: Storyville, 1975), 297. Bonnie Raitt, a young white folksinger, was instrumental in the revival of interest in and enthusiasm for artists such as Wallace, Sykes, and Montgomery in the early 1970s. That exposure to audiences all across the United States created a new demand for Wallace's style of blues singing—the shouting wail.

36     Sippie Wallace, interview with the author, Detroit, November 1983.

37     Sippie Wallace, interview with the author, Detroit, January 1977.

38     Wallace interview, 1975.

39     Ibid.

40     Refer to Cone, *Spirituals,* for discussion on this topic.

41     James T. Jones, "Sippie: Two Roads to the Blues," *The Detroit News,* 9 November 1986, 1B and 8B.

# Billie Jean Young

## "This Little Light of Mine": Dramatizing the Life of Fannie Lou Hamer

In 1962, at age forty-five, when Fannie Lou Hamer walked off a cotton row to attempt to register to vote, only a handful of Mississippi Blacks (or poor whites for that matter) had the privilege of suffrage enjoyed by other Americans. Trapped on the huge Delta plantations in Mississippi, Blacks toiled from "kin to can't," from sunup ("can see") to sundown ("can't see"), working for a mere pittance, filling their bosses' pockets with wealth and their lives with leisure. How could Fannie Lou Hamer think of "getting to Washington to the Congress, Justice Department, FBI?" The vision of most of her contemporaries could not transcend the endless cotton rows and the struggle to survive! Who was this woman?

In physical form, Fannie Lou Hamer was, by her description, a short (5'4"), squat, plain woman, wife of a sharecropping husband, born Fannie Lou Townsend in 1917, of the union of Jim and Louella Townsend in Mississippi. Not blessed to bear children biologically, she was already mother to the children of others long before she picked up the mantle of civil rights, shouldered it, and inspired thousands to freedom by her example. Being the last child in a family of twenty, one might say she was the "runt" of the family. Her unimposing stature was made the more so by a limp caused by polio in her youth. Mrs. Hamer was a pillar of community support and leadership *before* 1962, even as she wore the manacles of oppression and sharecropping, for she was the timekeeper and keeper of cotton weights on the plantation. People came to her for information and reassurance. Such was the life of Fannie Lou Hamer.

When Mrs. Hamer went with seventeen other Blacks to the Sunflower County seat of Indianola, Mississippi, to register to vote on August 31, 1962, she once again demonstrated the kind of leadership of which she was capable, this time outside of the "protective" and sanctioned realm of plantation life. Afraid to move once they had reached the courthouse, the eighteen Blacks remained on the bus, fully aware of the danger posed to them by the sheriffs and state troopers who were ringing the courthouse in anticipation of their group's arrival. And then, "All of a sudden, this little short woman got up and switched off the bus, and marched into the courthouse to register." Others followed immediately. That was Fannie Lou Hamer, an extraordinary, ordinary woman of faith, leading.

On other occasions, Mrs. Hamer used song to quell fear. Fannie Lou Hamer raised her voice in song to teach, to dispel fear, and to bring solace and uplift to the vanquished. Fannie Lou Hamer, woman of faith, believed in the essence of humanity. She believed that integrity could conquer death, and, by her example, proved that truth and goodness can triumph over evil. Even in jail, beaten until "her skin was hard," she could say of those who beat her: "You know, I can't hate nobody. These sheriffs is sick. They need God's help. They foaming at the mouth. I can't hate nobody and hope to see God's face."

Outwardly pious, Mrs. Hamer understood earthly matters very well. She was prophet enough to use scriptures to cause others to think, contemplate, and reexamine that which they considered secular. Fannie Lou Hamer understood the preoccupation of her own people with the hereafter and religion in general. She, however, wanted to experience some of earth's joys in the present. Her message was essentially this: "God is Good and Great, has a place for all humanity; we are all brothers and sisters under the skin. He would not want us to suffer." She quoted from Acts 17:26 often: "Hath made of one blood *all* nations for to dwell on the face of the earth." It was hard for downtrodden Blacks to dismiss their own inferiority as this notion was engrained in their psyche, but Mrs. Hamer was relentless in her efforts to have *all* humanity understand their God-given equality.

Fannie Lou Hamer, by her example, her long suffering, and her humility, demonstrated the power of faith and commitment to change.

Dying of breast cancer in 1977, essentially alone, she had had fifteen productive years in the struggle. But her work did not stop there; it is carried on by those who love and revere her. Indeed, there are those of us who invoke her name to bring ourselves and others back, sometimes, when we stray off course, back to the true issue at hand. Her very name, *Fannie Lou Hamer,* epitomizes for us goodness, compassion, trustworthiness, love, perseverance; we recoil at our own tenuousness, our own fallibility. Such was the work of the seers of old and of Fannie Lou Hamer, Mississippi Sharecropping Woman, Mother, Wife, Worker, Prophet, Seer, Saint, who lived among us.

The idea to do "This Little Light of Mine: A Dramatization of the Life of Fannie Lou Hamer" arose on a day in early December 1982, on a Delta Airlines flight out of Washington, D.C. Because books and progressive magazines are hard to come by in Mississippi, I'd gone to a bookstore and bought several copies of *Sojourner Magazine* which had run a series of articles about Fannie Lou Hamer. I planned to give them to Mississippians for Christmas presents. On the plane, headed home, I finally got a chance to settle down and read a copy myself. I was again brought face to face with her—Mrs. Hamer. It was prophetic. In the months and now years to come, I was to be continually reminded that she exerted the control and provided the impetus for my work. Fannie Lou Hamer continues to speak to people today through "This Little Light . . . ," through her life, by her example. But I'm getting ahead of myself.

Back on the plane, I cried, I wept for myself because I had remained so ignorant for so long and I had only had a shadowy glimpse of this great woman before, even though I had, in fact, met her on more than one occasion. I wept also for countless others who had been denied knowledge of her greatness; so little was said about her life and work even in Mississippi where I'd been living for the past year. Oh, in our women klatches, we "conscientious" sisters would bring her up, talk about her sassiness, how she didn't *ever* learn, and therefore, could not *accept,* the "place" reserved for her as a Black and a woman. I cried unabashedly. The person sitting next to me, a white gentleman from the South, inquired quizzically with his eyes if something was amiss and asked could he help. I never spoke. I looked at him. I couldn't even shake my head "no." I hope he understood. I turned my back, looked out the window, and let the tears lap under my chin and run onto my dress.

I owed Fannie Lou those tears, I thought. No need to explain to anyone. How to rectify? What to do to make this woman known? How can I make recompense? As director then of the Southern Rural Women's Network (SRWN), the first thoughts to enter my head were community and organization. How to involve southern rural women and the community in general?

It occurred to me that a series on Fannie Lou in the SRWN quarterly newsletter would be a means of making people aware of her significance. Mollified somewhat, I began to think about the kind of articles that would attract the most readers: perhaps a cover feature for the first articles; maybe interview some people. I let my mind wander. Nagging at the back of my brain, however, was the thought, "You need to reach more people, and reading *ain't* the medium." Suddenly, a light bulb went off in my head. "You can act, girl! Fannie Lou's life lends itself to a one-woman show. And this is one role you don't need to look like Twiggy to do. Do it!" After that, it was only a question of how, when, where. Money was never a question (since I had the practical experience of producing theater with children for four years on a shoestring budget in Selma, Alabama).

I first spoke to girlfriends, to women in the Southern Rural Women's Network and I received encouragement from them. In particular, when I spoke to Virgia Brock-Shedd, she responded with a "Right on!" and a question: "Can I get a contract on that?" "Contract" was introduced to us in Alabama by writer Toni Cade Bambara who understands its psychological value in accomplishing an objective; Virgia was, in effect, asking me to write out an agreement to enact Mrs. Hamer's life and become the promisor to myself by signing it and having the girlfriends witness it. She's a real Mississippian (I'm only a transplant from Alabama), so I felt I was home free. Besides, she's a librarian at Tougaloo College, and she had already made a personal commitment to collect Hamer memorabilia through the library herself. Her help was invaluable: films, boxes of information, news clippings, and so on. It was a perfect place to start.

I began January 15, 1983. I figured if there were any way to sanction the whole affair with good, Dr. Martin Luther King, Jr.'s birthday would do it. I have been fortunate enough, since Dr. King's death, to work for agencies that have always celebrated his birthday as a holiday, and I never squander it. I went to see Pap, Fannie Lou's husband, Mr. Perry Hamer of Ruleville, Mississippi. I needed the family's blessings as well as their permission to do the show. I knew I couldn't do it otherwise.

My decision to do "This Little Light . . ." was not made without some trepidation. First, it takes a lot of temerity to portray an important person whom everybody remembers; and second, Mississippians were always talking about how the Hamer family had been exploited since Mrs. Hamer's death, how they were bitter and didn't want to see a lot of people from the struggle, and how some people had actually raised money after the death for a memorial fund which had never materialized (nor the money!). I resolved these two main concerns this way: On the first, I would insure historical integrity by doing as thorough a job as possible in researching Mrs. Hamer's life and work. I lived among the people who should know it best; at least, I felt so. My visit to Pap and the children was to obtain permission to perform his late wife's life story, to write the drama itself. I was prepared for whatever they would say. I did not expect to be very warmly received. I drove into the flat Mississippi Delta, still marveling that someone would cut down so many trees for King Cotton, leaving shacks sitting out in the bare sun. It was nice though, despite the barrenness, and a breezy day.

Pap and the girls, Jackie and Lynora, Mrs. Hamer's adopted daughters, were seated in the den. They welcomed me quietly. I got out who I was, what SRWN was, and what I wanted to do—summed up in about ten minutes. Occasionally, they looked at me with interest, but they didn't say much. I went on. I told them about my inspiration and gave Pap the *Sojourner* article, which he didn't know about. "Did he mind?" He didn't mind. "Good idea," he said quietly, and looked down.

Perry Hamer is a gentle man. His looks belie this. He is tall, ebon, large. Not fat. One does not think fat when one encounters Perry Hamer (everybody calls him Pap). He likes to joke, be "sociable," as he calls it, and make others feel good. It is hard for him to talk about Fannie Lou, and he does so sparingly. I wouldn't push him. We talked about Unita Blackwell instead and others who had been in the struggle with Her. I asked if he would show me the grave. He agreed without hesitation.

She is buried in an open field on the land the freedom co-op owns, a single grave. A beautiful headstone bears the inscription: "Fannie Lou Hamer: 1917–1977: Sick and Tired of Being Sick and Tired."

When we approached the grave, Pap told me that ugly people would sometimes come out and tear up the flowers, or worse, take them away. This he told me as he picked up a bouquet and rearranged it.

I was reminded that two years ago, I had looked at twenty-two bullet holes on Jimmy Lee Jackson's grave in Alabama.[1] This had prompted Albert Turner, an associate, to say: "You know, it's a sick person who will try to kill a dead man." Presently, I walked around Mrs. Hamer's grave. Awed somewhat, I knelt. Pap turned his back and walked back to the car. I cried some more, wiped up my tears, and joined Pap with only telltale moisture. He didn't need reminding. I tried to strike a light note: "If you'd known she was gonna be a helluva woman like that, Pap, would you have been scared to marry her?" He looked at me, grinned a gold-toothed grin: "Damn straight, baby."

Then I knew Pap would talk. I needed to be real gentle with him. We got back to the house and sat in the yard a few minutes. I couldn't leave without more information; didn't want to leave at all. I decided to ask him about Mrs. Hamer's leaving the plantation—getting put off for trying to register to vote. He laughed. It was okay. He could talk about it now. I needed this piece of information badly. One of the questions worrying my mind was how to treat Pap in the script. The bragging we women used to do earlier about Mrs. Hamer was usually about how she walked off the plantation and left her husband there, made the decision herself, we would say, and left. Well, in talking to Pap, I found some facts that gave a different interpretation to the story. The truth led me to better understand Mrs. Hamer's relationship with her husband; it enabled me to see the kind of positive relationship that is possible among people engaged in struggle. (So often, it has been impossible for civil rights activists to reconcile work with home and hearth.) As is borne out in the drama, the decision for Pap to remain on the plantation was an economic one, until his crops could be gathered; when that was done, he came off the plantation and rented a house for the family in Ruleville. This information proved invaluable in guiding the piece and setting the tone of their relationship, as portrayed in the drama.

It was hard to work on the piece after that. Returning from a fact-finding tour of war-torn Nicaragua, I needed space to think and to write down the poetry that came. I was still directing the Southern

Rural Women's Network, running around the country, trying to organize rural women, and raising money to do so at the same time. As I looked at one foundation program officer or executive director after the other across cold, impersonal desks in D.C. or New York, I was reminded of Fannie Lou Hamer again and again. "She probably went through this—and she *could* have if she didn't": foundation folk telling her that what she's doing is not a "women's issue." How would she have responded, handled it? She would have kept on keeping on, I would remind myself. Nobody could stop her. Thinking of the foundations and their "feminist" directors and program officers who always asked the last question in the form of: "What will you do if you don't get *Our* money?" I knew my answer: "We will do this with or without you. You can help us if you will." It became my standard answer to their standard question! During that period, writing poems and keeping in focus the determination of Fannie Lou Hamer and contemporary women of courage—from the Nicaraguan mothers to the voter registration activists in Alabama to my own mama— strengthened my resolve to make the project a reality.

The "Fannie Lou Hamer Portrait," as it was called in my mind that year, was constantly in the back of my mind, waiting for me to do something about it. The notes with Pap were a constant reminder. I knew I had to do more interviews, talk to Pap some more as well. Besides, by July, my assistant, Julia Winn, was becoming downright nasty about the whole thing, wanting me to firm up my date book so she could schedule the rest of the interviews. I relented; she did it. I conducted the interviews that summer with old colleagues of Mrs. Hamer, civil rights workers, Mississippi folk. I went back to see Pap, Jackie, and Lynora, and we talked some more. Others would give me numbers to call and ask that I talk to such and such person about what happened in the Mississippi Freedom Democratic Party, or at Atlantic City in 1964 at the Democratic National Convention, or about SNCC (Student Nonviolent Coordinating Committee). There was so much information. I kept gathering, all the while wondering what in the world I would do with it and how I would put it into some artistic form and expect somebody to want to see it. And, "when, oh when would I ever find time?"

In August, I was graciously invited to the Women's Farm at Eco-theater—Maryat Lee's house in the mountains of West Virginia—to write the first draft. Underneath the skirts of the huge mountains that look like women and Maryat's watchful eye (she's a slave-driver, one of the girlfriends who, if you tell her you're working, will see to it that you *do*. Invaluable.) I concocted the first draft, and Maryat took the publicity shots. We were both proud, as proud as newborn parents, I for the birth, Maryat for being the midwife.

I left the Women's Farm with a draft of the script in hand. Came back to Mississippi. Talked to some more folk. Went to see John O'Neal, playwright, who gave me tapes of community meetings when Mrs. Hamer had spoken. From these tapes, I was to pull powerful script material, mostly extemporaneous speech which exemplified Mrs. Hamer's progression from a sharecropping woman to a leader, philosopher, and spokesperson. John helped me with the structure, the form of the drama itself. "Fannie Lou wouldn't say those things about herself," he reminded me. "We must have another voice, take the show out of the first person." I agreed. And, thus, the storyteller for "This Little Light . . ." Issaquena Hopewell, was born.

The title came in the mountains: Maryat Lee liked the song so much and, God bless her, actually thought I could sing! I began to research other songs Mrs. Hamer liked, talking especially to Hollis Watkins and Wazier (Willie) Peacock, veteran songsters of the civil rights era. The songs began to mean something to the script. The script was gradually changing still in several parts, but becoming a thematic whole, nonetheless. John O'Neal raised so many questions that needed answers which I had not articulated to myself: "Why are you doing this? Who is Issaquena? Who are you telling this story to? Why? Why them?" He was a basket of questions! I inevitably came to realize that the questions had to be answered before I could complete my work with the material. I went into solitude around the end of August and began to write some more, to rearrange. In the middle of it all, I received a call from a church group asking me to go to Brazil for a week in the middle of September. It would mean returning to the United States only one week before the premiere. And I had to finish the show and put it on stage by October 1 for a premiere at Tougaloo College. I could do both. I must be crazy! Fannie Lou could do it. (Rather, Mrs. Hamer. By this time, enough Mississippians had reminded me that she was *Mrs.* Hamer, person, NOT Fannie Lou, "star.")

I returned from Brazil. Too much poverty, drought, famine, sick people. What to make of it all? How does it fit with what I'm doing with southern rural women? How can I help people make the connection? Will Jackie, Lynora, Pap, and the rest of Mrs. Hamer's family like "This Little Light . . ."? On top of all that, with one week, an unfinished script, and a speech to be delivered the day before the opening, I knew I was in for it. The speech was *not* my biggest problem. The play was another matter.

I went to Jackson State University where I asked Tommie Stewart for space to rehearse. I looked terrible. Wild-eyed, worried, four days from production, leotards, headrag, jean skirt, script in hand was the way I met Tommie that morning. She had classes. She led me to a large room (next day, she gave me an attic). I sang, I let loose in that room, I recited lines I'd never heard out loud before. That first day people stuck their heads in the door. I didn't care. I needed the space. During those two days, I got in four whole hours of practice, in spurts, never able to perform the whole. The script was *not* above revision once I started to act and feel the show. The day before the show opened, I took a hotel room. I needed to memorize the script if nothing else. I learned the script in those six hours.

Girlfriends promised to come by after finishing their last-minute work for the conference and the premiere to be my first audience in rehearsal. (They had played central roles throughout the production's development; they had bought my costume, Ivory Williams purchased the hairpiece I was to use for a year, Julia Winn picked out the dress, and Sharon Miles, Dana Alston, Sandra Woods, along with Ivory, Virgia, and Julia, formed a program committee.) When girlfriends dragged their tails into the room around midnight, I was too pooped to perform, and they were too pooped to listen. "I was going on stage without a first dress rehearsal. I must be crazy!" In all my years of producing community theater with schoolchildren in musty church basements and community centers, I had never gone on stage with a first dress. My kids in the theater would be disdainful of such transgressions, breaking cardinal rules I'd taught them. Dress rehearsal was like opening night, to be done, without mishap! But the words of Dana shored up my courage: "You'll be good, Billie Jean; just give 'em what you got, girl."

October 1, 1983, I went on stage. At 6:30 that evening and for a full thirty minutes, a candlelight ceremony in song was held for old and young, rich and poor, meek and proud. I could hear their voices—loud and clear, soft at times, and reverent, as they sang freedom songs—wafting through the mahogany rafters of the chapel and reaching me backstage. They were making me feel good. I gave vent to it. Prayed a "get down on your knees prayer," not standing up. When I finished asking the Creator for help, the voices were closer, and I realized that the women, a hundred or so of them, many in white dresses, were entering the chapel with candles, singing "This Little Light of Mine, I'm Gonna Let It Shine." It was a heart-stopping moment. And "This Little Light . . ." took stage.

I sweated. The house was full. Mississippi folk. I sweated, acted, remembered lines, sang songs. I acted with everything I had—unrehearsed. I was satisfied. I felt dignified when I left the stage. But backstage I was still wondering. "What did Mississippi folks really think? You're from Alabama, still. A Mississippi resident, not a Mississippian." But they were going wild; they came backstage, waited outside. Mrs. Hamer's daughters, Jackie and Lynora, were there, Mrs. Annie Devine, her close sister in the struggle, was there, Reverend Edwin King, Unita Blackwell, her co-worker, Hollis Watkins and Wazir Peacock, Dr. Margaret Walker Alexander, and on and on. They liked it!

In the program notes, I had asked for more stories, anecdotes, information from anybody who possessed it, as I had decided "This Little Light . . ." would not be a finished, static piece, but a work-in-progress. I wanted to continue working on it in my spare time. My major goal was to speak to women and Mississippians about Mrs. Hamer. The response surpassed even my own sometimes rather grandiose aspirations. Calls came from all over for "This Little Light . . ." Before 1983 was over, I had performed "This Little Light . . ." in Ruleville, Mississippi; Washington, D.C.; Alabama, and California, and before diverse audiences of people: all Black, all white, mixed Black and white, Asian, Caribbean, Puerto Rican. The pervading responses were: "Amazing!" "Keep it up!" "She's powerful; she teaches us!" "We need to recall her suffering *and* her struggle!" "She helps us recommit ourselves to the struggle today."

Nineteen hundred and eighty-four arrived. Requests were coming in for "This Little Light . . ." on a very regular basis even from Mississippi. (Mississippians are really closet Missourians and don't believe anything unless they're shown, especially from non-Mississippians!)

Nevertheless, there we were getting calls from local grassroots folk for "This Little Light . . ."

Black History Month arrived. Twenty-one performances all over the country. Folk in Bangor, Maine: Yellow Springs, Ohio; New York City; Pennsylvania; Georgia; Washington, D.C.; South Carolina; North Carolina; Oklahoma, and the Caribbean, and many other places saw the show that year. We were still not doing any marketing; the drama was marketing itself among those who cared to remember. "This Little Light . . ." is a lesson for young *and* old folk; motivation and inspiration for those with waning energy; a sermon for those who require spiritual sustenance.

SRWN continued to produce "This Little Light . . . ," with large foundations and many small ones still pretending that our work was not a "women's issue." This is a running battle between women of color and Caucasian women in the women's movement. Women of color tend to address issues of concern to women and children, and families, including men. The mainstream women's movement concentrates instead on sex-specific issues like sexual harassment in the workplace. The comment of one Black woman is illustrative: "I *can* and *will* handle the situation when somebody slaps me on the rump at work; that's not my problem. I can't even *experience* sexual harassment in the workplace unless I have a *job* in the first place."

In 1984, Blue Mountain Center in upstate New York invited me for a six-week residency. "This Little Light . . ." was my project as I had continued to treat the show as a work-in-progress. But I could not do much with it. "This Little Light . . ." had a will all its own. I could dot an "i" or cross a "t" to make or clear up a point here and there, but, by and large, I could not change what had been created. It was of itself, unto itself, on its own. I performed the show that summer before artists at Blue Mountain Center and in Atlanta for ROOTS. The sensitive, constructive criticisms were helpful, and the reviews continued to be good. I also continued to visit with Pap and the girls, my way of letting them know how "This Little Light . . ." was progressing, and for spiritual sustenance. I always gain strength from visits to Mrs. Hamer's home.

Finally, 1985 rolled around. January, February, and March I was on the road most of the time performing the show: for Dr. King's birthday at Morehouse College, for International Women's Day in

Belize, another week of performances at prisons, schools, halfway houses, and churches in Washington, D.C., among a host of others.

I cannot begin to relate all the positive experiences I had performing "This Little Light . . . ," but some of the highlights deserve mention. Going to Mrs. Hamer's hometown of Ruleville, Mississippi, for the second performance after Tougaloo was memorable. We'd chosen to do "This Little Light . . ." as a fundraiser for the Fannie Lou Hamer Day Care Center in Ruleville. The SRWN produced "This Little Light . . ." because Fannie Lou Hamer exemplified the kind of leadership the SRWN would wish to see fostered among rural women. "This Little Light . . ." is a part of the SRWN Leadership Skills and Development Institute (LSDI). Besides, if the Tougaloo experience was really what I thought it had been, Ruleville was the place to validate it. We drove to the Mississippi Delta early in the day on October 15, 1983, to Pap's house. Pap and the girls were waiting for us. "Was Pap coming?" He couldn't. Of course, I was disappointed. I needed him to see it. His high blood pressure wouldn't let him. He'd had to turn off the recent PBS television documentary on Mrs. Hamer. It had been too much. Jackie was in charge of things. Both she and Lynora have the solid nature of good rural women, both studious, both serious.

The amenities over, Jackie asked me if I needed a room. I did. She led me to a room with a king-sized bed and with pictures of Mrs. Hamer on the walls. I knew instantly that it was Her room. I got chills. Jackie disappeared. I stayed in that room. I looked at her on the wall, looking down. I prayed. I asked the Creator for help. "Lord, help me not to make a fool of myself in Mrs. Hamer's hometown!" I was scared, really scared of the task I'd undertaken. I got up from praying and crying and realized the house was still, no voices. I ventured out. Nobody. Everybody was gone. "They didn't really leave me here alone," I thought. I searched the house. They had. I went back to the room, sat down on the bed, looked at my costume, held my head in my hands, and looked at Her. And I became peaceful.

When Julia came to take me to the community center for the performance, I was ready. After the performance, one of Mrs. Hamer's friends came up to congratulate and thank me. She was simply wonderful: "Baby, me and Fannie Lou was girls together; I knowed her before she married. Thank you, baby, thank you, Jesus." Other women have come backstage to hold my hand and pray for me after the performance, to give me strength to carry the message on, both before and after, but none has provoked the feelings of this woman in me. See, country people don't say much. I know that. She'd said a mouthful to me in her own way.

In Washington, D.C., Mayor Marion Barry, himself born in Mississippi, proclaimed the week of February 17th through 23rd, 1985, as Fannie Lou Hamer Week in the District of Columbia, to mark my week of performances there, issuing a beautifully worded proclamation to that effect prior to one of my performances. "This Little Light . . ." was shining all over the evening news the next day!

My trip to Belize was another memorable experience—replete with pomp and circumstance and positive receptions by the National Women's Commission, the prime minister, first lady Mrs. Kathy Esquivel, the American ambassador, and the Belizean people. The highlight of the three performances of "This Little Light . . ." in Belize was in Dangriga, where the population is made up largely of Garifuna Blacks, a mixture of African and Carib Indian peoples. Belize is a small Central American country populated largely by Blacks. The people in Southern Belize, Dangriga, look to me very much like American Blacks. But for the palm trees and the beautiful ocean, it could have been a town in the rural United States. Practically nobody had heard of Fannie Lou Hamer. But the townspeople came out in force, standing-room only, to the town hall in Dangriga, with the vice mayor there to welcome me.

I had worried that people would not understand the heavy dialect of the Deep South as spoken by Fannie Lou in "This Little Light . . ." (Fannie Lou Hamer's "dialect" is my first language, the language I speak to my mama when I return to Alabama.) Would the Belizeans understand? I need not have feared. The people who live in Dangriga understood, even better, it seemed, than the city folk in Belize City. Their response was terrific. They got it *all*. I was on a high; I felt them, everything. I felt what they were, and they me. I was at home; we were all speaking some variation of somebody else's language. Dangrigans were used to adjusting to variations on the King's ("Queen's," they say) English! And they had no trouble.

I finished the curtain calls, escaped to the balcony, and let loose a flood of tears. It was one of the greatest communication experiences of my life. I was theirs, Fannie Lou was theirs. I felt the connecting click. Sowa, a Dangrigan woman who brought me bread she'd baked the next day, said to the woman with her as she departed my host's house: "I like that gal; what she stand for; I like that gal's ways." Cousin Thurla, back home in Alabama, would have said it the same way!

These experiences characterize my first three years with "This Little Light . . ." And, yes, John O'Neal, we were right: "Integrity conquers death."

## Notes

1    Jimmy Lee Jackson was killed during the Civil Rights Movement and is recognized as a martyr by Black communities.

## Part II

## Redefining the Veil

A Mother's Day march, May 10, 1981, in Brooklyn, New York, organized by the Coalition of Concerned Black Women to protest the disappearances and murders of more than two dozen Black youths in Atlanta, Georgia. Photo: David Vita/Impact Visuals

# Andrée Nicola McLaughlin

# Black Women, Identity, and the Quest for Humanhood and Wholeness: Wild Women in the Whirlwind

One of the last poems I wrote was based on an old song called 'Every time me 'memba Liza. . . .' I changed that into 'Every time me 'memba Elaine (Elaine Clair),' 'Every time me 'memba Colin (Colin Roach) . . .' and I talk about the youths in Soweto and Atlanta, Georgia, all the young Black people who are being killed. And what I'm saying in that poem is that they're killing Black children because they are trying to wipe out the part of the race which is militant. And although it's not stated openly, I'm also saying that the youths are coming up militant, thanks to the Black women who raised them.

> Nefertiti, poet, quoted in *Heart of the Race: Black Women's Lives in Britain* by Beverley Bryan, Stella Dadzie, and Suzanne Scafe

Nnu Ego had allowed herself to wonder where she had gone wrong. She had been brought up to believe that children made a woman. She had had children, nine in all and luckily seven were alive, much more than many women of that period could boast of. . . . Still, how was she to know that by the time her children grew up the values of her country, her people and her tribe would have changed so drastically, to the extent where a woman with many children could face a lonely old age, and maybe a miserable death all alone, just like a barren woman? She was not even certain that worries over children would not send her to her grave before her *chi* was ready for her. Nnu Ego told herself that she would have been better off had she had time to cultivate those women who had offered her hands of friendship; but she had never had the time.

> *The Joys of Motherhood* by Nigeria's Buchi Emecheta

How can a magistrate judge determine whether an Aboriginal tribal mother is looking after her child properly. It is not for him to decide. Aboriginal people tie the removal of their children closely with the taking of the land. The children are the only resource we've got. We're fighting to get our land back but, we say, what's the use of it if they're taking our children.

> Marjorie Thorpe, national co-ordinator of the Secretariat of Aboriginal and Islander Child Care in Aboriginal Island (Australia)

By 1927 the French had reduced the Kanak population 200,000 to 26,000. Our grandmothers used to hide their children from the massacring colonial army, and thanks to them we are 56,000 strong today. We are organised, and we are ready to fight.

> Sousanna Ounei, revolutionary independence activist, Kanaky (New Caledonia)

The basic unit for change is the mother and her child, and the turning around of Te Kohanga Reo ["Language Nests"—preschool Maori language programs], from a palliative into a tidal wave of self-determination, rests basically on the efforts and struggle of thousands of young Maori mothers. It will be up to them to heal the breach formed by the wedge white culture has forced through our young and old. Leadership can be simply defined as leading. And it is women in every sphere and in all current phases who are doing it.

> *Maori Sovereignty* by Donna Awatere, Maori activist of Aotearoa (New Zealand)

It is imperative that young people be told that we have come a long way, otherwise they are likely to become cynical. A cynical young person is almost the saddest sight to see, because it means that he or she has gone from knowing nothing to believing in nothing. Young people must not get to the point of saying, "You mean to tell me we had Malcolm X, Martin Luther King, Medgar Evers? You mean to tell me we had the Kennedys, Fannie Lou Hamer and Mary McLeod Bethune? You mean to tell me we had all these men and women and we have made no progress? Then what the hell—there is no progress to be made. It can't be made." So it must be simultaneous—how far we have come and how far we have to go.

> Maya Angelou, artist, quoted in *I Dream a World: Portraits of Black Women Who Changed America* by Brian Lanker

You could smell gunfire everywhere. Children were dying in the street, and as they were dying, the others marched forward, facing guns. No one has ever underestimated the power of the enemy. We know that he is armed to the teeth. But the determination, the thirst for freedom in children's hearts, was such that they were prepared to face those machine guns with stones. This is what happens when you hunger for freedom, when you want to break those chains of oppression. Nothing else seems to matter. We couldn't stop our children. We couldn't keep them off the streets.

> *Part of My Soul Went with Him* by Winnie Mandela, on the June 1976 Uprising of Soweto, Azania (South Africa)

I came down from the Sierra / to put an end to capital and usurer / to generals and to bourgeois / Now I exist: only today do we own, do we create / Nothing is foreign to us / The Land is ours / Ours the sea and the sky / the magic and the vision.
"The Black Woman" in *Where the Island Sleeps Like a Wing* by Nancy Morejón, Cuban poet

B lack women's realities, concerns, and analyses are being brought to world attention today by their political activism globally and by their artistic and written expression.[1] In spite of pervasive illiteracy and still limited opportunities for publication, distribution, or translation of their writings, many more Black women are making their stories known in print. The significance of this work is evident in the fact that the theories expressed in Black women's writings have become a part of the general discourse regarding the major questions of our times—social justice and human freedom.

The power of the theory being put forth by these writers largely rests in the interpretative penning of the Black female experience through the prism of their activism. An enhanced role in the political struggles of the modern world has given Black women an embryonic prominence as social and political theoreticians, and their writings are motivating further efforts to creatively render, explicate, or redress Black women's existence. A cross-cultural discussion of Black feminism by two Black women writers in Britain, for example, notes that theoretical works by Amerafrican women in the United States "have acted as a catalyst for discussion, and reaffirmed that similar kinds of consciousness were being explored."[2] As a result of increased literary endeavors, the correlative and comparative dimensions of Black women's lives and issues are perceptible in ways that previously they have not been.

This intercontinental surge of consciousness reflects a variety of complementary factors: a desire by Black women to foster understanding of their lives and legacies in a durable form; a will to build links with Black women and other people; and a passion to stir hu-

man consciousness through accounts of political struggles, exposi-
tions of history, present events and trends, and visions of new social
orders. Black women's literature, by purposeful intent, emerges as a
force in the dialogue about the quality and future of all human existence. Of equal primacy with their literary voices, however, are the
societies Black women create and the identities they simultaneously
forge to attain their aims of humanhood and wholeness.

The philosophic world-views guiding Black women's new self-
definitions bring into focus a consciousness movement. Signaled by
the resurgence in Black female activism and expression, this intercontinental Black women's consciousness movement is a motion to
have power of the *word, the idea,* and *the ideal.* Black women, thus
engaged, are not only redefining themselves and society but also the
realm of resistance and, ultimately, the future. These Wild Women
in the Whirlwind strive to create a new global culture by a pro-active
connection to the universe, working across real boundaries of human existence while challenging those which are artificial.

The following discussion presents a cross-cultural treatment of
the consciousness and theory undergirding socio-political identities
Black women have adopted in endeavoring to govern their destinies.
It contextualizes the Black female experience before offering another
theoretical paradigm for exploring variations in self-definition relating to the term "Black" and to different identities Black women
have chosen. A survey of how Black women—primarily in English-
speaking, economically developed nations—have named themselves
and defined their experiences is instructive about their distinct socio-political realities and the diversity and complexity of the Black
female experience. The examination concludes by analyzing the social applicability of Black women's activism and self-definition to the
quality of global order that is required for a truly liberated humanity.

## Multiple Jeopardy and the Human Experience

The human experience in the twentieth century has been significantly shaped by two interrelated but divergent factors: economic
class oppression and the quest for self-determination. In this regard,
the United Nations' *Universal Declaration of Human Rights* and *Dec-*

*laration on the Granting of Independence to Colonial Countries and Peoples* have comprised a primary basis of legitimization, if not an actual impetus, for continuing political movements for social justice. The breadth of efforts by the world's women to transform unjust systems is rivaled only by the scope of their experiences of oppression.

While the condition of most women's lives has been attributed to economic class oppression based upon race (racialism) or nationality (colonialism and imperialism) and gender (sexism and patriarchy), such a view is too simplified. Women's lives—as they experience them—are far more complex. For instance, the oppression of Burakumin women in Japan suggests a unique configuration of "triple jeopardy" in an industrialized society—gender, economic class, and caste. More pervasively, women experience national *and* racial oppression, not one to the exclusion of the other. Some examples are: indigenous women who belong to internal colonized groups and, in this way, suffer both racial and national oppression, such as Namibian, South African, (Japan's) Ainu, Palestinian, Northern Irish; Amerindian, and many Pacific women; Latin American women of African descent who experience imperialist domination along with their fellow nationals and, because of their countries' racial hierarchies, also experience racial oppression; and a large number of migrant women who were among the economically "locked-out" (or politically repressed) in their native countries and who, because of race, remain locked out in the developed societies to which they have immigrated. Reinforced and maintained by the world economic order, diverse configurations of structural inequities exist in both industrialized and developing nations. To look at the concept of women's class oppression as one solely based on race or nationality and gender is a Western notion that does not speak to the intricacy of class contradictions in other societies.

Symptomatic of the array of tensions in the world community are the possibilities for women experiencing *multiple jeopardy*. On a large scale, the oppression of women is compounded by various structural inequities which have their origins in colonialism or feudalism: differences of religion (e.g., Muslim vis-à-vis Catholic Philippine society) and ethnicity (e.g., Tamil minority vis-à-vis Sinhalese majority of Sri Lanka); and the contradictions of region (e.g., rural vis-à-vis urban Ugandans), caste (e.g., "untouchables" vis-à-vis post

Gandhian India), social class (e.g., descendants of Americo-Liberian immigrants vis-à-vis indigenous peoples of Liberia), and color (e.g., status determined by complexion vis-à-vis Jamaica). Even as the bases for these structural inequities and divisions are being undermined by political revolutions, new ones are being produced by the globalization of capital (moving into those regions of "the periphery" traditionally outside "the center" of concentrated capital) and of labor (whereby new populations are relocating in foreign contexts as cheap labor). Furthermore, patriarchal oppression ensures that women experience any other oppression twice over—as a member of the dominated group and as a woman. To the extent that multiple structural inequities dictate human existence, they also define the experience of Black women.

If these forces are not complex enough already, Black women's multiple jeopardy is further complicated by a great range of geopolitical realities such as, for example, famine in the Sudan, discriminatory immigration laws in France, foreign military intervention in Nicaragua, an upsurge in racist violence in the United States, political repression in Haiti, counterrevolution in Mozambique, military occupation of East Timor, narco-terrorism in Colombia, civil war in Ethiopia, radioactive uranium mining on Aboriginal lands in Australia, nuclear testing in the Marshall Islands, apartheid in South Africa. The temptation to oversimplify and generalize about Black women's experiences and issues originates from several sources: 1) the pathos and insignificance ascribed to the cultures and lives of people of colony and promoted by Western cultural chauvinism and racism;[3] 2) the patriarchal devaluation of all women and the trivialization of their lives; 3) the great emphasis oppressed groups put upon both the commonalities in the roots of their respective circumstances and the unity of representations of their subordinate station—a means of garnering moral, political, and material support for social change; and 4) a wide-scale proclivity by many people and institutions to resort exclusively to pre–twentieth-century social thought for evaluating contemporary social phenomena.

Within the frameworks of historically evolved variations in their societies and concerns, Black women initiate new, socio-political identities, commonly spurred by the imperative of social transformation. They define themselves according to their experiences of oppression and their unique priorities for achieving a higher quality of life. These experiences and priorities in their own societies also constitute the bases for Black women's determining the relative importance of nationality, ethnicity, race, social class, culture, gender, sexuality, and so forth to their struggles for social justice.

## Black As Political-Class Identification

Many scholars have documented that, in antiquity, "black" was a physical characteristic, a color. "Black" first developed as a social category of low station when the Arab trade in African slaves increased; a hierarchy that valued cultural, religious, and social homogeneity assigned a negative status to slaves.[4] With Europeans' subordination of world peoples as laboring classes in subsequent centuries, the designation of social groups by color and nationality was entrenched in the Western psyche. "Black," in this context, shifted in the seventeenth century from mere association with color. As a term and a social category, "black" came to form part of a system of oppositional and hierarchical cultural constructs that patterned and justified power constellations of the colonizer and the colonized, the slave owner and the slave. That which was "white" (or Anglo, male, Christian, wealthy) was extolled and infused with connotations of benevolence and superiority, while that which was not white (or not Anglo, female, non-Christian, poor) was debased and associated with malevolence and inferiority. As such, the concept of "race" as ideological taxonomy, with "white" occupying the apical position, has represented a social construction inherent in Anglo-Saxon racism. Imposing racial identity had, in many instances, the impact of dual processes, deculturation as well as racialization of economic class arrangements. The varying sets of assumptions which Black people today assign to "black" identity mirror the range of their historical experiences and point to "Black" as a political-class identification.

Poignant evidence of the diversity of the Black experience is the difficulty in applying just one term or one definition to label or define the collective realities of Black women. For example, Black women in English-speaking North America employ a definition of Black identity which assumes that all women of African descent are Black and, conversely, that all Black women are of African descent. Yet, the majority of women in the African nations of Algeria, Tunisia, Mauritania, and elsewhere represent a cultural heritage distinct from Africans south of the Sahara and claim "Arab," not Black, identity, based on linguistic and cultural unity (although there are obviously black-skinned Arabs). Furthermore, phenotypically black (physiologically classified as "Negroid") people of islands in the Pacific—many of whom embrace Black identity—are indigenous to this region, not the African continent (speculatively, a result of a glacial epoch). In areas of Europe, Black self-definition is increasingly inclusive of women of Asian, Middle Eastern, and Pacific as well as African ancestries. The Black Dutch of Holland, for instance, include immigrants and descendants of peoples from "Indonesia, South Africa, Nigeria, Turkey, the Moluccans, the Caribbean, China and other parts of the world where Black people are aboriginals."[5]

While assigning Black identity to Asian, Middle Eastern, and Pacific women in North America would invariably be interpreted as a misnomer, these women and those of African ancestry in both Canada and the United States are, to a large extent, linked by the shared designation of "women of color." But, in parts of southern Africa, stark political realities have included schematic stratifications of privileges based upon racial classification; referring to a Black woman as a "woman of color" in South Africa, for example, may lead her to believe that the referent assumes she is of the so-called "colored" category of inhabitants or that she accepts the apartheid regime's practice of legalized racialism. In Latin America, the literal translation of "woman of color" similarly has negative associations. Even so, some Latin American and Caribbean countries possess intricate racial hierarchies based on phenotype (and, sometimes, social status) in which black is a low-status social classification. Exemplary of Black self-identification in this situation is Afro-Brazilians' descriptive definition that includes those who "possess Black racial characteristics in skin color, facial characteristics and hair texture" among Brazil's more than three dozen racial categories.[6] Black identity can also break down along lines of ethnicity: those of English-speaking Caribbean background in Central America's Panama consider themselves to be Black in contrast to Spanish-speaking descendants of African slaves. In various regions of the world where self-definition is exclusively linked to nationality, tribal affiliation, and/or kinship systems (family and/or clan), the relevance of Black identity can span associations of no meaning at all, color, material condition, and/or cultural unity. Thus, there are limitations to the applicability of Black women's terms for and definitions of themselves when they move outside given social contexts.

In the absence of a universally applied taxonomy, however, Black still exists as culture, social class, and political class. As a cultural group, Black people, in their distinct geographical and interactive historical contexts, are bound by what Frantz Fanon defined as "the whole body of efforts made by a people in the sphere of thought to describe, justify and praise the action through which that people has created itself and keeps itself in existence," including its belief systems, social structures, idioms, aesthetics, art, customs, traditions, and technology.[7] As a social class, Black people are among the world's disfranchised whose plight is characterized by a condition of poverty, violence, misery, and inequality. A Black political class exists when the oppressed—self-defined as "Black"—act in behalf of their social class to oppose the prevailing socio-economic interests of the dominant group. There is a dialectical relationship among all three— culture, social class, and political class—with each influencing the way the others are expressed.

According to sociologist Oliver C. Cox, a political class seeks "control of the state" in order to fulfill the aspirations of a social class. "Different political factions may represent the same political class" when they share the same motivating premise; in this case, the factions are only separate organs for meeting the demands of the same social class.[8] Cox further argued that "*as a function of the economic order, the political class has potential existence, but as the result of agitation it becomes organized for conflict*" (emphasis mine).[9] While economic determinants are common to both classes, the political class—unlike the social class—exhibits "social solidarity" and is an actual "power group," not merely a concept. Basically, social class defines status whereas political class organizes and performs political action to empower a social class. The absence of political power to reorder unsatisfactory economic arrangements is the catalyst for political-class movement.[10] Within this theoretical framework, then, from the mid-1960s to the present, "Black" has constituted a political-class identity internationally adopted in disparate ways by oppressed women (and men) as a vehicle for liberating themselves from man-made systems of human suffering.

## Black Women of South Africa

For Black women of South Africa, Black political-class has been a crucial dimension of the process of change, encompassing Africans, Asians, and so-called coloreds—that is, people of mixed-race backgrounds. Together, these groups comprise the critical mass of opposition to domination of the Black majority population by the white minority descendants of European colonial settlers.

Evolving out of the Black Consciousness Movement, Black self-definition is a basis upon which Black women have strengthened their three-hundred-year resistance against the encroachment upon and dispossession of African ancestral land. As Blacks, they seek no less than the total eradication of a system which sanctions—through a series of laws—Black economic underdevelopment, political disfranchisement, and dehumanization. Black political-class identity promotes the united front for self-determination across racial backgrounds, ethnicity, religion, ideology, social status, and, by virtue of solidarity with external oppressed groups, across nationality. As Black women have mounted their independence struggle with the objective of "one man, one vote, majority rule!" or "Azania will be free!" they approach their foremost aim of participatory democracy by means of a national consciousness of political class, defining themselves in relation to a common cause to liquidate the deadly apartheid system of white privilege.

Black women's social class forms one basis for paramountcy of "Black" political-class identification. On the one hand, Black women's relationship to the apartheid economy is substantially predetermined by the impoverishment of the reserves and townships to which they have been consigned, and by a migratory labor system in which they have been economically marginalized—mostly as domestic servants or farm workers—and denied a family existence. On the other hand, racist legislation, backed by military force, proscribes their status and precludes their participation in the nation's political system.

Instructively, Black women of South Africa interpret their racial oppression under apartheid "from its social power base, imperialist colonialism, . . . the conditions upon which racism, in the form of apartheid, is possible."[11] According to Black women, their struggle is one against settler colonialism as well as against racism, monopoly capitalism, and sexism: "Owing to the colonial character of the 'South African' state and to apartheid, women's oppression in our country is *quadrupled* where African women are concerned" (emphasis mine).[12]

The colonial character of South Africa renders economic class relations—via its political system of apartheid—beneficial to all whites, including women, at the expense of all Blacks. Black women, therefore, particularize that the nature of the state "places white women in a social position to oppress African men. This, in turn, unites the 'maid' and the 'boy' against the masters and madams."[13] In effect, categorical social, political, and economic privilege of white women and men in South Africa diminishes, if not eliminates, any possibility of whites comprising a political class organized to transform the state and the situation of a social class *except in relation to the existing Black political-class*. It is Blacks who form the essential socioeconomic antagonism (vis-à-vis the state) as, largely, the one and the same group of colonized, racially victimized, and exploited masses. On this basis, Dabi Nkululeko argues that understanding "national oppression as the fourth colonialism" exposes the cause and effect of Black women's condition and how they became maids and white women 'madams': Colonization and, consequently, Black women's "landlessness" predisposed them to national, racial, and economic oppression, and also reconstituted relations between women and men.[14] Thus, South African Black women's *Black* political-class identity is summarily rooted in colonialism and its development whereby "because of new methods of production . . . , economic power has been shifted to some section of the population [whites] without at the same time shifting the political power" to Blacks.[15]

By rejecting identification as "non-whites," "coloreds," and "Bantus," Black women's political motion to decolonize the soil has been complemented by a process which has sought to end the circumscribing of Black people's humanity. Indeed, culture—the distinguishing character of a group's humanity—is another important basis for Black political-class identity. Winnie Mandela does more than suggest that the colonization and attendant vilification of Black culture have contributed to the progression of Black revolt: "To say that [Black] culture, which in fact meant respecting your elders, was atheism, that your belief in your ancestors, your respect for your grandfathers was atheist and ungodly, that was where things went wrong."[16] Inasmuch as the process of liberating the land necessitates resisting Western political domination, Black women's contemporaneous decolonizing of culture implies not being wedded to systems of Western thought. By their measure, true freedom must entail the unencumbered and authentic expression of group character.

Through reclaiming their histories and indigenous ethos, Black women have drawn upon the egalitarian and nonsectarian aspects of their cultural heritages as guideposts for liberation. Discussing the foresight of a Black woman leader who implored Africans to "not live above your people, but live with them," Ellen Kuzwayo speaks to the real measure of leadership that contravenes the social chauvinism required by systems of human exploitation.

> Even in those early years, 'tribalism' was recognized as a danger by the black community. It was no coincidence that the leadership of the black people in those days was consciously chosen on the basis of merit and not ethnicity, an evil which has come with the Nationalist government regime. I suppose it is used as an instrument to divide and rule blacks. These were the warnings given by one of the leading black women in South Africa as long ago as 1938.[17]

Merit, then, not ethnicity—the latter of which the apartheid regime has seized on to frustrate Black political-class movement—is part of the formula for freeing South Africa of *apartheid colonialism* and establishing the democratic nation envisioned by Black women. Similarly, traditional moral values of group connection and collective responsibility, which are contained in Africa proverbs but are being eroded by the dislocation of Black communities, have a place in Black women's political struggle and their society of the future:

> Proverbs to a very great extent were regarded as an undefined code of law. Many are frequently used to this day and still retain their social and ethical importance. [Some] are used in all black communities south of the Sahara. . . . "No man is an island." The communal way of

life of the black people of this nation is based upon this [Setswana] saying.[18]

With the recognition that much of precolonial society could not meet the requirements of this epoch, Black women correspondingly acknowledge that oppression is a precondition of Black political-class/self-definition.[19] In this regard, Black women express that the nonracialist movement does not view humanity in terms of race, but is compelled—by reason of the inimical state and its structures—to use descriptive terminologies to define their modal existence. Clearly, it is on the foundation of the democratic principles of Black women's cultural heritages and through the action of democratic forces, catalyzed by Black political-class movement, that Black women of South Africa build their new society.

## Maori Women of New Zealand

The Maori women, indigenous Polynesian people of New Zealand, endure, as the Black women of South Africa do, circumstances profoundly conditioned by Western colonialism. This experience, in combination with the forty-year reality of prolific nuclearization and militarization of their region by Western powers, has shaped the goal of Maori sovereignty; in this sense, self-determination is expressly articulated in terms of their relationship to the land. Donna Awatere states that Maori sovereignty entails "the Maori ability to determine our destiny and to do so from the basis of our land and fisheries."[20] In popular terms, this translates to mean a "Nuclear Free and Independent Aotearoa."

Grounded in Maori women's pursuit of social justice, Black self-definition is one of several political-class identities they have assumed. In New Zealand (or Aotearoa, "the ancestral land of Long White Cloud"), Black identity signifies a conceptual and practical alliance among Maoris, New Zealand-born Pacific Islanders, and Pacific Island immigrants.[21] Having originated to seek the empowerment of Polynesians (through groups like the Polynesian Panthers), the Black political-class movement today agitates around civil rights issues. While Maori women and other Black people are commonly

affected by separate development policies of the state, and consequently relegated to a common social class, the question of culture
has dictated the primacy of *Maori* political-class identity.

Atareta Poananga writes of the relationship of Maori culture to the
land:

> Maoris valued the land not only as a source of food, but also because
> of its permanence and connections with the ancestors. The mana
> [sovereignty] of the tribe was bound up with the land. Tribal history
> and songs referred to it, and members died to protect its sacred burial
> grounds, shrines, marne, gardens and villages.[22]

That the culture of Maori women is linked to the life forces of the
soil, forests, and seas, which they have traditionally honored as
sources of spiritual energy and consciousness, stands central to Maori
political-class identity and movement. Maori women's separation
from the communal land, caused by a broken treaty, large-scale colonial settlement, transnational corporate penetration, and nuclearism,
threatens the existence of the 2,000-year-old Maori culture. Endeavors for group survival, preservation of culture, control of the land
and waters, and determination of their destinies are interchangeable.
In this regard, Maori women's way of life as well as their standard of
living is tied to colonialism and the struggle for Maori sovereignty.

For Maori women who rebuke the notion that their struggle is
merely an issue of race relations, the "conflict between Maori and
Pakeha [whites; literally, "strangers"] is the natural outcome of the
colonial experience."[23] The recognition that social justice cannot be
achieved without Maori land rights underscores the preeminence of
Maori political-class identity: "We are *Maori* before anything. What
does cancer, sexuality, rape, individual survival, death or anything
mean without the survival of the Maori as a Nation? It is empty.
Meaningless."[24]

In response to Maori women's economic underdevelopment and
ensuing cultural alienation (through 150 years of colonization) and
in the absence of electoral political power (aided by the restrictive
Maori Representation Act), Maori nationalism emerges as a political
class movement. "This cultural, economic and political nationalism
is the assertion of an indigenous people, the Maori, who along with
others of color make up the majority of the world's population."[25]

Hence, Maori political-class identity and Black political-class identity are interactive expressions of the same political class which agitates for the oppressed social class.

Cultural unity, shared political goals, and the common condition of being "internal colonies" (often as minorities) in their own lands form the bases for Maori and other groups' self-definition as *indigenous people*. This represents a transnational political-class identity, reflected in alliances with Amerindians as well as the Aborigines of Australia, Hawaiians, and other Pacific (also known as Melanesian, Micronesian, and Polynesian) peoples. The cultural postulate for political-class identification is that indigenous peoples observe the "same laws: Respect for Mother Earth, religion of natural laws, the wisdom of ancestors and elders, human life and those yet unborn."[26]

On a regional level, this observance of similar life principles takes the form of a campaign for what indigenous people in the Pacific consider to be two inseparable tasks: "denuclearization and independence." Inherent in indigenous women's cooperation to regain the land for "living needs" is a resolve to hasten eradication of their misery and poverty. At the 1985 Non-Governmental World Meeting of Women (Nairobi), they declared mutual resistance to having "been exposed to radiation dangers, made a dumping ground for contraceptives and dangerous medicines and pesticides, subjected to over-advertising of inferior imported foods, drugs and alcohol, and made dependent on the wage economy."[27] They are united in opposition to the exploitation, radiation, and privatization of their lands, namely *nuclear colonialism*. Politically, through diplomatic initiatives, joint actions, and regional and international networks for peace, global nuclear disarmament, and self-determination, the political-class movement of indigenous peoples aims to transform not simply the socio-economic order of their respective states but, ultimately, the structural inequities in the world economic order.

The cultural base of Maori women's self-definition as Maori and indigenous people informs their conception of the political struggle in their homeland and the world. In *Maori Sovereignty*, Awatere reasons that focusing upon any one of the structural inequities of racism, sexism, or capitalism is a "fragmented" means of rectifying the condition of Maori women who experience these phenomena inclusively. Maori women's struggle, Awatere posits, fundamentally represents a "massive confrontation of two opposing ways of life": that which recognizes "spiritual reality is infused in the very earth around us" versus that which has "determined the rules" and dehumanizes and jeopardizes the survival of all life—humanity and the living environment.[28]

Awatere goes further to suggest that Maori/Black/indigenous women's emancipation requires their stepping outside the frame of Western culture in which "parts of reality are seen as separate from the whole." She argues that Western culture is the means by which the dominant group, "captives of their own culture," do not view Maori/Black/indigenous women as cultures—only as races with the latter's concerns perceived as "racial matters." Self-definition, then, for indigenous/Maori women, entails reclaiming a "holistic cultural view" to "break the habit of seeking to rectify grievances one at a time and instead formulate a battle plan based on full knowledge of the battle conditions as the confrontation of two ways of life."[29] The holistic character of the indigenous world-view exposes and confutes the confrontational cultural base of the isms and fragmented ways of existing, which oppressed women resist. For the Maori system of reference "reorders reality," extolling the unity of the universe as well as the invariable power of "human connections" over "spatial and temporal constriction":

> The elemental forces of Maoridom [Maori self-determination] are based on human connections, on the dynamics of human exchange, of pooling resources and pulling together, of mutual exchanges of thought and actions, of interweaving and interlocking patterns of human connections, of all skills, knowledge, talent and "things" belonging to the group not the individual.[30]

The indigenous world-view inexorably interlinks the past, nature, the dead, the omnipresent and living reality of all humanity; women, as custodians of culture, represent the whole. By contrast, Western secular culture compartmentalizes the universe and approaches women as a fragmented part. Overcoming oppression necessitates disengaging a Western world-view which prompts fragmented solutions and, thereby, abets discontinuity, isolation, and powerlessness. Based on this "full knowledge," Awatere contends that the route to full liberation from multiple jeopardy can be formulated and attained.

## Black Women in Britain

Black women in Britain include "Africans, continental and of the diaspora, and Asians primarily of Indian sub-continent descent."[31] Prevalently, they do not define themselves as "Britons" despite the centuries-old Black presence on the island nation, the existence of a distinct "Black British" culture, or the fact that the majority of Black people are British citizens by birth. Based on a history of antagonism whereby Blacks have not been "recognized as legitimate and equal inhabitants . . . and are continuously fighting for [their] right to be [in British society]," Black people reject British self-definition and correspondingly adopt Black identity.[32] The concept of "blackness," however, continues evolving, "as yet unmatured and inadequately defined" in contemporary Britain, according to women editors of *Charting the Journey: Writings by Black and Third World Women.* The idea patterns change and growth to reflect material unity in political action among various oppressed groups and to "collectivize" diverse experiences and struggles.[33]

A Black political-class was born in Britain when people of African and South Asian descent began to mobilize collectively for Black Power and to oppose their social, political, and economic marginalization. A then largely migrant Black populace confronted rife vigilantism and racial discrimination in housing, employment, education, police enforcement, and immigration and citizenship legislation. More recently, Black political-class, by definition and practice, shifts to include Arabs, Latin Americans, and other people with histories of Western imperialist domination. In this respect, the experience of colonialism as well as that of racism is a key factor in Black political-class identification.

Some of the assumptions of Black political-class identity are made evident in the statements of one Black woman of Caribbean origin: "When we use the term 'Black,' we use it as a political term. It doesn't describe skin colour; it defines our situation here in Britain. We're here as a result of British imperialism, and our continued oppression in Britain is a result of British racism."[34] Her reproach that, "We're here as a result of British imperialism," emphasizes a basic presupposition of Black identity in Britain: A common circumstance of de facto displacement from one's home of heritage. The presence of four million Black people in Britain is associated with Great Britain's historical colonization of African, Asian, and native American peoples; its coterminous role in the African slave trade; its transporting of Asian labor to facilitate the postslavery expansion of the Empire; and its centrality to structural inequities in the economies of former colonies or spheres of influence (i.e., neo-colonialism).

For many, Black consciousness attributes the poverty of underdeveloped nations and the consequent migrations of labor toward Western metropoles to capitalist economic expansion. Furthermore, by tracing the dynamic of racism in capitalism's evolution, from the colonial experience to their plight as exploited settlers or migrants in Britain, Black people combine "an understanding of how colonialism had divided the Asian and African and Caribbean peoples (coolie, savage and slave) with an awareness of how that same colonialism made them one people now . . . all Blacks."[35] To Black women like those who, in 1978, launched the first national Black women's organization (the Organization of Women of Asian and African Descent [OWAAD]), Black political-class expresses "federalist opposition" to exploitation by the victims of Britain's colonial legacy.[36]

Parita Trivedi interprets the operative principle of Afro-Asian unity in Britain as "a mark of rising strength and confidence in a bid to break with the divisive ethnic boundaries and evolve common political strategies to face institutionalised racism and right-wing attacks."[37] Without the prospect of transforming their condition electorally, Black people cooperate with each other across ethnic lines to increase their base of resistance. For example, the harbinger of numerous "Black" organizations, the Black People's Alliance (BPA), united tens of thousands of inhabitants of African, South Asian, and Caribbean origin under one national umbrella to counteract discriminatory immigration laws and attendant racist assaults that were fueled by a receding economy. In like fashion, defining the Black political-class more broadly to include Latin Americans, Arabs, and Middle Easterners augments this ability to oppose injurious social policies; it also augurs noncomplacency with *domestic neocolonialism,* that is—external (state) manipulation of Black communities using select members within them who have no commitment to the Black political-class and who employ their status to thwart needed systemic change. Allied, these groups enhance the possibilities to control their destinies, combating rising unemployment, their fixing into citizens and aliens, separation of families, transfer of their children, disproportionate incarceration, and institutional abuse. The political class both intensifies its struggle and ensures its longevity by "social solidarity," or practically valuing the immutable need to attract members to itself for a common goal.

Pointing to "the diverse cultural, religious, and socio-political histories" out of which Black women in Britain have evolved, Amina Mamma writes that they politically support struggles for social justice and national liberation in Africa, Asia, and the Caribbean.[38] In addition, Black women support the Irish liberation struggle and other anti-imperialist movements in Latin America, the Middle East, and the Pacific. Because they link the erosion of the British welfare state with economic and political crises around the world, many Black women similarly identify with the international women's movement for "equality, development, and peace." The contention by Black feminists that "imperialist relations . . . also determined the emotional, sexual and psychological aspects of Black women's lives" forms a basis for support of the gay liberation movement of the western world.[39] Grounded in the premise that the extant economic order cannot be reformed, the internationalism of Black women impels multilateral cooperation for empowerment to create a new world economic system.

An integral aspect of Black identity and struggle is validating Black women's heritages. Black women perceive that the suppression of Black history and culture chiefly supports British domination:

> Some Black people forget about their culture and bring up their children with this society's values, so that they know nothing about their history. . . . Black people need to be more positive and more together. If we're not together here in this culture, then there's no future for us. Black people are getting wiped out, physically and mentally.[40]

By this analysis, survival and liberation hinge upon eradicating the despair and alienation engendered by Western acculturation. Such an enterprise involves actively repudiating the stereotypes, myths, and violence by which Black people's life existence has been detrimentally cast. Within the framework of a Black feminist consciousness, traversing sexism is an important part of this process. Black women argue that achieving social justice entails transforming all Black people's experiences into an affirmative statement of self-worth, unity, and direction. To this end, reversing denial and derogation of their "ways of being" figures prominently in protecting Black life and culture.

The first Black female publishing press in Britain, established by a collective of unemployed Black women, introduced its premiere publication, *Blackwomantalk* (1987), with a poetic declaration:

> Women
> Black women
> of different—
> ages colours nationalities religions classes
> backgrounds cultures . . .
> have entrusted us their work.
>
> Pulled from dusty history
> dusty draws chewed envelopes tablenapkins . . .
> Laying down words to record
>     that we do not forget—
> forget how much is different in our paths.
>
> . . . These are the words,
> quartered, divided, and whole
> whose contradictions
> line our souls.
> Words of resistance
> which in sharing
> we more forward—
> claiming what is ours.[41]

As the excerpt from this poem suggests, the activism of Black women approaches "the simultaneity of class exploitation and race and sex oppression," aiming to create "a synthesis" to extend beyond race, gender, class, and sexuality "as single factors."[42] Pursuing wholeness, Black women lay claim to their diverse pasts and present, the ancestors and each other, and their unique life expressions and circumstances. More exactly, they challenge the totality of their oppression and exploitation by political activity that addresses numerous issues and that, where possible, coalesces their particular "cultural agendas": workers' rights, welfare benefits, violence against women, affordable housing, equal education, culture, language, citizenship policy, AIDS education, peace, nuclear disarmament, national liberation support work, among others.

In assuming collective responsibility for each other, Black women consciously mend their estrangement from traditions. It is an undertaking of "woman-purpose," guarding the transplanted and adapted ethos which has sustained Black people as they forge a culture and a destiny that brings them closer to total freedom. By their own account, Black women are "preserving, extending and redefining [themselves] in order to create a situation in which 'blackness,' as commonly understood, has no social meaning."[43] Accordingly, Black women have characterized their political-class movement for self-determination as a "coherent and coordinated rebellion."[44]

## Black Women in the United States

The adoption of Black identity by African-American women in the United States, as true elsewhere, emerged in a context of political resistance which was inspired by post–World War II struggles for independence and liberation, particularly those on the Asian and African continents. What distinguishes Black self-definition in the United States is that it identifies the same political class which has historically had different names. Connoting a meshing of African culture and political class, "Black" is one of a progression of terms describing the same people identified as African, Colored, Negro, Afro-American, and African-American.[45] The name of the political class has changed when the power structure co-opted the term and made it meaningless as an identification for counteracting the status quo. A Black political theorist in Britain analyzes that the evolution of Black as a "political color" and the Black nationalist impulse that has shaped it were profoundly influenced by the character of political resistance in the United States: This movement for Black Power "showed up the essential unity of the struggles against white power and privilege."[46]

During the first half of the decade of the 1960s, it was Malcolm X (El-Hajj Malik El-Shabazz), a spiritual leader, revolutionist, and progenitor of the philosophy of Black nationalism, who brought into widespread use the terms Black, Afro-American, and African-American which he used in juxtaposition to the term "Negro." Stressing the African origins of Black people in the United States, which he believed Western society deliberately obfuscated, he characterized Negro self-definition (effectively applied by Marcus Mosiah Garvey in earlier years) as an abyss of nonbeing: "It's a person who has no history, and by having no history, he has no culture. . . . We have nothing to identify ourselves as part of the human family."[47] Malcolm X advocated identification by the terms Afro-American and African-American to link, historically and culturally, people of African descent with the African continent and the Pan-African world community.

According to Malcolm X, however, Black self-definition was not based on ancestry. Black identity could be associated with all people battling Western domination due to the global doctrine of white supremacy:

> . . . when I say Black, I mean non-white. Black, brown, red, or yellow. . . . Our brothers and sisters in Asia, . . . Africa, . . . and in Latin America, the peasants, . . . have been involved in struggle . . . to get the colonizing powers, the Europeans, off their land, out of their country.[48]

He thus called for the development of a new power group defined as Black—not based on a common social class but on a united political opposition to the social class condition and to the system responsible, an "international power structure." In this, Malcolm extended to a broader base the precepts of national self-determination and individual liberty—two of the original principles of the twentieth-century Pan-Africanist movement (as espoused by W.E.B. Du Bois). As significant as his identification of the political-class stood Malcolm's vision of a new world order and his strategy for achieving Black economic, political, and social empowerment.

Malcolm envisaged a world free of the economic structural inequities which divided the human race into the haves and have-nots. He internationalized social justice issues in the United States, imploring Black people to see their plight in the "world context,"—that is, as part of a majority oppressed people globally. Drawing on the model of unity forged at the 1955 Afro-Asian Conference in Bandung, Indonesia, Malcolm appealed for unity among Black people "despite their religious or nonreligious beliefs" or their "economic or political differences" to achieve the goal of Black Power.

Black became a new political-class identity in actuality when the consciousness of Black nationalism and the ethic of African-American mass resistance converged—with Fannie Lou Hamer, Angela Davis, Assata Shakur, and many more Black women as part of the front-lines—forming the parameters of the Black Power movement. African-American women have been among the millions galvanized by Black political-class, confronting the state apparatus with the sheer power of morally committed numbers.

Black identity, for more than two decades, remains the major, but not exclusive, political frame for the protection of civil and human rights. Declaring "change [as] the immediate responsibility of each of us wherever and however we are standing, in whatever arena we choose," Audre Lorde writes that "while we wait for another Malcolm, another Martin, another charismatic Black leader to validate our struggles, old Black people are freezing to death in tenements, Black children are being brutalized and slaughtered in the streets, or lobotomized by television, and the percentage of Black families living below the poverty line is higher today."[49] At stake, as Lorde points out, are the lives and minds of Black people. Widespread upheaval in Black communities and families—caused by homelessness, unemployment, crime, institutionalization, substance abuse, illiteracy, infirmity, and unnatural deaths—begets the urgency for Black women's political-class movement.

Black women contend that their group condition commenced with separation from the land of their birthright. European colonialism *in the form of slavery* brought about the uprooting of their African ancestors for use as human chattel. Further, "emancipation found the freedwoman empty-handed, without home or land or mule for plowing."[50] Historical abrogation of the privileges of citizenship and the rights of humanity has ensured Black people's extensive confinement to the underclass.

Discussing the failure of the mid-twentieth-century Civil Rights Movement to rectify Black people's social class position, Assata Shakur incriminates the "rich [who] have always used racism to maintain power."[51] She points out that legislation and enforcement do not serve all sectors of the country, owing to the wealthy's inordinate influence on campaigns for and persons seeking executive, legislative, or judicial office.

Instrumental to Black women achieving a new balance of power for life, liberty, and security implies far-reaching social transformation. Gloria Joseph stresses that primary deterrents to liberation struggles include "the web of class-controlled technologies, corporate and multinational interests, propaganda, and pervasive hierarchical and class ideologies."[52] In this respect, challenging the ruling elite's political domination requires rebuffing the economic and cultural superstructures, the latter of which rationalizes and, thereby, promotes Black people's subjugation.

Western cultural disparagement of Africa and of things and peoples African is a decisive factor in Black women's political-class movement. By reason of its biased memory system, Western culture grossly distorts the history and the character of African peoples, encourages Black people to assimilate, and fosters a genocidal milieu with regard to them. Fundamentally, the culture inspires hatred toward and among people of African descent, inducing destructive behaviors and an equally adverse disconnection from anything not Western. This is manifested in how institutions of the dominant society function. They undermine Black communities, families, and individuals through, for example: a preponderance of negative media images, pejorative labeling of cultural difference, double standards in the allocation and administration of resources for education, health, and housing, and support for police violence and murder. Psychic rage or despair in Black communities turns in on itself, producing crises of mental illness, drug abuse, crime, and self-mutilation.

On this basis, Shakur insists that Black people "have got to constantly make positive statements about ourselves. Our desire to be free has got to manifest itself in everything we do and are."[53] This entails forgoing Western values, namely the cult of the individual that forsakes cooperative existence and exalts money, fame, glory, and status. Shakur states that Black women must reforge a connection with their foremothers: "Under the guidance of Harriet Tubman and Fannie Lou Hamer and all of our foremothers, let us rebuild a sense of community. Let us rebuild the culture of giving and caring on the tradition of fierce determination to move on closer to freedom."[54] Black women must "rebuild" their culture by restoring the communal heritage "of giving and caring" which fostered survival and resistance. This also means debunking a plethora of Western images and ideas which rally against the humanity of all who do not conform to the white, Anglo-Saxon, male, Christian, and wealthy hierarchical apex. To safeguard the future and "move on closer to freedom" necessitates healing the disjunction Western culture has exacted between Black people and their community, history, and African ethos.

Rooted in Black women's "manifold and simultaneous oppressions," the African-American feminist movement is committed to opposing harmful institutions and fashioning a destiny based on humane values. The consonant political activity resists oppression based on gender, race, class, sexuality, nationality, religion, age, disability, "at the same time that it challenges militarism and imminent nuclear destruction."[55] Given the size of the Black population, approximately 40 million, and its demographic concentrations, Black women work within their own communities for "community control" and development of independent social, political, and economic structures. They impact domestic and foreign policy through religious organizations and by formation of such bodies as the National Black Women's Health Project, the African-American Women's Political Action Caucus, and the National Rainbow Coalition; or by solidarity with such diverse struggles as those for Nicaraguan sovereignty, Namibian independence, AIDS research, and reproductive rights. Other noteworthy manifestations of the push for social change are the contemporary renaissance in Black women's literature and art, the surge in new Black women's organizations and enterprises, the Black-led anti-apartheid movement, and the institutionalization of Black Women's Studies. Reinterpreting, reasserting, and reproducing their heritage, Black women invoke the possibilities for social change through cooperation and coalition. In this manner, Black identification in the African-American community continues to command dint of authority as, in the words of Gwendolyn Brooks, "an open, wide-stretching, unifying empowering umbrella" and "familyhood."[56]

An impetus to broaden Black political-class identity and movement in the United States has been propelled by heightened tensions and concerns for survival in response to nuclearism, a growing global economic recession, and the proliferation and intensification of struggles for self-determination. While Black consciousness spurred many Black people to define themselves as "Africans" and "Muslims," the extension of Black identity to other peoples was arrested by several factors, among them: the predominate association of Black with African culture and Pan-Africanism and, not least, the cultural apparatus's stigmatizing of Black nationalism as "racism in reverse." As Black people have called for other oppressed peoples to join their struggle, and are themselves called to show political solidarity, they increasingly exercise multiple political-class identities. These identities include "Third World" people and "people of color."[57]

The growing popular use of the terminologies "people of color" and "women of color" in the United States links peoples of African, Asian, Pacific, and indigenous American descent, Latinos and, more recently, certain Middle Eastern populations. Asoka Bandarage comments on the significance of the term, "people of color," in selected Western societies: "The term "people of color" helps transcend the divide-and-conquer strategies of white supremacy which have kept the black, brown, yellow, and red peoples of the world separate and powerless."[58] The expression "people of color" is based on the assumption of a commonality in the situation of peoples world over who are victims of white supremacy, while the term "women of color" presupposes an added reality of patriarchal oppression. Bandarage further states that these political-class identities provide "a unifying conceptual formula and a direction for political organizing."[59]

In 1988, a commission of political, business, educational, and civic leaders confirmed the shared status of people of color in the United States. Its report, "One-Third of a Nation," cited that widening gaps persist between people of color and the majority population "in education, employment, income, health, longevity and other basic measures of individual and social well-being."[60] In a similar vein, women of color have pointed to the common plight of people of color internationally, victimized by nuclear weapons and militarism. Such being the case, African-American activist Lenora Fulani, speaking in Britain, stated that "the international movement for disarmament and nonintervention, while supported by many peace-loving people, must be and will be led by people of color."[61]

As a power group in the United States, people of color are, through the practice of struggle, inverting the former, negative connotations associated with the terminology ("of color"). One example of their force for change was the successful election of the late Harold Washington, Chicago's first Black mayor (in 1983). Another is Kitchen Table: Women of Color Press, the only publishing firm owned and operated by women of color, which continues to print and make available the diverse histories, cultures, and ideas of people of the colonial experience—indigenous people, descendants of slaves, and migrants and settlers and their descendants.

In the last two decades, the internationalizing of Black political-class has stirred the energies of other oppressed groups, bringing the world face-to-face with the manifold oppressions of the human experience, including those not based on white supremacy and not solely exhibited in economic relations. Lorde cites those "movements for change among women, other peoples of Color, gays, the handicapped—among all the disfranchised peoples of . . . society."[62] Although Malcolm's death predated the birth of these movements (including the United States Black Power Movement itself!), he foresaw the problematic nature of Black nationalism from an international perspective.

Responding to a question on the definition of Black nationalism in an interview just months before he was killed in early 1965, Malcolm revealed how a conversation in 1964 with the Algerian ambassador to Ghana, Taher Gaid, had made him recognize that the concept of Black nationalism excluded oppressed people of Algeria, Morocco, Egypt, Iran, and Mauritania. In fact, it alienated these "people who were true revolutionaries dedicated to overturning the system of exploitation that exists on this earth."[63] He further stated:

> So I had to do a lot of thinking and reappraising of my definition. Can we sum up the solution to the problems confronting our people as black nationalism? And, if you notice, I haven't been using the expression for several months. But I still would be hard-pressed to give a specific definition of the overall philosophy which I think is necessary for the liberation of the black people in this country.[64]

As Malcolm appreciated, the substance of Black political-class had significant meaning to other peoples whose unique histories or oppressions (as religious, cultural, or multiracial national groups, for example) precluded their adoption of Black political-class. Black nationalism was smaller than the times. Subsequently referring to political-class movements of the oppressed as those for "self-determination," instead of for Black nationalism, Malcolm was gone before he could define the comprehensive philosophy to implement his spiritual insights: "It takes *all* of the religious, political, economic, psychological and racial ingredients, or characteristics, to make the Human Family and the Human Society complete."[65]

## Wild Women in the Whirlwind

The overall philosophy of Black liberation for which Malcolm searched in his final days takes shape in the ongoing movement of Black women intercontinentally. They have sought to extend the body politic of Black nationalism to other oppressions not specific to race, and to develop an even broader frame for political-class movement. This motion, which aims to address biological life, the standard of living, and their ways of life, motivates Black women's continual redefinition of self as Azanians, indigenous people, feminists, and people and women of color.

Culture being the only real expression of human existence, the derogation and impairment of group character and, consequently, the threatened survival of the group propel Black women to move from being a class *in* itself—a social class, to a class *for* itself—a political class. Both social class and political class are aspects of culture, and oppressed women in either case are responding to what they are in the culture differently. However, Black women are conscious of the need for political power to ensure a future, embodied in the children, which spurs Black women's political-class identification and movement. In global perspective, Black political-class exhibits no particular geographic, racial, ethnic, religious, sexual, phenotypical, or ideological reference point outside of a uniform political opposition to imperialism, namely monopoly capitalism, colonialism, and racism, which relegates Black people to a life-threatening condition.

The political-class consciousness of Black women cross culturally evinces a quintessential unity. As a popular means through which they empower themselves, political-class, most profoundly, expresses a sentiment for autonomy. This moral sensibility demands freedom from social homogenization by means of new economic arrangements and a new definition of the human community. It insists on the reunification of the universe based on the inseparability of body, mind, and spirit, and the interdependence of all living things and life sources, and asserts a will to be self-determining in every situational locus—the home, workplace, community, and broader society. This quest for autonomy ultimately translates as a desire to free culture at the levels of the group and the individual.

The universal import of Black women's political-class action lies in both its political premise and its intrinsic sentiment for autonomy. The battle against multiple jeopardy—that is, the international and national divisions of labor with all their attendant configurations, including racialism, sexism, ethnocentrism, colorism, sectarianism, regionalism, and caste—embodies the struggle of and for humanity. The modern epoch also brings to light the contest for freedom of culture—that is, real existence: from the Tibetans in China to the Eritreans in Ethiopia, the Basque in Spain to the Kurds in Iraq, the French Canadians to the Sikhs in India, and many other peoples. The struggle for autonomy embraces to another degree the world's women who, living under patriarchal domination, seek to liberate their respective women's cultures.

Black women's activism manifests multiple consciousness, indicating a recognition that political class is a demand for the end of oppression *whatever* the basis and, further, that the vision for autonomy is shared by *all* people. Moreover, their contemporaneous political-class identities suggest qualitative change is brought about by the community who opposes domination and not by a 'nationality,' a 'race,' a 'gender,' or an ethnic group per se. Multiply-identified, Black women in various regions of the world are offering a holistic conception of the struggle for social justice and human freedom. This poses another challenge to transcend the vocabulary and limitations of Western language and secularism.

Political-class identity, even as it is necessary to achieve humanhood, obscures the basis of humanhood—culture. For if culture is the commonly real expression of human existence, then, in the final analysis, true human identity will not be based upon social class or political class. This premise makes Fanon's contention ring with import: What does it mean to be Black when the person who created the nigger is losing control of the world?[66] Overcoming domination requires that Black women leave aside the imperialist-derived secularism of Western culture that fragments the universe, including human existence, the struggle for human freedom, and human identity.

To establish a new relationship to the planet and cosmos, Black women are not redefining women-qua-women but redefining themselves in their entirety and, hence, the men, children, Earth, and the universe. By symbolmaking, ideamaking, and worldmaking, they are creators in the preeminent sense. Through this activity, Black women—from Holland to Brazil, South Africa to New Zealand, Britain to the United States, and elsewhere—expose the truths of their existence. Demythified by the intensity of their own actions, they turn Western imagery of Black women and their experiences on its head. Their primary instruments are the traditional world views and fearlessness of their maligned foremothers. Assuming the mantle of the foremothers to regain their lost autonomy, these Wild Women in the Whirlwind make real change in the real world through real means.

With this reassertion of their world-views in tandem with efforts to reorder the world economy, Wild Women in the Whirlwind are attempting to establish a meaningful and nondestructive basis for human interaction and all life's coexistence. In so doing, they reclaim their land, labor, fellow human being, history, language, and culture—elements of humanhood and wholeness. They are receptive to multiple perspectives and concepts of being, cognizant that there is not one truth but many, and, thereby, they represent a humanistic social force. These Black women's proactive connection to the living global community is grounded in the acceptance of the diversity and integrity of life as a means and ends for existence. The political-class movement of Black women conveys that autonomy must be true for all people and that human fulfillment rests in the harmonious integration of all life systems. Their visions instruct that there is only one humanity, one Earth, one cosmos, one reality.

Creating a new identity in the course of creating a new world, Wild Women in the Whirlwind invoke the birth of a new global culture based on an ethos of human liberation and harmony with the universe. In the lyric of Gwendolyn Brooks's prophecy, they urgently impart that

. . . we are the last of the loud.
Nevertheless, live.
conduct your blooming in the noise and whip of the whirlwind.[67]

## Notes

1     Sections of this paper are based on a presentation, "Redefining Parameters for Comparative Research on Black Women," for the Centre for Multicultural Education and the Centre for Research and Education on Gender, the University of London Institute of Education, June 4, 1986.

2     Dorothea Smartt and Val Mason-John, "Black Feminists Organizing on Both Sides of the Atlantic," *Spare Rib: A Women's Liberation Magazine* [London], no. 171 (October 1986), 22.

3     "People of colony" in this context designates peoples who currently are or have formerly been subjugated by European colonialism.

4     For discussion of concerns for homogeneity in the Muslim order as they apply to "the men of low estate," namely African slaves, see Fatna A. Sabbah, "The Omnisexual Woman in Action: Subversion of the Social Order," in *Women in the Muslim Unconscious* (New York: Pergamon Press, 1984).

5     Black Women's Centre, Amsterdam, Holland, letter to attendees of the 1985 Non-Governmental World Meeting of Women in Nairobi, Kenya (n.d.).

6     Niani [Dee Brown], "Black Consciousness vs. Racism in Brazil," *The Black Scholar* 11, no. 3 (January/February 1980), 68.

7     Frantz Fanon, "On National Culture," in *The Wretched of the Earth* (New York: International Publishers, 1968), p. 233.

8     Oliver C. Cox, "The Political Class," in *Caste, Class & Race: A Study in Social Dynamics* (New York: Modern Readers Paperbacks, 1948), pp. 156, 155. In this Chapter 10 of his work, Cox distinguished "political class" and "social class" as two different phenomena. He contended that social class was a type of "social-status system": "Social classes form a system of co-operating conceptual status entities; political classes, on the other hand, do not constitute a system at all, for they are antagonistic." Regarding political class, he said "the designation 'economic class' might have been used, but economic determinants are evidently at the base of social classes also."

9     Ibid., p. 157.

10    Ibid., pp. 154, 155, 159.

11    "Zephania Mothopeng Operated on Illegally," interview with Mama Bebe Mothopeng, wife of PAC founding member Zephania Mothopeng, *Azania Woman* [London] 1, no. 2 (August 1986), 2.

12    Editorial, *Azania Woman* 1, no. 2 (August 1986), 1.

13    Ibid.

14    Dabi Nkululeko, "Books of Women in Azania," *Azania Woman* 1, no. 2 (August 1986), 12–14.

15    Cox, "The Political Class," p. 159.

16    Winnie Mandela, "The Chapter of Dialogue Is Finally Closed: The Political Situation," in *Part of My Soul Went With Him* (New York: W. W. Norton & Company, 1984), p. 126.

17    Ellen Kuzwayo, *Call Me Woman* (San Francisco: Spinsters Ink, 1985), p. 103.

18    Ibid., p. 16.

19    See Nkululeko, "Books of Women," pp. 12–14 and Mandela, "Chapter of Dialogue," pp. 120–123. Nkululeko refers to "traditional African forms of male domination" and a need to examine how "sexes related in pre-capitalist African society." Mandela discusses that, although there is a present need to continue use of the terms "Black" and "White" to describe the social class antagonisms, the South Africa of the future is being created by a multiracial political-class which opposes the dominant political-class.

20    Donna Awatere, *Maori Sovereignty* (Auckland: Broadsheet Magazine, Ltd., 1984), p. 10.

21    Ibid., p. 36.

22    Atareta Poananga, "Colonisation: The Maori Experience and Resistance," a paper presented at the Australia/New Zealand Association of Aboriginal Studies (ANZAAS) Conference, Melbourne, Australia, August 1985, p. 8.

23    Ibid., p. 7.

24    Awatere, *Maori Sovereignty*, p. 45.

25    Poananga, "Colonisation," p. 14.

26    "Nga Iwi O Te Moana-Nui-A-Kiwa," in *Te Hui Oranga* (Otara: Te Reo Oranga O Te Moana-Nui-A-Kiwa, 1984), p. 29.

27    Seona Martin, "Pacific Women Pull Together," *Forum 85* [Nairobi] (July 18, 1985), 10.

28    Awatere, *Maori Sovereignty*, pp. 9, 62, 70, 98.

29    Ibid., p. 9.

30    Ibid., pp. 101, 102.

31    Amina Mamma, "Black Women, the Economic Crisis and the British State," *Feminist Review*, no. 17 (Autumn 1984), 23.

32     Beverley Bryan, Stella Dadzie, and Suzanne Scafe, *Heart of the Race: Black Women's Lives in Britain* (London: Virago Press, 1985), p. 210.

33     Shabnam Grewal, Jackie Kay, Liliane Landor, Gail Lewis, and Pratibha Parmar, eds., *Charting the Journey: Writings by Black and Third World Women* (London: Sheba Feminist Publishers, 1988), pp. 1, 4.

34     Bryan et al., *Heart of the Race,* p. 170.

35     A. Sivinandan, "From Resistance to Rebellion," in *A Different Hunger: Writings on Black Resistance* (London: Pluto Press, 1982), p. 21.

36     Gail Hart, "Remembering OWAAD," *Woman of Power* [Cambridge], no. 4 (Fall 1986), 63.

37     Parita Trivedi, "To Deny Our Fullness: Asian Women in the Making of History," *Feminist Review,* no. 17 (Autumn 1984), 43, 44.

38     Mamma, "Black Women," p. 24.

39     Carmen, Gail, Shaila, and Pratibha, "Becoming Visible: Black Lesbian Discussions," *Feminist Review,* no. 17 (Autumn 1984), 87.

40     Bryan et al., *Heart of the Race,* p. 201.

41     Da Choong, Olivette Cox Wilson, Bernadine Evaristo, and Gabriela Pearse, eds., *Black Womantalk Poetry* (London: Black Womantalk, 1987), pp. 11, 12.

42     Carmen et al., "Becoming Visible," p. 67.

43     Grewal et al., *Charting the Journey,* p. 5.

44     Mamma, "Black Women," p. 25.

45     Don Quinn Kelley, "History of the Black Liberation Struggle, 1712–1982," paper presented at Medgar Evers College of the City University of New York, Martin Luther King, Jr. Memorial Conference, Brooklyn, January 14, 1984.

46     Sivinandan, "Black Power and Black Culture," in *A Different Hunger,* p. 55.

47     "Malcolm X on Afro-American History," in *Malcolm X on Afro-American History* (New York: Pathfinder Press, Inc., 1970), p. 16.

48     "The Black Revolution," in *Malcolm X Speaks,* ed. George Breitman (New York: Merit Publishers, 1965), p. 50.

49     Audre Lorde, "Learning from the Sixties," in *Sister Outsider* (Trumansburg, N.Y.: The Crossing Press, 1984), p. 141.

50     Dorothy Sterling, *We Are Your Sisters: Black Women in the Nineteenth Century* (New York: W. W. Norton & Company, 1984), p. x.

51     Assata Shakur, *Assata: An Autobiography* (Westport, Conn.: Lawrence Hill & Company, 1987), p. 139.

52     Gloria I. Joseph and Jill Lewis, *Common Differences: Conflicts in Black and White Feminist Perspectives* (Garden City, N.Y.: Anchor Press/ Doubleday, 1981), p. 274.

53      Shakur, *Assata,* p. 175.

54      Assata Shakur, "Women in Prison: The Way We Are," *The Black Scholar* 9, no. 7 (April 1978), 15.

55      Barbara Smith, ed., "Introduction," in *Home Girls: A Black Feminist Anthology* (Albany, N.Y.: Kitchen Table/Women of Color Press, 1983), p. xxix.

56      Gwendolyn Brooks, "Familyhood," an open letter, January 1989.

57      The term Third World, although European in origin, has been widely used to identify peoples and nations that suffered histories of western colonial exploitation. Today, as the colonial era recedes, the term is increasingly the object of scrutiny, criticism, and rejection by those it identifies.

58      Asoka Bandarage, "Women of Color: Towards a Celebration of Power," *Woman of Power,* no. 4 (Fall 1986), 8.

59      Ibid.

60      "Commitment to Minorities Fading in U.S., Study Says," *New York Times,* Late City Edition, May 24, 1988, Sec. A, p. 16, col. 4, 5.

61      Iqbal Wahhab, "First Black Woman to Run for U.S. Presidency," *African Times* [London] (July 31, 1987), 15.

62      Lorde, "Learning from the Sixties," p. 138.

63      *Malcolm X Speaks,* p. 212.

64      Ibid., pp. 212, 213.

65      Malcolm X and Alex Haley, *The Autobiography of Malcolm X* (New York: Grove Press, Inc., 1964), p. 375.

66      Fanon, "On National Culture," p. 234.

67      Gwendolyn Brooks, "Second Sermon on the Warpland," in *In the Mecca* (New York: Harper & Row, 1964); *Blacks* (Chicago: The David Company, 1987), p. 456.

# Régine Altagrâce Latortue

# In Search of Women's Voice: The Woman Novelist in Haiti

H aiti is the first Black republic of the Western Hemisphere, and the second country—after the United States—to achieve nationhood in the Americas. Yet, from the War of Independence (1791–1803), "the first time a Napoleonic army had ever been defeated, a fact still carefully kept out of French history school books"[1] to the aftermath (in 1986) of the Duvalier era and the *tonton macout,* which fulfilled the Western media's penchant for sensationalism, the image of Haiti has been largely negative. Further, the Hollywood image of the *vodun* religion, with its macabre and unrealistic associations, reinforced this image in the Western imagination. Haiti's literature has been similarly misunderstood, or worse, simply ignored, although Haitians have published more books per capita since the beginning of the nineteenth century than any other country in the Americas, except the United States.[2]

The Haitian writer is caught in a web of paradox that involves problems of language, literacy, socio-political change, and cultural identity. Her work is accessible primarily to the small, educated, French-speaking elite. This dilemma is complicated by the fact that even when the writer uses Créole, the language spoken by the entire population, the massive illiteracy of the Haitian makes the vernacular as transcribed into written language inaccessible to the general public. Moreover, the writer who raises issues that suggest socio-political change is confronted with the contradiction of message and audience—that is, her readers are precisely the group most heavily invested in preserving the status quo. No longer is the problem that of writing in French but, rather, the problem of the relationship of writer to audience. No longer is it a question of Haitian writers adopting a certain tradition or form of literature which reflects or imposes the sensibilities of different history and culture, namely French. Generations of Haitian writers have incorporated into their texts the spoken language and the cultural national experiences of the Haitian people. Nevertheless, the problem of literacy appears to be overwhelming.

More than the poet or the playwright, the novelist in Haiti is isolated because of a limited audience. Whereas the poet can theoretically reach a large audience by having her poems set to music and popularized, as illustrated by the immortality of Oswald Durand's "Choucoune" (1869)—which has been well rendered in English by Harry Belafonte's "Yellow Bird"—and whereas the playwright, through the audio-visual art of the stage, can also reach the masses, as attests the popularity of Frankétienne's last play *Pélin tèt* (1978), the Haitian novelist, whether writing in French or in Créole, must rely on the small fringe of the population that can read and makes up most of the elite.

An investigation of the woman in the Haitian narrative confirms that women are characterized according to a class ideology, which is not surprising considering that the novel in Haiti has always been strongly anchored in the "realist" tradition. Predictably, in the Haitian novel, women are depicted differently according to the gender of the writer. The male writers, by social precedence and numerical dominance, have charted the imaginative landscape in which the female writer lives and writes. In the novels of the male writers, the woman is rarely the major protagonist. In those instances, she remains merely the projection of an ideology created by male bourgeois society. She is most often depicted either as "l'ange" (the peasant and proletarian woman, the passive bourgeoise) or "la bête" (the bourgeoise, when she is not passive as she is supposed to be). However, women writers have begun to assume their own voice and to create their own authority through the text in Haiti. Unable to find female representations in which they could locate meaning and identity within the literature of their country, they rightly deduced they had to create their own, and they have earned their rightful place in the literary canon of their country by creating often unconventional but always rich and diverse Black female characters with pivotal roles.

## L'Ange—The Amazon

In the physical descriptions of Haitian women, certain clichés, certain terms and images recur frequently. They fall into two clear categories depending on whether the woman character is from the poorer classes or from the middle and upper classes. This uniformity with which only two representative types of Haitian women, each endowed with a physical appearance which remains essentially subordinate to their class in society, are described, leads to some interesting conclusions. All the more so since it is closely linked to the role the woman character is destined to play in the novel.

The phenomenon of color and how it affects the protagonists' self-perception and perception by others is also equally important. The "angel" is generally a dark-skinned peasant or proletarian woman: she has "la peau noire très fine" ("a very fine dark skin") like Annaise in Jacques Roumain's *Gouverneurs de la rosée* (1944; translated by Mercer Cooke and Langston Hughes as *Masters of the Dew,* 1947), or "la peau d'un noir riche" ("a rich dark skin") like Claire-Heureuse in Jacques Stephen Alexis's *Compère Général Soleil* (1955). These women enjoy a special rapport with nature, a rapport inaccessible to man. In fact, they are nature itself; they connote the Mother Earth image, like Céline in Roger Savain's *La Case de Damballah* (1939), with her "black skin, soft like a tropical night": "Céline était une belle négresse, saine et forte. Fruit incestueux des grands pins et de la terre brune et grasse, elle avait leur parfum et leur sauvage luxuriance."[3] ("Céline was a beautiful black woman, healthy and strong. Incestuous fruit of the tall pine trees and the brown and rich soil, she had their perfume and savage luxuriance.")[4] For Hilarion in *Compère Général Soleil,* Claire-Heureuse is "la fraicheur d'un matin d'été, la douceur d'une eau limpide. Tout était naturel, la façon dont ils avaient fait l'amour, sa démarche dans les rues de Carrefour."[5] ("[Claire-Heureuse was] the freshness of a summer morning, the softness of clear water. Everything was natural with her, the way they had made love, her walk in the streets of Carrefour.") In fact, woman becomes synonymous with nature, the earth in particular. In *Masters of the Dew,* "the earth's just like a good woman: if you mistreat her, she revolts."[6] Women are perpetually compared to flowers, trees, the earth, fruits, food. For Viejo in Maurice Casséus's *Viejo* (1935) for instance, his lover Olive is "cette nourriture servie à son appétit tous les soirs . . . c'était la nourriture secrète qui entretenait sa vie, l'amplifiait."[7] ("[Olive was] the nourishment served to his appetite every night; . . . it was the secret nourishment which fed his life, amplified it.") Commenting on this recurring motif, Léon-François Hoffman aptly remarks that the sexual symbolic identifies the fruit one eats with the woman one possesses, the act of eating becomes one of possession.[8]

Further, these women are tall, strong, robust, true amazons with "des dures mains de travailleuses" ("strong, hard-working hands") like those of Claire-Heureuse and Zétrenne in *Compère Général Soleil* or Annaise in *Masters of the Dew,* where we witness the following exchange between Annaise and her future lover Manuel: "He took her hand. She tried to withdraw it, but she had no strength: 'You're a hard worker, one would say.' 'Yes,' she said proudly, 'my hands are rough.'"[9]

Young or old, these women are strong, work hard all their lives, and have a powerful instinct for survival. In fact, just as woman becomes synonymous with nature, strength becomes synonymous with beauty, and indeed, at times, strength transcends beauty. Here are Hilarion's reflections about Claire-Heureuse as she faces the daily trials and tribulations of proletarian life in Haiti, following her *plaçage* (common-law marriage) with him in *Compère Général Soleil:*

> Claire-Heureuse s'était bien débattue, toute fatiguée, toute enceinte qu'elle était. Elle avait lutté comme une vraie négresse d'Haiti, de toutes ses forces. Dans ce combat quotidien, sa petite bouche violacée s'était pincée, ses yeux s'étaient entourés d'un cerne gris, son sourire commençait à s'écorcher, sa peau à se ternir, mais sa beauté n'en était que plus forte, plus humaine, moins céleste.[10]

> (Although tired and pregnant, Claire-Heureuse had struggled valiantly. She had fought like a real Haitian black woman, with all her strength. In this daily struggle, her little purple mouth had become tight, her eyes were bordered with a grey circle, her smile had be-

come tight-lipped, her skin dull and lifeless, but her beauty was only stronger, more human, less heavenly.)

This physical strength reveals itself to be a moral and spiritual force qualifying the peasant and proletarian women as well. The image of Mother Earth mentioned above is particularly apropos when one realizes that the most important domestic role of woman in the Haitian novel is that of mother. Often, she gives birth on the side of the road, on the way to the market which is several kilometers away from her home, and proceeds to the market on the same day she gives birth, like Céline in *La Case de Damballah* who cannot afford the luxury of staying home, even on such an occasion, for "que voulez-vous? Pouvait-elle, pauvre négresse, jouer à la bourgeoise?"[11] ("What do you want? Could she, a poor negress, pretend to be a bourgeoise?") The peasant and proletarian woman usually becomes a devoted mother, the sole breadwinner of her family, who sacrifices herself for the sake of her children. Examples abound: Madame George in Antoine Innocent's *Mimola* (1906), Thémistocle's mother in Frédéric Marcelin's *Thémistocle Epaminondas Labasterre* (1901), Mansia in Paulette Poujol-Oriol's *Le Creuset* (1980). Julie Legros in Roger Dorsainville's *Mourir pour Haiti* (1980) "avait embrassé la vie sans amour, on pourrait dire presque sans joie, comme un immense et incompréhensible devoir au sein duquel figurait un devoir précis: élever ce fils."[12] ("[Julie Legros] had embraced life without love, one could almost say without joy, like an immense and incomprehensible duty in the midst of which figured a precise duty: bring up this son.") And Lamercie in Marie-Thérèse Colimon's *Fils de misère* (1974) commits the greatest, noblest sacrifice: she gives up her life in order to save her son whom she believes to be in mortal danger.

## La Bête—The Bourgeoise

In the stereotype of "la bête," the woman is usually bourgeoise—an upper-middle- or upper-class woman—a golden-skinned mulatto, like Madeleine in *Viejo*, characterized by "une peau d'or où dans le filigrane naissaient les veines d'un beau vert fané"[13] ("a golden skin where the veins of a beautiful faded green appeared in the filigree"). The bourgeoise is not compared to nature like the peasant and proletarian woman. In *Compère Général Soleil,* Hilarion thinks that Domenica Betances resembles "une vieille *Mater Dolorosa* de bois polychrome" ("an old *Mater Dolorosa* of polychromatic wood"). He finds her "glaçant" (chilly, icy), to be contrasted with "the freshness of a summer morning, the softness of clear water" which characterizes Claire-Heureuse in the same novel. In Colimon's *Fils de misère* Mlle. Réza Régulier is a "light form," a "ghost," a "shadow." Her body is "asexual, sexless": "Son visage blême avait la pâleur des cierges qui garnissaient la table sainte et semblait pétri de la même cire."[14] ("Her sallow face was as pale as the candles which garnished the holy altar and seemed moulded from the same wax.") Madeleine's fingers in *Viejo* are also compared to candles, "luxurious little candles."

Generally speaking, the bourgeoises are gracious, thin, elegant, not strong and robust like the peasant and proletarian women. They have soft, elegant hands, like those of Madeleine, "long, artistic fingers." The soft hands of the bourgeoises immediately reveal their social class. Here are the thoughts that assail Hilarion as he contemplates Domenica's hands: "S'il avait quelque chose de clair en lui, c'était la conscience des oppositions de classe, une méfiance invincible contre une certaine sorte de vêtements, contre la finesse et le soigné de certaines mains."[15] ("If one thing was very clear to him, it was the consciousness of class oppositions, an invincible distrust of a certain sort of clothes, of certain polished, well-groomed hands.") In Jean-Baptiste Cinéas' *L'Héritage Sacré,* (1945), the *houngan* (priest of the *vodun* religion) Aïza Cédieu, simply by examining the "soft hand" of his veiled client, realizes that "such an inaccessible princess" would never accept the love of a mere *houngan*.

> Ah! la douceur perfide de ces mains! Ces mains fines, nerveuses, d'une élegante maigreur! Le délicat fuseau de ces doigts! Ces ongles, naturellement beaux, soignés avec coquetterie, rosés avec goût, sans excès.[16]

> Ah! the misleading softness of these hands! These fine, sinewy, elegantly thin hands! These fingers so delicately tapered! These nails, naturally beautiful, so coquettishly finished, polished with taste, without excess.

Soft, delicate, well-groomed hands, unlike the peasant and proletarian women, because the bourgeoises do not work. Since their maids take care of the housework, they are free to spend idle, care-free lives in a world where clothes, jewelry, and the way one looks take precedence over everything else. For instance, in Annie Desroys' *Le Joug* (1934):

> Dès huit heures du matin, [Fernande] était libre d'employer à son gré ses longues matinées. . . . Fernande, gâtée par un mari laborieux, passait son temps à confectionner ces brimborions charmants qui occupent les mains de toute jolie femme sans empêcher cependant les idées de vaguer.[17]

> (From eight a.m. on, [Fernande] was free to spend her days as she pleased. . . . Spoiled by an industrious husband, Fernande spent her time manufacturing these charming knick-knacks which keep busy the hands of every beautiful woman while her thoughts wander aimlessly.)

Félicia in Marie Chauvet's *Amour, colère et folie* (1968) is similarly portrayed: "Comme toutes les femmes indolentes, elle est plutôt partisane du laisser-aller, et croit tout régler en brodant inlassablement la layette de son futur enfant."[18] ("Like all idle women, she is rather slovenly, and thinks she is putting everything in order by tirelessly embroidering the layette of her future child.")

Nevertheless, the principal domestic role of the bourgeoisie is also that of mother. However, generally, the bourgeoise has a difficult pregnancy, unlike Céline in *La Case de Damballah,* or Délira, Manuel's mother, in *Masters of the Dew,* who both continue to work the same day they give birth. In *Amour, colère et folie,* Claire, who is jealous of her sister Félicia, is enchanted by the latter's terrible physical appearance when pregnant:

> La grossesse dessert Félicia . . . Elle est décidément allergique à cet état . . . Sa mine cadavérique fait peine à voir. . . . Elle est squelettique . . . elle a l'air d'une condamnée. . . . Félicia est si pâle qu'elle a l'air d'une morte.[19]

> (Pregnancy is really unflattering to Félicia. . . . She is decidedly allergic to that state. . . . Her cadaverous face is pitiful to see . . . She looks like a skeleton . . . she looks like a doomed woman. . . . Felicia is as pale as a dead woman.)

In Colimon's *Fils de misère,* Mme. Ledestin becomes so cantankerous when she finds out she is expecting another baby that, on a whim, she fires the heroine Lamercie, thus depriving the latter of her only means of support for her own son.

The bourgeoise is supposed to be passive, devoted to her husband and her children, like Mme. Ledestin who ignores the infidelities of her husband and treats him as a child, or Mme. Roumel in *Compère Général Soleil,* who returns tirelessly each day to the prison where her son is incarcerated, asking for permission to see him, a permission always denied. Unlike the peasant and proletarian women, however, the bourgeoises are rarely able to assist their children. Mme. Catullus Pernier Alcibiade of Jean-Baptiste Cinéas's *Le Choc en retour* (1948), Mme. Normil of Chauvet's *Amour, colère et folie,* and Mme. Labédoyère of Colimon's *Le Chant des sirènes* (1976) remain powerless when faced with their husbands' financial ruin and the corollary bleak future of their children. Or else, if they do act, it is only to guarantee the unhappiness of their children. The bourgeoise then truly becomes "la bête." The blond Christiane Landsfeld in Poujol-Oriol's *Le Creuset,* for instance, manages things so well that her daughter Mica can no longer marry the young man she loves, a dark-skinned doctor whose grandmother was a market woman. As a result, her daughter Mica, disabused and cynical, becomes a member of the international jet set and follows the model proposed by her mother. Living in Europe and alienated from all things Haitian, she marries and divorces at an accelerated rate, neglecting her only son Paul who resides in Haiti, and knows of her only through a letter from his aunt: "Ta mère a divorcé trois ans après ta naissance, te laissant à ton père et te voyant entre deux avions."[20] ("Your mother divorced your father three years after your birth, leaving you with your father, and only seeing you between the arrival and departure times of two planes.")

## The Woman Novelist in Haiti

This stereotypical depiction of the woman does not necessarily reflect the mirror image the bourgeoise holds of herself, and certainly not that of the peasant and proletarian woman who has yet to write her-story in Haiti. On the other hand, the woman writer has, in

Haiti, been in quest of the bourgeoise's own story, and has attempted to shatter the mirror that has so long reflected what she was supposed to be. Even though the earlier works of Haitian women novelists, such as Annie Desroys' *Le Joug* (1934) and Cléanthe Valcin's *La Blanche Négresse* (1934), follow the model proposed by the male writers, in general, the more recent women writers reveal their authorial anger and their frustration directed against the patriarchal institutions which they see as governing their lives. Even when they do not openly criticize these institutions, they invariably create characters who do and therefore act out the authors' own repressed or hidden anger.

The actions (overt and covert, passive or violent) and silence of the major female protagonists encode a system of accommodation and resistance in their domestic and social roles, an opposition between "l'ange et la bête," or between "the angel in the house" and "the madwoman in the attic" as Sandra Gilbert and Susan Gubar argue in *The Madwoman in the Attic* (1976). Further, even apparent accommodation is often a mask for more covert rebellion, and the heroines ultimately escape into neurotic or antisocial behavior.

Contemporary women novelists almost obsessively give birth to female characters who seek to escape their predictable fate in Haitian society and rebel against the status quo. Marie-Ange in Marie Chauvet's *Fonds-des-Nègres* (1960) is rebellious to the point of nearing mental derangement. She feels entrapped by the life of the peasants that she is forced to share and by the rigid cultural traditions outlined for her by her grandmother and the "papa," the patriarchal *houngan* of the community. But she is eventually forced to resign herself and to adapt to her situation, if only for the sake of physical survival. Mansia's very conformity in Paulette Poujol-Oriol's *Le Creuset* constitutes in itself a revolt against the status quo: she escapes in the norm, devoting herself self-sacrificingly to her family, which eventually leads to an early demise. All the female protagonists of Marie-Thérèse Colimon's *Le Chant des sirènes* escape from their society for the promise of a freer life abroad, in the United States—the promised land. Colimon's Lamercie in *Fils de misère* rebels and dies challenging the army representative of the oppressive male forces of her society.

In fact, the world presented to us in this novel is a closed female universe, where the men appear only briefly to spread disaster. All the female protagonists are victims, in one way or another, of the men in power: Mme. Ledestin, the bourgeois wife and mother, harried and subject to the whims of her frustrated husband, an ex-secretary of state; Mlle. Régulier, the upper-class spinster who never recovered from the loss of her fiancé, killed twenty years earlier in a political demonstration against the government one month before their wedding date, and who has consequently become a religious fanatic; Ti-Tante, the young single peasant woman, who barely after her arrival in the capital city of Port-au-Prince, is dismissed by her aunt Lamercie because of her liaison with Sergeant Pierrélus; and finally, the single proletarian mother, the major protagonist, Lamercie, killed by Sergeant Pierrélus who had sworn to avenge himself of the insults hurled at him by Lamercie.

Often, the heroines adopt the first-person narrative, suggesting a clear *dédoublement* between author and heroine. Annie in Nadine Magloire's *Le Sexe mythique* (1975) angrily and openly voices her frustration at and rejection of the sexual double standard of the society. Significantly, "Annie" is an almost perfect acronym of the author's first name.

Annie is a liberated woman, economically independent, a mathematics teacher, who has chosen not to marry, and is determined not to follow the conventional path proposed for the young bourgeoise, either as wife or mistress: "L'homme devait l'accepter comme une partenaire à part entière et égale"[21] ("A man had to accept her completely and equally as his partner"), she declares. Annie's lover, Frantz, is married, and as he is unable to be with her on a regular basis, Annie decides to take a second lover—Yves, a young, pedantic and pretentious diplomat. Although she dissolves that affair soon thereafter, Annie realizes that for her emotional well-being, she will have to maintain two relationships simultaneously, but she regrets the fact that she cannot confide in Frantz, for, in Haiti:

Il fallait accepter la règle du jeu. Un homme peut tromper sa femme ouvertement mais la proposition ne s'inverse pas. La femme, par un décret prétendu naturel, se doit de n'appartenir qu'à un seul mâle.[22]

(One had to accept the rules of the game. A man could openly be unfaithful to his wife, but the proposition could not be reversed. Woman, according to an allegedly natural decree, can only mate with one male.)

In *Amour, colère et folie,* Marie Chauvet exposes brilliantly and subtly the utter powerlessness of the bourgeoises, unable to control their own lives because of the sexual double standard of a color-conscious society. They are consequently forced to direct and rechannel their energies in other ways which abort and become fruitless due to their inherent frustrations.

Not only is Claire, the heroine, telling her story in the first person, clearly the author's double, Claire herself is aware of her own double nature. She is quite conscious that the image she carefully constructs for "the other" is not at all a reflection of her true self: "Vais-je porter toute ma vie ce masque étouffant?" ("Will I wear this stifling mask all my life?") Looking at herself in the mirror—her mirror image—she ponders:

Je me découvre, surprise, un faciès asymétrique: Profil gauche, rêveur, tendre; profil droit, sensuel, féroce. Est-ce moi ou ce que je vois de moi? Mes mains aussi me semblent tout à coup, dissemblables; celle faite pour agir, plus épaisse, plus lourde.[23]

(Surprised, I discover unsymmetrical features: left profile, dreamy, tender; right profile, sensuous, ferocious. Is it me or the way I see myself? My hands too seem suddenly dissimilar; the one made to act, thicker, heavier.)

Claire is a thirty-nine-year-old spinster, tired of "ce sexe, vierge et rance entre mes cuisses" ("this virgin and rancid sex between my legs"), obsessed by her dark skin color which clashes in the tight circle of light-skinned mulattoes frequented by her family. She is jealous of her two younger sisters, Félicia and Annette, "des mulâtresses-blanches" ("white mulattoes"). As a child, she is constantly punished by her father who sees his "white" blood "in regression" in the dark color of his daughter. As a young woman, she falls in love with a young impoverished mulatto, Frantz Camuse, but the observations of her parents and other relatives about the prospective union create such complexes that Claire refuses to marry Frantz, convinced he could only want her because of her father's financial situation and prestigious position in society. Claire, whose very name is ironic as it means "light," begins to hate the black ancestor whom she sees as responsible for her present plight, a situation which eventually culminates in self-hatred.

Living in a restricted, small-town, aristocratic milieu, Claire is dark skinned when she is supposed to be light skinned, is unmarried when she is supposed to be a wife and mother, according to the dictates of her society. She is offered no positive mirror image from her mother, has no female bonding, no artistic outlet, no place—except for the confining space of her home, the space of the woman *par excellence*. She is therefore frustrated to the point of madness and her neurotic attempts to escape her confinement lead her to criminality.

For Claire, at thirty-nine, is determined to make up for her lost youth and the happiness she feels has escaped her. Envious of her sister Felicia's French husband, "the handsome Jean-Luze," she tries to instigate an affair between Jean-Luze and her youngest sister Annette, an affair that she intends to experience vicariously. When this plan fails, Claire decides to kill Félicia in order to marry the grieving widower herself. Significantly, she prepares to murder Félicia with a dagger—supreme phallic symbol—given her by Jean-Luze. However, at the decisive moment, she finds herself unable to murder her own sister. Disgusted with herself at what she considers to be a weakness in her character, she decides to kill herself with the dagger. Ultimately, a rapid succession of events cause her to kill someone else instead, namely Calédu, the newly appointed chief of police, and the representative of the terrorist regime.

Calédu's job is precisely to keep society in check, to control and limit the actions of the members of the community. A sadist whose name, in Créole, means "the one who beats hard" (*calé* means to beat; *du* means hard), Calédu is particularly hard and vengeful against the ladies of the "haute bourgeoisie," especially those who, like Claire, refuse to recognize him as their equal and persist in snubbing him. He has arrested and beaten several of them so severely between the legs that none can have sexual intercourse anymore. Thus, he deprives them not only of their womanhood but of their ability to give birth as well. He is the external, concrete symbol of the upper-class woman's oppression, and he embodies for Claire the dictates of a society blatantly favorable to men, which declares that a dark-skinned woman is often not attractive and that an honest woman should not enjoy sex outside of marriage . . . or even inside of it.

In this instance, Claire is both the victim and the executioner. Although she hates and fears Calédu who is as dark-skinned as she is, she nevertheless has vivid erotic dreams every night, in which she couples with a faceless man whose body is reminiscent of Calédu's, and not Jean-Luze's, although he had been the previous protagonist of those dreams.

As Claire is about to plunge the dagger into her breast, the yells of a mob make her pause. Just then, she sights Calédu being cornered by a horde of famished, angry beggars, and being driven accidentally to her house. She swiftly opens the door, and plunges the dagger destined for herself in Calédu's back. He struggles back to the street and dies. By turning the dagger against Calédu, she turns it against its proper target, against the forces which have denied her, and women like her, freedom, erotic dignity, and full womanhood.

This act which constitutes the dénouement of the novel exorcises Claire's frustrations to such a point that she is even rid of her obsession for Jean-Luze, sole witness of her crime, who now finds himself irremediably attracted to her. At the end of the novel, Claire has at least achieved self-respect and appreciation.

Gilbert and Gubar contend in *The Madwoman in the Attic* that the madwoman in women's fiction is often the author's double, and that the madwoman's violence expresses the author's own anxiety and rage in her attempts to escape from male texts.[24] Indeed, Haitian women authors encode covert rebellion, anger, and resistance in characters who appear to accept what society has prescribed for them. They have achieved their own authority through the text to finally give voice to the experience of being black and female in a world dominated by European middle-class ideology. Yet the intent of Marie Chauvet and other contemporary Haitian women novelists is not to glorify individual action per se, but to point out the inequities of color and gender that trigger the individualistic, (self-)destructive reactions of their protagonists.

## Notes

1    Léon-François Hoffmann, *Essays on Haitian Literature* (Washington, D.C.: Three Continents Press, 1984), pp. 5–6.

2    Edmund Wilson, *Red, Black, Blond and Olive* (New York: Oxford University Press, 1956), p. 110.

3    Roger Savain, *La Case de Damballah* (Port-au-Prince: Imprimerie de l'Etat, 1939), p. 15.

4    Except where otherwise indicated, all translations are mine, and strive for exactitude rather than elegance.

5    Jacques Stephen Alexis, *Compère Général Soleil* (Paris: Gallimard, 1955), pp. 79–80.

6    Jacques Roumain, *Masters of the Dew,* translated from the French, *Gouverneurs de la rosée* (Port-au-Prince: Imprimerie de l'Etat, 1944) by Mercer Cooke and Langston Hughes (New York: Macmillan, 1947, 1971), p. 45.

7    Maurice Casséus, *Viejo* (Port-au-Prince: Imprimerie de l'Etat, 1935), pp. 55, 58.

8    Léon-François Hoffmann, "L'Image de la femme dans la poésie haïtienne," *Présence Africaine,* #34–35, 1960–61, p. 201.

9    Roumain, *Masters,* p. 83.

10   Alexis, *Compère Général,* p. 199.

11   Savain, *La Case de Damballah,* p. 12.

12   Roger Dorsinville, *Mourir pour Haiti* (Paris: L'Harmattan, 1980), p. 114.

13   Casséus, *Viejo,* p. 69.

14   Marie-Thérèse Colimon, *Fils de misère* (Paris: Editions de l'Ecole, Port-au-Prince: Editions Caraïbes, 1974), p. 22.

15   Alexis, *Compère Général,* pp. 291–93.

16   Jean-Baptiste Cinéas, *L'Héritage Sacré* (Port-au-Prince: Editions Henri Deschamps, 1945), p. 148.

17   Annie Desroys, *Le Joug* (Port-au-Prince: Imprimerie Modèle, 1934), p. 15.

18   Marie Chauvet, *Amour, colère et folie* (Paris: Gallimard, 1968), p. 72.

19   *Ibid.,* pp. 160–62 and 172–73.

20   Paulette Poujol-Oriol, *Le Creuset* (Port-au-Prince: Editions Henri Deschamps, 1980), p. 184.

21   Nadine Magloire, *Le Sexe mythique* (Port-au-Prince: Editions du Verseau, 1973), p. 56.

22   *Ibid.,* p. 47.

23   Chauvet, *Amour,* p. 185.

24   Sandra Gilbert and Susan Gubar, *The Madwoman in the Attic: The Woman Writer and the Nineteenth-Century Literary Imagination* (New Haven: Yale University Press, 1976), pp. 78, 85.

# Calvin Hernton

## The Sexual Mountain and
## Black Women Writers

> We younger Negro artists who create now intend to express our individual dark-
> skinned selves without fear or shame. If white people are pleased we are glad. If they
> are not, it doesn't matter. We know we are beautiful. And ugly too. The tom-tom
> cries and the tom-tom laughs. If colored people are pleased we are glad. If they are
> not, their displeasure doesn't matter either. We build our temples for tomorrow,
> strong as we know how, and we stand on top of the mountain, free within ourselves.
> —Langston Hughes, "The Negro Artist and the Racial Mountain"

Though black and white men stand on opposing sides of the racial mountain in America, they tread on common ground when it comes to the mountain of sex. Traditionally, the world of black literature in the United States has been a world of black men's literature. The fathers and purveyors of black writing have been men, and the male authors have portrayed male heroes, male protagonists. The complexity and vitality of the black female experience have been fundamentally ignored.

Black women have been involved in the development of Afro-American writing since its inception, yet no pre-twentieth-century black women writers are treated as major contributors to the history of black literature. The back-burner status of female writers persists into the twentieth century too. Despite women writers such as

Effie Lee Newsome, Georgia Douglas Johnson, Anne Spencer, Alice Dunbar-Nelson, Nella Larsen, Jessie Fauset, Dorothy West, Helene Johnson, and others, it has been almost impossible to read the critical works and general history of the New Negro/Harlem Renaissance of the 1920s and get any impression other than that the "New Negroes" were entirely of the male sex. The only female of the period to receive substantial recognition is Zora Neale Hurston—but only as an "oddball" eccentric who wrote folktales and ran around measuring Negro heads. Until recently Hurston's most significant books, *Their Eyes Were Watching God* and *Jonah's Gourd Vine,* were neglected.

Despite the legacy of this double standard, black women, like black men, continued to write through the Depression years on into the 1960s. But unlike men, some of whom rose to heights of literary prominence, the women received the usual secondary treatment. *Native Son* (1940), devoted to the plight of America's black male youth, was and is hailed as a masterpiece, and has remained in print. Ann Petry's 1946 novel *The Street,* devoted to the tragedy of a young black female who is crippled, exploited, and driven to murder by the oppressive misogynous systems of the white *and* black man, seems always to be out of print. Unlike Wright's fiction, Petry's work has, until recently, been known by an increasingly small number of blacks (and whites) since the 1950s.

The same situation has prevailed regarding the works of other black women writers whose female protagonists stand as timeless examples of the autonomous humanity of their sex, such as the transplanted West Indian woman in Paule Marshall's *Brown Girl, Brownstones,* Merle Kinbona in Marshall's *The Chosen Place, The Timeless People,* Mariah Upshur in Sarah Wright's *This Child's Gonna Live,* and Vyry in Margaret Walker's *Jubilee,* the first contemporary slave narrative novel, a portion of which mysteriously found its way into the pages of *Roots.*

Except for Gwendolyn Brooks, and perhaps Margaret Walker, the name of not one black woman writer and not one female protagonist was accorded a worthy status in the black literary world prior to the 1970s. Gwendolyn Brooks was *the* exception. Her age, her numerous prizes and awards and honors from the white literary world, the prestige she *already* had, plus her unquestionable genius, made her, *per force,* the acceptable exception.

Although the 1960s witnessed a plethora of black female writers, especially poets, the legacy of male chauvinism in the black literary world continued to predominate. In fact, during the Black Power/ Black Arts Movement of the 1960s, the unequal recognition and treatment of women writers was enunciated more bigotedly than perhaps ever before. "The only position in the revolution for women is the prone position!" "The women's place is seven feet behind the men!" Pronouncements like these were reflected again and again in the writings, and deeds, of the males of the period. In Stokely Carmichael's and Charles Hamilton's *Black Power: The Politics of Liberation in America,* not one black woman is mentioned significantly, not even Angela Davis. In Harold Cruse's encyclopedic masterpiece *The Crisis of the Negro Intellectual,* about thirty women are mentioned, largely in passing; most are entertainers such as Josephine Baker and Lena Horne. There also occurred, if one remembers, the sudden proliferation of macho pimp films and books, *Superfly, Sweetback, Shaft, Nigger Charlie;* Nathan Heard's *Howard Street* and Iceberg Slim's autobiographical works enjoyed lively sales. During the heyday, moreover, of the Black Power/Black Revolution/Black Arts Movement, one could go through the Black Studies Curriculum and learn all about the Black Experience—and encounter less than a handful of black females.

The first issue of *The Black Scholar* magazine came out in 1969. Entitled "The Culture of Revolution," each of its nine articles was authored by a man. On the inside cover the editorial states:

> A black scholar . . . is a man of both thought and action, a whole man who thinks for his people and acts with them, a man who honors the whole community of black experience, a man who sees the Ph.D., the janitor, the businessman, the maid, the clerk, the militant, as all sharing the same experience of blackness, with all its complexities and its rewards. THE BLACK SCHOLAR is the journal for such a man.

Precisely, black men have historically defined themselves as sole interpreters of the black experience. They have set the priorities, mapped out the strategies, and sought to enforce the rules. Yet, as in the past, black women during the 1960s doggedly continued to write. Just as there were more male writers, there were more women writers than ever before. They found publishers and got read. They made recordings of their works which solid in the tens of thousands. Many of them took to the road, lecturing and reading. A number of them achieved unprecedented recognition. Unmistakably, the recognition was achieved because black women, particularly the poets, consituted a formidable phalanx of the consciousness-raising activities of the 1960s.

The macho philosophy of the Black Power/Black Arts Movement resulted in so many demeaning experiences for the women that many of them began to protest and eventually break away. Older women who had been raising children and servicing husbands all of their lives—Sarah Webster Fabio, for example—began actualizing their talent. In the process they became peers, and teachers of the young. Activists, students, and lone sideliners alike—all joined in what was now a more thorough consciousness of themselves as black women.

Then, in 1970, Toni Cade Bambara published an anthology, *The Black Woman,* in which twenty-seven women writers expressed, according to the jacket notes, "the rising demand by women for liberation from their chattel-like roles in a male-dominated society." Significantly, a preponderance of the writers had backgrounds in the Civil Rights *cum* Black Power Movement. It was this anthology that signaled the decline of the historical inequality of women writers in Afro-American literature.

Today, the women of the 1960s are writing in an increasingly pioneer fashion; among them are Audre Lorde, June Jordan, Vertamae Smart-Grosvenor, Jayne Cortez, Maya Angelou, Ann Shockley, Sonia Sanchez, Alice Walker, and Toni Cade Bambara. Women who were writing before the 1960s, such as Paule Marshall, Gwendolyn Brooks, Margaret Walker, Margaret Danner (1915–1984), and Sarah Wright, broke ground for the generation of the 1960s, and are now griots of song and letters, foremothers of ancient testament and new truths. There are also the women who were around during the 1960s and 1970s, but are just now coming into publication, including Barbara Masekela, Hattie Gossett, Regina Williams, and Barbara Christian; and new black women authors, Thylias Moss, Donna K. Rushin, Hillary Kay, Cheryl Jones, Gloria T. Hull, Patricia Jones, Pat Parker, and Lorraine Bethel are but a few. Their writings exhibit a freshness of style, sensitivity, and language; a boldness of subject and stance;

and a newness of treatment imbued with exciting promise. The works of these women, and many more like them, constitute the celebration of the black women's literary Fourth of July for the first time in the United States.

Though Bambara's *The Black Woman* anthology in 1970 heralded the weakening of male literary dominance over females, it was not until 1978 that the straw which actually broke the billy goat's back appeared in the form of the Broadway production of Ntozake Shange's *for colored girls who have considered suicide when the rainbow is enuf*. In fact, there were two straws, the second being the 1979 publication of Michele Wallace's book *Black Macho and the Myth of the Superwoman*.

## Hell Breaks Loose

Black males took severe offense over the rave reviews Shange's *colored girls* received from the critics who, the blacks said, were mostly Jewish males. Shange, the black men said, was a goddamn traitor to the race. In a time when black men were striving for respect, here comes some middle-class, light-skinned bitch, putting black men down before the eyes of the white world. Resentment was also expressed over Shange's quick rise to fame—off of a bullshit, nothing-ass recitation of some fucking, man-hating poems! Nothing but a ripoff. That's all it was, the men said.

The air had not begun to clear over *colored girls* when *Ms.* magazine hit the newsstands with prepublication excerpts of *Black Macho,* announcing on the cover that Wallace's book would determine the central issue for blacks during the 1980s. A few days later the book topped the bestseller list. The feelings black men expressed about *colored girls* were expressed more widely and more intensely about *Black Macho.* A noticeable number of reactions also came from black women writers, intellectuals, and political activists. Dissent and controversy reigned. June Jordan, reviewing *Macho* in *The New York Times Book Review,* seemed outraged over *Ms.*'s assertion that *Macho* would sound the main issue for blacks in the 1980s. Wallace was to be interviewed by Jordan on a New York radio station. But, according to Wallace's sister, who phoned the station, Wallace became paranoid en route and never arrived.

The mobilization against Wallace, and in the process Shange too, was quick and solid. It came from all sectors of the black population: the press, the literary and scholarly journals and magazines; on black and white college campuses, and in the ghettoes as well. Wallace and Shange were invalidated as writers, scholars, and most of all they were put down as black women. Vernon Jarrett in the *Chicago Defender* equated Shange's play with "that classic pro–Ku Klux Klan achievement of 1915, 'Birth of a Nation'!" Jarrett went on to assert that *colored girls* was, "a degrading treatment of the black male . . . a mockery of the black family." Stanley Crouch wrote in *The Village Voice* that the whites within the media were "promoting a gaggle of black female writers who pay lip service to the women's movement while supplying us with new stereotypes of black men and women." The word went out: White males were using black women as a backlash against the black male's dynamic assertion of manhood during the 1960s. Rumors sizzled: One of the more popular was that some white woman at *Ms.* had actually written Wallace's book, *Black Macho and the Myth of the Superwoman.*

The upshot of the Shange and Wallace affair—which had been generalized to include not only women writers but intellectuals and activists as well—eventuated in the 1979 May/June issue of *The Black Scholar,* "The Black Sexism Debate."

There were seventeen writers and intellectuals represented in the issue—Ron Karenga, Robert Staples, Askia Touré, Harry Edwards, Audre Lorde, June Jordan, Ntozake Shange, Alvin Poussaint, Kalamu ya Salaam, Julianne Malveaux, Sarah Fabio, and Pauline Stone among them. The specific initiative for the "debate" issue had been a review of *Macho,* by Robert Staples, "The Myth of Black Macho: A Response to Angry Black Feminists," in the previous issue of the *Scholar.*

In both issues of the *Scholar,* it was clear that the men were the ones who were angry. They were also less honorable than the women. The words in the title of Staples's review of Wallace's book were twisted and turned against the women. The men claimed that the women had fallen prey to white feminist propaganda. They said that black women, like white women, had been duped into turning against their men. The most truculent assertion was that the writings of black women were "divisive" to the cohesion of the black community.

The men said that black women writers were aiding the white

male-dominated, racist, capitalist society in the historical oppression of black people. Unanimous among the men was the view that instead of making up lies and half-truths about black males, black women should be about the all-important business of exposing and fighting racism and capitalism so that the successful struggle of black men rising to their rightful position of power and dominance in their families, in their communities, and in America in general would be hastened. (A notable exception to black male hostility against *Black Macho* was an endorsement on the book's inside cover by Ishmael Reed, often branded a "male chauvinist," praising the book as "a stunning achievement.")

The resentful emotions that black men feel toward black women writers are due to four unprecedented eventuations: 1) Black women writers are declaring their independence as never before; 2) black women writers are gaining autonomous influence over other black women; 3) black women writers are causing their existence to be seen and felt in areas of American society and culture which have heretofore been barred to them; and 4) black women writers are at last wresting recognition from the white literary powers that be.

The telling thing about the hostile attitude of black men toward black women writers is that they interpret the new thrust of the women as being "counter-productive" to the historical goal of the Black Struggle. Revealingly, while black men have achieved outstanding recognition throughout the history of black writing, black women have not accused the men of collaborating with the enemy and setting back the progress of the race.

## Double Standard

After the publication of *Soul on Ice,* black women did not go berserk denouncing Eldridge Cleaver as an unscholarly, overgeneralizing sensationalist, or as a rapist, hater, and batterer of black women, all of which were and are true. Yet, when Gayl Jones, author of *Eva's Man* and *Corregidora,* or Alice Walker in *The Third Life of Grange Copeland* and *The Color Purple,* or Ann Shockley, author of *Loving Her*—when these and other writers depict the hateful attitudes and violent treatment of black men toward black women, the men accuse these women of being black-men-haters, bull-dykes, and perverse lovers of white men and women.

Black men write a lot about the "castrating" black female and feel righteous in doing so. But when black women write about the incest, rape and sexual violence committed by black men against black females of all ages, and when black women write that black men are castrators and oppressors of black women, black men accuse them of sowing seeds of "division" in the black community. When black male writers write of the brotherhood of black men in the struggle for manhood, this is viewed as manly and fitting. But when black women write about the sisterhood of black women, black men brand them as "feminist bitches."

Too often black men have a philosophy of manhood that relegates women to the back burner. Therefore it is perceived as an offense for black women to struggle on their own, let alone achieve something independently. Thus, no matter how original, beautiful, and formidable the works of black women writers might be, black men become "offended" if such works bear the slightest criticism of them, or if the women receive recognition from other women, especially from the white literary establishment. They do not behave as though something of value has been added to the annals of black literature. Rather, they behave as though something has been subtracted, not only from the literature, but from the entire race, and specifically, from *them*.

One of the most galvanizing examples of this is the hostility most black men have toward Toni Morrison. Morrison has won many prizes and awards. She sits in chairs of mainstream American literary organizations and is often the principal speaker at major literary gatherings. Long-time senior editor at Random House, she has published four highly acclaimed novels, *The Bluest Eye, Sula, Song of Solomon,* and *Tar Baby*. In 1981, articles about Morrison appeared in *The New Republic, Essence, Nation,* the *Soho News, The New York Times Book Review, Vogue,* and other publications, culminating in the March 30th issue of *Newsweek,* on the cover of which appeared Morrison's photograph.

Toni Morrison is among the foremost Afro-American writers of all times. Since she is among the first black women to achieve this kind of status, one would think that black men would be proud of her accomplishments. On the contrary, I have witnessed black men—intellectuals, professors, and writers alike—express resentments against Morrison, ranging from the profound to the most petty. Variously she has been accused of "selling out," of turning back the clock of racial progress, of being a tool of white feminism, of being a black-man-hater, and of engendering sexual immorality among black women.

## Pens as Spades

Meanwhile, there are black women writers—poets, novelists, dramatists, critics, scholars, researchers, intellectuals, politicos, and ideologues—hard at work. They are wielding their pens like spades, unearthing forbidden treasures buried in old soil. They are bringing forth new, uncut literary jewels of their lives, in which are reflected for the first time the truer wages of our history and our conduct. It is an exciting, adventurous literature and scholarship. There are both traditional and pioneer women writers, professed feminists and nonfeminists, and those who refuse to accept any label at all. Collectively, it is the *mass presence* of literature written by black women that is unprecedented. In the past one had to search for black-women-authored literature. Today the literature seeks you out.

Similar to women's writings in general, writings by black women enjoy a large popular audience, a heterogeneous readership comprising both blacks and whites, women and men. The works of Toni Morrison, Alice Walker, June Jordan, Toni Cade Bambara, Maya Angelou, Margaret Walker, Ntozake Shange, along with those of such newly recognized writers as Octavia Butler (science-fiction author) and Mildred Taylor (novelist), usually appeal to the popular female writer's audience.

There is, on the other hand, a readership within the popular audience which can be delineated as subpopular. Barbara Smith, Audre Lorde, Ann Shockley, Pat Parker, Gloria T. Hull, Lorraine Bethel, and other lesbian feminist authors are read more often than not by a subpopular audience of conscientious feminist black and white women, and a few men. While the writers appealing to the wider popular audience may or may not be lesbian feminists or feminists of any sort, the writers appealing to the subpopular readership are nearly all declared feminist women. Their works most often appear in publications with a limited circulation.

But the line between popular and subpopular readership—and between lesbian feminists, feminists, and non-declared feminists—is very thin. Just as the declared lesbian feminist writers are a part of the general pool of black women writers, so too is the subpopular audience a part of the larger readership. In other words, the people who read the works of lesbian feminist authors also read works of black women writers in general. The people who read black women writers in general, however, do not necessarily read the explicitly lesbian feminist writings. Depending on the subject and treatment of a particular piece of writing, a writer may be read by the popular audience, including the conscientious feminist readers. In another instance, the readership for the same author may comprise only that portion of the general audience that is consciously involved with feminist issues. Many writers appeal to a "universal" audience. Alice Walker and Toni Morrison, for example, are usually read both by feminist readers as well as by non-feminist ones. Occasionally, a writer may "cross over." In 1984, Mary Helen Washington, a declared feminist writer, published an article dealing with the television images of black performers in *TV Guide,* which is read by millions of television viewers.

The declared and lesbian black feminist writers are pioneering a black feminist criticism. This is not to take away from other writers. All are blazing new trails. But especially the declared feminists and lesbian feminists—Barbara Smith, Ann Shockley, Cheryl Clarke, Wilmette Brown, and the rest—are at the forefront of the critics, scholars, intellectuals, and ideologues of our time.

But let us return to the sexual mountain. What is historically distinct about the present state of black writing in America is where it is coming from and where it seems inexorably to be going.

In 1937, in *New Challenge* magazine, Richard Wright published an essay entitled "Blueprint for Negro Writing" in which he asserted that a Marxist black-male-oriented aesthetic and politics against racism and capitalism should be the all-consuming perspective of the black wrter. Accordingly, the central character in all the Wright novels and stories is a young black male ensnared in the nightmare of a white racist capitalistic world. Wright was the first black writer to incorporate Marxism in a formulated black male aesthetic statement. But the masculine perspective itself, concerning the manhood of the black race, has always occupied center stage in the drama of Afro-American literature.

Along with its male-centered aesthetic, it is the hegemony of the masculine perspective that is now being changed—in and through the writings of black American women. In 1903, Du Bois pointed out that the Negro, being both black and American, shoulders a double consciousness. Black women have contended with the mountain of racism in America. But being at once black, American, and female, they have also been victimized by the mountain of sexism, not only from the white world but from the men of the black world as well. Black women are bearers of what Barbara Smith calls "geometric oppression." They are, therefore, bearers of a triple consciousness. To take but one of many examples, the perspective in the works of Alice Walker (*The Third Life of Grange Copeland, Meridian, In Love & Trouble, The Color Purple,* etc.) is consistently informed with this consciousness. Since, however, the white feminist movement is ridden with racism, and since black men have tabooed the word *feminism* and invested it with negative stigmas, many black women avoid calling themselves *feminists.* Alice Walker says she is a "womanist."

## Woman to Woman Approach

Whether you and I like it or not, both on the subpopular and popular levels the de facto situation is that a black feminist perspective pervades contemporary Afro-American literature. The perspective governs the aesthetic, and the aesthetic informs the landscape and the vision. The literature, moreover, marks a significant juncture in the character of relations between black male writers and black female writers. For the first time, the status of black women writers is no longer relegated below the status of the males. Black women writers are taking the initiative. Instead of being constrained by and secondary to the literary dominance of black males, the literature of the women is expansive and liberating.

Unlike the past, when women were supposed to be seen but not heard, the women of today have become recognized writers in all fields and genres. Most importantly, black women are dealing with

the sexual beliefs, feelings, and actions that black men have maintained toward black females—in the street, in the family, and in the
bedroom. And they are dealing with the political machinations of
these sexual beliefs and practices. Their perspective is faithful to the
actual experiences of black women in America.

Consistent with the perspective is the aesthetic. Rather than a
woman-to-man approach, it is a woman-to-woman approach. It is a
black feminist aesthetic in which the form, language, syntax, se-
quence, and metaphoric rendering of experience are markedly different and expansive in comparison to those of the male-authored
literature. This can be witnessed in the works of Toni Morrison, especially in her *Bluest Eye,* in Toni Cade Bambara's *The Salt Eaters,*
in Alice Walker's *Meridian,* and in Gloria Naylor's *The Women of
Brewster Place.*

The women are also engaged in research and scholarship. Works
of black women long ignored are now being sought out and acclaimed. Having been castigated and dismissed as not being a "black"
poet, particularly during the Black Power era of the 1960s, Phillis
Wheatley is being reappraised by the women of today. Though
she did not write much out of a black consciousness of slavery,
Wheatley's works are imbued with a sensitivity that is specifically female. Similarly, works of Zora Neale Hurston, Dorothy West, Paule
Marshall, and Rosa Guy are being republished and seriously assessed
for the first time.

In the Winter 1980 issue of *Black American Literature Forum,*
Margaret B. McDowell, Claudia Tate, and Janet E. Sims published
materials devoted to works by Ann Petry, Nella Larsen, and Jessie
Fauset. Jean Carey Bond edited the Fourth Quarter 1979 issue of
*Freedomways,* devoted to Lorraine Hansberry. There is also a great
deal of material coming out on Anne Spencer. "The Heart of a Woman,"
by Harlem Renaissance poet Georgia Douglas Johnson, is another example of the buried treasures that are being unearthed. Black women
of heroic deeds are also being raised from behind the mountain of
sexism—Anna Julia Cooper, Maria Stewart, Mary Terrell, Mary Mc-
Cleod Bethune, and Ida Wells, to mention a few.

In the past, it was the men who wrote the sociology, history, political tracts, expository essays, and ideological treatises. The traditional authorities on black women were overwhelmingly black

males—the Du Boises, Fraziers, Bennetts, Staples, Poussaints, and Hares. A Black scholar was automatically assumed to be a black male. Even white women were more likely to be scholars on black women than black women were.

## Black Women Scholars

Today all of this is changing. Black women are scholars on themselves and on black men as well. There are the works of Joyce Ladiner, Doris Y. Wilkinson, Carlene Young, Angela Davis, Lee Rainwater, Jean Carey Bond, Sharon Harley, Rosalyn Terborg-Penn, Paula Giddings, Johnnella Butler, and many others. Edited by Gloria T. Hull, Patricia Bell Scott, and Barbara Smith, the book *But Some of Us Are Brave* marks a primal attempt to demythify the traditional male-oriented sociology on black women and men, and offers a blueprint for organizing a black women's studies curriculum.

What we are witnessing is an entire movement on the part of contemporary black women in general, and not just on the part of the so-called creative writers. Many of the women are renaissance women, multiple in talent and endeavors, at once poets, novelists, mothers, scholars, workers, professors, intellectuals, and activists. Their efforts at the typewriter and in the world are toward reshaping the way we view the past and live in the present, and how we socialize our children for the future. When a child picks up a book called *Civil Wars*, by June Jordan, it is hoped that the child will encounter something more thorough of the black experience, in addition to what she or he will encounter in, say, a book by James Baldwin or Calvin Hernton. *Civil Wars* demonstrates that black women live generically in the world and relate generically to all things in the world—just as any black man does.

Traditionally, we have been unaccustomed to books of socio-cultural and political analysis authored by black women from a black feminist, or womanist, perspective. In their ambitious anthology, *Black Writers of America*, Barksdale and Kinnamon designate a section in the contents for "Racial Spokesmen"—Martin Luther King, Malcolm X, and Eldridge Cleaver. No spokeswomen are included. Since the tacit and spoken assumption has been that the black race is a race of men, black women have had to specify their own existence, as represented by the titles of Mari Evans's *I Am a Black Woman* and Sonia Sanchez's *I've Been a Black Woman*.

More and more women are assuming the task of being spokes-women of black people, and writing socio-culture/political essays and books. Hattie Gossett has completed a formidable, yet-to-be-published work of this nature. Paula Giddings has published *When and Where I Enter*. *Conditions: Five,* produced in 1979, contains the work of about thirty women poets and writers. Edited by Lorraine Bethel and Barbara Smith, the issue represents some of the best of the new writings on realities which black women and men live with everyday, but which few of us have dared to write about. Elaine Brown, for ten years of high rank in the Black Panther Party, is searching for a publisher.

It is, significantly, the conscientious feminists who are the most autonomous in their thinking and writing. They are the most chal-lenging, and are forging unprecedented breakthroughs. Black women are now emerging as the foremost critics of our literature and our lives. Barbara Smith's "Toward a Black Feminist Criticism" and Deborah E. McDowell's "New Directions for Black Feminist Criti-cism" are primal efforts in building the new criticism and aesthetics.

In her *Black Women Novelists: The Development of a Tradition, 1892–1976,* Barbara Christian exhibits painstaking analysis and of-fers cogent perceptions from a black womanist perspective in illu-minating the works of Frances Ellen Watkins Harper, Paule Marshall, Toni Morrison, and Alice Walker. Margaret Walker is readying *The Daemonic Genius of Richard Wright* for publication.

An integral part of what black women are doing consists of bring-ing to the forefront what has been extant all along, a humanity of black women in their writings that has been historically, system-atically overshadowed by the sexual mountain. In the July 1981 issue of *Essence,* Alexis DeVeaux expressed the task of today's black women as follows: "A struggle to express ourselves. To be heard. To be seen. In our own image. To construct the words. To name the deeds. Confront the risks. Write the history. Document it on radio, television and satellites. To analyze and live it."

Because much of the writing of contemporary black women is critical of black men, both in the literary sphere and in real life, the men find it unpalatable. But black writing owes its very nature to the oppressive conditions under which blacks were and are subjected in America. The function of black literature has always been, as Langston Hughes declared, to illuminate and elevate the condition of black people.

It is altogether consistent with the heritage of black writing that black women write about the meanness they have experienced and still experience at the hands of black men as well as white men. It is inescapable that women writers seek to illuminate and elevate the condition of black women, their whole condition. How is one to meaningfully participate in the struggle between the races if one is the victim of subjugation within the race?

## Challenging Racism *and* Sexism

Today black women writers are challenging racism *and* sexism in all spheres of life and culture. Women having no avowed truck with feminism are increasingly engaged in literary activities that nevertheless fall within the scope of contemporary black womanist consciousness. Assisted by Margaret Potter of *The New York Times,* the New Bones group of New York women has sponsored literary affairs at Small's Paradise involving poets Lucille Clifton, Brenda Connor-Bey, Anasa Jordan, Jeraldine Wilson, and others. The book *Black Women Writers at Work,* edited by Claudia Tate, contains interviews with fourteen outstanding black women writers. *Home Girls: A Black Feminist Anthology,* edited by the indefatigable Barbara Smith, contains some of the most woman-oriented black writers of today.

The scaling of the historic mountain of sexism on the part of contemporary black women writers does not mean that there are no differences or controversy among them. It certainly does not mean that their works are flawless. Some of their assertions are downright bombastic, some of their scholarship is questionable, and some of their quotations are very biased and misleading. The prolific propagation of literature by black women does mean that the sexual mountain need not remain as a barrier behind which black women writers must languish forever. But there remains much work to be done. The mountain must not merely be scaled: it must be destroyed.

Harsh sanctions on the part of black males exist against black feminism itself, and against joint feminist efforts between black and white women. But, while combating racism within the white women's movement, more and more black women are accepting genuine cooperation from white feminists. Edited by Gloria I. Joseph and Jill Lewis, *Common Differences: Conflicts in Black and White Feminist Perspectives* is an example of black and white women's efforts to iron out their problems.

It is through women's publishing outlets—*Essence, Ms., Off Our Backs, Heresies,* Kitchen Table Press, and so forth—that many black women are combating the sexual mountain. The Combahee River Collective in Boston is a group of dedicated black feminists who dominated the hallmark black women's issue of *Conditions: Five.* As editor of The Feminist Press, Florence Howe has been responsive to the needs of black women by publishing and republishing black women's works of yesterday and today that have been obscured by the sexual mountain. It is, moreover, not in the established media but in black magazines and periodicals and noticeable in white feminist media that black women are accorded the all-important acknowledgment of having their writings seriously reviewed.

The present innovations in Afro-American literature are not isolated. They are part and parcel of the expanding consciousness of subjugated women all over the planet, particularly in Africa. Black feminist writers are engaged in a literature of demythification and liberation on a global scale. An examination of the perspective and landscape of the global literature of women of color reflects the same two tasks of which Elise McDougald spoke in 1925: 1) The demythification/*illumination* of white male and female racism and imperialism over dark people, and 2) the specific liberation/*elevation* of women of color from the fetters of both white and black male supremacy. For the last ten years the poetical works of Jayne Cortez have constituted a one-woman arsenal designed to accomplish these two tasks.

The globalization of the two tasks means fostering alliances and promoting cooperative literary efforts between Afro-American women and women of the so-called Third World. In her 1981 *Essence* article, Alexis DeVeaux writes:

. . . like the women of Algeria, Cuba and Vietnam . . . Zimbabwean women often find themselves alienated from the society they helped liberate. In the so-called Third World it is a familiar pattern . . . the constraints of roles based on sex. . . . Black women in America and African women in Zimbabwe . . . share the need for news of other women/cultures; the need to be active, and creative. . . . and we shake hands. We hug. We stretch the distance. . . .

The book *This Bridge Called My Back: Writings by Radical Women of Color,* edited by Cherrie Moraga and Gloria Anzaldúa, with a foreword by Toni Cade Bambara, contains prose, poetry, personal narratives, and social analyses by Afro-American, Asian-American, Latina, and Native American women. It is one of the many cooperative efforts reflecting an expanding "melting pot" of women's consciousness. The works of Latin and African women writers in particular are now being brought to the foreground of black feminist consciousness. *Maru* and *A Question of Power,* by Bessie Head of South Africa; *Efuru,* by Flora Nwapa of Nigeria: *No Sweetness Here,* by Christina Ama Ata Aidoo of Ghana; *Three Solid Stones,* by Martha Mvengi of Tanzania; plus the scholarly work by Christine Obbo, *African Women: Their Struggle for Economic Independence;* and the collectively edited work by Latin American women, *Slaves of Slaves: The Challenge of Latin American Women*—these and other African, Latin, and third world publications are having an impact upon black women writers and black women's studies in the United States. Of course, the most widely read woman-identified African writer of today is the Nigerian born Buchi Emecheta, who has published five novels in rapid succession: *In the Ditch, The Bride Price, Second Class Citizen, The Slave Girl,* and *The Joys of Motherhood.*

We have always heard about the brotherhood of man. Now, for the first time, we are witnessing a literature, the pervasive aesthetic of which is the sisterhood of women. In *Civil Wars,* June Jordan has written:

I am a feminist, and what that means to me is . . . that I must undertake to love myself and to respect myself as though my very life depends upon self-love and self-respect . . . and that I am entering my soul into a struggle that will most certainly transform the experience of all the peoples of the earth, as no other movement can, in fact, hope to claim: because the movement into self-love, self-respect, and self-determination is the movement now galvanizing the true, the un-arguable majority of human beings everywhere.

The literature of contemporary black women writers is a dialectical composite of the unknown coming out of the known. It is an up-heaval in form, style, and landscape. It is the negation of the nega-tive. And it proffers a vision of unfettered human possibility.

# Barbara Smith

# The Truth That Never Hurts: Black Lesbians in Fiction in the 1980s

I n 1977, when I wrote *Toward a Black Feminist Criticism,* I wanted to accomplish several goals. The first was simply to point out that Black women writers existed, a fact generally ignored by white male, Black male, and white female readers, teachers, and critics. Another desire was to encourage Black feminist criticism of these writers' work, that is, analyses that acknowledged the reality of sexual oppression in the lives of Black women. Probably most urgently, I wanted to illuminate the existence of Black Lesbian writers and to show how homophobia insured that we were even more likely to be ignored or attacked than Black women writers generally.

In 1985, Black women writers' situation is considerably different than it was in 1977. Relatively speaking, Black women's literature is much more recognized, even at times by the white, male literary establishment. There are a growing number of Black women critics who rely upon various Black feminist critical approaches to studying the literature. There has been a marked increase in the number of Black women who are willing to acknowledge that they are feminists, including some who write literary criticism. Not surprisingly, Black feminist activism and organizing have greatly expanded, a precondition which I cited in 1977 for the growth of Black feminist criticism. More writing by Black Lesbians is available, and there has even been some positive response to this writing from non-Lesbian Black readers and critics. The general conditions under which Black women critics and writers work have improved. The personal isolation we face and the ignorance and hostility with which our work is met have diminished in some quarters but have by no means disappeared.

One of the most positive changes is that a body of consciously Black feminist writing and writing by other feminists of color actually exists. The publication of a number of anthologies has greatly increased the breadth of writing available by feminists of color. These include *Conditions: Five, The Black Women's Issue* (1979); *This Bridge Called My Back: Writings by Radical Women of Color* (1981); *All the Women Are White, All the Blacks Are Men, But Some of Us Are Brave: Black Women's Studies* (1982); *A Gathering of Spirit: North American Indian Women's Issue* (1983); *Cuentos: Stories by Latinas* (1983); *Home Girls: A Black Feminist Anthology* (1983); *Bearing Witness/ Sobreviviendo: An Anthology of Native American/Latina Art and Literature* (1984); and *Gathering Ground: New Writing and Art by Northwest Women of Color* (1984). First books by individual authors have also appeared, such as *Claiming an Identity They Taught Me to Despise* (1980) and *Abeng* (1984) by Michelle Cliff; *Narratives: Poems in the Tradition of Black Women* (1982) by Cheryl Clarke; *For Nights Like This One* (1983) by Becky Birtha; *Loving in the War Years: Lo Que Nunca Pasó por Sus Labios* (1983) by Cherríe Moraga; *The Words of a Woman Who Breathes Fire* (1983) by Kitty Tsui; and *Mohawk Trail* (1985) by Beth Brant (Degonwadonti). Scholarly works provide extremely useful analytical frameworks, for example, *Common Differences: Conflicts in Black and White Feminist Perspectives* by Gloria I. Joseph and Jill Lewis (1981); *Black Women Writers at Work* edited by Claudia Tate (1983); *When and Where I Enter: The Impact of Black Women on Race and Sex in America* by Paula Giddings (1984); and *Black Feminist Criticism: Perspectives on Black Women Writers* by Barbara Christian (1985).

Significantly, however, "small" or independent, primarily women's presses published all but the last four titles cited and almost all the authors and editors of these alternative press books (although not all of the contributors to their anthologies) are Lesbians. In his essay, "The Sexual Mountain and Black Women Writers," critic Calvin Hernton writes:

> The declared and lesbian black feminist writers are pioneering a black feminist criticism. This is not to take away from other writers. All are blazing new trails. But especially the declared feminists and

lesbian feminists—Barbara Smith, Ann Shockley, Cheryl Clarke, Wilmette Brown, and the rest—are at the forefront of the critics, scholars, intellectuals, and ideologues of our time.[1]

Yet Hernton points out that these writers are "subpopular," published as they are by nonmainstream presses. In contrast, non-Lesbian Black women writers have been published by trade publishers and are able to reach, as Hernton explains, a "wider popular audience."

In her excellent essay, "No More Buried Lives: The Theme of Lesbianism" in Audre Lorde's *Zami,* Gloria Naylor's *The Women of Brewster Place,* Ntozake Shange's *Sassafras, Cypress and Indigo,* and Alice Walker's *The Color Purple,* critic Barbara Christian makes a similar observation. She writes:

> Lesbian life, characters, language, values are *at present* and *to some extent* becoming respectable in American literature, partly because of the pressure of women-centered communities, partly because publishers are intensely aware of marketing trends. . . . I say, *to some extent,* because despite the fact that Walker received the Pulitzer for *The Color Purple* and Naylor the American Book Award for *The Women of Brewster Place,* I doubt if *Home Girls,* an anthology of black feminist and lesbian writing that was published by Kitchen Table Press, would have been published by a mainstream publishing company.[2]

Significantly, Christian says that "Lesbian life, characters, language, values" are receiving qualified attention and respectability, but Lesbian writers themselves are not. No doubt, this is why she suspects that no trade publisher would publish *Home Girls,* which contains work by women who write openly as Lesbians, and which defines Lesbianism politically as well as literarily.

The fact that there is such a clear-cut difference in publishing options for Black Lesbian writers (who are published solely by independent presses) and for non-Lesbian and closeted Black women writers (who have access to both trade and alternative publishers) indicates what has *not* changed since 1977. It also introduces the focus of this essay.[3] I am concerned with exploring the treatment of Black Lesbian writing and Black Lesbian themes in the context of Black feminist writing and criticism.

Today, not only are more works by and about Black women available, but a body of specifically Black feminist writing exists.

Although both the general category of Black women's literature and the specific category of Black feminist literature can be appropriately analyzed from a Black feminist critical perspective, explicitly Black feminist literature has a unique set of characteristics and emphases which distinguishes it from other work. Black feminist writing provides an incisive critical perspective on sexual political issues that affect Black women—for example, the issue of sexual violence. It generally depicts the significance of Black women's relationships with each other as a primary source of support. Black feminist writing may also be classified as such because the author identifies herself as a feminist and has a demonstrated commitment to women's issues and related political concerns. An openness in discussing Lesbian subject matter is perhaps the most obvious earmark of Black feminist writing and not because feminism and Lesbianism are interchangeable, which of course they are not.

For historical, political, and ideological reasons, a writer's consciousness about Lesbianism bears a direct relationship to her consciousness about feminism. It was in the context of the second wave of the contemporary feminist movement, influenced by the simultaneous development of an autonomous gay liberation movement, that the political content of Lesbianism and Lesbian oppression began to be analyzed and defined. The women's liberation movement was the political setting in which anti-Lesbian attitudes and actions were initially challenged in the late 1960s and early 1970s and where, at least in theory, but more often in fact, homophobia was designated unacceptable, at least in the movement's more progressive sectors.

Barbara Christian also makes the connection between feminist consciousness and a willingness to address Lesbian themes in literature. She writes:

> Some of the important contributions that the emergence of the lesbian theme has made to Afro-American Women's literature are: the breaking of stereotypes so that black lesbians are clearly seen as *women*, the exposure of homophobia in the black community, and an exploration of how that homophobia is related to the struggle of all women to be all that they can be—in other words to feminism.
>
> That is not to say that Afro-American women's literature has not always included a feminist perspective. The literature of the seventies, for example, certainly explored the relationship between sexism and racism and has been at the forefront of the development of feminist

ideas. One natural outcome of this exploration is the lesbian theme, for society's attack on lesbians is the cutting edge of the anti-feminist definition of women.[4]

Black feminist writers, whether Lesbian or non-Lesbian, have been aware of and influenced by the movement's exploring, struggling over, and organizing around Lesbian identity and issues. They would be much more likely to take Black Lesbian experience seriously and to explore Black Lesbian themes in their writing, in contrast with authors who either have not been involved in the women's movement or who are antifeminist. For example, in her very positive review of *Conditions: Five, The Black Women's Issue,* originally published in *Ms.* magazine in 1980, Alice Walker writes:

> Like black men and women who refused to be the exceptional "pet" Negro for whites, and who instead said they were "niggers" too (the original "crime" of "niggers" and lesbians is that they prefer themselves), perhaps black women writers and nonwriters should say, simply, whenever black lesbians are being put down, held up, messed over, and generally told their lives should not be encouraged, *We are all lesbians.* For surely it is better to be thought a lesbian, and to say and write your life exactly as you experience it, than to be a token "pet" black woman for those whose contempt for our autonomous existence makes them a menace to human life.[5]

Walker's support of her Lesbian sisters in real life is not unrelated to her ability to write fiction about Black women who are lovers, as in *The Color Purple.* Her feminist consciousness undoubtedly influenced the positiveness of her portrayal. In contrast, an author like Gayl Jones, who has not been associated with or seemingly influenced by the feminist movement, has portrayed Lesbians quite negatively.[6]

Just as surely as a Black woman writer's relationship to feminism affects the themes she might choose to write about, a Black woman critic's relationship to feminism determines the kind of criticism she is willing and able to do. The fact that critics are usually also academics, however, has often affected Black women critics' approach to feminist issues. If a Black woman scholar's only connection to women's issues is via women's studies, as presented by white women academics, most of whom are not activists, her access to movement analyses and practice will be limited or nonexistent. I believe that the most accurate and developed theory, including literary theory, comes from practice, from the experience of activism. This relationship between theory and practice is crucial when inherently political subject matter, such as the condition of women as depicted in a writer's work, is being discussed. I do not believe it is possible to arrive at fully developed and useful Black feminist criticism by merely reading about feminism. Of course every Black woman has her own experiences of sexual political dynamics and oppression to draw upon, and referring to these experiences should be an important resource in shaping her analyses of a literary work. However, studying feminist texts and drawing only upon one's *individual* experiences of sexism are insufficient.

I remember the point in my own experience when I no longer was involved on a regular basis in organizations such as the Boston Committee to End Sterilization Abuse and the Abortion Action Coalition. I was very aware that my lack of involvement affected my thinking and writing *overall.* Certain perceptions were simply unavailable to me because I no longer was doing that particular kind of ongoing work. And I am referring to missing something much deeper than access to specific information about sterilization and reproductive rights. Activism has spurred me to write the kinds of theory and criticism I have written and has provided the experiences and insights that have shaped the perceptions in my work. Many examples of this vital relationship between activism and theory exist in the work of thinkers such as Ida B. Wells-Barnett, W. E. B. Du Bois, Lillian Smith, Lorraine Hansberry, Frantz Fanon, Barbara Deming, Paolo Freire, and Angela Davis.

A critic's involvement or lack of involvement in activism, specifically in the context of the feminist movement, is often signally revealed by the approach she takes to Lesbianism. If a woman has worked in organizations where Lesbian issues have been raised, where homophobia was unacceptable and struggled with, and where she had the opportunity to meet and work with a variety of Lesbians, her relationship to Lesbians and to her own homophobia would undoubtedly be affected. The types of political organizations in which such dialogue occurs are not, of course, exclusively Lesbian and may focus upon a range of issues, such as women in prison, sterilization abuse, reproductive freedom, health care, domestic violence, and sexual assault.

Black feminist critics who are Lesbians can usually be counted upon to approach Black women's and Black Lesbian writing non-homophobically. Non-Lesbian Black feminist critics are not as dependable in this regard. I even question at times designating Black women—critics and noncritics alike—as feminist who are actively homophobic in what they write, say, or do, or who are passively homophobic because they ignore Lesbian existence entirely.[7] Yet such critics are obviously capable of analyzing other sexual and political implications of the literature they scrutinize. Political definitions, particularly of feminism, can be difficult to pin down. The one upon which I generally rely states: "Feminism is the political theory and practice that struggles to free *all* women: women of color, working-class women, poor women, disabled women, lesbians, old women—as well as white, economically privileged, heterosexual women. Anything less than this vision of total freedom is not feminism, but merely female self-aggrandizement."[8]

A Black gay college student recently recounted an incident to me that illustrates the kind of consciousness that is grievously lacking among nonfeminist Black women scholars about Black Lesbian existence. His story indicates why a Black feminist approach to literature, criticism, and research in a variety of disciplines is crucial if one is to recognize and understand Black Lesbian experience. While researching a history project, he contacted the archives at a Black institution that has significant holdings on Black women. He spoke to a Black woman archivist and explained that he was looking for materials on Black Lesbians in the 1940s. Her immediate response was to laugh uproariously and then to say that the collection contained very little on women during that period and nothing at all on Lesbians in any of the periods covered by its holdings.

Not only was her reaction appallingly homophobic, not to mention impolite, but it was also inaccurate. One of the major repositories of archival material on Black women in the country of course contains material by and about Black Lesbians. The material, however, is not identified and defined as such and thus remains invisible. This is a classic case of "invisibility [becoming] an unnatural disaster," as feminist poet Mitsuye Yamada observes.[9]

I suggested a number of possible resources to the student and in the course of our conversation I told him I could not help but think of Cheryl Clarke's classic poem, "Of Althea and Flaxie." It begins:

In 1943 Althea was a welder
very dark
very butch
and very proud
loved to cook, sew, and drive a car
and did not care who knew she kept company with a woman.[10]

The poem depicts a realistic and positive Black Lesbian relationship which survives Flaxie's pregnancy in 1955, Althea's going to jail for writing numbers in 1958, poverty, racism, and, of course, homophobia. If the archivist's vision had not been so blocked by homophobia, she would have been able to direct this student to documents that corroborate the history embodied in Clarke's poem.

Being divorced from the experience of feminist organizing not only makes it more likely that a woman has not been directly challenged to examine her homophobia, but it can also result in erroneous approaches to Black Lesbian literature, if she does decide to talk or write about it. For example, some critics, instead of simply accepting that Black Lesbians and Black Lesbian writers exist, view the depiction of Lesbianism as a dangerous and unacceptable "theme" or "trend" in Black women's writing. Negative discussions of "themes" and "trends," which may in time fade, do not acknowledge that for survival, Black Lesbians, like any oppressed group, need to see our faces reflected in myriad cultural forms, including literature. Some critics go so far as to see the few Black Lesbian books in existence as a kind of conspiracy and bemoan that there is "so much" of this kind of writing available in print; they put forth the supreme untruth that it is actually an advantage to be a Black Lesbian writer.

For each Lesbian of color in print there are undoubtedly five dozen whose work has never been published and may never be. The publication of Lesbians of color is a "new" literary development, made possible by alternative, primarily Lesbian/feminist presses. The political and aesthetic strength of this writing is indicated by its impact having been far greater than its actual availability. At times its content has had revolutionary implications. But the impact of Black Lesbian feminist writing, to which Calvin Hernton refers, should not be confused with easy access to print, to readers, or to the material perks that help a writer survive economically.

Terms like "heterophobia," used to validate the specious notion that "so many" Black women writers are now depicting loving and sexual relationships between women, to the exclusion of focusing on relationships with men, arise in an academic vacuum, uninfluenced by political reality. "Heterophobia" resembles the concept of "reverse racism." Both are thoroughly reactionary and have nothing to do with the actual dominance of a heterosexual white power structure.

Equating Lesbianism with separatism is another error in terminology, which will probably take a number of years to correct. The title of a workshop at a major Black women writers' conference, for example, was "Separatist Voices in the New Canon." The workshop examined the work of Audre Lorde and Alice Walker, neither of whom defines herself as a separatist, either sexually or racially. In his introduction to *Confirmation: An Anthology of African American Women,* co-editor Imamu Baraka is critical of feminists who are separatists, but he does not mention that any such thing as a Lesbian exists. In his ambiguous yet inherently homophobic usage, the term 'separatist' is made to seem like a mistaken political tendency, which correct thinking could alter. If "separatist" equals Lesbian, Baraka is suggesting that we should change our minds and eradicate ourselves. In both these instances the fact that Lesbians do not have sexual relationships with men is thought to be the same as ideological Lesbian "separatism." Such an equation does not take into account that the majority of Lesbians of color have interactions with men and that those who are activists are quite likely to be politically committed to coalition work as well.

Inaccuracy and distortion seem to be particularly frequent pitfalls when non-Lesbians address Black Lesbian experience because of generalized homophobia and because the very nature of our oppression may cause us to be hidden or "closeted," voluntarily or involuntarily isolated from other communities, and as a result unseen and unknown. In her essay, "A Cultural Legacy Denied and Discovered: Black Lesbians in Fiction by Women," Jewelle Gomez asserts the necessity for realistic portrayals of Black Lesbians:

> These Black Lesbian writers . . . have seen into the shadows that hide the existence of Black Lesbians and understand they have to create a universe/home that rings true on all levels. . . . The Black Lesbian writer must throw herself into the arms of her culture by acting as student/teacher/participant/observer, absorbing and synthesizing the meanings of our existence as a people. She must do this despite the fact that both our culture and our sexuality have been severely truncated and distorted.
>
> Nature abhors a vacuum and there is a distinct gap in the picture where the Black Lesbian should be. The Black Lesbian writer must recreate our home, unadulterated, unsanitized, specific and not isolated from the generations that have nurtured us.[11]

This is an excellent statement of what usually has been missing from portrayals of Black Lesbians in fiction. The degree of truthfulness and self-revelation that Gomez calls for encompasses the essential qualities of verisimilitude and authenticity that I look for in depictions of Black Lesbians. By verisimilitude I mean how true to life and realistic a work of literature is. By authenticity I mean something even deeper—a characterization which reflects a relationship to self that is genuine, integrated, and whole. For a Lesbian or a gay man, this kind of emotional and psychological authenticity virtually requires the degree of self-acceptance inherent in being out. This is not a dictum, but an observation. It is not a coincidence, however, that the most vital and useful Black Lesbian feminist writing is being written by Black Lesbians who are not caught in the impossible bind of simultaneously hiding identity yet revealing self through their writing.

Positive and realistic portrayals of Black Lesbians are sorely needed, portraits that are, as Gomez states, "unadulterated, unsanitized, specific." By positive I do not mean characters without problems, contradictions, or flaws, mere uplift literature for Lesbians, but instead, writing that is sufficiently sensitive and complex, which places Black Lesbian experience and struggles squarely within the realm of recognizable human experience and concerns.

As African-Americans, our desire for authentic literary images of Black Lesbians has particular cultural and historical resonance, since a desire for authentic images of ourselves as Black people preceded it long ago. After an initial period of racial uplift literature in the nineteenth and early twentieth centuries, Black artists during the Harlem Renaissance of the 1920s began to assert the validity of fully Black portrayals in all art forms including literature. In his pivotal essay of 1926, "The Negro Artist and the Racial Mountain," Langston Hughes asserted:

> We younger Negro artists who create now intend to express our individual dark-skinned selves without fear or shame. If white people are pleased we are glad. If they are not, it doesn't matter. We know we are beautiful. And ugly too. The tom-tom cries and the tom-tom laughs. If colored people are pleased we are glad. If they are not, their displeasure doesn't matter either. We build our temples for tomorrow, strong as we know how, and we stand on top of the mountain, free within ourselves.[12]

Clearly, it was not always popular or safe with either Black or white audiences to depict Black people as we actually are. It still is not. Too many contemporary Blacks seem to have forgotten the universally debased social-political position Black people have occupied during all the centuries we have been here, up until perhaps the Civil Rights Movement of the 1960s. The most racist definition of Black people has been that we were not human.

Undoubtedly every epithet now hurled at Lesbians and gay men— "sinful," "sexually depraved," "criminal," "emotionally maladjusted," "deviant"—has also been applied to Black people. When W. E. B. Du Bois described life "behind the veil," and Paul Laurence Dunbar wrote,

> We wear the mask that grins and lies,
> It hides our cheeks and shades our eyes,—
> This debt we pay to human guile;
> With torn and bleeding hearts we smile,
> And mouth with myriad subtleties.
>
> Why should the world be overwise,
> In counting all our tears and sighs?

> Nay, let them only see us, while
> We wear the mask. . . .[13]

what were they describing but racial closeting? For those who refuse to see the parallels because they view Blackness as irreproachably normal, but persist in defining same-sex love relationships as unnatural, Black Lesbian feminist poet, Audre Lorde, reminds us: "'Oh,' says a voice from the Black community, 'but being Black is NORMAL!' Well, I and many Black people of my age can remember grimly the days when it didn't used to be!"[14] Lorde is not implying that she believes that there was ever anything wrong with being Black, but points out how distorted "majority" consciousness can cruelly affect an oppressed community's actual treatment and sense of self. The history of slavery, segregation, and racism was based upon the assumption by the powers-that-be that Blackness was decidedly neither acceptable nor normal. Unfortunately, despite legal and social change, large numbers of racist whites still believe the same thing to this day.

The existence of Lesbianism and male homosexuality is normal, too, traceable throughout history and across cultures. It is a society's *response* to the ongoing historical fact of homosexuality that determines whether it goes unremarked as nothing out of the ordinary, as it is in some cultures, or if it is instead greeted with violent repression, as it is in ours. At a time when Acquired Immune Deficiency Syndrome (AIDS), a disease associated with an already despised sexual minority, is occasioning mass hysteria among the heterosexual majority (including calls for firings, evictions, quarantining, imprisonment, and even execution), the way in which sexual orientation is viewed is not of mere academic concern. It is mass political organizing that has wrought the most significant changes in the status of Black and other people of color and that has altered society's perceptions about us and our images of ourselves. The Black Lesbian feminist movement simply continues that principled tradition of struggle.

A Black woman author's relationship to the politics of Black Lesbian feminism affects how she portrays Black Lesbian characters in fiction. In 1977, in *Towards a Black Feminist Criticism,* I had to rely upon Toni Morrison's *Sula* (1974), which did not explicitly portray a

Lesbian relationship, in order to analyze a Black woman's novel with a woman-identified theme. I sought to demonstrate, however, that because of the emotional primacy of Sula and Nel's love for each other, Sula's fierce independence, and the author's critical portrayal of heterosexuality, the novel could be illuminated by a Lesbian feminist reading. Here I will focus upon three more recent works—*The Women of Brewster Place, The Color Purple,* and *Zami: A New Spelling of My Name*—which actually portray Black Lesbians, but which do so with varying degrees of verisimilitude and authenticity, dependent upon the author's relationship to and understanding of the politics of Black Lesbian experience.

Gloria Naylor's *The Women of Brewster Place* (1983) is a novel composed of seven connecting stories. In beautifully resonant language Naylor makes strong sexual political statements about the lives of working poor and working-class Black women and does not hesitate to explore the often problematic nature of their relationships with Black men—lovers, husbands, fathers, sons. Loving and supportive bonds between Black women are central to her characters' survival. However, Naylor's portrayal of a Lesbian relationship in the sixth story, "The Two," runs counter to the positive framework of women bonding she has previously established. In the context of this novel a Lesbian relationship might well embody the culmination of women's capacity to love and be committed to each other. Yet both Lesbian characters are ultimately victims. Although Naylor portrays the community's homophobia toward the lovers as unacceptable, the fate that she designs for the two women is the most brutal and negative of any in the book.

Theresa is a strong-willed individualist, while her lover Lorraine passively yearns for social acceptability. Despite their professional jobs, they have moved to a dead-end slum block because of Lorraine's fears that the residents of their two other middle-class neighborhoods suspected that they were Lesbians. It does not take long for suspicions to arise on Brewster Place, and the two women's differing reactions to the inevitable homophobia they face is a major tension in the work. Theresa accepts the fact that she is an outsider because of her Lesbianism. She does not like being ostracized, but she faces others' opinions with an attitude of defiance. In contrast, Lorraine is obsessed with garnering societal approval and would like nothing more than to blend into the straight world, despite her Lesbianism.

Lorraine befriends Ben, the alcoholic building superintendent, because he is the one person on the block who does not reject her. The fact that Ben has lost his daughter and Lorraine has lost her father, because he refused to accept her Lesbianism, cements their friendship. Naylor writes:

> ". . . When I'm with Ben, I don't feel any different from anybody else in the world."
> "Then he's doing you an injustice," Theresa snapped, "because we are different. And the sooner you learn that, the better off you'll be."
> "See, there you go again. Tee the teacher and Lorraine the student, who just can't get the lesson right. Lorraine who just wants to be a human being—a lousy human being who's somebody's daughter or somebody's friend or even somebody's enemy. But they make me feel like a freak out there, and you try to make me feel like one in here. That only place I've found some peace, Tee, is in that damp ugly basement, where I'm not different."
> "Lorraine." Theresa shook her head slowly. "You're a lesbian—do you understand that word?—a butch, a dyke, a lesbo, all those things that kid was shouting. Yes, I heard him! And you can run in all the basements in the world, and it won't change that, so why don't you accept it?"
> "I have accepted it!" Lorraine shouted. "I've accepted it all my life, and it's nothing I'm ashamed of. I lost a father because I refused to be ashamed of it—but it doesn't make me any *different* from anyone else in the world."
> "It makes you damned different!"
>
> . . . . . . . . . . . . . . . . . . . . . . . .
>
> "That's right! There go your precious 'theys' again. They wouldn't understand—not in Detroit, not on Brewster Place, not anywhere! And as long as they own the whole damn world, it's them and us, Sister—them and us. And that spells different!"[15]

Many a Lesbian relationship has been threatened or destroyed because of how very differently lovers may view their Lesbianism, for example, how out or closeted one or the other is willing to be. Naylor's discussion of difference represents a pressing Lesbian concern. As Lorraine and Theresa's argument shows, there are complicated elements of truth in both their positions. Lesbians and gay men are objectively different in our sexual orientations from heterosexuals. The society raises sanctions against our sexuality that range from inconvenient to violent, and that render our social status and life experiences different. On the other hand we would like to be recognized and treated as human, to have the basic rights enjoyed by heterosexuals, and, if the society cannot manage to support how we love, to at least leave us alone.

In "The Two," however, Naylor sets up the women's response to their identity as an either/or dichotomy. Lorraine's desire for acceptance, although completely comprehensible, is based upon assimilation and denial, while Naylor depicts Theresa's healthier defiance as an individual stance. In the clearest statement of resistance in the story, Theresa thinks: "If they practiced that way with each other, then they could turn back to back and beat the hell out of the world for trying to invade their territory. But she had found no such sparring partner in Lorraine, and the strain of fighting alone was beginning to show on her." (p. 136) A mediating position between complete assimilation or alienation might well evolve from some sense of connection to a Lesbian/gay community. Involvement with other Lesbians and gay men could provide a reference point and support that would help diffuse some of the straight world's power. Naylor mentions that Theresa socializes with gay men and perhaps Lesbians at a bar, but her interactions with them occur outside the action of the story. The author's decision not to portray other Lesbians and gay men, but only to allude to them, is a significant one. The reader is never given an opportunity to view Theresa or Lorraine in a context in which they are the norm. Naylor instead presents them as "the two" exceptions in an entirely heterosexual world. Both women are extremely isolated and although their relationship is loving, it also feels claustrophobic. Naylor writes:

> Lorraine wanted to be liked by the people around her. She couldn't live the way Tee did, with her head stuck in a book all the time. Tee didn't seem to need anyone. Lorraine often wondered if she even needed her. . . .
>
>     . . . She never wanted to bother with anyone except those weirdos at the club she went to, and Lorraine hated them. They were coarse and bitter, and made fun of people who weren't like them. Well, she wasn't like them either. Why should she feel different from the people she lived around? Black people were all in the same boat—she'd come to realize this even more since they had moved to Brewster—and if they didn't row together, they would sink together. (p. 142)

Lorraine's rejection of other Lesbians and gay men is excruciating, as is the self-hatred that obviously prompts it. It is painfully ironic that she considers herself in the same boat with Black people in the story, who are heterosexual, most of whom ostracize her, but not with Black people who are Lesbian and gay. The one time that Lorraine actually decides to go to the club by herself, ignoring Theresa's warning that she won't have a good time without her, is the night that she is literally destroyed.

Perhaps the most positive element in "The Two" is how accurately Naylor depicts and subtly condemns Black homophobia. Sophie, a neighbor who lives across the airshaft from Lorraine and Theresa, is the "willing carrier" of the rumor about them, though not necessarily its initiator. Naylor writes:

> Sophie had plenty to report that day. Ben had said it was terrible in there. No, she didn't know exactly what he had seen, but you can imagine—and they did. Confronted with the difference that had been thrust into their predictable world, they reached into their imaginations and, using an ancient pattern, weaved themselves a reason for its existence. Out of necessity they stitched all of their secret fears and lingering childhood nightmares into this existence, because even though it was deceptive enough to try and look as they looked, talk as they talked, and do as they did, it had to have some hidden stain to invalidate it—it was impossible for them both to be right. So they leaned back, supported by the sheer weight of their numbers and comforted by the woven barrier that kept them protected from the yellow mist that enshrouded the two as they came and went on Brewster Place. (p. 132)

The fact of difference can be particularly volatile among people whose options are severely limited by racial, class, and sexual oppression, people who are already outsiders themselves.

A conversation between Mattie Michaels, an older Black woman who functions as the work's ethical and spiritual center, and her lifelong friend, Etta, further prods readers to examine their own attitudes about loving women. Etta explains:

> "Yeah, but it's different with them."
> "Different how?"

"Well . . ." Etta was beginning to feel uncomfortable. "They love each other like you'd love a man or a man would love you—I guess."

"But I've loved some women deeper than I ever loved any man," Mattie was pondering. "And there been some women who loved me more and did more for me than any man ever did."

"Yeah." Etta thought for a moment. "I can second that but it's still different, Mattie. I can't exactly put my finger on it, but . . ."

"Maybe it's not so different," Mattie said, almost to herself. "Maybe that's why some women get so riled up about it, 'cause they know deep down it's not so different after all." She looked at Etta. "It kinda gives you a funny feeling when you think about it that way, though."

"Yeah, it does," Etta said, unable to meet Mattie's eyes. (pp. 140–41)

Whatever their opinions, it is not the women of the neighborhood who are directly responsible for Lorraine's destruction, but six actively homophobic and woman-hating teenage boys. Earlier that day Lorraine and Kiswana Browne had encountered the toughs who unleashed their sexist and homophobic violence on the two young women. Kiswana verbally bests their leader, C. C. Baker, but he is dissuaded from physically retaliating because one of the other boys reminds him: "'That's Abshu's woman, and that big dude don't mind kickin' ass,'" (p. 163). As a Lesbian, Lorraine does not have any kind of "dude" to stand between her and the violence of other men. Although she is completely silent during the encounter, C. C.'s parting words to her are, "I'm gonna remember this, Butch!" That night when Lorraine returns from the bar alone, she walks into the alley which is the boys' turf. They are waiting for her and gang-rape her in one of the most devastating scenes in literature. Naylor describes the aftermath:

Lorraine lay pushed up against the wall on the cold ground with her eyes staring straight up into the sky. When the sun began to warm the air and the horizon brightened, she still lay there, her mouth crammed with paper bag, her dress pushed up under her breasts, her bloody pantyhose hanging from her thighs. She would have stayed there forever and have simply died from starvation or exposure if nothing around her had moved. (p. 171)

She glimpses Ben sitting on a garbage can at the other end of the alley sipping wine. In a bizarre twist of an ending Lorraine crawls through the alley and mauls him with a brick she happens to find as she makes her way toward him. Lorraine's supplicating cries of "'Please. Please.' . . . the only word she was fated to utter again and again for the rest of her life," conclude the story (p. 171, 173).

I began thinking about "The Two" because of a conversation I had with another Black Lesbian who seldom comes in contact with other Lesbians and who has not been active in the feminist movement. Unlike other women with whom I had discussed the work, she was not angry, disappointed, or disturbed by it, but instead thought it was an effective portrayal of Lesbians and homophobia. I was taken aback because I had found Naylor's depiction of our lives so completely demoralizing and not particularly realistic. I thought about another friend who told me she found the story so upsetting she was never able to finish it. And of another who had actually rewritten the ending so that Mattie hears Lorraine's screams before she is raped and saves her. In this "revised version," Theresa is an undercover cop, who also hears her lover's screams, comes into the alley with a gun, and blows the boys away. I was so mystified and intrigued by the first woman's defense of Naylor's perspective that I went back to examine the work.

According to the criteria I have suggested, although the Lesbian characters in "The Two" lack authenticity, the story possesses a certain level of verisimilitude. The generalized homophobia that the women face, which culminates in retaliatory rape and near murderous decimation, is quite true to life. Gay and Lesbian newspapers provide weekly accounts, which sometimes surface in the mainstream media, of the constant violence leveled at members of our communities. What feels disturbing and inauthentic to me is how utterly hopeless Naylor's view of Lesbian existence is. Lorraine and Theresa are classically unhappy homosexuals of the type who populated white literature during a much earlier era, when the only options for the "deviant" were isolation, loneliness, mental illness, suicide, or death.

In her second novel, *Linden Hills* (1985), Naylor indicates that Black gay men's options are equally grim. In a review of the work, Jewelle Gomez writes:

> . . . one character disavows a liaison with his male lover in order to marry the appropriate woman and inherit the coveted Linden Hills

home. . . . We receive so little personal information about him that his motivations are obscure. For a middle-class, educated gay man to be blind to alternative lifestyles in 1985 is not inconceivable but it's still hard to accept the melodrama of his arranged marriage without screaming "dump the girl and buy a ticket to Grand Rapids!" Naylor's earlier novel [*The Women of Brewster Place*] presented a similar lim-itation. While she admirably attempts to portray black gays as integral to the fabric of black life she seems incapable of imagining black gays functioning as healthy, average people. In her fiction, although they are not at fault, gays must still be made to pay. This makes her books sound like a return to the forties, not a chronicle of the eighties.[16]

Gomez's response speaks to the problems that many Lesbian femi-nists have with Naylor's versions of our lives, her persistent message that survival is hardly possible. I do not think we simply want "happy endings," although some do occur for Lesbians both in literature and in life, but an indication of the spirit of survival and resistance which has made the continuance of Black Lesbian and gay life possible throughout the ages.

In considering the overall impact of "The Two," I realized that be-cause it is critical of homophobia, it is perhaps an effective story for a heterosexual audience. But because its portrayal of Lesbianism is so negative, its message even to heterosexuals is ambiguous. A semi-sympathetic straight reader's response might well be: "It's a shame something like that had to happen, but I guess that's what you get for being queer." The general public does not want to know that it is possible to be a Lesbian of whatever color and not merely survive, but thrive. And neither does a heterosexual publishing industry want to provide them with this information.

The impact of the story upon Lesbian readers is quite another matter. I imagine what might happen if a Black woman who is grap-pling with defining her sexuality and who has never had the oppor-tunity to read anything else about Lesbians, particularly Black ones, were to read "The Two" as a severely cautionary tale. Justifiably, she might go no further in her exploration, forever denying her feelings. She might eventually have sexual relationships with other women, but remain extremely closeted. Or she might commit suicide. As a Black Lesbian reader, I find Naylor's dire pessimism about our possi-bilities to be the crux of my problems with "The Two."

Alice Walker's portrayal of a Lesbian relationship in her novel *The*

*Color Purple* (1982) is as optimistic as Naylor's is despairing. Celie and Shug's love, placed at the center of the work and set in a rural southern community between the World Wars, is unique in the history of African-American fiction. The fact that a book with a Black Lesbian theme by a Black woman writer achieved massive critical acclaim, became a bestseller, and was made into a major Hollywood film is unprecedented in the history of the world. It is *The Color Purple* which homophobes and antifeminists undoubtedly refer to when they talk about how "many" books currently have both Black Lesbian subject matter and an unsparing critique of misogyny in the Black community. For Black Lesbians, however, especially writers, the book has been inspirational. Reading it we think it just may be possible to be a Black Lesbian and live to tell about it. It may be possible for us to write it down and actually have somebody read it as well.

When I first read *The Color Purple* in galleys in the spring of 1982, I believed it was a classic. I become more convinced every time I read it. Besides great storytelling, perfect Black language, killingly subtle Black women's humor, and an unequivocal Black feminist stance, it is also a deeply philosophical and spiritual work. It is marvelously gratifying to read discussions of nature, love, beauty, God, good, evil, and the meaning of life in the language of our people. The book is like a jewel. Any way you hold it to the light you will always see something new reflected.

The facet of the novel under consideration here is Walker's approach to Lesbianism, but before going further with that discussion, it is helpful to understand that the work is also a fable. The complex simplicity with which Walker tells her story, the archetypal and timeless Black southern world in which it is set, the clear-cut conflicts between good and evil, the complete transformations undergone by several of the major characters, and the huge capacity of the book to teach are all signs that *The Color Purple* is not merely a novel, but a visionary tale. That it is a fable may account partially for the depiction of a Lesbian relationship unencumbered by homophobia or fear of it and entirely lacking in self-scrutiny about the implications of Lesbian identity.

It may be Walker's conscious decision to deal with her readers' potentially negative reactions by using the disarming strategy of writing as if women falling in love with each other were quite ordinary, an average occurrence which does not even need to be specifically remarked. In the "real world" the complete ease with which Celie and Shug move as lovers through a totally heterosexual milieu would be improbable, not to say amazing. Their total acceptance is one clue that this is indeed an inspiring fable, a picture of what the world could be if only human beings were ready to create it. A friend told me about a discussion of the book in a Black writers' workshop she conducted. An older Black woman in the class asserted: "When that kind of business happens, like happened between Shug and Celie, you know there's going to be talk." The woman was not reacting to *Purple* as a fable or even as fiction, but as a "real" story, applying her knowledge of what would undoubtedly happen in real life where most people just aren't ready to deal with Lesbianism and don't want to be.

Because the novel is so truthful, particularly in its descriptions of sexual oppression and to a lesser extent racism, the reader understandably might question those aspects of the fable which are not as plausible. Even within the story itself, it is conceivable that a creature as mean-spirited as Mr. —— might have something to say about Shug, the love of his life, and Celie, his wife, sleeping together in his own house. For those of us who experience homophobia on a daily basis and who often live in fear of being discovered by the wrong person(s), like the teenage thugs in "The Two," we naturally wonder how Celie and Shug, who do not hide their relationship, get away with it.

Another fabulous aspect of Celie's and Shug's relationship is that there are no references to how they think about themselves as Lesbian lovers in a situation where they are the only ones. Although Celie is clearly depicted as a woman who at the very least is not attracted to men and who is generally repulsed by them, I am somewhat hesitant to designate her as a Lesbian because it is not a term that she would likely apply to herself and neither, obviously, would the people around her. In a conversation with Mr. —— in the latter part of the book Celie explains how she feels:

> He say, Celie, tell me the truth. You don't like me cause I'm a man?
> I blow my nose. Take off they pants, I say, and men look like frogs

to me. No matter how you kiss 'em, as far as I'm concern, frogs is what they stay.

I see, he say.[17]

Shug, on the other hand, is bisexual, another contemporary term that does not necessarily apply within the cultural and social context Walker has established. There is the implication that this is among her first, if not only sexual relationship with another woman. The first and only time within the novel when Shug and Celie make love, Walker writes:

She say, I love you, Miss Celie. And then she haul off and kiss me on the mouth.

*Um,* she say, like she surprise. I kiss her back, say, *um,* too. Us kiss and kiss till us can't hardly kiss no more. Then us touch each other.

I don't know nothing bout it, I say to Shug.

I don't know much, she say. (p. 109)

Despite her statement of inexperience, Shug is a wonderfully sensual and attractive woman who takes pleasure in all aspects of living from noticing "the color purple in a field" to making love with whomever. When Shug tries to explain to Celie why she has taken up with a nineteen-year-old boy, the two women's differing perspectives and sexual orientations are obvious. Walker writes:

But Celie, she say. I have to make you understand. Look, she say. I'm gitting old. I'm fat. Nobody think I'm good looking no more, but you. Or so I thought. He's nineteen. A baby. How long can it last?

He's a man. I write on the paper.

Yah, she say. He is. And I know how you feel about men. But I don't feel that way. I would never be fool enough to take any of them seriously, she say, but some mens can be a lots of fun.

Spare me, I write. (p. 220)

Eventually Shug comes back to Celie and Walker implies that they will live out their later years together. The recouplings and reunions that occur in the novel might also indicate that the story is more fantasy than fact. But in Celie and Shug's case, the longevity of their relationship is certainly a validation of love between women.

The day Shug returns, Celie shows her her new bedroom. Walker writes:

> She go right to the little purple frog on my mantelpiece.
>     What this? she ast.
>     Oh, I say, a little something Albert carve for me. (p. 248)

Not only is this wickedly amusing after Celie and Mr. ——'s discussion about "frogs," but Mr. ——'s tolerance at being described as such to the point of his making a joke-gift for Celie seems almost too good to be true. Indeed Mr. ——'s transformation from evil no-count to a sensitive human being is one of the most miraculous one could find anywhere. Those critics and readers who condemn the work because they find the depiction of men so "negative" never seem to focus on how nicely most of them turn out in the end. Perhaps these transformations go unnoticed because in Walker's woman-centered world, in order to change, they must relinquish machismo and violence, the very thought of which would be fundamentally disruptive to the nonfeminist reader's world-view. It is no accident that Walker has Celie, who has become a professional seamstress and designer of pants, teach Mr. —— to sew, an ideal way to symbolize just how far he has come. In the real world, where former husbands of Lesbian mothers take their children away with the support of the patriarchal legal system, and in some cases beat or even murder their former wives, very few men would say what Mr. —— says to Celie about Shug: "I'm real sorry she left you, Celie. I remembered how I felt when she left me" (p. 238). But in the world of *The Color Purple* a great deal is possible.

One of the most beautiful and familiar aspects of the novel is the essential and supportive bonds between Black women. The only other person Celie loves before she meets Shug is her long-lost sister, Nettie. Although neither ever gets an answer, the letters they write to each other for decades and Celie's letters to God before she discovers that Nettie is alive, comprise the entire novel. The work joyously culminates when Nettie, accompanied by Celie's children who were taken away from her in infancy, return home.

Early in the novel Celie "sins against" another woman's spirit and painfully bears the consequences. She tells her stepson, Harpo, to beat his wife Sofia if she doesn't mind him. Soon Celie is so upset about what she has done that she is unable to sleep at night. Sofia, one of the most exquisitely defiant characters in Black women's fiction, fights Harpo right back and when she finds out Celie's part in Harpo's changed behavior comes to confront her. When Celie confesses that she advised Harpo to beat Sofia because she was jealous of Sofia's ability to stand up for herself, the weight is lifted from her soul, the women become fast friends, and she "sleeps like a baby."

When Shug decides that Celie needs to leave Mr. —— and go with her to Memphis, accompanied by Mary Agnes (Squeak), Harpo's lover of many years, they make the announcement at a family dinner. Walker writes:

> You was all rotten children, I say. You made my life a hell on earth. And your daddy here ain't dead horse's shit.
>
> Mr. —— reach over to slap me. I jab my case knife in his hand.
>
> You bitch, he say. What will people say, you running off to Memphis like you don't have a house to look after?
>
> Shug say, Albert. Try to think like you got some sense. Why any woman give a shit what people think is a mystery to me.
>
> Well, say Grady, trying to bring light. A woman can't git a man if peoples talk.
>
> Shug look at me and us giggle. Then us laugh sure nuff. Then Squeak start to laugh. Then Sofia. All us laugh and laugh.
>
> Shug say, Ain't they something? Us say um *hum,* and slap the table, wipe the water from our eyes.
>
> Harpo look at Squeak. Shut up Squeak, he say. It bad luck for women to laugh at men.
>
> She say, Okay. She sit up straight, suck in her breath, try to press her face together.
>
> He look at Sofia. She look at him and laugh in his face. I already had my bad luck, she say. I had enough to keep me laughing the rest of my life. (p. 182)

This marvelously hilarious scene is one of countless examples in the novel of Black women's staunch solidarity. As in *The Women of Brewster Place,* women's caring for each other makes life possible; but in *The Color Purple* Celie and Shug's relationship is accepted as an integral part of the continuum of women loving each other, while in the more realistic work, Lorraine and Theresa are portrayed as social pariahs.

If one accepts that *The Color Purple* is a fable or at the very least has fablelike elements, judgments of verisimilitude and authenticity are necessarily affected. Celie and Shug are undeniably authentic as Black women characters—complex, solid, and whole—but they are not necessarily authentic as Lesbians. Their lack of self-consciousness as Lesbians, the lack of scrutiny their relationship receives from the outside world, and their isolation from other Lesbians make *The Color Purple*'s categorization as a Lesbian novel problematic. It does not appear that it was Walker's intent to create a work that could be definitively or solely categorized as such.

The question of categorization becomes even more interesting when one examines critical responses to the work, particularly in the popular media. Reviews seldom mention that Celie and Shug are lovers. Some critics even go so far as to describe them erroneously as good friends. The fact that their relationship is simply "there" in the novel and not explicitly called attention to as Lesbian might also account for a mass heterosexual audience's capacity to accept the work, although the novel has of course also been homophobically attacked.[18] As a Black Lesbian feminist reader, I have questions about how accurate it is to identify Walker's characters as Lesbians at the same time that I am moved by the vision of a world, unlike this one, where Black women are not forced to lose their families, their community, or their lives, because of whom they love.

A realistic depiction of African American Lesbian experience would neither be a complete idyll nor a total nightmare. Audre Lorde terms *Zami: A New Spelling of My Name* (1982) a "biomythography," a combination of autobiography, history, and myth. I have chosen to discuss it here, because it is the one extended prose work of which I am aware that approaches Black Lesbian experience with *both* verisimilitude and authenticity. *Zami* is an essentially autobiographical work, but the poet's eye, ear, and tongue give the work stylistic richness often associated with well-crafted fiction. At least two other Black women critics, Barbara Christian and Jewelle Gomez, have included *Zami* in their analyses of Black Lesbians in fiction.[19] Because *Zami* spans genres and carves out a unique place in African-American literature as the first full-length autobiographical work by an established Black Lesbian writer, it will undoubtedly continue to be grouped with other creative prose about Black Lesbians.

The fact that *Zami* is autobiographical might be assumed to guarantee its realism. But even when writing autobiographically, an author can pick and choose details, can create a persona that has little or nothing to do with her own particular reality, or she might fabricate an artificial persona with whom the reader cannot possibly identify. A blatant example of this kind of deceptive strategy might be an autobiographical work by a Lesbian that fails to mention that this is indeed who she is; of course there are other less extreme omissions and distortions. Undoubtedly, Lorde has selected the material she includes in the work, and the selectivity of memory is also operative. Yet this work is honest, fully rounded, and authentic. It is not coincidental that of the three works considered here, *Zami* has the most to tell the reader about the texture of Black Lesbian experience and that it is written by an out Black Lesbian feminist. The candor and specificity with which Lorde approaches her life are qualities that would enhance Black Lesbian writing in the future.

*Zami* is a Carriacou word "for women who work together as friends and lovers."[20] Just as the title implies, *Zami* is woman-identified from the outset and thoroughly suffused with an eroticism focusing on women. Lorde connects her Lesbianism to the model her mother, Linda, provided—her pervasive, often intimidating, strength; her fleeting sensuality when her harsh veneer was lifted—and also to her place of origin, the Grenadian island of Carriacou, where a word already existed to describe who Linda's daughter would become. As in the two novels *The Color Purple* and *The Women of Brewster Place,* in *Zami* relationships between women are at the center of the work. Here they are complex, turbulent, painful, passionate, and essential to the author's survival.

Although Lorde continuously explores the implications of being a Black Lesbian and she has an overt consciousness about her Lesbianism which is missing from Naylor's and Walker's works, she does not define Lesbianism as a problem in and of itself. Despite homophobia, particularly in the left of the McCarthy era; despite isolation from other Black women because she is gay; and despite primal loneliness because of her many levels of difference, Lorde assumes that her Lesbianism, like her Blackness, is a given, a fact of life which she has neither to justify nor explain. This is an extremely strong

and open-ended stance from which to write about Black Lesbian experience, since it enables the writer to deal with the complexity of
Lesbianism and what being a Black Lesbian means in a specific time
and place. Lorde's position allows Black Lesbian experience to be revealed from the inside out. The absence of agonized doubts about
her sexual orientation and the revelation of the actual joys of being a
Lesbian, including lush and recognizable descriptions of physical
passion between women, make *Zami* seem consciously written for a
Lesbian reader. This is a significant point because so little is ever
written with us in mind, and also because who an author considers
her audience to be definitely affects her voice and the levels of authenticity she may be able to achieve. Writing from an avowedly
Black Lesbian perspective with Black Lesbian readers in mind does
not mean that a work will be inaccessible or inapplicable to non-
Black and non-Lesbian readers. Works like *Zami,* which are based in
the experiences of writers outside the "mainstream," provide a vitally
different perspective on human experience and may even reveal new
ways of thinking about supposedly settled questions. Or, as Celie
puts it in *The Color Purple:* "If he [God] ever listened to poor colored
women the world would be a different place, I can tell you" (p. 175).
It would be more different still if "he" also listened to Lesbians.

The fact that *Zami* is written from an unequivocally Black Lesbian
and feminist perspective undoubtedly explains why it is the one book
of the three under discussion that is published by an alternative
press, why it was turned down by at least a dozen trade publishers,
including one that specializes in gay titles. The white male editor at
that supposedly sympathetic house returned the manuscript saying,
"If only you were just one," Black or Lesbian. The combination is
obviously too much for the trade publishing establishment to handle.
We bring news that others do not want to hear. It is unfortunate that
the vast majority of the readers of *The Women of Brewster Place* and
*The Color Purple* will never have the opportunity to read *Zami.*

Lorde's description of Black "gay-girl" life in the Greenwich Village of the 1950s is fascinating, if for no other reason than that it
reveals a piece of our cultural history. What is even more intriguing
is her political activist's sense of how the struggles of women during
that era helped shape our contemporary movement and how many
of our current issues, especially the desire to build a Black Lesbian
community, were very much a concern at that time. The author's

search for other Black Lesbians and her lovingly detailed descriptions of the fragments of community she finds give this work an atmosphere of reality missing in "The Two" and *The Color Purple.* Unlike Lorraine and Theresa and Celie and Shug, Lorde is achingly aware of her need for peers. She writes:

> I remember how being young and Black and gay and lonely felt. A lot of it was fine, feeling I had the truth and the light and the key, but a lot of it was purely hell.
>
> There were no mothers, no sisters, no heroes. We had to do it alone, like our sister Amazons, the riders on the loneliest outposts of the kingdom of Dahomey. . . . There were not enough of us. But we surely tried. (pp. 176–177)

> Every Black woman I ever met in the Village in those years had some part in my survival, large or small, if only as a figure in the headcount at the Bag on a Friday night.
>
> Black lesbians in the Bagatelle faced a world only slightly less hostile than the outer world which we had to deal with every day on the outside—that world which defined us as doubly nothing because we were Black and because we were Woman—that world which raised our blood pressures and shaped our furies and our nightmares. . . . All of us who survived those common years have to be a little proud. A lot proud. Keeping ourselves together and on our own tracks, however wobbly, was like trying to play the Dinizulu War Chant or a Beethoven sonata on a tin dog-whistle. (p. 225)

The humor, tenacity, and vulnerability which Lorde brings to her version of being in "the life" are very precious. Here is something to grab hold of, a place to see one's face reflected. Despite the daily grind of racism, homophobia, sexual, and class oppression, compounded by the nonsolutions of alcohol, drugs, suicide, and death at an early age, some women did indeed make it.

Lorde also describes the much more frequent interactions and support available from white Lesbians who were in the numerical majority. Just as they are now, relationships between Black and white women in the 1950s were often undermined by racism, but Lorde documents that some women were at least attempting to deal with their differences. She writes:

However imperfectly, we tried to build a community of sorts where we could, at the very least, survive within a world we correctly perceived to be hostile to us; we talked endlessly about how best to create that mutual support which twenty years later was being discussed in the women's movement as a brand new concept. Lesbians were probably the only Black and white women in New York City in the fifties who were making any real attempt to communicate with each other; we learned lessons from each other, the values of which were not lessened by what we did not learn. (p. 179)

Lorde approaches the meaning of difference from numerous vantage points in *Zami*. In much of her work prior to *Zami* she has articulated and developed the concept of difference which has gained usage in the women's movement as a whole and in the writing of women of color specifically. From her early childhood, long before she recognizes herself as a Lesbian, the question of difference is *Zami's* subtext, its ever-present theme. Lorde writes: "*It was in high school that I came to believe that I was different from my white classmates, not because I was Black, but because I was me*" (p. 82). Although Lorde comes of age in an era when little if any tolerance existed for those who did not conform to white male hegemony, her stance and that of her friends is one of rebellion and creative resistance, including political activism, as opposed to conformity and victimization. *Zami* mediates the versions of Lesbianism presented in *The Women of Brewster Place* and *The Color Purple*. It is not a horror story, although it reveals the difficulties of Black Lesbian experience. It is not a fable, although it reveals the joys of a life committed to women.

Since much of her quest in *Zami* is to connect with women who recognize and share her differences, particularly other Black Lesbians, it seems fitting that the work closes with her account of a loving relationship with another Black woman, Afrekete. Several years before the two women become lovers, Lorde meets Kitty at a Black Lesbian house party in Queens. Lorde writes:

One of the women I had met at one of these parties was Kitty.
When I saw Kitty again one night years later in the Swing Rendezvous or the Pony Stable or the Page Three—that tour of second-

string gay-girl bars that I had taken to making alone that sad lonely spring of 1957—it was easy to recall the St. Alban's smell of green Queens summer-night and plastic couch-covers and liquor and hair oil and women's bodies at the party where we had first met.

In that brick-faced frame house in Queens, the downstairs pine-paneled recreation room was alive and pulsing with loud music, good food, and beautiful Black women in all different combinations of dress. (p. 241)

The women wear fifties dyke-chic, ranging from "skinny straight skirts" to Bermuda and Jamaica shorts. Just as the clothes, the smells, the song lyrics, and food linger in the author's mind, her fully rendered details of Black Lesbian culture resonate within the reader. I recalled this party scene while attending a dinner party at the home of two Black Lesbians in the deep South earlier this year. One of the hostesses arrived dressed impeccably in white Bermuda shorts, black knee-socks, and loafers. Her hair straightened, 1980s style much like that of the 1950s, completed my sense of déjà vu. Contemporary Black Lesbians are a part of a cultural tradition which we are just beginning to discover through interviews with older women such as Mabel Hampton and the writing of authors like Ann Allen Shockley, Anita Cornwell, Pat Parker, and Lorde.

When she meets Afrekete again, their relationship helps to counteract Lorde's loneliness following the break-up of a long-term relationship with a white woman. The bond between the women is stunningly erotic, enriched by the bond they share as Black women. Lorde writes:

By the beginning of summer the walls of Afrekete's apartment were always warm to the touch from the heat beating down on the roof, and chance breezes through her windows rustled her plants in the window and brushed over our sweat-smooth bodies, at rest after loving.

We talked sometimes about what it meant to love women, and what a relief it was in the eye of the storm, no matter how often we had to bite our tongues and stay silent. . . .

Once we talked about how Black women had been committed without choice to waging our campaigns in the enemies' strongholds, too much and too often, and how our psychic landscapes had been plundered and wearied by those repeated battles and campaigns.

"And don't I have the scars to prove it," she sighed. "Makes you tough though, babe, if you don't go under. And that's what I like about you; you're like me. We're both going to make it because we're both too tough and crazy not to!" And we held each other and laughed and cried about what we had paid for that toughness, and how hard it was to explain to anyone who didn't already know it that soft and tough had to be one and the same for either to work at all, like our joy and the tears mingling on the one pillow beneath our heads. (p. 250)

The fact that this conversation occurs in 1957 is both amazing and unremarkable. Black Lesbians have a heritage far older than a few decades, a past that dates back to Africa, as Lorde herself documents in the essay, "Scratching the Surface: Some Notes on Barriers to Women and Loving."[21] Lorde's authentic portrayal of one segment of that history in *Zami* enables us to see both our pasts and futures more clearly. Her work provides a vision of possibility for Black Lesbians surviving whole, despite all, which is the very least we can demand from our literature, our activism, and our lives.

Despite the homophobic exclusion and silencing of Black Lesbian writers, the creation of complex, accurate, and artistically compelling depictions of Black Lesbians in literature has been and will continue to be essential to the development of African-American women's literature as a whole. The assertion of Black women's right to autonomy and freedom, which is inherent in the lives of Black Lesbians and which is made politically explicit in Black Lesbian feminist theory and practice, has crucial implications for all women's potential liberation. Ultimately, the truth that never hurts is that Black Lesbians and specifically Black Lesbian writers are here to stay. In spite of every effort to erase us, we are committed to living visibly with integrity and courage and to telling our Black women's stories for centuries to come.

## Notes

1    Calvin Hernton, "The Sexual Mountain and Black Women Writers," *The Black Scholar* 16, no. 4 (July/August 1985). 7. Reprinted in this volume.

2    Barbara Christian, *Black Feminist Criticism: Perspectives on Black Women Writers* (New York: Pergamon, 1986), p. 188.

3     Audre Lorde and Ann Allen Shockley are two exceptions. They have published with both commercial and independent publishers. It should be noted that Lorde's poetry is currently published by a commercial publisher, but that all of her works of prose have been published by independent women's presses. In conversation with Lorde I have learned that *Zami: A New Spelling of My Name* was rejected by at least a dozen commercial publishers.

4     Christian, *Black Feminist Criticism,* pp. 199–200.

5     Alice Walker, "Breaking Chains and Encouraging Life," in *In Search of Our Mothers' Gardens: Womanist Prose* (New York: Harcourt Brace Jovanovich, 1984), pp. 288–289.

6     In her essay, "The Black Lesbian in American Literature: An Overview," Ann Allen Shockley summarizes Jones's negative or inadequate treatment of Lesbian themes in her novels *Corregidora* and *Eva's Man* and in two of her short stories. Ann Allen Shockley, "The Black Lesbian in American Literature: An Overview," in *Home Girls: A Black Feminist Anthology,* ed. Barbara Smith (Latham, N.Y.: Kitchen Table Press, 1982), p. 89.

7     In her essay "The Failure to Transform: Homophobia in the Black Community," Cheryl Clarke comments: "The black lesbian is not only absent from the pages of black political analysis, her image as a character in literature and her role as a writer are blotted out from or trivialized in literary criticism written by black women." Clarke also cites examples of such omissions. In *Home Girls,* ed. Smith, pp. 204–205.

8     Barbara Smith, "Racism and Women's Studies," in *All the Women Are White, All the Blacks are Men, But Some of Us Are Brave: Black Women's Studies,* ed. Gloria Hull, Patricia Bell Scott, and Barbara Smith (New York: Feminist Press, 1981), p. 49.

9     Mitsuye Yamada, "Invisibility Is an Unnatural Disaster: Reflections of an Asian American Woman," in *This Bridge Called My Back: Writings by Radical Women of Color,* ed. Cherrie Moraga and Gloria Anzaldua (Latham, N.Y.: Kitchen Table Press, 1984), pp. 35–40.

10     Cheryl Clarke, *Narratives: Poems in the Tradition of Black Women* (Latham, N.Y.: Kitchen Table, 1983), p. 15.

11     Jewelle Gomez, in *Home Girls,* ed. Smith, p. 122.

12     Langston Hughes, "The Negro Artist and the Racial Mountain," in *Voices from the Harlem Renaissance,* ed. Nathan Huggins (New York: Oxford, 1976), p. 309. It is interesting to note that recent research has revealed that Hughes and a number of other major figures of the Harlem Renaissance were gay. See Charles Michael Smith, "Bruce Nugent: Bohemian of the Harlem Renaissance," in *In the Life: A Black Gay Anthology,* ed. Joseph F. Beam (Boston: Alyson, 1986), pp. 213–214 and selections by Langston

Hughes in *Gay and Lesbian Poetry in Our Time: An Anthology,* ed. Carl Morse and Joan Larkin (New York: St. Martin's, 1988), pp. 204–206.

13      Paul Dunbar, "We Wear the Mask," in *The Life and Works of Paul Laurence Dunbar,* ed. Wiggins (New York: Kraus, 1971), p. 184.

14      Audre Lorde, "There is No Hierarchy of Oppressions," in *The Council on Interracial Books for Children Bulletin, Homophobia and Education: How to Deal with Name-Calling,* ed. Leonore Gordon, Vol. 14, nos. 3 & 4 (1983), 9.

15      Gloria Naylor, *The Women of Brewster Place* (New York: Penguin, 1983), pp. 165–166. All subsequent references to this work will be cited in the text.

16      Jewelle Gomez, "Naylor's Inferno," *The Women's Review of Books* 2, no. 11 (August 1985), 8.

17      Alice Walker, *The Color Purple* (New York: Washington Square, 1982), p. 224. All subsequent references to this work will be cited in the text.

18      In his essay, "Who's Afraid of Alice Walker?" Calvin Hernton describes the "hordes of . . . black men (and some women)" who condemned both the novel and the film of *The Color Purple* all over the country. He singles out journalist Tony Brown as a highly visible leader of these attacks. Brown both broadcast television shows and wrote columns about a book and movie he admitted neither to have read nor seen. Hernton raises the question, "Can it be that the homophobic, nitpicking screams of denial against *The Color Purple* are motivated out of envy, jealousy and guilt, rather than out of any genuine concern for the well-being of black people?" Calvin Hernton, *The Sexual Mountain and Black Women Writers* (New York: Anchor, 1987), pp. 30–36.

19      Christian, *Black Feminist Criticism,* pp. 187–210. Gomez, in *Home Girls,* ed. Smith, pp. 118–119.

20      Audre Lorde, *Zami: A New Spelling of My Name* (Freedom, Calif.: Crossing, 1983), p. 255. All subsequent references to this work will be cited in the text.

21      Audre Lorde, *Sister Outsider* (Freedom, Calif.: Crossing, 1984), pp. 45–52.

# Joanne V. Gabbin

# A Laying On of Hands: Black Women Writers Exploring the Roots of Their Folk and Cultural Tradition

Contemporary black women writers, like many of their heroines, have gone deeply into themselves to discover who they are, to urge forth a voice too long silenced by a male-centered literary tradition, and to heal wounds inflicted by racism, oppression, and indifference. Their willingness to explore the very loam of their emotional lives as Sula did in Toni Morrison's novel and their courage to bare their scars as Vyry did in Margaret Walker's *Jubilee* have resulted in a powerful infusion of health and vitality into today's American literary scene. With their writing they are challenging the premises upon which women have been defined and, inevitably, are smashing icons in a struggle toward self-definition. They are telling their stories, born in intimacy and nourished by communal revelation, by drawing upon a rich legacy of storytelling and myth-making. Transforming these oral forms into innovative literary structures, black women writers are giving evidence of another aesthetic experience and, in the process, using particularly womanist forms of thought and expression, are rocking the foundations of a Euro-centric male hegemony which has dominated American literature.

In Paule Marshall's *Praisesong for the Widow,* the protagonist Avey Johnson goes through a transforming experience brought on by "a laying on of hands" that may serve as an appropriate analogy to the transformation that is taking place in Afro-American literature. Like

Avey Johnson, whose memory of the past forces her "to embark on her own personal ritual of cleansing, healing and empowerment,"[1] black women writers have begun to explore the roots of their cultural tradition and, as symbolic agents in a kind of ritualistic laying-on-of-hands experience, are cleansing, healing and empowering the images of themselves. What is the point of using this cultural ritual as a metaphor to discuss black women writers' exploring of folk and cultural traditions? Before an answer becomes apparent, an interpretation of the term "a laying on of hands" is essential. The term signifies an ancient practice of using hands in a symbolical act of blessing, healing, and ordination. By its very act it appears to bestow some gift. Some identify the practice with one of the gifts of the Spirit that Paul speaks of in Corinthians. Thus it is associated with the healing power of Christ as he lays his hands on sufferers and they are cured. Others see the practice as central to the African concept that the body and spirit are one. "Thus sensuality is essential to the process of healing and rebirth of the spirit."[2] For the purpose of this discussion, the practice represents the transmission of a miraculous power that heals, restores, and transforms all that it touches. However mystical the practice appears, the existence of such powers is readily accepted by initiates who have experienced a laying on of hands.

Paule Marshall in her novel *Praisesong for the Widow* provides a striking illustration of the dimensions of the ritual and its purpose. Avey Johnson, the novel's central character, has this sensual/spiritual experience while on holiday in Carriacou, a small island in the Caribbean. Drawn into the island's annual festival of spiritual rejuvenation, this middle-aged, middle-class woman receives the laying-on-of-hands experience from Rosalie Parvay, who skillfully coaxes away Avey's self-consciousness and aversion to having someone interfere with her "obsessive privacy." Parvay prepares Avey for her later Big Drum conversion, which will have the final effect of expelling the artificiality, the aridity, and the falseness from her suburban existence.

After Parvay's vigorous kneading and pummeling, "Avey Johnson became aware of a faint stinging . . . and a warmth."

> Then slowly, they radiated out into her loins. The warmth, the stinging sensation that was both pleasure and pain passed up through the emptiness at her center. Until finally they reached her heart. And as

they encircled her heart and it responded, there was the sense of a
chord being struck. All the tendons, nerves and muscles which strung
her together had been struck a powerful chord, and the reverberation
could be heard in the remotest corners of her body.[3]

Through this experience Avey Avatarra Johnson is brought to health
and wholeness and is spiritually prepared for the atavistic ceremony
that will transform her existence and restore her name.

The same way that Rosalie Parvay is the channel for Avey's spiritual rebirth, black women writers are transforming Afro-American
literature. By exploring the roots of their folk and cultural tradition
they have discovered an aesthetic foundation upon which to build
art that is vital, original, and rich in emotional and spiritual depth.
Zora Neale Hurston lays on hands and takes it as her sacred task to
keep alive Afro-American oral traditions in the living memories of
black people. In her now classic novel of a black woman's journey
into womanhood and self-possession, *Their Eyes Were Watching God,*
she surrounds Janie Crawford's story with the lore she had heard as a
child in the all-black town of Eatonville, Florida. Margaret Walker
lays on her hands and retrieves the Afro-American past, whole and
true, in her epic novel *Jubilee.* She exorcises the devils of stereotyp-
ing that had relegated too many images of black women to the roles
of mammies, harlots, and confused and tragic mulattoes. Urging out
of her personal history and painstaking research a sensibility that
eschewed racial timidity, she creates the memorable portrait of her
great grandmother and, concomitantly, an authentic portrait of a
race that loves freedom. Toni Morrison, with the power of her hands,
reveals the way black people see the world of the flesh and the world
of the spirit. She writes about their superstitions, their rituals, their
cosmology with cherished objectivity. In *Sula,* her second novel, she
examines the community of Medallion, the lives of the Peace women,
and the complex relationship that Sula and Nel share with a rigor
and tough-mindedness familiar to folk who knew the blues as well as
the spirituals.

Hurston, Walker, and Morrison are three of a long list of black
women writers including Gwendolyn Brooks, Maya Angelou,
Ntozake Shange, Mari Evans, Paule Marshall, Sonia Sanchez, Alice
Walker, Kristin Hunter, Toni Cade Bambara, Nikki Giovanni, and
Gloria Naylor, whose works are bringing a vitality to American

literature that has been sorely needed. This vitality is rooted in their determination to possess their images, to name themselves, and to establish their place. It is rooted in their unabashed confrontation with the past and clear-eyed vision of the future, in their inclination away from empty protest toward revelation and informed social change. Particularly in Hurston's *Their Eyes Were Watching God,* Walker's *Jubilee,* and Morrison's *Sula,* the considerable impact of these works can be traced to the writers' fulfillment of their artistic selves as they explore form, content, and imagery in the context of a rich Afro-American folk culture.

Hurston is foremost among black women writers of the 1930s and 1940s and a pioneer in the use of folklore in her fiction. Critic Sterling Brown said fifty years ago that her short stories, "Drenched in Light," "Spunk," and "The Gilded Six-Bits," all published between 1924 and 1931, "showed a command of folklore and idiom excelled by no earlier Negro novelist."[4] Though she has been dead since 1960, interest in her work has grown exponentially. This revival of interest can be attributed to her sound cultural aesthetic and her ingenious grasp of craft. Her accomplishments have encouraged Alice Walker, Robert Hemenway, Barbara Smith, and Mary Helen Washington, among others, to give serious critical attention to her work.

Born in the lap of Floridian folk culture, Hurston used the stuff of rural life to fill her stories. In most of her fiction, the center of interest is Florida, whether it is Orlando, Maitland, the swamps of the Everglades, or her native Eatonville. In the setting of a little factory town near Orlando, Missie May and Joe, the affectionate young couple in "The Gilded Six-Bits," have their marital bliss briefly interrupted by a city slicker whose apparent easy way with money offers a dangerous temptation to the naive wife. The story is notable because of the typically sympathetic view Hurston gives of the life of rural folk and the profusion of folk expressions that inform her narrative. Hurston writes in her autobiography, *Dust Tracks on a Road,* that she picked up many of these expressions on the porch of the town store where as a girl she "dragged" her feet so that she could get an ear-full of adult "double talk": "For instance, somebody would remark: Ada Bell is ruint, you know. Yep, somebody was telling me. A pitcher can go the well a long time, but it's bound to get broke sooner or later."[5] She also gathered into her imagination the tales told in the "lying sessions." With an obvious joy of recollection, Hurston describes these sessions and their participants "straining against each other in telling folk tales." "God, Devil, Brer Rabbit, Brer Fox, Sis Cat, Brer Bear, Lion, Tiger, Buzzard, and all the wood folk walked and talked like natural men."[6] The folksy vernacular, the hyperbole, and the irony are always there as she recounts stories about Big John de Conquer and other folk heroes who reign supreme in the imaginations of her hometown folk.

Such material plays a significant role in the creation of her best known novel, *Their Eyes Were Watching God.* Emphasizing the importance of nature in folk life, Hurston introduces the protagonist Janie Crawford with an array of nature symbols. Hurston shows the possibilities for Janie's love and marriage in the blossoming pear tree, for her freedom and fulfillment with the beckoning horizon, and for her sensuality in the hum of the singing bees. From Janie's unfortunate marriage to Old Man Logan Killicks, who succeeds in killing her dreams about romance, through her twenty-year marriage to Joe Starks, Hurston enlists the aid of natural symbols to show her development. She also uses the tales and "lying sessions" to advance her plot and to reveal the emotional texture of her characters. For instance, skillfully juxtaposing the sensual, lively play-acting of the porch against the reality of the spiritless marriage that Janie and Joe Starks share, Hurston effectively reveals Janie's frustration and disappointment in her loveless marriage and the empty years of striving and climbing. After hearing one of the porch regulars use exaggerated though amorous terms to court the beautiful, disinterested Daisy, Janie reflects on her own marriage bed: "The bed was no longer a daisy field for her and Joe to play in. It was a place where she went and laid down when she was sleepy and tired" (62).[7] Her marriage to Joe is doomed to failure because the freedom that Janie first envisioned is trampled by her husband's insecurity and his chauvinism.

After Joe dies and she is a respectable, middle-aged widow, she falls in love with and marries a good-hearted, fun-loving man named Tea Cake Woods. Yet fate and nature are in devilish league, and their dream marriage is short-lived. The two are caught in a violent hurricane that rips through the Everglades and destroys and kills much in its path. As the couple struggles to reach safety, Tea Cake is bitten by a rabid dog. Janie, in what is called "the meanest moment of eternity" (152) is forced to shoot him. The tragic circumstances that lead to the shooting of Tea Cake are brilliantly conceived and reflect Hurston's rooting in the beauty, form, and vitality of folk art. Like some time-honored spiritual, the following passage combines an awareness of a personal, even intimate, relationship with God and a deep sense of the inexorable limitations of mortal life:

> The wind came back with triple fury, and put out the light for the last time. They sat in company with the others in other shanties, their eyes straining against crude walls and their souls asking if He meant to measure their puny might against His. They seemed to be staring at the dark, but their eyes were watching God. (131)

Janie embodies a black woman's search for personhood within the bounds of a specific black community. Hurston, in having Janie tell her story to Phoeby, allows Janie to affirm and to challenge her community's definition of her. As she enlists the power of storytelling to defend herself against the gossip and disapprobation of the townsfolk, she learns about the power of language to recreate reality, to reconstruct the past, and, thus, to construct the parameters of the future. Nanny, Janie's grandmother, knew about this power. As "mind-pictures brought feelings and feelings dragged out dramas from the hollows of her heart," Nanny told her granddaughter of her tumultuous passage from slavery and of the crushing feeling of resignation and impuissance that she did not want to leave as a legacy. Therefore, when Nanny pleads, "Have some sympathy fuh me. Put me down easy, Janie, Ah'm a cracked plate" (21), Janie's response is predictable. As Janie's story replicates her grandmother's in persuasive force and intent, the tradition continues.

Exploring traditional orality, Hurston also invents an effective narrative frame in *Their Eyes Were Watching God*. Elizabeth A. Meese in her book *Crossing the Double-Cross: The Practice of Feminist Criticism* suggests that Hurston constructs a narrative frame in which only the Janie who has looked upon chaos and disaster as well as experienced love and personal fulfillment can tell the story. She argues that any other strategy "would have diminished the power of Janie's having come to speak, one of the highest forms of achievement and artistry in the folk community."[8] As the reader hears Janie say to Phoeby, "You got tuh *go* there tuh *know* there" (158), Hurston reminds the reader of the narrative authority bequeathed to ancestral black folk who held in trust the cultural value that speaking is equivalent to knowing. When Janie finishes her story, she says to her friend, "Ah'm back home agin and Ah'm satisfied tuh be heah. Ah done been tuh de horizon and back and now Ah kin set heah in mah house and live by comparisons" (158). Her comment, rich in racial vernacular and philosophy, sends the reader back to the opening comparison of men and women. Janie, like Hurston herself, has used language to push back the horizon; she has culled from it all of its power to outwit time with remembering, to create life and transform death, and to secure the dream and make it truth.

> Tea Cake, with sun for a shawl. Of course he wasn't dead. He could never be dead until she herself had finished feeling and thinking. The kiss of his memory made pictures of love and light against the wall. Here was peace. She pulled in her horizon like a great fish-net. Pulled it from around the waist of the world and draped it over her shoulder. So much of life in its meshes. She called in her soul to come and see. (159)

As Hurston achieves a language and structure that evince her rooting in the Afro-American folk tradition, Margaret Walker gathers the shards of the black historical experience and fashions them into art. In her novel *Jubilee,* she envelops the story of her maternal great-grandmother Margaret Duggans Ware Brown with a rich cloak of rituals, myths, songs, and lore passed down through generations of racial memory. As Walker chronicles Vyry's life, she amplifies its meaning with sacred and secular songs that voice the anguish, anger, and exultation felt by black people during the fateful years of the Civil War and Reconstruction. Eleanor Traylor in her essay, "Music as Theme: The Blues Mode in the Works of Margaret Walker," identifies music as a significant reference in Afro-American narrative and fiction. Claiming for sacred and secular songs the importance of "ancestral touchstone," she writes, "The oracular, evocative, incantatory elliptical songs of African-American oral literature form a base of traditional reference which may be called the blues mode of Afro-American narrative and fiction."[9] As Traylor recognizes, Walker has made music her leitmotif. She has revealed in the songs a paradigm

for life and, with songs that are jubilant, ironic, irreverent, and sanctified, has signaled the complexity of the people who sang them.

The lyrics of the spiritual "Swing low, sweet chariot / Coming for
to carry me home . . ." begin the story of Vyry, one of several children, born to Hetta and her white master, John Dutton.[10] Death
hovers over Hetta, who is worn out with childbirth. When death finally arrives, Brother Ezekiel, the spiritual leader of the slave community, sings the death chant: "Soon one morning / Death come
knocking at my door" (14). As Vyry begins her journey as a motherless child—a servant in her father's house—she is not prepared for
the vitriol of the master's wife Salina or the cruel neglect of a master-
father who disinherits his own flesh and blood.

However, in this hostile setting Vyry discovers that she has the
power to absorb the incongruities of slave life and deal with the
chaos by seeking identity with her community. The community's
greatest hope, freedom, is hers. "Flee as a bird to your mountain / Ye
who are weary of sin / Go to the clear flowing fountain / Where you
may wash and be clean" (32). As she sings her favorite hymn, filter-
ing her emotions through song while cultivating her own voice,
Vyry, the novitiate, is brought into the circle of folk wisdom in the
slave community whose existence was a testament to its survival
mechanisms. Aunt Sally tells her about "who she was and where she
came from and what life was like and how to live in the Big House
and get along with Big Missy" (36). Brother Ezekiel teaches her the
funny stories about the spider and the cat, the wise donkey and the
silly man. Mammy Sukey teaches her the use of herbs, and the wise
elders of the quarter teach the lessons of dissimulation.

Yet there are times when the community cannot protect its own.
When Vyry is caught after trying to run away to meet her husband
Randall Ware, the community cannot prevent the whip that cuts
seventy-five lashes on her naked back. When her ordeal is over she
wonders why she is still alive: "'Why has God let me live?' All the
black people must be scared to come and get me till it is black dark.
Maybe they think I'm dead. Lawd, have mercy, Jesus! Send somebody to get me soon, please Jesus!" (144) Walker, remembering the
WPA stories of ex-slaves that she had read, as they told of the horrors of slavery and remembering the tales handed down in her family, does not take the easy route to sentimentality even in these most

searing scenes. Rather, she captures the folk's deep sense of their limitations in the face of a universe they do not control. She concludes that chapter with restraint and understatement: "She was too weak to speak above a whisper, and when she was able to examine herself she saw where one of the lashes had left a loose flap of flesh over her breast like a tuck in a dress. It healed that way" (145).

With similar material lesser writers have been tempted to recast stereotypes for purposes of idealization and denigration or to write obvious propaganda to protest or to justify. In an interview with Claudia Tate in *Black Women Writers at Work*, Walker suggests that this false, stereotypical treatment of black women in literature stems from the mangled roots of the plantation tradition:

> The plantation tradition is the source of female characters as the mammy, the faithful retainer, the pickaninny, Little Eva and Topsy, the tragic mulatto, conjure-woman or witch, the sex object, the bitch goddess, the harlot and prostitute and, last but not least, the matriarch. These are typical and stereotypical roles of black women in American fiction, poetry, and drama. Furthermore, black as well as white writers have worked within this tradition. It was on the plantation that the brutalizing of black women was at its greatest.[11]

Because of the many years that it took to research and write *Jubilee,* Walker recognizes that truthful revelation is the best approach to character portrayal and serves the cause of freedom as stereotypes and propaganda never can. Therefore, Walker's protagonist breaks the mold of mammy, the white folk's nigger, the powerless victim, because Walker puts into Vyry's character a shrewd pragmatism, a tongue laced with irony, and a spirit of love that empowers her. As the reader hears Vyry say to her son, "Love stretches your heart and makes you big inside," one recognizes a woman who has been through dissolution and chaos but who, in accepting the role of suffering, has retained her humanity.

Walker is a forceful portrayer of characters in literature mainly because she puts into her portraits the same strengths that she found in members of her family and in herself. Perhaps *Jubilee* remains such a book of truth and inspiration because it is a product of Walker's mature perspective of the folk heritage she treasures and of her life with all its patterns of struggle, achievement, and determination.

Toni Morrison, author of *The Bluest Eye, Sula, Song of Solomon, Tar Baby,* and *Beloved,* shares with Walker and Hurston a firm grounding in black cultural traditions and aesthetics. With depth and subtlety, Morrison makes the folk tradition the impulse behind her creative approach and her means of sharing crucial messages for the black community.

In *Sula,* her second novel, Morrison shows her willingness to trust black folk roots. Like Richard Wright, Ralph Ellison, Sterling Brown, Zora Neale Hurston, Langston Hughes, Margaret Walker, and others, Morrison is convinced that original, profound, significant literary expression can sprout from these sturdy, humble roots. An obvious consequence of her approach is realness. In *Sula* she creates a blues-tinged world in which people of the Bottom mask their pain with "a shucking, knee-slapping, wet-eyed laughter."[12] It is a world of National Suicide Days, broomsticks across doors to ward off evil, and conjure women acquainted with High John the Conquer, Devil's Shoe String, footstep dust, and fingernail parings. It is a place where folks preserve naming rituals. Tar Baby, Plum, the deweys, Boy Boy, Chicken Little—ironic, diminutive, affectionate names—ring with the familiarity of annual family reunions and front-stoop games. In the Bottom, the haunts of the people and their business establishments—the Elmira Theatre, Irene's Palace of Cosmetology, Reba's Grill, the Time and a Half Pool Hall, and Edna Finch's Mellow House—have a raucous reality stamped upon them. Even the "nigger joke" explaining why the white people lived in the rich, fertile valley and blacks lived in the hills above, which accounts for the origin of the Bottom, assumes the level of myth. The joke, which Morrison created out of a family reminiscence told to her by her mother, recalls other self-mocking tales in which blacks lose out.[13] Sometimes dismissed with a laugh out of hell and sometimes functioning as Ellison's blues in keeping a painful incident alive in the group's consciousness, the joke was emblematic of the mood and temperament of the place.[14]

This vivid, raucous, and tragicomic world of the Bottom is Sula's antagonist and remains alive during three generations of Peace women who stride like giants into the reader's imagination. Eva Peace, Sula's grandmother, is a powerful woman whose mystery and will accommodate bizarre acts of self-sacrifice and maternal authority. Hannah Peace, Sula's mother "who simply refused to live without the attentions of a man," is as generous and natural in her manlove as the mythical earth mother in spring. Her daughter, Sula, is different. She is the image of a woman in possession of herself. Her difference makes her at once the pariah of the Bottom and its most precious and needed symbol of evil. Sula is the center. It is through Sula that her friend Nel Wright completes herself. Sula is also Shadrack's vision of unextinguishable life, the lingering spirit bird. For many years Shadrack, the Bottom's hermit and resident lunatic, kept her belt as a momento of her frantic visit to his shack. Morrison writes,

> It hung on a nail near his bed—unframed, unsullied after all those years, with only the permanent bend in the fabric made by its long life on a nail. It was pleasant living with that sign of a visitor, his only one. And after a while he was able to connect the belt with the face, the tadpole-over-the-eye-face that he sometimes saw up in the Bottom. His visitor, his company, his guest, his social life, his woman, his daughter, his friend—they all hung there on a nail near his bed. (135)

Through these relationships, Morrison wraps Sula in the haunting otherworldliness of the spirituals, making her comforter and friend.

As Morrison subtly weaves in rituals, manners, myths, and customs that make the Bottom and the people who live there real, she has a clear-eyed approach to the tradition. Rejecting idealization and sentimentality, she avoids the pitfalls of attributing all that is good to the tradition. In *Sula* the proverbial collective wisdom of the folk is held up to Morrison's spotlight and collective ignorance often appears. A prime example is Eva Peace's treatment of the Deweys, her adopted sons. As the folk expression goes, "I treats all my children just the same." This bit of folk "wisdom" led Eva to treat each Dewey, distinctly different in character, exactly the same, until gradually one could not be distinguished from the others.

> Slowly each boy came out of whatever cocoon he was in at the time his mother or somebody gave him away, and accepted Eva's view, becoming in fact as well as in name a dewey—joining with the other two to become a trinity with a plural name . . . inseparable, loving nothing and no one but themselves. When the handle from the icebox fell off, all the deweys got whipped, and in dry-eyed silence watched their own feet as they turned their behinds high up into the air for the stroke. (33)

The Deweys are bludgeoned into insipid sameness by folk love and indifference. Morrison appears to a take deadly aim, according to critic Odette C. Martin, against distortions of the values of kinship, survival of the tribe, and collective responsibility, especially reflected in such thinking as "ain't none of my children no better than the others" and "one more child ain't gonna make no difference."[15]

Toni Morrison also holds suspect the folk family that has prided itself on enduring and surviving. Eva Peace, the epitome of survival values, sacrifices her leg for money to support her children and then kills Plum, her drug addict son, when he tries to crawl back into her womb. The highly touted control and authority of black mothers captured in the half-serious threat "I brought you into this world and I'll take you out," takes on a sinister quality as the reader hears Hannah scream, "'Plum! Plum! He's burning, Mamma! We can't even open the door! Mamma!' Eva looked into Hannah's eyes. "'Is? My baby? Burning?'" (41).

As keenly as Morrison brings the reader to ask "what should be the quality of life and how steep a price is to be paid for survival?," she also convinces the reader of her effectiveness in adapting the elements of folklore to tell, enrich, and deepen her story. Though Morrison uses elements of folklore in creating tone and setting and in advancing the events of the plot, she appears most ingenious in drawing the portraits of Sula and Nel and in depicting their relationship. Sula and Nel have a friendship that was forged in the intensity of childhood needs, fantasies, and shared intimacies. Nel is the manipulated daughter of Helene Wright whose entire life was spent in pursuit of conventional safety and refinement for herself and her daughter. Subjecting Nel to the demeaning ritual of pinching her nose, she wanted to make her daughter "presentable" but was grateful that Nel did "not inherit the great beauty that was hers," for such beauty was dangerous. "Under Helene's hand the girl became obedient and polite. Any enthusiasms that the little Nel showed were calmed by the mother until she drove her daughter's imagination underground" (16). Nel's impuissance in the face of her mother was relieved when Helene was humiliated by a white train conductor on a trip south. Nel recognized a vulnerability, an obsequious, smiling acceptance of caste that was obscene. The "custard" that she sensed underneath her mother's gorgeous dress led her to claim, "I'm me. I'm not their daughter. I'm not Nel. I'm me, me" (24).

When Sula and Nel begin their friendship, Sula finds Nel to be lonely and timid. Once when they are confronted by four Irish boys who had intimidated Nel in the past, Sula, in order to frighten the boys away, slashes off the tip of one of her fingers. As the boys stare incredulously at the scrap of flesh curling up "like a button mushroom," she says, "If I can do that to myself, what you suppose I'll do to you?" (47). Morrison appears to bequeath to Sula the bravado and craziness of badmen celebrated in folk ballads. Stagolee, Long Gone, Lost John, Wild Bill, to name a few, who "outtrick and outspeed" the law, were celebrated by Blacks who were often victims of white man's law and his lawlessness.[16] However, Sula's toughness, though necessary, is not the quality that most possessed her or her friend. Adventurousness is. Together they discover boys and dream about Prince Charming and exhilarate with the new sensations of maturation. Their adventurousness brings on startling consequences in the accidental drowning of Chicken Little. After Sula coaxes the little boy to the very top of a tree, Nel warns them to come down. But when Sula swings Chicken Little, still bubbly with laughter, out over the water and he slips from her hands and sinks, Nel simply watches, feeling what she could only later admit to as a kind of contentment that comes after excitement. Johanna Grimes suggests that this incident, although somewhat implausible, seems to underscore the freedom and adventurousness that characterize the two young girls, "who are laws unto themselves."[17]

The secret of Chicken Little's drowning would usher them into womanhood. Their closeness continued until Nel married Jude, and Sula left for a ten-year odyssey into the world beyond Medallion. When she returned and slept with her best friend's husband, the friendship—as the values of the community demanded—had to end. That is when Nel first saw the gray ball—Morrison's magnificent symbol for the evidence of loss, of disconnection, and the nagging awareness of something missing. The symbol is enmeshed in the moorings of conjure and superstition. The ball of muddy strings, fur, and hair stayed with her. It was terrible in its malevolence. For years, through Nel's separation from Jude, through Sula's illness and death, and through that terrible day when Shadrack led the people of the Bottom to the mouth of the tunnel where many of them perished when the tunnel collapsed, the nightmare of the gray ball that was just out of sight disquieted her. That is, until the day Nel encountered Shadrack and thoughts of Sula bring on her revelation.

> Leaves stirred; mud shifted; there was the smell of overripe green things. A soft ball of fur broke and scattered like dandelion spores in the breeze.
>
> "All that time, all that time, I thought I was missing Jude." And the loss pressed down on her chest and came up into her throat. "We was girls together," she said as though explaining something. "O Lord, Sula," she cried "girl, girl, girlgirlgirl." (149)

In a 1983 interview in *Contemporary Literature,* Morrison made clear her intentions in writing novels, "I am simply trying to recreate something out of an old art form in my books—the something that defines what makes a book 'black.'"[18] Morrison wants her language to reflect the way black people talk which, as she explained, is "not so much the use of non-standard grammar as it is the manipulation of metaphor." She wants to tell stories as the folk would tell them, "meanderingly, constantly retold, constantly imagined within a framework."[19] Her skill at recreating the folk voice and spirit is everywhere present in Eva's tale about her leg. One day she tells the children in the village that it got up by itself and walked away, or how she hobbled after it but it ran too fast, or how she had a corn that grew until it traveled up the leg to her knee before it stopped (26).

Morrison's is not a didactic voice, for black folk "have never taken directions well, they've always participated . . . whether it was political or blues singing, or jazz . . . you have to share that with them."[20] Therefore, if Morrison is to communicate messages that are crucial to black people—and to all people, she must share the experience of black folk, aware of a different cosmology that reflects their "vast imagination." Her treatment of good and evil in *Sula* reflects her awareness of a different cosmology. In an interview with Claudia Tate, Morrison explains why she is intrigued with the concept of evil.

> When I was writing about good and evil, I really wasn't writing about them in Western terms. It was interesting to me that black people at one time seemed not to respond to evil in the ways other people did, but that they thought evil had a natural place in the universe;

they did not wish to eradicate it. They just wished to protect them-selves from it, maybe even to manipulate it, but they never wanted to kill it.[21]

Sula becomes the metaphor for evil in the Bottom. Her return to Medallion is announced by "a plague of robins," because of her, Teapot falls and breaks his arm. Mr. Finley chokes on a chicken bone, rumors fly that she watched poor Hannah burn and that she put Eva in an old folk's home, that she comes to church suppers without underwear, and worst of all, that she sleeps with white men. Yet, they treat Sula as they did all other evil, "with an acceptance that bordered on welcome" (77). Sula is a pariah in the Bottom, but, as Morrison says, "she is nevertheless protected there as she would not be elsewhere."[22]

Through *Sula,* Morrison moves with authority into her own voice, her own structure, her own cosmology. And when she speaks of love, her abiding theme, the reader is ever aware that her imagina-tion straddles the real world and the world of the supernatural. When she sings, she allows Tar Baby to sing "In the Sweet By and By" with the sweetest hill voice imaginable. When she sings, the blues float unhampered over the Time and a Half Pool Hall to Reba's Grill. What she does is organic, growing out of a love that replicates itself. It is the process of black and unknown bards who sang and joked, and lied, and scandalized. Because of writers like Morrison they live. Toni Morrison promises that she will continue this way for the young who are to come and for all those "unceremoniously buried people made literate in Art."[23]

Hurston, Walker, and Morrison are bound by a tradition that shapes their art. Like the women in Ntozake Shange's *for colored girls who have considered suicide when the rainbow is enuf,* they recog-nize a single heritage and a common bond. In the finale of the poem, Shange forces home the intensity and intent of her theme—the need for sisterly healing and wholeness—by using the ritual of a laying on of hands. After many scenes of dissolution, disappointment, and de-spair, Shange has the women say:

> lady in red
> i waz missing somethin

lady in purple
somethin so important

lady in orange
somethin promised

lady in blue
a layin on of hands

lady in green
fingers near my forehead

lady in yellow
strong

lady in green
cool

lady in orange
movin

lady in purple
makin me whole

lady in orange
sense

lady in green
pure

lady in blue
all the gods comin into me
laying me open to myself

lady in red
i waz missin somethin

lady in green
somethin promised

lady in orange
somethin free

lady in purple
a layin on of hands

> lady in blue
> i know bout/layin on bodies/layin outta man
> bringin him alla my fleshy self & some of my pleasure
> bein taken full eager wet like i get sometimes
> i waz missin somethin
>
> lady in purple
> a layin on of hands
>
> lady in yellow
> layin on
>
> lady in purple
> not my mama/holdin me tight/sayin
> i'm always gonna be her girl
> not a layin on of bosom & womb
> a laying on of hands
> the holiness of myself released[24]

Shange shows women who have been separated from each other, as well as from and by every manner of man and circumstance, as they come together and recognize the bonds that have brought them together and the ties that will keep them close.

I see the same coming together among black women writers. Their seeking to mine the vast reservoir of folk material, their need to fulfill their artistic selves, and their desire to share messages of healing, wisdom, power, and love with others are the bonds that unite them in a great literary tradition and that make their writing some of the most exciting literature being read and studied today.

## Notes

1     Barbara Christian, "Ritualistic Process and the Structure of Paule Marshall's *Praisesong for the Widow*," in *Black Feminist Criticism: Perspectives on Black Women Writers* (New York: Pergamon Press, 1986), p. 152.

2     Ibid., p. 156.

3     Paule Marshall, *Praisesong for the Widow* (New York: G. P. Putnam's Sons, 1983), p. 224.

4     Sterling A. Brown, *The Negro in American Fiction* (1937; Reprint, New York: Atheneum, 1969), p. 159.

5      Zora Neale Hurston, *Dust Tracks on a Road* (1942; Reprint, New York: Arno Press and the New York Times, 1969), p. 69.

6      Ibid., pp. 71–72.

7      Zora Neale Hurston, *Their Eyes Were Watching God* (1937; Reprint, Greenwich, Conn.: Fawcett Premier Book Fawcett Publications, Inc.), p. 62. Subsequent references are included in the text.

8      Elizabeth A. Meese, *Crossing the Double-Cross: The Practice of Feminist Criticism* (Chapel Hill: University of North Carolina Press, 1986), p. 50.

9      Eleanor Traylor, "Music as Theme: The Blues Mode in the Works of Margaret Walker," in *Black Women Writers (1950–1980): A Critical Evaluation,* ed. Mari Evans (Garden City, N.Y.: Anchor Press/Doubleday, 1984), p. 513.

10      Margaret Walker, *Jubilee* (New York: Bantam Books, 1966), p. 3. Subsequent references are included in the text.

11      "Margaret Walker," in *Black Women Writers at Work,* ed. Claudia Tate (New York: Continuum, 1983), p. 203.

12      Toni Morrison, *Sula* (New York: Knopf, 1973), p. 4. Subsequent references are included in the text.

13      Johnanna Lucille Grimes, "The Function of the Oral Tradition" in "Selected Afro-American Fiction" (Ph.D. diss., Northwestern University, 1980), p. 144.

14      Ibid., p. 147.

15      Odette C. Martin, "*Sula,*" *First World* 1 (Winter 1977), p. 39.

16      Sterling A. Brown, "Negro Folk Expressions: Spirituals, Seculars, Ballads, and Work Songs," *Phylon* 14 (1953), p. 53.

17      Grimes, "The Function of the Oral Tradition," p. 153.

18      Nellie McKay, "Toni Morrison: Interview," *Contemporary Literature* 24 (Winter 1983), p. 425. Hereafter cited as *Contemporary LIterature.*

19      Ibid., p. 427.

20      Gloria Naylor and Toni Morrison, "A Conversation." *The Southern Review* 21 (July), p. 574. Hereafter cited as *The Southern Review.*

21      "Toni Morrison," in *Black Women Writers at Work,* ed. Tate, p. 129

22      *Contemporary Literature,* p. 426.

23      *The Southern Review,* p. 585.

24      Ntozake Shange, *for colored girls who have considered suicide when the rainbow is enuf* (New York: Macmillan Publishing Co., Inc., 1975), pp. 60–62.

# Nellie Y. McKay

# The Autobiographies of Zora Neale Hurston and Gwendolyn Brooks: Alternate Versions of the Black Female Self

D uring the first seventy-five years of the twentieth century more than sixty black women published autobiographies. Only four of them, Zora Neale Hurston, Maya Angelou, Nikki Giovanni, and Gwendolyn Brooks are otherwise women of letters, and two, Hurston, in *Dust Tracks on a Road* (1943), and Brooks, in *Report from Part One* (1972), have, through form and content, stepped outside of the boundaries of conventional patterns in black autobiography.[1] It is not unusual that the group of black female autobiographers should contain only a small number of literary women. Studies of American autobiography show that across lines of race and gender, among creative writers, the production of autobiography is small. Nor is it surprising that only two of the women named here chose to explore the personal self through verbal constructions that do not fit the models in the tradition.

Black autobiography, originating in the religious, captivity, and slave narratives, emerged in full strength in the nineteenth century as the form that permitted Afro-Americans to voice their disapproval of and protest against a political, social, and economic system that treated them in ways that violated the premises on which it was founded. This expedient motivation for the rise of the genre, which extends into the twentieth century, has given credence to the notion of the collective nature of the endeavor, and in turn has defined its paradigms for close to two hundred years. As a result, the deliberate search for a black self beyond the parameters of polemic has been undertaken by only a few black autobiographers. Instead, the representative individual black self opposed to the large forces of racial oppression is the central focus in such well-known autobiographies as Richard Wright's *Black Boy* and Claude Brown's *Manchild in the Promised Land,* as is the black self in the making and shaping of history, in a similar struggle, in those of W. E. B. Du Bois or Malcolm X.

While there have always been significant differences between the writings of men and women within this tradition, the racial impulses in male narratives also define the autobiographies of representative women like Angela Davis, Shirley Chisholm, Anne Moody, and Mary Church Terrell. Among literary women, poet Nikki Giovanni, who came of age in the early years of the black revolution that began in the 1950s, followed the familiar pattern and devoted her autobiography and other work to questions and issues coming out of the militant nationalistic black liberation movement of the 1960s and early 1970s. Electing to do otherwise, Maya Angelou, poet, dramatist, and performer, has eschewed the overtly political narrative for a literary model, and made excellent use of the traditional *Bildungsroman* as it is commonly appropriated in black women's fiction. In her 1969 autobiography, *I Know Why the Caged Bird Sings,* she followed the chronological story of her life from age three through her eighteenth year, when she became a mother. Her account is a sympathetic unfolding of the pains, anxieties, and positive elements in the personal growth and development of the individual black female from girlhood into womanhood. Angelou's is the best account of its kind in the black autobiographical canon.

On the other hand, Hurston, an anthropologist and fiction writer, and Brooks, a poet and author of one novel, employ other kinds of techniques and have produced nontraditional representations of the black female textual self. What readers observe initially in Hurston's book is that she distances all but her intellectual self from the life-in-writing by maintaining silence on some of the most crucial events in her young adult biography, and instead, gives over a part of her story to a set of impersonal essays on various topics. Contemporary readers would better appreciate the effort had she "shown" rather than "told"—had she woven her ideas on these subjects into the fabric of her personal experiences, as later writers such as June Jordan and

Audre Lorde have successfully done by way of the essay. In her manner of self-construction Hurston ignores events and incidents readers expect to be integrated into the recalling of her life.

There are two almost-opposing aspects of the created self in this autobiography. In one, in its early chapters, as ethnographic interpreter of black folk culture outside of racial oppression, Hurston particularizes and contextualizes her identity by connecting herself to the social archaeology of her region and family background. In the other, in the topical chapters, she fiercely and explicitly defends her position as an individual, with a larger group identity within the human race. Both sides are bonded by Hurston's silences on and evasions of her personal life. Brooks, whose narrative accommodates more to the imagistic demands of the modernist text than to a realistic portrayal of the self, likewise, exercises extreme selectivity in what she reveals about her private life. Her priority rests with the effects of form and language in presentation, not on the details of the account.

Hurston was the first black woman writer to venture on the uncertain path of creating the self outside of the group framework in which black autobiography had existed since the late eighteenth century. By the time she did this, however, her best fiction and her work in folklore had already been favorably appraised. Although *Dust Tracks* sold well when it appeared, and even won a prize from the *Saturday Review* for its contributions to race relations, then and now, it has received a good deal of negative criticism from inside of the black intellectual community. In the first instance, Hurston's contemporaries complained that it broke with the tradition in which Afro-Americans identified with racial oppression, and not only failed to contribute positively to the ongoing struggle against racism, but had a counterproductive effect on it. In the second instance, today's critics find it frustrating and wanting in its lack of self-disclosure, and they disparage its silences, evasions, and distortions, its deliberate suppression of the author's personal history.

Gwendolyn Brooks, the first black American to receive the Pulitzer Prize, was also well established as a poet before her autobiography appeared. In place of negative criticism from the literary community, blacks and whites have treated it mainly with benign neglect. The complaints about and reticence on the part of many critics to explore these texts place both *Dust Tracks* and *Report from Part One* in the category of "problems" in the tradition. However, the difficulties they present are valuable to the ongoing scholarship on black autobiography, because they force us to return to several questions relative to the field at large. An examination of works in which black female authors deliberately avoided the most obvious manifestations of collective black autobiography and fashioned selves more akin to their intellectual and artistic concerns can be a profitable avenue from which to ponder the makeup, role, and function of autobiography; its differences from biography; and the place of reader-expectations in the critical evaluation of individual autobiographical works.

The most common types of Afro-American autobiography are the confessional/conversion narratives and the overt historical/political documents of individual struggle and triumph over racial and sexual oppression. *Dust Tracks* and *Report* do not fit these models but they openly celebrate their authors and the roots of the culture from which they come. In that respect, they make aesthetic and political statements. For Hurston and Brooks, whatever else they say, situate, claim, and applaud the independent selves they created within the context of black female identity. In doing so, their books demonstrate that black lives also include a powerful dimension outside of the oppression of black people as a group. In other words, these two writers set out, self-consciously, to use selected elements in their lives in such a way that they created personal identities that discover and reveal alternate versions of the black female self to those already prevalent in black autobiographical literature. This is not to suggest that other black autobiographers have not consciously shaped their life stories to embody their unique individual selves, but that Hurston and Brooks, more than most, revised the terms of the Afro-American female autobiographical impulse through verbal constructions that diverged from patterns set by their predecessors. Unlike the eminent W. E. B. Du Bois, for whom "the Negro problem" was "more important than . . . literary form,"[2] but whose autobiographies achieved high literary status nevertheless; for Brooks, attention to form was preeminent, and Hurston went further by rejecting the "problem" as the central issue of her life and writing.

Writing almost thirty years apart, both Hurston and Brooks were at the mid-points of their lives when their autobiographies were published. Born and raised in different parts of the country, and coming from different backgrounds, their childhood and adult experiences were different, yet it is not surprising that they chose to deviate from some of the patterns in traditional black autobiography. For one thing, neither came to the literary mode as the result of struggle to define herself in relationship to a hostile world, and authenticating the self in autobiography was, for them, only another manifestation of the power of words that they had discovered much earlier. Writing verse and spinning tales were familiar activities of their youth, and we can locate autobiographical threads in their previously published fictional and poetic writings.

As children, Brooks and Hurston had the privilege of stable family situations removed from the traumas of daily confrontations with the hostility of overt racism. In addition, when they were very young, their imaginative talents were encouraged, especially by their mothers. Hurston was born and grew up in the all-black town of Eatonville, Florida, the first incorporated "Negro" township in America. Eatonville, located in central Florida, came into being after the Civil War, as the black counterpart of the white town of Maitland, a prosperous community which took its name from the beautiful lake along whose shores it was built. Maitland began as the search for new frontiers in a "dark and bloody country [where], since the 1700s, French, English, Indian, and American blood had been bountifully shed" (*Dust Tracks*, 4). Three young, well-educated white men, from northern families of wealth and fame, decided to settle there instead of following dreams of adventure in Brazil. They quickly attracted settlers from New York State, Minnesota, and Michigan. Black people were initially recruited to clear the land and perform the heavy construction labors for what became a "center of . . . fashion" . . . [with] wealthy homes, glittering carriages behind blooded horses . . . [and] well-dressed folk [who] presented a curious spectacle in the swampy forests so dense that they were dark at high noon" (*Dust Tracks*, 7). On the other hand, black workers, in search of a less racially oppressive environment than the states in which they had recently been enslaved, found profitable employment in the new white town, and settled around St. John's Hole, which later became Lake Lily. In the liberal atmosphere they encountered, life fulfilled many of the promises of freedom. "No more back-bending over rows of cotton; no more fear of the fury of Reconstruction. Good pay, sympathetic white folks and cheap land. . . . Relatives and friends were sent for" (*Dust Tracks*, 8). Eatonville received its charter in 1886, and in this "raw, bustling frontier, the experiment of self-government for Negroes was tried." Through the time of Hurston's childhood, the contiguous white and black towns existed in harmony and mutual interdependence with each other.

In this environment, in her growing-up years, Hurston escaped the terror and victimization of segregation and racism in the southern ex-slave states and the northern industrial centers which Richard Wright and others describe in their autobiographies. Her parents, originally from Alabama, flourished materially and spiritually in Eatonville, where her father, a successful preacher as well, served as mayor for three terms and helped to write the local laws. They owned land with an abundance of fruit trees, cultivated a five-acre garden, raised chickens, and had more than adequate housing for themselves and their eight children. Hurston's mother encouraged her children to "jump at de sun," and with her insistence that they remain close to home, play with, and entertain each other, Zora grew up with the sense of security that comes from the closeness of such a family unit (*Dust Tracks*, 20). Hurston's mother died when she was nine years old, and the impact of this tragedy on her and the family is evident in the way she laments the subsequent fragmentation of her siblings from each other. "That night [the one following her mother's funeral], Mama's children were assembled together for the last time on earth" is a painful memory of the experience of great loss (*Dust Tracks*, 93). Years later, while she was on a research trip to the South, she had a happy reunion with two of her brothers who lived in Memphis. The three exchanged information on the rest of the Hurston children. She wrote:

> It was a most happy interval for me. . . . I felt the warm embrace of kin and kind for the first time since the night after my mother's funeral . . . that house had been a hovering home . . . [then] it had turned into a bleak place of desolation. . . . But now that was all over. We could touch each other in the spirit if not in the flesh. (*Dust Tracks*, 173)

In meeting and overcoming adversities later, she had the sustaining strength of the early years that were sheltered from the worst aspects of family instability, and race and class oppression. Under very different circumstances, Zora Neale Hurston in Eatonville, Florida, W. E. B.

Du Bois in Great Barrington, Massachusetts, and James Weldon Johnson, in Jacksonville, Florida, shared more edenic experiences in early childhood than the majority of black Americans of their times.[3]

Gwendolyn Brooks grew up in a very different environment from Hurston. In addition to a mother who, when she discovered her daughter's "ability to write," voluntarily did most of the housework herself, Brooks also had the advantage of a father, David Brooks, who felt equally as positive toward her talent. This was not true of Hurston's father who attempted to temper her ambitions while she was a child. When Brooks was thirteen years old her father gave her an old desk "with many little compartments, . . . long drawers at the bottom, and a removable glass-protected shelf at the top, for books." Here she kept her reading materials and her notebooks, and wrote "a poem everyday? Sometimes *two* poems?" (*Report,* 56). David Brooks, son of a runaway slave, grew up in Oklahoma City and attended Fisk University for one year after he completed high school. His ambitions to pursue a medical career never materialized, and he spent most of his working years as a janitor. In spite of this signal disappointment, throughout his life he "revered books and education" and encouraged his children to do likewise. In 1916 he married Keziah Wims, a schoolteacher from Topeka, Kansas. She gave up her profession after the birth of her first child. When Gwendolyn was five weeks old the family moved to Chicago and that city became her life-long home. In spite of poverty and northern segregation, the Brookses, with education and urban social sophistication, internalized the values of the American middle class and passed them on to their two children. This included, for the young Brooks, proper feminine deportment. Where Hurston, growing up in rural Florida, had preferred to and did play with boys because they were "tougher" than girls, and she was as tough as they were, Brooks reports: "I did not fight brilliantly, or at all, on the playground. I was not ingenious in gym, carrying my team single-handedly to glory. I could not play jacks. I could not ride a bicycle" (*Report,* 38). On the other hand, neither girl enjoyed school while they were in the lower grades, although for different reasons. Hurston was bored by what was happening around her and wanted to "read ahead" of the other children; Brooks felt like an outsider among her peers who took great delight in teasing the dark-skinned, "not-pretty," quiet child. And like

Hurston, Brooks enjoyed love within the family circle, and writes with great warmth of happy birthday parties, holiday celebrations, and larger family gatherings.

Both girls loved books, and the absence of constant racial oppression allowed them to "dream freely" in their young years. But again, their interests and imaginative spheres were not alike. Hurston made up stories from fragments she selected from the tales told on the "store porch," where the men held "lying" sessions; or she fabricated her own. Brooks's well-supervised Hyde Park city house, with its small, no doubt, very neatly kept front and back yards that guarded the privacy of the family was very different from the open folk community of Eatonville. Sitting on the steps of the back porch of her house, secure from the view of the world, Gwendolyn conjured up poetic images of "Gods and little girls, angels and heroes and future lovers" that she saw in the clouds (*Report,* 55). In her time, Zora sat "on top of the gate-post" to her family's widespread property and watched the world go by. Sometimes she accompanied passersby a short distance on their way. But mostly, she dreamed of riding to the horizon on a fine black horse, or thought about the stories of Greek and Roman myths, of Moses and King David that she loved to read. "My soul was with the gods and my body in the village," she wrote of those years (*Dust Tracks,* 56). She longed for large adventure. In her teens, Brooks, still extremely timid in social situations, was "fonder of paper dolls than of parties," and she used her large collection of them to entertain herself. Hurston, on the other hand, made dolls from corn cobs, soap, door knobs, and other handy items. She gave them active lives, and they "stayed around the house [with her] for years holding funerals and almost weddings and taking trips . . . to where the sky met the ground" (*Dust Tracks,* 77). Hurston's and Brooks's childhood relationships to their environments, especially their imaginative appreciation of what they saw around them and the spiritual freedom they enjoyed from the harsher realities of white racism, were factors that had a great influence on the selves in the autobiographies they created.

Clearly a less ebullient child than her precursor, and perhaps also because of the constraints of the urban environment, her family background, and the fact that her only sibling was sixteen months younger than herself, Brooks had a more restrained adolescence than the older woman. However, the opening lines of *Report:* "When I was a child, it did not occur to me, even once, that the black in which I was encased (I called it brown in those days) would be considered, one day, beautiful. . . . I always considered it beautiful" (*Report,* 37) shows that she had a positive sense of herself. Thus, the two women came to writing autobiography from long-standing positions of self-acceptance growing out of the strengths of familial love, the security of feeling that they had a place of their own in the world, and assurances that they were valuable in themselves. While not unaware of the problems of the world around them, neither desired to order time or history through the expression of her individual self in writing. Any rebellion in their autobiographies is the struggle to maintain individual autonomy in a world in which race and gender have prevented black women from achieving full self-realization. In a direct reversal of both the nineteenth and twentieth century escape-from-the-South narratives, Hurston's pressing motivation to leave her native Florida, was not to escape overt racial oppression, but to separate herself from the pathetic fragmentation of her family after the death of her mother. Throughout her life the South remained her source of spiritual strength, the locus of her genius, and always the place to which she returned. The consuming anger and bitterness in Wright's *Black Boy,* or the sense of frustration and injustice that Anne Moody emits in *Coming of Age in Mississippi* are not a part of Hurston's consciousness in turn-of-the-century, all-black Eatonville, Florida. In a similar manner, Brooks, born in Kansas and raised in Chicago, which she chose to make her adult home as well, suffers no alienation from the community of which she is a part. In childhood the closeness was with her immediate family, later, through friendship networks, it expanded much farther outward. In a number of personal interviews she has noted that this "city" is the inspiration for her artistic output.

The early interests of Hurston and Brooks took them in different intellectual directions. Not surprisingly, Hurston, more of an extrovert, studied anthropology at the same time that she nurtured an interest in literature, and became the first formally trained black woman to examine the roots of the black folk culture; while Brooks, the more private person, followed the muse consistently and experienced stunning literary successes. At the same time, it is somewhat ironic that the social scientist/litterateur chose an ambiguous metaphor for the title of her autobiography, while the poet decided to name her own in a more literal way. The precise meaning of "Dust Tracks on a Road" has been as baffling for readers as the title of Hurston's most well-known novel, *Their Eyes Were Watching God.* Few have wondered at the meaning of "Report from Part One," published by the author in her fifty-fifth year. On the contrary, many have been awaiting the report beyond the first part of such an exciting life.

*Dust Tracks on a Road* informally divides into three sections. In the first, consisting of six chapters, we have an account of the writer's childhood from which it is possible to extrapolate some of the factors in her environment that had a profound impact on the adult person she became. We learn a good deal of the history of Eatonville and of the people who lived there. The section closes shortly after the death of Hurston's mother, when circumstances force the young girl to leave home. The second part of the narrative covers the years following that death until the author's graduation from Barnard College, and takes readers through the 1920s and into the early 1930s. The third and longest section of the book, abandons narrative form for essays which express Hurston's opinions on various subjects. In the original edition of the work, some of these pieces were omitted or drastically edited by the publisher. As the Appendix, they were restored in the 1984 edition of the book, for which we are grateful to Robert Hemenway, Hurston's biographer.

The text opens: "Like the dead-seeming rocks, I have memories within that came out of the material that went to make me. Time and place have had their say" (*Dust Tracks,* 3). This "material," which she explains in Parts I and II of the book is the introduction to its third part. Her aim is not to recite personal biography, or to make us confidants to her secrets, but to present us with ideas. What readers miss in the portrayal is the sense of emotional involvement that many autobiographers have with their texts as they struggle to present themselves in the lights in which they wish to be perceived. We have come to expect at the heart of autobiography the revelation of a part of the private self, formed by influence and action, as the writer seeks meaning in individual experience. We want to feel that we know the person behind the ideas or the deeds. Thus, in reading Anne Moody's *Coming of Age in Mississippi,* for instance, although Moody remains a very private person, and tells us only those things which have a bearing on why and how she became involved with the Civil Rights Movement, she struggles in the telling to discover for herself how and why some of the Movement's efforts met with success and others with failure. The self in the text enables us to identify with the anger, pain, and frustration she felt during those years. Although the story is told from the perspective of one removed from the action, she is still vitally connected to the emotions she experienced in the earlier time.

Hurston's narrative is descriptive, not reflective. She begins with the origins of the all-Negro town Eatonville and moves to the history of her family's settlement there. She enters the picture in the third chapter of the book. We learn from the first section of this book, which is told largely through anecdotes, that the "materials" that form the self who speaks in the third section include the collective psychology of Eatonville and the heritage of the oral culture; the family love and security that Hurston experienced in her early years; her active overt and covert resistance to gender roles even in childhood; learning to confront personal difficulties with an eye on long-term goals; having a spirit of daring and adventure; and recognizing the value of the folk culture. We perceive elements of the woman in the child, as we know her from her biography, but only in a few selected situations do we see her interacting with her world.

Silence surrounds the life of the writer in the three chapters of the second section of the book. We discover nothing of Hurston's feelings about such important events as the Harlem Renaissance and the people who were involved in or promoted it, although she was one of its principals; no details of what it was like to be a black student at Barnard College in the late 1920s; and almost nothing about anything connected to her personal life. By the time *Dust Tracks* was complete she had published three novels, two books of folklore, and a large number of essays and short stories. We also know that she had financial difficulties, differences with other black intellectuals, and had been married at least twice. The events of both the private and public life are never fully explored in the autobiography, and the appropriate space in the narrative encloses only spare and dispassionate mentions of selective experiences.

If, as I am arguing, the essays in the third section of this book are what Hurston wants us to focus on regarding her autobiography, then what she constructs is an intellectual rather than an emotional self—a fully-formed philosophical self rather than the self taking shape in interaction with external stimuli and circumstances. Among these essays, "Research" and "Books and Things" recognize the value of the black folk culture not only in the United States, but also in Africa and the West Indies. In "Books and Things" she also declares her artistic independence from group psychology by repudiating social pressures that attempt to force her to write about the "Race Problem." Although never given the credit it deserves for this, in promoting the idea of a U.S./Africa/West Indian literary and cultural connection, Hurston was in fact engaged in a discourse that complemented the political work of scholars like W. E. B. Du Bois.

"My People, My People!" both in the original text and as part of the Appendix in the second edition, criticizes the black intelligensia; "Two Women in Particular" focuses on the celebration of friendships; "Love" disclaims any useful knowledge of the subject by the author; and in "Religion" she declares her independence from related institutions, while she expresses respect for the beliefs of people associated with the institutions. The most powerful piece in the group is "Seeing the World As It Is," the earlier unpublished version of "Looking Things Over," in the 1943 text. This only recently printed essay is scathing in its condemnation of political greed and the abuse of white patriarchal power. Beginning with a condemnation of black nationalism, it moves through the history of Western Civilization's imperialism, castigating Europe for colonialism, and the United States for its past and present abuses of power, and for the mockery it has made of the ideals of democracy. This essay significantly alters earlier perceptions of Hurston as politically uninformed, conservative, or naive, and there is little surprise that in 1943 her publisher would have refused to print it.

Still, consistent with her philosophy of life, Hurston concludes the essay on a note that reinforces her individualism. Claiming to be "shaped by the chisel in the hand of Chance," she observes that she had lived fully and well, and craved only the simplicity of fulfilling the ideals of a good human being. Using the metaphor that has made her famous in fiction, she brings the volume to a close with: "I have touched the four corners of the horizon, and from hard searching it seems to me that tears and laughter, love and hate, make up the sum of life" (*Dust Tracks,* 348).

In assessing this book, it is not the life of Hurston, in any conventional way, that we have to judge—certainly not from her delineation of it. Fiercely guarding her private history, and even the active intellectual life in which she engaged, she gives us instead fragments of carefully shaped philosophy. Anger appears only in the final chapter, where, in an impersonal manner, she turns to global issues—to the historical abuses of race, politics, and power conjoined. In her direct relationships with others she appears remarkably free of bitterness or negative impulses. From reading Hurston's fiction and her biography, however, we know that this was a woman of strong feelings whose life did not follow smooth paths. The essays lack the passion and emotion we associate with her life. The voice in the text stands apart from the text, disembodied from the forces that give power to Hurston's fiction. We are disappointed and even offended by her dispassionate presentations, and by her refusal to tell us the "facts." It is as though in writing her life she claimed the order, and calm, and emotional neatness that eluded her daily reality. What emerges from these essays that we can identify with her, nevertheless, is a strong sense of her acceptance of the frailties of the human condition, her respect for and insistence on individualism in a pluralistic society, faith in the possibilities for positive change, and a realization of the complicated nature of race relations. Black women before her had dared to scan the horizon of human thought and action and pass judgement on it, but none had made such a disinterested perception the focal point of what readers expect to be a personal narrative.

On the other hand, *Report from Part One* has a more fragmented structure than *Dust Tracks on a Road*. This book contains two prefaces by persons other than Brooks, and five other sections, each constructed differently. The first, "Report from Part One," with linear chronology but including a variety of narrative interruptions, is an account of Brooks's life from childhood through her fiftieth year, written in ten short sections. "African Fragment," travel vignettes resembling journal entries, in twenty-five (some very short) parts, originates from a trip that Brooks took to East Africa in the late 1960s. "Photographs" present visual images of the life-in-writing, and "Interviews," enables readers to see the writer in direct interaction with others inside of the autobiography. "Appendix," serves as footnotes. The diversity of forms and methods of portrayal causes interruptions in narrative flow, and creates discontinuities within the text. However, these also symbolize the effort to integrate the many parts of the life into a whole.

The inclusion of prefaces, written other than by the autobiographer, goes back to the nineteenth-century tradition in black autobiography, in which Afro-American writers were authenticated by white people who knew and vouched for them and their stories. The practice continued into the twentieth century, and occurs in the works of such well-known writers as Richard Wright. Brooks deviates from the earlier tradition by having her prefaces done by black men: Don L. Lee (now Haki Madhibuti) and George Kent, who, in the 1960s and 1970s supported and participated in the search for a separate black aesthetics. Nor did she need these men to authenticate her. Rather, their presence in her book creates an artistic and intellectual unity between black men and women. Nor are these the only external voices in her book. Later, in the first section we encounter those of her parents and her children, which emphasize the author's connections to family in the creation of the self; and beyond these, there are letters, book reviews, and other memorabilia of the life. If Brooks moves outside of traditional patterns to construct her life in writing, then she still maintains the collective quality of conventional Afro-American autobiography through the separate voices of the members of her family who speak in her text. The seemingly chaotic quality in this work is directly opposite to the major aspects of Brooks's life and Hurston's autobiography. Brooks, unlike Hurston, never suffered the distress of family disintegration as a result of untimely death or other unforeseen difficulties, and stability of place and people has given her the opportunity to continue to share her life with her closest kin. With fewer disruptions in her living patterns, the rhythms of her life have been steadier, more predictable, and have involved less risk taking than Hurston's.

Brooks's early life revolved around the close community of home, which appears to have expanded mainly to include distant members of her immediate family who sometimes came to visit. One of the interesting things that this book illustrates is how, in the transition from folk to urban life, elements in black culture changed. For Brooks there was no public life of the store porch of Eatonville, and no oral tradition which held the community together. Earlier in this century, during periods of black migration North, the church was a bridge between the old and new patterns of life. Brooks makes no mention of experiencing this in her Chicago childhood. Her parents were from Kansas, and close ties with the South had previously been broken. Although she had been sheltered from many of life's harsher aspects, for Brooks reality resided in the drawbacks and possibilities of urban life.

"Report from Part One" takes in elements of the writer's adolescence and early adulthood, her first efforts to write poetry, her marriage, children, publishing successes, special professional and personal friendships, and the momentous change in her life and politics that occurred toward the end of the 1960s. Having lived for almost fifty years as a proud "Negro" woman, in the wake of the black revolution and the Black Arts Movement she became a proud African woman. Although fragmented and full of interruptions, the section has elements of the Bildungsroman through which we can trace the intellectual and spiritual development of Gwendolyn Brooks in this piece. It is the delineation of a quest for wholeness which takes place almost wholly inside of the black community.

The trip that precipitated "African Fragment" belongs in the tradition of Afro-Americans returning to Africa in search of connections to ancestral roots. For Brooks, as for many others, it is a journey full of anxious pleasure and pain. That dichotomy is sharply represented by the insertion of twenty-four pages of photographs of the writer's life into the text of "African Fragment" at its halfway point. Interestingly, there are no pictures of the African trip. Among the things that give Brooks pain in the land of her forefathers is her inability to communicate with Africans in any of their languages—the loss of voice to slavery and the West.

Another section, "Interviews," covers the time between 1967 to 1971. The first and second of these were conducted by white men, the third by a black woman. Until 1967, Brooks, using topics from urban black life, worked with traditional Western poetic forms. In that year, while attending a conference of black writers in Nashville, Tennessee, she realized a different aesthetic and awakened to a new understanding of race. This changed her life. The 1967 and 1969 interviews, recorded during a period of transition for her, lack the political fervor of the third, in 1971. The first two present an image of the successful, traditional black woman poet in a white world, a model of the process and outcome of her achievements. The third is different. She is more open, more relaxed, more sure of her political groundings. A more integrated Gwendolyn Brooks, for whom art and life come together, is evident in this portrait. The "Appendix" to *Report from Part One,* in two sections, "Marginalia" and "Collage," serves as the "footnotes" to the earlier parts of the book, making additional comments and adding new aspects to already explored areas of the life.

Where Hurston appears to have aimed for an intellectual portrait of the black female self, Brooks concentrates on shaping her own through an artistic rendering. *Report* is much like a prose poem, marked by conciseness and a careful economy of words. In this text, Brooks welds her own voice with external ones, not to authenticate herself, but to authorize the self in the image its creator desires. She never loses control of her materials, and constantly manipulates them for the best advantage to herself. This work constantly reminds us of Brooks's skill as a poet. Like Hurston, the biographical details are few, but where the first book used the discussion of topics outside of the personal life to construct an image of the writer, Brooks manages to keep the spotlight on herself and yet permit readers only "privileged glimpses" into her personal life.

In their autobiographies, Hurston and Brooks have created alternate versions of the black female self that go well beyond refuting the negative stereotypes of black women in much of American literature. Hurston, we know, did not wish to present herself as a victim of race and gender, and could not write a narrative that cast her in the role representative of the living struggle against the social oppression of blacks and black women. This attitude set her outside of the literary expectations of her peer group. On the other hand, more contemporary readers would accept that aspect of her reasoning had she used her autobiography to reveal more of her personal self, and had she engaged in fewer suppressions or distortions of the facts of her experiences. However, this too, she deliberately did not do. Instead, she chose to create a self molded out of the certainties of her own being and her concerns with ideas connected to a larger world outside of herself. On the other hand, Brooks chose to manipulate and control language as the central feature of her book. The liberties she takes

with form move her text from any comparison with traditional autobiographical narrative and structure and create an artistic image
of the self which stands in opposition to the readily perceptible
external realities of the life. What both books demonstrate is an independence on the part of their writers to disregard external expectations and shape their autobiographical selves in images of their
own making. They empower themselves to name themselves in their
own voices.

Books like these force us, as readers, to continue to reevaluate the
personal and cultural meanings of autobiography. As theories of
Western autobiography proliferate and take a prominent place in our
understanding of history and literature, it is necessary for readers
to maintain flexibility in their reception of texts, especially those
by minorities, when they do not fit the models we have come to expect from the genre. For black women, in particular, the ability to
name the self autonomously is an important part of their historical
identity, a means of reclaiming and affirming selves novelist Toni
Morrison described as having

> [Edged] into life from the back door. Everybody in the world was in
> position to give them orders. White women said, "Do this." White
> children said, "Give me that." White man said, "Come here." Black
> men said, "Lay down." The only people they need not take orders
> from were black children and each other. But they took all of that and
> re-created it in their own image. They ran the houses of white people,
> and knew it. When white men beat their men, they cleaned up the
> blood and went home to receive abuse from the victim. They beat
> their children with one hand and stole for them with the other. . . .
> They had carried a world on their heads.[4]

Their generations earned the right, through them, to write themselves as they wished. Neither Brooks nor Hurston pretended to
write memoirs to complement the biographies that others have and
will continue to write about them. Autobiography need not fill the
role of exemplar of the will to survive in spite of difficulties, nor does
it have to be the sharing of more than the writer wishes to do. Creative autobiography may well be no more than the author's wish to
imagine the self in a specific way at a specific moment—an exploration of the possibilities of self-perception. These books are literary
ventures which experiment with the boundaries of the genre. We

need not agree on whether they succeeded or failed—they exist as they are. *Dust Tracks on a Road* and *Report from Part One* are alternate but valid self-representations of the black female self.

## Notes

1    Zora Neale Hurston, *Dust Tracks on a Road,* ed. Robert Hemenway (Urbana: University of Illinois Press, 1984). Gwendolyn Brooks, *Report from Part One* (Detroit: Broadside Press, 1972). Subsequent references to these texts are taken from these editions.

2    Albert E. Stone, *Autobiographical Occasions and Original Acts: Versions of American Identity From Henry Adams to Nate Shaw* (Philadelphia: University of Pennsylvania Press, 1982), p. 32.

3    In their autobiographies, both Du Bois and Johnson also speak of the ways in which their childhoods were free of the fears and hostilities of racial strife. Both men grew up in communities in which blacks were a small minority of the populations, and their families were as economically well off as most of their white neighbors. In Du Bois's case, he learned early that his color meant something different from that of his playmates, but that fact did little to diminish his self-image. He compensated for his feelings of "difference" by excelling in school beyond the level of many of those he knew, and was one of the few young people of his age, from Great Barrington, Massachusetts, to leave home for college. Johnson did not come to an awareness of the disadvantages of his race until he was a young man on his way out into the world.

4    Toni Morrison, *The Bluest Eye* (New York: Washington Square Press, 1972), p. 110.

# Barbara Omolade

## The Silence and the Song: Toward a Black Woman's History through a Language of Her Own

She was central to the slave economy which was central to the development of the Americas, north and south, and critical to the intimate and personal dynamics of the white families for whom she worked. She was at the center of the struggles and the whirlwinds, the ups and downs of Black life: its families, its churches, its organizations, and its ideas. She dared to walk union picket lines, sign antiwar petitions, begin schools, and stand up for the downtrodden and less fortunate. She has danced and sung her way across the Americas and Europe for at least a century. And she has been writing books, making speeches, and creating poetry for more than two hundred years on this continent and since the beginning in her homeland. Yet there are no history books that tell her story on her own terms, few history books that sing her songs.

Colleges and universities have promised to teach white men, and recently white women, and men and women of color universal truths and useful knowledge. The very universality of their claims have always been false and their "truths" and "knowledge" have been most often used to oppress and silence most of the world's people. Black women attending colleges have been taught to instruct, but not to teach, to learn but not to know, to research the works of others, but not to create their own. Though there have been noble attempts by Black women to succeed—to break through and overcome these barriers against creating new languages, new perspectives and knowledge—the unique voice of Black women and their experiences has been silenced.

History books and social scientific studies about Black women have yet to capture, touch, or transmit their historical experiences and visions with the truth and depth of the poetry, songs, and novels written by Black women about Black women. The Black woman is certainly a historical being, but where is her history? Where are the books for high school and college reading that tell her story? Where are the lengthy discussions about her political philosophy, her religious theology, her sociological methods? How did she become so central, yet so invisible; so outspoken, yet so silenced?

A pioneer Black woman historian of the eighties writes:

> Despite the range and significance of our history, we have been perceived as token women in Black texts and as token Blacks in the feminist ones. Most of the books that focus on Afro-American women are of the "contributions" type: the achievements of Black women, who despite double discrimination and oppression, were able to duplicate the feats of Black men or White women.

> What I learned by reading these texts was important and illuminating. But it wasn't enough. For Black women have a history of their own, one which reflects their distinct concerns, values and the roles they have played as both Afro-Americans and women. And their unique status has had an impact on both racial and feminist values.

> So I set out to write a narrative history on Black women, tracing their concerns—and what they did about them—from the 17th century to the contemporary period. It is thematic in approach, using a broad canvas to illustrate the nature and meaning of the Black women's experience.[1]

In writing *When and Where I Enter,* a narrative history of Black women, Paula Giddings has begun our search for our own historical language. She has built upon the documentary histories of Gerda Lerner, Bert Loewenberg, and Ruth Bogin; the historical surveys of Angela Davis and Jeanne Noble; and the more distant legacies of diaries, speeches, papers of Black women.[2]

Inevitably, Black women's history will fully emerge only when Black women become "griots" speaking and creating a historical language of their own. The Black woman griot historian actually is not a reflection of the "griot's" historical role in West African traditional society, where they were usually male, and attached to the courts to praise royal lineage. Here the "griot" is a symbolic conveyor of African oral and spiritual traditions of the entire community. A "griot historian" is a scholar in any discipline who connects, uses, and understands the methods and insights of both Western and African world-views and historical perspectives to further develop a synthesis—an African American woman's social science with a unique methodology, sensibility, and language. The "griot historian" is and must be a warrior breaking down intellectual boundaries along with the destruction of political limitations to her people's—and, indeed, all humanity's—liberation. She is a challenger to the university's way of operating. She carves out new lands of the mind while reaching back to her spiritual and cultural sources, the major one of course being Africa, with its rivers and memories. One river named for the African orisha, Oshun, a symbol of female power and sensuality is a guiding power for the griot-historian's quest.

## The Silence

*The African woman had been baptised. Since the beginning of time, the power of woman came through her. The lives of men and of women were seen through her eyes. She sang and danced their story. But then she was raped and became chattel and then she became silent. First she dared to moan from memory the songs of her African mother. She sang out in her own words the tunes she recalled. She moaned and sang while tending fields, washing clothes, preparing food, and caring for her kin. Some dared to write diaries and letters. Some spoke out against the pain, "but none but Jesus heard." Her sisters heard her whisper, her brothers heard her sing the blues, while others wailed out in spirituals.*

*Black women poets and writers heard all of them and combined their voices into books and poetry. Black women fought against the silencing. A few tried to tell the history and moved toward being a "griot" while remembering the river where the first African woman had been baptised long before the horror of her sentence of silence.*

Before a new language, which captures the experience of Black women in the Americas, can be created, the griot-historian must "break de chains" of Western thought which controls the methods and visions of the historical process. The Black woman griot-historian must be baptised by some force outside the tradition of Western civilization and become submerged in the waters of Black women's pain, power, and potential. In order to tell their story, the griot-historian must acknowledge and reach beyond the shame of being the embodiment of the "underclass" and the mother of the "teenage mother." She must overcome her fear of the stigma of being the daughter of Aunt Jemima, the granddaughter of "negra wenches," and the great granddaughter of Africans called "primitive and animal-like." Seeing the woman beyond the shame affirms the use of historical truths to sing praise songs which resurrect the lives and experiences of the orisha, the warrior, and the "drylongso" Black woman.

The history, study, and writing of Black women is shaped by two conflicting paradigms existing within the United States of America; a culture and a nation that she and her brother unwillingly helped to create and that they both willingly struggle to transform and change into a more humane society. The Black woman griot-historian must be shaped by an African world-view which evolved within democratic/consensus tribal societies where the oral tradition of transmitting information and knowledge is interwoven among music, art, dance, and crafts, and everyday activities intermix with communication and connection with both the spiritual world and the ancestral past.

Rites and rituals, along with intuition, feelings, seeing, speaking, and singing embody a tremendous repertoire of historical methods. The griot-historian who recognizes and uses these methods as well as reading and writing is in opposition to the paradigm of Western intellectual history and its civilization. The ways of knowing which have developed in the West betray an obsession with rational thought; an inability to connect body, mind, and spirit; and a preoccupation with domination based simultaneously upon violence and impotence.

Since the nineteenth century, history has been the most powerful discipline within the academy, spawning all other social sciences— psychology, anthropology, political science, economics—and shaping their conceptual framework and methodologies. The control of history and the writing of history is the means of controlling how people think about themselves and their place in the world and in time.

There have been three significant developments in the discipline of history during the last hundred years. First, German historian Leopold von Ranke helped establish history as a discipline in the universities, making it the "Queen of the Sciences." He promoted the concept that all "sound history must use primary sources and rigorous scientific methods." Second, Karl Marx's historical method, which relies on materialism as a basis for explaining the development of nation states from "primitive [sic] communalism," examines the contradiction of class under capitalism. Third, during the twentieth century, many historians have broken with traditional history to study social history: the everyday experiences of average men and women. Social history evolved from the protests and movements of the working class, people of color, and white women in Western societies.

In the West the scientific approaches of both social and natural scientists are based upon isolating and concentrating on data, atoms, and facts. Placing the observer in an ivory tower with pen and pad, telescope or books to observe the comings and goings of the lowly is at the locus of Western thinking. Western thought, especially in the social sciences, rests upon reading, writing, and thinking, in an ivory tower removed from human distractions. The function of distance is to enable the observer ostensibly to objectify, but actually to dominate the observed. In this manner, the observer-scholar has become connected to the conquistador and the slave master, for his observations became useful data for explaining and justifying the domination of the observed. As subjects of Western scientific research, the African in the New World is transformed into an entity who constitutes the silent and the missing of history—the slave, the negress, and the nigger. For nearly four hundred years, including the contemporary present, Black women have been used by white men simultaneously as slaves and servants and as whores and workers. The accompanying history and other social sciences of the West are preoccupied with racist pathology which views Black life and history, when it views it at all, as problematic. Thus, a Black woman historian of Black women is not merely a contradiction in terms, but an ontological impossibility, for all Black women within the academy are regarded as nonbeings and therefore without a history outside of the white world.

Black women who attempt to study Black women using the discipline of history are students in an institution whose entire raison d'être, philosophy, methods, purpose, and history have never allowed her voice to be heard, her body to be respected, or her existence to be recognized. Black women writing Black women's history outside the academy are unduly pressured and, at least, influenced by the academy's definitions and methods of "doing history." The authentic historian of Black women, therefore, cannot reside in the ivory tower or its shadows trying to see Black women through her master's telescope. From way up there, all the observer will see is a shadow. She will not be able to hear Black women moan and sing.

Black women scholars in the shadows or the rooms of the ivory tower get caught too tightly within their training to see and feel the serious involvement of their sisters' and mothers' scientific commitment to the past and the future (because their science is derived from traditional African, Indian, and women's culture which uses and combines information about mind and body, feelings and thought, the seen and unseen into a holistic understanding of the world).

Most Black women scholars have been trained by white men or by those who have been trained by white men. At first, she gets overtaken by a passion to become scholarly to please those who have trained her, then she develops the scholar's love of learning, the search for truth, and the concern with "objectivity." She spends long hours in the library verifying her every instinct and thought. Seminars and lectures are religiously attended and she takes copious notes. Books and sources are read and reread; papers are written in that precise and professional style in which the "I" and "me" and "she" have been changed into a discussion about subjects, clients, and "theys." After all, she is competing in the white man's world and must prove herself to him in order to pass the course, get the job on the faculty, get her grant funded, receive a book contract, or simply to justify all that time spent studying and postponing her life.

Black colleges and institutions of higher education which have housed and educated many Black scholars have also failed to produce significant Black women griot-historians—scholar-warrior-women who could liberate Black people as well as defend and produce Black intellectual and cultural traditions. Black colleges influence Black public opinion and policy through their training and recognition of

Black social scientists in Black periodicals, journals, and other publications. Black historians, both male and female, have been confined to a vision usually concerned with restoring Black manhood and pride by demonstrating the equality or superiority of Black "civilization" to white "civilization." In nationalistic, patriarchal, and bourgeois terms, they chronicle Black contributions to American society usually in terms of "great" Black male leaders who have uplifted the race out of poverty into the middle class. Furthermore, increased numbers of Black female social scientists in both "Black" and "white" publications have focused a considerable amount of their writings on Black male-female relations and the Black family in little more than idealistic lamentations of the passing of the patriarchal family. Their historical writings have documented the legacies of supposedly "exceptional" Black women, most of them like Mary McCleod Bethune, who pulled themselves out of poverty into powerful, middle-class positions, or women like Mary Church Terrell, strong middle-class fighters for Black social justice. What about the nameless members of Ms. Bethune's National Council of Negro Women? What about Black women domestics and labor leaders, blues artists and mothers? What about those extraordinary, ordinary Black women of the past and present who are our mothers, our sisters, and daughters? For although Black women have been professional social scientists, instructors, and students in Black colleges for over a century the Black academy and the Black church have taught Black women to devalue their sexuality, African philosophical perspectives (especially spiritualism), radical culture and politics, and "low class" women and "no count" men—that is, the poor and working class. They learned to write and study with and about Black men and viewed Black women from that vantage point, neither particularizing Black women's experiences nor taking them seriously enough to institutionalize Black women's scholarship. Could that be why Zora Neale Hurston died a forgotten woman in an unmarked grave? Or why it took Spelman College, a Black female institution of higher learning, over a century to develop a Black women's center for research and study?

No institution of "higher learning," and few publications and magazines allowed the Black woman to speak, to write her own story in her own way. Daughter after daughter, both inside and outside the academy, grew up ignorant and mute about themselves. They always deferred the more important historical places to their men. They wrote histories and documented experiences of themselves that were incomplete, and dulled by years of silence. They forgot the griot-historians that came before them and their sister scholars were unknown to them. They omitted the blood of their sister's abortion, their sister's lesbian lover, the gele-lapa wrapped women, the warriors who became "sick and tired of being sick and tired," the singers who shouted in church and the silent musings of dancers, teenagers, and workers. She could not hear her own heart and voice. The academy had successfully trained Black women against herself and her sisters.

And unlike her brothers, Carter G. Woodson, Arthur Schomburg, W. E. B. Du Bois, Ivan Van Sertima, and John Henrik Clarke, she had little room to collect the facts and write books telling her story. For even with a degree she was first a worker and a mother. She had no companion to type her records, save money for books, to care for the children so she could study, or to cook for her while she wrote and thought. Her life was caught up in babies and work and men and struggle. With few exceptions her story would remain silenced and unwritten, or if written unpublished; *except for Zora Neale*.

The Black woman griot-historian in the West, even more so than her brother, had to fight for the right and the time to think and to know, the right and the time to learn and to be literate, the right to come together with her sisters in serious discourse about their-selves—examining, analyzing, criticizing any and all aspects of the world. She had to struggle for the right "to see" what she saw, and to speak about it in her own way.

## The Song

> *The woman stood up with ghosts on her shoulders . . . she reached inside and a voice rose up and a story came through her which spoke of our past . . . and the old people tapped their feet while the eyes of children shined . . .*

The Black woman griot-historian must wrestle herself free of the demons of the discipline of history which deny her. Eventually she must break the fetters of the academy and its shadow on Black's woman thought. She must retrace the steps of our people, allowing the capacity of her dreams and her struggle to guide her through the raw material and data of our history. She must embrace the men and women of the past who push their voices into her body and mind, ignoring time and death to do so.

The Black woman scholar faces the index cards of facts and references as she sits down to write, and the voices of the academy come to haunt: "Bad history are those set of assertions which cannot be verified with primary sources." "Your language is too subjective." "Quote from authorized sources!" "Demonstrate how this is significant to the entire society, not just Black people." "Don't be a generalist!" "Your work is too rhetorical, too lyrical." She sits immobilized caught between those voices and the voices of her mothers and fathers. Her writing becomes paralyzed and stunted, stillborn within her psyche.

Yet Black women novelists, poets, activists, dramatists, artists, singers, and dancers use their ancestral voices, serve them, and allow them to become a medium for "brutal honesty" about the Black experience. Their honesty and passions enable their readers, in turn, to use the Black experience as an explication of the struggle of the human spirit to be free. The Black woman's cultural and literary renaissance of the 1970s and 1980s has demonstrated the model for Black women in social science, especially historical writing. These "wild women" have been able to use a combination of historical voices, spiritual consciousness, liberation politics within creative mediums and works designed to empower and enlighten. Their example should urge social scientists to use simultaneity, multiple consciousness, and diverse approaches in their work.

Dialogues, letters, and family histories are some of the tools historians use to build their theories of human movement through time and space. In the hands of Alice Walker, Gayl Jones, and Toni Morrison these tools take us straight into the insides of Black women, drawing attention to the immediacy of their pasts with their "twists of fate" and the incredible sense of justice going and coming around.

Many renaissance women use slavery as a reference point—the "slave within us" as a present place of confusion and limitation while emancipation, the "laying down of the world," comes from reliance on feelings and passion. That holocaust can never become objectified. It is always remembered in the way they touch it gently with lines from spirituals and memories of chains. The father's ravishings in *Corregidora* and the slave love of *Sally Hemings* are not allowed to become self-righteous and simplistic, but rather human dilemmas and tragedies brought about when human beings become sexual chattel. The holocaust of the renaissance women is a personal, not merely a political statement of enslavement.

Using the language of the people of everyday Black life without apology or adherence to the "underclassness and poverty" of Black life, renaissance writers and singers reinforce the dignity of Black women as brilliant, insightful philosophers and commentators on the human experience around them. The responsibility of the chronicler is to hear what people truly are saying about their experiences. To use their rhythm and cadence of expression to define and describe and not delete it from the retelling. The retelling should not be blindly copied. The language of the people should become shaped and honed into a conscious statement of both the writer and her people. The words must become musical notes and beats in the hands of the musician who can then put all the parts together.

The language of the social sciences tends to be mechanical and fraught with fear because the words do not have life. So much of the research material is dry and lifeless, few can or want to read it unless they are forced. Social science information repeated in magazine articles is vivid, but hardly accurate and, in no way, is it "brutally honest." The people they discuss get lost in charts and data, overshadowed by language constructs designed to hide their humanity rather than illuminate and celebrate it. The people who need the truth the most, for example, Black women, get turned off because there are few social scientists who are trained to translate and write clearly and passionately of their lives. Articles by Black women social scientists that are committed to eradicating poverty and strengthening the Black family are often passionless discourses unlike the music, poetry, and writings of Black women of the renaissance of the 1970s and 1980s.

Many of those renaissance women rely upon African culture—orisha power, rites, rituals, colors, and sounds. Toni Cade Bambara's description of the dialogue between the healer and "her old hag" beautifully illustrates the work and the world of the spiritualist in the African tradition. Many Black artists stand in awe of the great human mysteries which can't be explained in rational terms. (Just how did Harriet manage to free all those slaves?) The reliance on the spiritual center for answers, explanations, and focus is the strongest opposition to Western social and natural science. All questions can't be answered through objectivity, and certainly the Black woman's power and knowing can't be understood without a knowing of her spirit and spiritual life. Black spiritual and gospel music seems to impart the most perfect notes to match the internal rhythm of Black women's prayers and visions. Wasn't it the prayers of Black mothers that placed Black daughters in the academy in the first place? And once there, Black women were able to push these mothers aside for the first time in their lives and became lost and confused without them. Social scientists in their search for reasons, theories, themes, and explanations of human history have always dismissed the concept of inner spiritual life as a force in a material world, though any truly scientific understanding would have to acknowledge it. Resurrecting those prayers and dreams is the most difficult wrestling Black women scholars have to do . . . though it is all too necessary for any sensible understanding of the world and Black woman's place within it.

Renaissance women blaze a path of spirituality and sexuality which moves us all to defy the limits placed upon our lives, especially upon our gender, our race, and our heterosexuality. The biomythography, poems, and essays of Audre Lorde implore us not to use the master's tools any more, but to seek the power of the erotic along with other powers of our liberation. These artists defy our mothers' fear of sexuality and its power and force us to link sexual freedom with liberation politics. As organizers and activists altering movements for social and political change, the renaissance artists have renounced the thoughts of the white and Black patriarchs. Their political warriorship infuses their writings. They have also worked in myriad low-paying, demeaning jobs to survive. Many have been secretaries, waitresses, maids, and lonesome travelers from city to town, seeing and learning. As pioneers they painfully had to create the space to stand. Like Nina Simone and Miriam Makeba, they had to create ways to sing their own song. Nothing was given to them. They had to expand their reach by recalling the powerful Black women of the past as they drew strength from their sisters in collectives, friendships, love affairs, and organizations. Many were escapees from the ivory tower thrown off paths of legitimacy to become word warriors and documenters of the Black woman's world.

To be thrown off the path to and from the ivory tower is no longer stigma, but part of the baptismal needed to empower Black women and to demystify the West's way of knowing. And once outside in the "real world," they discover there could be no scholarship or writing on behalf of the oppressed unless it pointed toward liberation, no real writings except those which lead to revolution and freedom. Justifications and rationalization of oppression without a class stand with working people; without affirming Blackness and the language, history, and cultures of other people of color; without explicitly loving women and telling their story; and without using common sense and our mothers' wit about life, is an inexcusable travesty of both scholarship and politics. Yet the writings of Black women social scientists who, meaning no harm, uphold whiteness, maleness, and privilege, do harm, furthering the oppression of their sisters. Black women who author historical studies which use whiteness as the model and reference point when discussing the suffrage movement, radical organization, and education demonstrate the poor training and lack of consciousness of these sisters. Yet the politics of the renaissance women teach us to "lay down that world" and embrace the downtrodden and speak fearlessly of our people, our sisterhood, and the richness of our spirit and culture.

There are far too many lost legacies and sheroes whose stories lie obscured and hidden. The problem of publishing these works is another story of prejudice and jealousy. Clearly, Black women novelists have demonstrated the commercial success of Black women writing about Black women. Yet publishers still frown upon and reject social scientific writings by Black women about Black women. Our tasks as social scientists are to discover alternatives and possibilities, as well as new ways to speak to our sisters, while we fight the academy's partners in silence—the print and broadcast media.

Like gospel singers, the griot historian stands with her sisters, and those shadows of past women and men stand behind her singing words in her ears. She writes about the moving women, the warriors, and the silent women. She stops writing to go outside to march with her sisters and brothers, shaking their fists at the madness of those who enslave. She anonymously writes a leaflet for the march. She passes it out, separated from her authorship and ownership of the words. She meets with the others to plan, to cheer, to worry about the next time and the next time. She puts the children to bed, waits for her lover to come in, make love, and fall asleep. Then she returns to the typewriter and Zora Neale was there waiting for her—soothing her and urging her on. She, fighting the fatigue of her body with spirit energy, writes the history of what was and is. While writing about the slave, the words become the moans of women, sounds from the mourners bench in southern churches. She suddenly remembers why there was a bench and why her grandmother got up early to take her with her to sing and moan there in that old-timey way. Her grandmother was a slave and the words she writes and reads about slavery are about her, and she strains to remember the face of the oldest person in her family, for the story of slavery is in her blood, not just in the books. And the white men can never know it or teach it because it is in her beyond the words and the footnotes.

The next day our griot walks to the store and hears Black girls clapping the same rhythm as African drums. The girls look her up and down with disdain, and seeing how she's dressed and how old she is, they go back to sing and rap some more. These sisters, with their tough street selves, await her words in some future time and she must leave the words for them and their children's children. Each precious word becomes something for them and the time capsule Black women and men will need and seek.

She becomes multilingual. She understands and speaks the oppressor's language—Europeanese. She also speaks with Du Bois and learns. She speaks along with Bessie Smith, and Dinah Washington, and Billie Holiday. She does research using the poking-around method of Zora Neale. She interprets and translates a speech into a story which becomes a political program in the hands of some, a bedtime story for the mother, the document and scholarly paper for the library and conference, the legal defense of the fugitive, and all these forms become the song. And all of it becomes history, the recording of those who are, what was done, and will be done.

And when the sister griot writes these words which touch so many, especially other sisters, they become a part of her words and part of her grandmother's moans and the girl's clapping. They all smile after she hits the right chords, verifying and amening with the poets, the singers, and the dancers. Others translate her history into their own languages, and they further the story and the songs become extensions of the sister griot historian.

Her historical method is to take the melody and spread it to the singers in the chorus behind her, and as each one sings the melody and improvises upon it in her own way, the sounds come together. Each one becomes a griot, a storyteller of the past and future. They all learn to create a song loud enough to end the silence.[3]

## Notes

1     Paula Giddings, *When and Where I Enter: The Impact of Black Women on Race and Sex in America* (New York: William Morrow and Company, Inc., 1984), pp. 5–6.

2     A bibliography of key historical works on Black women: Angela Davis, *Women, Race And Class* (New York: Random House, 1981); Gerda Lerner, *Black Women in White America: A Documentary History* (New York: Pantheon, 1972); Bert James Lowenberg and Ruth Bogin, eds., *Black Women in 19th Century American Life* (State College: Pennsylvania State University Press, 1976); Jeanne L. Noble, *Beautiful, Also, Are the Souls of My Black Sisters: A History of the Black Women in America* (Englewood Cliffs, N.J.: Prentice Hall, Inc., 1978).

3     Since this essay was written there has been considerable movement of Black women in the academy which merits mention. Works pertaining to the special song of Black women include those by Terborg-Penn, Harley, and Rushing; Jones; Steady; and White. In addition, there is an Africana Women Studies Series at Atlanta University, founded by Shelby Lewis. Many fine monographs and bibliographies chronicling the experiences of women of color have been published by the Center for Research on Women (Memphis State University). Among the most significant writers and researchers are Bonnie Thorton Hill, Patricia Hill Collins, Elizabeth Higginbotham, and Maxine Baca Zinn.

# *Part III*

---

# Visions and Re-visions

Afro-Colombian children Johana (left) and Sayi, daughters of members of the Center of Study and Research for the Development of Afro-Colombian Women in Bogota, Colombia (December 1987). Photo: Berta Ines Perea Diaz

# Joanne M. Braxton

# Ancestral Presence: The Outraged Mother Figure in Contemporary Afra-American Writing

Ah wanted to preach a great sermon about colored women sittin' on high, but they wasn't no pulpit for me. Freedom found me wid a baby daughter in mah arms, so Ah said Ah'd take a broom and cook-pot and throw up a highway through the wilderness for her. She would expound what Ah felt. But somehow she got lost offa de highway and the next thing Ah knowed you was in de world. So whilst Ah was tendin' you of nights Ah said Ah'd save de text for you. Ah been waitin' a long time, Janie, but nothin' Ah been through ain't too much if you just take a stand on high ground lak Ah dreamed.

Nanny speaking to her granddaughter Janie Starks in<br>
Their Eyes Were Watching God by Zora Neale Hurston.

When I'm telling you something don't you ever ask if I'm lying. Because they didn't want to leave no evidence of what they done—so it couldn't be held against them. And I'm leaving evidence. And you got to leave evidence too. And your children got to leave evidence. And when it come time to hold up evidence, we got to have evidence to hold up. That's why they burned all the papers, so there wouldn't be no evidence to hold up against them.

From Corregidora, a novel by Gayl Jones

As Black American women, we are born into a mystic sisterhood, and we live our lives within a magic circle, a realm of shared language, reference, and allusion within the veil of our blackness and our femaleness. We have been as invisible to the dominant culture as rain; we have been knowers but we have not been known. This paradox is central to what I suggest we call the Afra-American experience.

Joanne Braxton in the Massachusetts Review

I n an essay called "Rootedness: The Ancestor as Foundation," novelist Toni Morrison speaks of her attempt to "blend the acceptance of the supernatural and a profound rootedness in the real world . . . with neither taking precedence over the other." In Morrison's view this artistic goal

> is indicative of the cosmology, the way in which Black people looked at the world. We are a very practical people, very down to earth, even shrewd people. But within that practicality we also accepted what I suppose could be called superstition and magic, which is another way of Knowing things. But to blend those two worlds together at the same time was enhancing, not limiting. And some of those things were 'discredited knowledge' that Black people had; discredited only because Black people were discredited and therefore what they *knew* was 'discredited.'[1]

Other aspects which Morrison uses to define the literary tradition of Black Americans include the "oral quality" of that body of writing and "the presence of an ancestor." Morrison views the inclusion of this figure as a "deliberate effort, on the part of the artist, to get a visceral, emotional response as well as an intellectual response as he or she communicates with the audience" in a literary pattern of "call and response" (341, 343).

The ancestral figure most common in the work of contemporary Black women writers is an outraged mother. She speaks in and through the narrator of the text to "bear witness" and to break down artificial barriers between the artist and the audience. Not only does this ancestor figure lend a "benevolent, instructive, and protective" presence to the text, she also lends her benign influence to the very act of creation, for the Black woman artist works in the presence of this female ancestor, who passes on her feminine wisdom for the good of the "tribe," and the survival of all Black people, especially those in the African diaspora created by the Atlantic slave trade. This essay examines the ancestral presence of the outraged mother as a primary archetype in the narratives of contemporary Black American women writers. The outraged mother embodies the values of sacrifice, nurturance, and personal courage—values necessary to an endangered group. She employs reserves of spiritual strength, whether Christian or derived from African belief. Implied in all her actions and fueling her heroic ones is outrage at the abuse of her people and her person. She feels very keenly every wrong done her children, even to the furthest generations. She exists in art because she exists in life.

Images of the outraged mother abound in the oral lore and early autobiographical narratives of persons of African descent enslaved in the Americas. For example, Jamaican Maroon folklore attributes many supernatural powers to Grandy Nanny, "a mythical ancestress from whom all present day Maroons (believe) they are descended." According to legend, Nanny was both a magician and a military leader in Maroon resistance to the British. In one story Nanny uses magic to neutralize a large British military force. "[S]he stooped down and tauntingly presented her rump toward their guns; as they fired on her, she proceeded to shock them by catching between her buttocks a full round of lead shot, rendering them inactive." Thus she both insults and overwhelms the enemy. British written history of Jamaica acknowledges the existence of "an important personage named Nanny," and refers to her as "a powerful obeah woman or sorceress." And when today's Mooretown Maroons refer to themselves as "Nanny's yo-yo, Nanny's progeny," they assert a connection with an outraged mother of the ancestral past, signifying both continuity and tradition.[2]

Throughout the slave narrative genre and even in the post-emancipation accounts of female former slaves, the outraged mother remains an ancestral presence. She is fully developed in Harriet "Linda Brent" Jacobs's *Incidents in the Life of a Slave Girl* (1861). Linda's conviction to save herself and her children moves her to act deliberately and decisively in planning a secret escape. As in Jamaica and elsewhere in the African diaspora, maroonage or running away from slavery, proved a viable form of rebellion for many enslaved in the United States. Like Grandy Nanny, Linda takes to the woods, and becomes, for a brief period, an American Maroon, a rebel and a fugitive from slavery. With the help of her maternal grandmother Aunt Marthy, a free woman, and another outraged mother, "Linda" was disguised as a sailor and taken to the "Snaky Swamp," a location she found more hospitable than landed slave culture. "[E]ven those large venomous snakes were less dreadful to my imagination than the white men in that community called civilized."[3] Such language and imagery set the tone for later developments in Afra-American narrative, with the protective and determined qualities of the outraged mother well established, and the "autobiographical act" performed in the presence of Aunt Marthy, an outraged female forebearer who dies during the course of the narrative.

Female slave narrators like "Linda Brent" planted the seed of contemporary Black feminist autobiography and "womanist" fiction early in Black American literary tradition. In fact, the slave narrator's outraged grandmother, Aunt Marthy, foreshadows Zora Neale Hurston's Nanny in *Their Eyes Were Watching God* (1937). A spiritual sister of the Mythical Grandy Nanny, Zora Neale Hurston's fictional Nanny shares many of the mythic character's rebellious and protective attributes. She emerges in *Eyes* as an ancestral presence.

Another American Maroon, Hurston's Nanny flees the slave plantation to create a new and better way of life for herself and her child. Nanny takes to the woods with her blond and gray-eyed newborn after the plantation mistress makes use of the master's absence to order Nanny whipped and the child sold. Repeating the story for her granddaughter Janie Starks (narrator of *Eyes*), Nanny reflects: "Ah knowed mah body wasn't healed, but Ah couldn't consider dat. In the black dark Ah wrapped mah baby the best I knowed how and made it to the swamp by the river. Ah knowed de place was full uh mocasains and other bitin snakes, but Ah was more skeered of what was behind me."[4] Here the words of Hurston's fictional heroine echo those of slave narrator Linda Brent: "[E]ven those large and venomous snakes were less dreadful to my imagination than the white men in that community called civilized." The outraged mother is more afraid of what is behind her than what is in front of her; she must create the New World and with it a new way of life. Like Linda's Aunt Marthy, Nanny dies and joins the ancestors in the course of her granddaughter's story. Although *Incidents* is a work of autobiography and *Eyes* a work of fiction, there are distinct similarities between the texts, especially in the pairings of the narrator-granddaughter with a protective and powerful grandmother.

The ancestral presence in Maya Angelou's autobiography *I Know Why the Caged Bird Sings* (1969) is represented by the narrator's paternal grandmother, who, though still living at the end of *Caged Bird*, embodies the "timeless" quality of the ancestor figure. Momma Henderson, a self-sufficient woman, provided for her two grandchildren and for her crippled son, Marguerite's Uncle Willie. "Momma intended to teach . . . the paths of life that she and all Negroes gone before had found, and found to be safe ones," Angelou writes.[5] Mrs. Henderson nurtured Marguerite and her brother, Bailey Jr., through their Stamps, Arkansas, childhood and beyond, doing what she could to protect her son's young children from frequent intrusions of "white reality."

In praising her grandmother's courage and spiritual strength, Angelou invokes the ancestral presence and strengthens the maternal archetype. Early in the narrative "Momma" hid a would-be lynch victim and provided him with supplies for a journey even though she jeopardized her own security to do so. On another occasion it was necessary for Mrs. Henderson to conceal her crippled son one night after an unknown Black man was accused of "messing with" a white woman: "With a tedious and fearful slowness Uncle Willie gave me his rubber tipped cane and bent down to get into the now enlarged bin. It took forever before he lay down flat, and then we covered him with potatoes and onions, layer upon layer, like a casserole. Grandmother knelt praying in the darkened store" (14–15). Through this description of her experience, Maya Angelou invites others to follow her grandmother's model—to stand courageously and full of faith—not to turn back and not to falter. In the role of nurturer and protectress, Momma, in the words of critic Stephen Butterfield, both protects and "inspires the urge to protect."[6]

Despite Mrs. Henderson's reliance on faith and her ingenuity in avoiding confrontations, her outrage bursts forth one day when a white dentist she had assisted with a loan denies Marguerite needed dental care because she is Black. Mrs. Henderson, a proud woman, pleads, not for herself but for her grandchild. "I wouldn't press on you like this for myself but I can't take No. Not for my grandbaby." The dentist's response is clear, "Annie, my policy is I'd rather stick my hand in a dog's mouth than in a nigger's" (159–160). Mrs. Henderson sends Marguerite down the stairs out of sight and earshot while she disappears into the inner sanctum of the dentist's office. Marguerite can only imagine the exchange between "Momma" and the dentist, but in so doing she endows her grandmother with supernatural strength:

Her eyes were blazing like live coals and her arms had doubled themselves in length. He looked at her just before she caught him by the collar of his white jacket. . . .

"I didn't ask you to apologize in front of Marguerite, because I don't want her to know my power, but I order you, now and herewith. Leave Stamps by sundown."

"Mrs. Henderson, I can't get my equipment . . ." He was shaking terribly now.

"Now that brings me to my second order. You will never again practice dentistry. Never! When you are settled into your next place you will be a veterinarian caring for dogs with the mange, cats with the cholera and cows with the epizootic. Is that clear?"

The saliva ran down his chin and his eyes filled with tears. "Yes, Ma'am. Thank you for not killing me. Thank you, Mrs. Henderson."

Momma pulled herself back from being ten feet tall with eight foot arms and said, "You're welcome for nothing, you varlet. I wouldn't waste a killing on the likes of you."

On her way out she waved her handkerchief at the nurse and turned her into a crocus sack of chicken feed. (161–162)

Of course, the actual exchange between the outraged Black grandmother and the white dentist could not have followed Angelou's imagined scenario. However, the powers Maya Angelou attributes to her grandmother recall Grandy Nanny's ancestral presence: Momma's turning herself into a woman ten feet tall with arms eight feet long, the defender and avenger of her people, recalls Grandy Nanny's magical powers and her ability to insult and overwhelm the enemy. The historical Mrs. Henderson could no more have turned the nurse into "a crocus sack of chicken feed" than the historical Grandy Nanny could have caught "between her buttocks a full round of lead shot." Yet both images are versions of the same Afra-American archetype; both are products of myth making and reflect the people's need for heroes who embody cultural values necessary to the survival of the group. Both figures transcend the generations to become "timeless people." Maya Angelou celebrates and performs her "autobiographical act" in the ancestral presence of an outraged grandmother who embodies the values of nurturance, protection, and self-sacrifice while exhibiting great personal courage. Thus, for Angelou and indeed for the readers of *I Know Why the Caged Bird Sings,* Momma Henderson assumes the mythical proportions of the archetypal outraged mother. Her benign ancestral presence shines through Angelou's first and best-known work.

*Caged Bird* incorporates the lyrical quality of Black folk language to achieve what Toni Morrison calls "orality," a quality common to "both print and oral literature" by Black Americans: "It should try deliberately," Morrison writes, "to make you stand up and feel something profoundly in the same way that a Black preacher requires his congregation to speak, to join him in the sermon, to behave in a certain way, to stand up and to weep and to cry and to accede or to change and to modify—to expand on the sermon that is being delivered."[7] In a very real sense, Angelou, like Linda Brent and Hurston's fictional Janie Starks, is delivering a sermon on the nature of the Black female experience in America. Brent, Hurston, and Angelou perform their creative acts in the presence of courageous and outraged female ancestor figures who want their stories told, both as a corrective to "white history" and as a means of unifying the tribe.

Reflecting on her work and the times, Toni Morrison asserts that the novel is a healing art form, that Black people need the novel "in a way that it was not needed before." In its function as a healing art form, the Black American novel carries a very special "sermon," and it fulfills the critical role of preserving cultural identity:

> We don't live in places where we can hear those stories anymore; parents don't sit around and tell their children those classical, mythological archetypal stories that we heard years ago. But new information has got to get out, and there are several ways to do it. One is the novel.[8]

Much of the contemporary fiction by Afra-American writers performs this important healing function of "bearing witness." In many cases this writing incorporates the figure who breaks down barriers between the narrator and the audience. For those familiar with the oral tradition, especially Black women, this feminine ancestral presence will usually be a comforting one. But for others accustomed to what Morrison calls "the separate, isolated ivory tower voice," this particular presence will often prove disturbing.[9]

Such a presence is "Great Gram," maternal great-grandmother of

Ursa Corregidora, the narrator of Gayl Jones's novel *Corregidora* (1975). Great Gram speaks to and through the character of Ursa, a contemporary blues singer, to bear witness to the outrages she suffered as a slave girl on a Brazilian coffee plantation. Great Gram speaks with an urgency that is nearly impossible to ignore:

> Yeah, I remember the day he took me out of the field. Some places they had cane and others cotton and tobacco like up here. Other places they had your men working down in mines. He would take me hisself first and said he was breaking me in. Then he started bringing other men and they would give me money and I had to give it over to him.[10]

This master, Corregidora, for whom the novel is named, was a "Portuguese seaman turned plantation owner" who had taken Great Gram "out of the field when she was still a child and put her to work in his whorehouse while she was still a child." Great Gram bore Corregidora's child, a daughter, and he used his child the same way. "My grandmama was his daughter," says Ursa, "but he was fucking her too. She said when they did away with slavery down there they burned all the slavery papers so it would be like they never had it." (9). But it was not like "they never had it" because the Corregidora women kept their history alive in "oral literature": "My great-grandmama told my grandmama the part she lived through that my grandmama didn't live through and my grandmama told my mama what they both lived through and my mama told me what they all lived through and we were supposed to pass it down like that from generation to generation so we'd never forget. Even though they'd burned everything to play like it didn't never happen" (9). Ursa's job is to make generations and to bear witness to the crimes of the past.

Gayl Jones's *Corregidora* is full of ancestral presence in the characters of Great Gram and Gram, outraged mothers and maternal forebearers of the narrator, Ursa. By incorporating their narratives into the text, Jones achieves "orality," the sense that the narrative is as much told as written. Retelling the Corregidora story is a form of healing for Ursa, who must recover from a beating at the hands of her husband—a beating which causes her to lose both her unborn child and her future ability to "make generations." Thus, where in some sense Ursa is what Mary Helen Washington might call "the woman suspended," she is in another very real sense a woman rooted in culture and history.

Although Toni Morrison's *Song of Solomon* (1977) is based on the mythical story of Solomon, a slave who flew back to Africa, it is Pilate Dead who represents the ancestral past in this text, and Morrison herself has identified Pilate as the ancestor figure in *Song of Solomon*.[11] One of the most imposing of all outraged mothers in fiction, Pilate embodies the heroism, self-sacrifice, and the supernatural attributes of her historical and mythical counterparts. Pilate (whose name her father chose from the Bible by random selection) is so self-sufficient she "borned herself"; she doesn't even have a navel. Pilate was "believed to have the power to step out of her skin, set a bush afire from fifty yards, and turn a man into a ripe rutabaga—all on account of the fact that she had no navel" (94). Pilate dressed strangely and symbolically: she wore her name in a brass box suspended from her ear. To make matters worse, she "had a daughter but no husband." At sixteen she had gone to work among a "colony of Negro farmers on an island off the coast of Virginia," and there she had taken a lover, from whom she had concealed her secret by managing always to keep her stomach covered. When she became pregnant, she "refused to marry the man," though he was eager to have her for his wife. "Pilate was afraid she wouldn't be able to hide her stomach from a husband forever. And once he saw that uninterrupted flesh, he would respond the same way everybody else had" (146–147). Pilate, her daughter Reba, and Reba's daughter Hagar later moved to the city where Pilate's brother Macon lived. There the three women made and sold bootleg wine and kept a wine house, which, although in the city, lacked electricity and such modern conveniences as plumbing. Pilate was a source of constant embarrassment to her brother Macon, himself a prominent businessman. But where Macon held the keys to houses and material wealth, Pilate held the keys to her own unique identity and a system of humane and protective values reminiscent of the ancestral outraged mother.

Pilate felt keenly the wrongs done to her children. She loved both Reba and her granddaughter Hagar fiercely; her generosity and protectiveness knew no bounds. Likewise, the three were generous with others; they lived always at the edge of poverty because they gave away everything they had. Once when one of Reba's male friends, "a newcomer to the city," asked her for a loan, she "told him that she didn't have any money at all." She told the truth, but he didn't believe her, and he quarreled with her and beat her in Pilate's backyard. Hagar saw her mother's distress and screamed, alerting Pilate, who picked up a kitchen knife and went to Reba's defense: "[A]pproaching the man from the back, she whipped her right arm around his neck and positioned the knife at the edge of his heart. She waited until the man felt the knife-point before she jabbed it skillfully, about a quarter of an inch through his shirt into the skin. Still holding his neck, so he couldn't see but could feel the blood making his shirt sticky, she talked to him" (92–93). Using the elements of fear and surprise, Pilate overwhelmed the man and spoke to him in the language of the outraged mother, a language of the heart:

> Women are foolish, you know, and mamas are the most foolish of all. And you know how mama's are don't you? You got a mama, ain't you? Sure you have, so you know what I'm talking about. . . . We do the best we can, but we ain't got the strength you men got. . . . You know what I mean? I'd hate to pull this knife out and have you try some other time to act mean to my little girl. Cause one thing I know for sure: whatever she done, she's been good to *you*. Still, I'd hate to push it in more and have your mama feel like I do now. . . . (94).

Finally the terrified man begged Pilate to release him, and she did, but only after he promised that they would never see him again. Pilate's speech and heroic actions are performed on behalf of her daughter and not herself. Pilate, the outraged and outrageous, uses the word 'foolish' where the word 'brave' would be better substituted. The outraged mother is brave in the defense of her child; lacking the physical strength of men, she does the best she can, even if she must jeopardize her own safety to protect the ones she loves. Such is the nature of ancestral presence in *Song of Solomon*.

Nowhere is the impulse to protect, even at the risk of personal danger, more obvious than in the character Sophia, a character made familiar to millions of Americans by the popular film version of Alice Walker's novel *The Color Purple* (1982). Ironically, it is Sophia's performance of the duties of motherhood which leads her into confrontation with white society and which eventually causes her to be separated from her children and sent to jail. Sophia and her friend Henry Broadnax, a boxer, have just driven Sophia's five children to town and gotten out of Henry's car "looking like somebody." Their proud appearance attracts the attention of the mayor's wife, who is looking for a maid, or perhaps just someone to subjugate. Celie narrates Sophia's story:

> All these children, say the mayor's wife, digging in her pocketbook. Cute as little buttons, though. Say, and such strong white teef.
>
> Sofia and the prizefighter don't say nothing, wait for her to pass. Mayor wait too, stand back and tap his foot, watch her with a little smile. Now Millie, he say. Always going on over colored. Miss Millie finger the children some more, finally look at Sophia and the prizefighter. She look at the prizefighter car. She eye Sophia wristwatch. She say to Sophia, All your children so clean, she say, would you like to work for me, be my maid.
>
> Sophia say, Hell no.
>
> She say, What you say?
>
> Sophia say, Hell no.[12]

For this display of "sass" and impertinence, Sophia is slapped by the mayor. According to Sophia's way, she balls up her fist and "knock the man down." When the police come, they start beating both Sophia and her children, who attempt to defend her. When Henry, the prizefighter, wants to jump into the fray, Sophia tells him "No, take the children home." Even in a moment of great passion and peril, she defends and protects her children. And she refuses to take an insult, for their sake more than her own.

Beaten unmercifully, knocked unconscious, and taken to prison, Sophia labors in the prison laundry from five in the morning until eight at night. Her outward behavior is that of a model prisoner, but her internal life is a different matter: "I dream of murder, she say, I dream of murder sleep or wake" (78). Ironically, Sophia is released to the custody of the mayor's wife, to work as her maid and to care for her children. Like Pilate, Nanny, Momma Henderson, and Great Gram Corregidora, Sophia is an outraged mother and the carrier of the maternal archetype. While there is no single figure in *The Color Purple* to represent the ancestral presence, there is yet a real sense in which Walker's work is performed in the presence of the ancestors.

*The Color Purple* offers the perfect illustration of how life offers models for art, for Sophia had a predecessor in the heroine of "The Revenge of Hannah Kemhuff," a short story, and another in the actual historical personage of Walker's mother, who endured a specific incident the analysis of which lends depth and clarity to the reading of both "The Revenge" and *The Color Purple.* Like Maya Angelou, Walker draws her primary model from life; her own mother is the ancestral presence behind both *The Color Purple* and "The Revenge of Hannah Kemhuff" (1974). In Walker's words:

> My mother tells of an incident that happened to her during the Depression. She and my father lived in a small Georgia town and had half a dozen children. They were sharecroppers, and food, especially flour, was almost impossible to obtain. To get flour, which was distributed by the Red Cross, one had to submit vouchers signed by a local official. On the day my mother was to go into town for flour she received a large box of clothes from one of my aunts who was living in the North. The clothes were in good condition, though well worn, and my mother needed a dress, so she immediately put on one of those from the box and wore it into town. When she reached the distribution center and presented her voucher she was confronted by a white woman who looked her up and down with marked anger and envy. "What'd you come up here for?" the woman asked. "For some flour," said my mother, presenting her voucher. "Humpf," said the woman, looking at her more closely and with unconcealed fury. "Anybody dressed up as good as you don't need to come beggin for food."[13]

Although the Walkers were denied their rightful share of food they "got by all right." "Aunt Mandy Aikens lived down the road from us and she got plenty of flour," her mother relates. "We had a good stand of corn so we had plenty of meal. Aunt Mandy would swap me a bucket of flour for a bucket of meal" (16). Like the New World Maroon, the southern Black woman must create her own tools of survival; Alice Walker's mother, like so many of her sisters, fashions that "way out of no way." Her experience informs her artist daughter's vision and that of those characters she creates.

Commenting on her mother's story, Walker writes: "[W]hen I listen to my mother tell and retell this story I find that the white woman's vindictiveness is less important than Aunt Mandy's resourceful generosity or my mother's ready stand of corn. For their lives were not about that pitiful example of Southern womanhood, but about themselves" (16–17). Walker views the world from within the Veil of the Black female experience, and she places that experience (and those women) at the center of her work, celebrating their feminine heroism and their controlled outrage. "My mother always told this story with a most curious expression on her face," Walker writes. "She automatically raised her head higher than ever—it was always high—and there was a look of righteousness, a kind of holy heat coming from her eyes. She said she had lived to see this same white woman grow old and senile and so badly crippled she had to get about on two sticks." Walker sensed in her mother's story "the possibilities . . . for fiction," and she wondered if her mother (herself a Christian) had voodooed the woman (9–10).

Walker wondered too "how a larger story could be created out of my mother's story; one that would be true to the magnitude of her humiliation and grief, and to the white woman's lack of sensitivity and compassion." Out of these wonderings, "The Revenge of Hannah Kemhuff" was born. Walker comments: "I wrote 'The Revenge of Hannah Kemhuff' based on my mother's experiences during the Depression, and on Zora Neale Hurston's folklore collection of the 1920's, and on my own response to both out of a contemporary existence. . . ." (12–13). Experience and story by Walker and Walker, plus folk magic by Zora Neale Hurston and the outraged mothers of the New World result in a story which speaks from the core of the Afra-American experience to connect the dead with the living and leave a legacy in writing for the as-yet unborn. In an essay called "Saving the Life That Is Your Own," Walker writes:

> In that story I gathered up the historical and psychological threads of the life my ancestors lived, and in the writing of it felt joy and strength and my own continuity. I had that wonderful feeling writers get sometimes, not very often, of being *with* a great many people, ancient spirits, all very happy to see me consulting and acknowledging them, and eager to let me know, through the joy of their presence, that, indeed, I am not alone."[14]

Walker successfully infuses her story with the "holy heat" of her mother's gaze. In writing "The Revenge of Hannah Kemhuff," Walker celebrates "Aunt Mandy's resourceful generosity" and her "mother's ready stand of corn." She does this by placing them at the center of her story, by acting as their medium, and by writing in a first-person voice, thereby *oralizing* her narrative. For in this story, Walker's mother becomes Hannah Kemhuff. Aunt Mandy is transformed into Tante Rosie (Ro'zee), root woman, diviner, and avenger of the outraged mother, and the narrator, who was not even born at the time of the Depression incident, becomes Tante Rosie's assistant.

Here's where the audience's discomfort comes in, where the mythological outraged mother employed supernatural means to overwhelm and defeat her foe. "The Revenge" suggests that "real" people—the common, ordinary people—had access to a similar balancing force in the uncommon and extraordinary means of folk magic. The uninitiated reader's discomfort is further increased by the role of the narrator, who seems to speak for Walker. Or is it Walker who speaks through the narrator and who hastens the destruction of her mother's enemy, realizing retribution for an act committed against her tribe before she was born? In any case, there is no "ivory tower" detachment here.

When "The Revenge of Hannah Kemhuff" opens, Mrs. Kemhuff is already a "very old woman." Wrapped in skirts and shawls, she visits Tante Rosie to rectify a great wrong that had been done to her when she was a twenty-five year old woman with four young children—when she was "young and pretty." The fictional Hannah Kemhuff lacks the resources of Alice Walker's historical mother. In the younger Walker's fiction, Mrs. Kemhuff's children slowly starve to death, and her husband deserts her for a prostitute who has plenty of money. The relief station incident and its repercussions broke Hannah Kemhuff's body and her spirit, and all she could remember or even dream about was the "grinning moppet." Mrs. Kemhuff waited on the Lord to right her wrongs, for she believed "all wrongs are eventually righted in the Lord's good time." But after many years of suffering, she "began to feel that the Lord's good time might be too far away." It was then she turned to Tante Rosie for assistance in realizing retribution for this one great wrong. "I could die easier if I knew something, after all these years, had been done to the little moppet. God cannot be let to make her happy all these years and me miserable. What kind of justice would that be? It would be monstrous!" (67).

Tante Rosie had the solution: "'Let me explain what we will do,' said Tante Rosie, coming near the woman and speaking softly to her, as a doctor would speak to a patient. 'First we will make a potion that has a long history of use in our profession. It is a mixture of hair and nail parings of the person in question, a bit of their water and feces, a piece of their clothing heavy with their own scents, and I think in this case we might as well add a pinch of goober dust; that is dust from the graveyard. This woman will not outlive you by more than six months'" (68–69). Other supplies necessary to the task included two large black candles (for Death), and a small bag of powder to be burned on an altar while reciting a powerful curse-prayer (taken directly from Hurston's *Mules and Men*). Tante Rosie told the outraged mother "that each morning and evening for nine days she was to light the candles, burn the powder, recite the curse-prayer from her knees and concentrate all her powers on getting her message through to Death. . . ." Mrs. Kemhuff leaves with complete confidence in Tante Rosie's work: "I will not live to see the result of your work, Tante Rosie, but my grave will fit nicer, having someone proud again who has righted a great wrong and by so doing lies straight and proud through eternity" (70).

It was the young assistant's job to secure the hair, nail parings, feces, water and clothing necessary to the potion. By this time the "moppet" was a married woman with children and grandchildren of her own. Following a disturbing visit by the participant/observer/narrator/assistant, Mrs. Holley began to hoard her hair, nails, feces, and water. She eventually went mad and died, following Mrs. Kemhuff to the next world by a few months.

Alice Walker has described her role as that of "author and medium," a mediator between this and the world of the ancestor spirits. As intermediary and avenger, she helps to right great wrongs and to unfold the meaning of her ancestors' lives. She works in the presence of those ancestors. In the dedication to *Horses Make a Landscape More Beautiful* (1984), Walker intones:

> Rest in Peace
> In me
> the meaning of your lives
> is still
> unfolding.
>
> Rest in peace, in me.
> The meaning of your lives
> is still
> unfolding.

Rest. In me
the meaning of your lives
is still
unfolding.

Rest. In peace
in me
the meaning
of our lives
is still
unfolding.

Rest.[15]

Alice Walker, "author and medium" fulfills a dual role: artistic and spiritual. As author, she both creates art and connects the ancestors with the living by distilling the oral wisdom, values, and unwritten history of those who have gone before into a written language to be preserved for future generations, and by making myths and images upon which the living may model their lives. For Alice Walker—like Hannah Kemhuff, Sophia, Tante Rosie, and all the Walker heroines—is a woman of power. She, like the young assistant in "The Revenge of Hannah Kemhuff," is a medium through whom peace and justice may be realized.

Afra-American writers like Zora Neale Hurston, Maya Angelou, Gayl Jones, Toni Morrison, and Alice Walker call on ancestors from whom they derive strength, and they perform in the "holy heat" of an ancestral presence. As often as not, especially in the case of these writers, the ancestor figure is an outraged mother who embodies the values of sacrifice, nurturance, and personal courage—values necessary to an endangered and embattled minority group. Black women writers employ "orality" as a literary device to enable the ancestor figure to speak directly to the audience and by so doing to "bear witness" to the unwritten history and wisdom preserved in the folklore and oral literature of Black Americans—that body of folk knowledge commonly referred to as "mother wit." These Black women writers borrow from archetypal imagery as well as the mood and the mind of common folk to create innovative fiction and contemporary myths to sustain a struggling people. In speaking for themselves, they extend the feminine version of the Black heroic archetype and nurture a tradition of Afra-American writing that is as mystical and real as life.

## Notes

1      Toni Morrison, "Rootedness: The Ancestor as Foundation," in *Black Women Writers (1950–1980),* ed. Mari Evans (New York: Doubleday, 1983), 342.

2      Kenneth Bilby and Filomena Chioma Steady, "Black Women and Survival: A Maroon Case," in *The Black Woman Cross-Culturally,* ed. Filomena Steady (Cambridge: Schenkman Publishing Company, 1981), 458–459.

3      Linda Brent, *Incidents in the Life of a Slave Girl: Written by Herself* (Boston: Thayer and Eldridge, 1861), 116.

4      Zora Neale Hurston, *Their Eyes Were Watching God* (New York: Lippincott, 1937), 34–35.

5      Maya Angelou, *I Know Why the Caged Bird Sings* (New York: Random House, 1969), 39.

6      Stephen Butterfield, *Black Autobiography in America* (Amherst: University of Massachusetts Press, 1974), 203.

7      Morrison, "Rootedness," 341.

8      Ibid., 340.

9      Ibid., 343.

10      Gayl Jones, *Corregidora* (New York: Random House, 1975), 11–12.

11      Toni Morrison, *Song of Solomon* (New York: Random House, 1977), 344.

12      Alice Walker, *The Color Purple* (New York: Harcourt Brace Jovanovich, 1982), 75–76.

13      Walker, *In Search of Our Mothers' Gardens* (New York: Harcourt Brace Jovanovich, 1983), 15–16.

14      Ibid.

15      Walker, *Horses Make a Landscape More Beautiful* (New York: Harcourt Brace Jovanovich, 1984), 9.

# Vashti Crutcher Lewis

## African Tradition in Toni Morrison's *Sula*

S terling Plumpp wrote in a 1975 review that "*Sula* is a suitable black edifice that came before critical blueprints for it."[1] He meant that critics measure Black fiction according to a Black aesthetic that uses touchstones such as assimilationism, combativeness, or revolution. Plumpp also suggested that most critics stress the need for Black writers to use their writing as a vehicle for teaching, and that they are most comfortable when Black writers depict Black people positively. He concluded that *Sula* is "written according to none of these recipes; it is too complex and mature a book to be classified."[2]

*Sula* is too complex to be classified because Toni Morrison writes from an African point of view—an African aesthetic. Names are a vital connection to life in traditional African culture, and Sula is an African name. In the Babangi language, it means any one or a combination of the following: 1) to be afraid, 2) to run away, 3) to poke, 4) to alter from a proper condition to a worse one, 5) to be blighted, 6) to fail in spirit, 7) to be overcome, 8) to be paralyzed with fear, or 9) to be stunned.[3] In the Kongo language Sula means electric seal[4]—a meaning which is highly applicable to the critical thrust of this analysis. Knowing the Africanness of the major character's name adds a dimension that clarifies much of the mystery of the novel for the reader and places a demand on the critic to search for a blueprint for the novel based upon an African world-view—a blueprint that is sorely needed for African-American fiction as people of

African descent wrestle with problems of identity, as we move into the twenty-first century.

Toni Morrison writes that her novels are rooted in an African past in that an ancestor is always present.[5] An African ancestral presence is not immediately obvious in *The Bluest Eye* (1970), but one is there in the presence of Mr. and Mrs. McTeer; it is strong in the characterization of Pilate in *Song of Solomon* (1977), and an African presence in both characterization and setting is more than obvious in Morrison's fourth novel, *Tar Baby* (1981).[5]

*Sula* (1973) is Morrison's most complex work in reference to traditional African culture. This is true because the African presence and cultural rootedness is woven into Black American culture without contrivance and with such extraordinary subtlety that neither the characters nor the reader are immediately aware of it; just as most of us are oblivious to the fact that after some three hundred plus years in America, African tradition continues to manifest itself in our lives. Black people in the Bottom of Medallion, Ohio, consider Sula and Shadrack pariahs of their community, and do not recognize their African presence.

Sula and Shadrack represent Black sons and daughters of America who would be more at home in Africa. In traditional African cultures, they would be neither pariahs nor mysteries, since both represent tradition and a profound rootedness in African cosmology. To the people of the Bottom, Sula is an enigma and Shadrack is a downright shame.

Appropriately, Shadrack is the first major character to be introduced in the novel. He is Sula's ancestral presence—a representation of an ancestral spirit, a husband, a father, a provider dispensed by the gods to "always"[6] be there for the displaced Sula. Theirs was a spiritual kinship—metaphorically, a marriage of a traditional West African water spirit/priest to a water priestess, both oracles of a river god.[7]

Shadrack's divine nature results from his state of unconsciousness as a victim of shell-shock during World War I. In traditional West African culture when one had lain unconscious for many days, people believed that that person's spirit left the physical body and entered the ancestral world where he or she became an active participant. Physically surviving the state of unconsciousness bestowed no insanity upon the person—no matter how eccentric or erratic the behavior following the onset. On the contrary, unconsciousness bestowed a specialness and a spirituality, since the unconscious person had communed directly with the ancestral spirits.[8]

When Shadrack returns to the Bottom from World War I, after having entered the spirit world of his ancestors, he establishes his residence on the banks of the river to earn his living as a fisherman. His spirituality, his residency near the river, and his calling as a fisherman place Shadrack squarely in the role of a divine river spirit, or more accurately, as a West African Water Priest who represents and speaks for a river god. According to Geoffrey Parrinder, "After the earth gods may come those very popular divinities of river and sea which play such a large part in West African thought, especially for fisherman and those who live near rivers . . . all the great rivers of Yoruba country have their presiding spirit."[9] Shadrack is the presiding river spirit for displaced African people in the Bottom who call Shadrack a lunatic and fear him. This would not have been so in traditional West African culture where lunatics were treated with awful respect,[10] since it was believed that they were nearest in contact with the unseen spiritual world, and that the ancestral spirits spoke through them.[11]

Lakes, streams, and rivers have always been associated with divinities and spirits among the Yoruba people in West Africa. They believe that in connection with every lake, stream, and river is a lord or owner. Shrines have been built throughout West Africa to honor water spirits. For example, the shrine of the river god, Ogun, at Oshogbo in Oyo, a state in Nigeria, is over five thousand years old, and people come there annually, by the thousands on pilgrimages, to pay homage to the river god and to be blessed by him.[12]

Many water spirits are said to look like men but their feet and hands are different.[13] People of the Bottom fear Shadrack not only because of his peculiar behavior but also because he does not look like them. Earlier, while he had lain in the hospital recovering from shell-shock and struggling with his identity "his fingers began to grow in higgly piggly fashion like Jack's beanstalk, all over the tray" (p. 7). Later, when Sula runs to Shadrack's hut overlooking the river where Chicken Little has been sacrificed, she notices his hands: "His hands were *different* [emphasis mine]. Relieved and encouraged, no one with hands like that, no one with fingers that curved around wood so tenderly could kill her" (p. 53). Sula leaves Shadrack's hut soothed by his hands which are different from other men's.

Sula's birthmark links her ontologically to Shadrack, the water spirit, priest, oracle of the river god. Some see Sula's birthmark as a rose, some see it as a serpent; Shadrack, her spiritual protector and kindred spirit, sees it correctly as a tadpole—a water creature. Priestesses of West Africa were often noted for their hierarchical body markings, which were often water creatures, and experts would know from the markings on a particular woman to what god the priestess had been vowed.[14] Sula, a water spirit/priestess, is vowed to the same river god as Shadrack and bound spiritually to Shadrack by the word "always."

In December 1985, when I stood at the shrine of the great River God, Ogun, which sits just above a serenely still river in Oshogbo, Nigeria, it was not difficult for me to sense the presence of Shadrack. Nor was it inconceivable to image Sula climbing one of the lofty trees, thousands of years old, to retrieve Chicken Little who is held spellbound by his view of the river. My imagination recaptured Sula swinging Chicken Little around and around in an attempt to amuse him after his dangerous climb in the great tree overlooking the river in the Bottom. When he slips from her grip into the water, he is sacrificed to the river god just as it was not uncommon for children to be sacrificed to river gods in Africa, throughout the Bight of Benin.[15] The sacrifice of Chicken Little to the river and therefore to the river god is yet another ontological linking of Shadrack and Sula. From that moment on, as representatives of traditional West African culture, their destinies are cojoined.

When Sula enters Shadrack's hut, he immediately recognizes and acknowledges her as a water spirit and priestess of the river god. He goes on to recognize their spiritual marriage and kinship. To quiet her terror over Chicken Little's drowning, he "smiles a great smile heavy with lust" (p. 55) of a marriage of a water priest and priestess: "He nods his head as though answering a question . . . and says in a pleasant conversational tone . . . 'always'" (p. 55). Sula will not understand the meaning of "always" and her spiritual kinship with Shadrack until some eighteen years later, in 1940, when she lies dying.

In 1941, after Sula's death, Shadrack feels that he has let Sula down. He is devastated by Sula's death because as her spiritual protector, provider, and husband, he has not provided the permanency that he had promised her—the permanency that his "always" had conveyed: "Another dying away of someone's face he knew" (p. 135). His soul-mate, his spiritual visitor is dead and will not return. However, if Shadrack could have communicated with Sula, he would have discovered that he had not let her down at all. One of her last thoughts before she dies is the promise of "always":

> She looks at the window from which Eva had jumped. . . . the boarded window soothed her with its finality. It would be here . . . held by this blind window high above the elm tree that she might draw her legs up to her chest, close her eyes, put her thumb in her mouth and float over and down the tunnels . . . down, down until she met a rain scent and the *water* was near, and she would know the *water* was near, and she would curl into its heavy softness and it would carry her and wash her tired flesh *always. Always.* Who said that? She tried hard to think. Who was it that has promised her a sleep of *water always.* (p. 128, emphasis mine)

It had been Shadrack, the fisherman, the priest, the oracle of the river god who had promised her a "sleep of water always." As Sula lies dying he is with her in a spiritual sense—remembrance of the "always" of her kindred water spirit comforts and consoles Sula as she moves into the spirit world. She realizes that there will be no pain: "She felt her face smiling. Well I'll be damned . . . it didn't even hurt" (p. 128).

The full significance of Sula as a water spirit/priestess is readily apparent at her grandmother Eva's burial in 1965, twenty-five years after Sula's death. Nel and a cluster of people from the Bottom linger at Eva's gravesite to sing "Shall We Gather at the River." Nel, Sula's childhood friend, who had felt betrayed by Sula at the time of her death, senses that Sula is already there at the river: "Their question clotted the October air. Shall We Gather at the River. The beautiful, beautiful river? Perhaps Sula answered them even then, for it began to *rain* and the women ran in tiny leaps through the grass for fear their straightened hair would beat them home" (pp. 148–149, emphasis mine).

As Nel leaves the cemetery, she recognizes Shadrack: He wonders where he has seen her before. He can't remember and continues his journey in the graveyard searching for Sula, his kindred water spirit, and Nel searches for answers to her turbulent relationship with Sula. According to traditional African cosmology, spirits linger in the most remote and desolate places, such as fields, forests, ravines, and in a western sense—graveyards.[16] Nel intuitively senses Sula's presence in the midst of the giant trees and the rain scent: "Nel suddenly stops, her eye twitches, and she whispers Sula's name while gazing at the tree tops. Leaves stirred; mud shifted; there was the smell of over-ripe green things. A soft ball of fur broke and scattered like dandelion spores in the breeze" (p. 149).

Feeling Sula's spiritual presence in nature, her physical remembrance presses down hard on Nel's chest and she recognizes that the spiritual love she had had for Sula transcends the sexual and romantic love that she had felt for her husband, Jude, whom she had accused Sula of taking. In this final scene, Morrison reunites Shadrack, Sula, and Nel. She links them in a spiritual and ontological sense in the world of nature—in the trees and the water that had inextricably bound them together some forty-three years earlier in the sacrifice of Chicken Little to the rivergod. This reuniting of Sula, Shadrack, and Nel in the graveyard reinforces the idea of permanency. Sula, as a spirit and daughter of the gods, is not literally dead, and Shadrack, a special son of the gods, will eventually join her in the ancestral world. Because Nel finally acknowledges her love for Sula and no longer damns her, she too will be accepted by the gods of their ancestors.

Sula and Shadrack would have a special kind of power that is revered in traditional West African Culture. Their power is clearly apparent in the confusion, pain, and even death that came to people who harass or criticize the two. Some die in the tunnel excavation that spans the river in 1965, and others have already experienced strange and ironic accidents as a direct result of their contact with this son and daughter of African gods.

Shadrack's name is an important indication of his specialness in reference to the gods and what might happen to those who defame him. His name also denotes his alien nature. As previously mentioned, Shadrack is a displaced African—out of time and out of place. His Old Testament namesake in biblical Hebrew history refuses to worship the alien gods of Babylon. Because he defies the king and will not follow alien law, he is thrown into a fiery furnace. But, fire has no power over Shadrack. Just as fire cannot consume water, it does not consume him, and Shadrack walks out of the furnace unscathed, untouched, and unburned. He walks amidst the fire unharmed. The king is astonished and awed by this miracle, and he decrees that anyone who speaks against Shadrack will be torn limb from limb.[17]

After Sula's death, Shadrack reluctantly leads the joyous people of the Bottom in their last third of January Suicide Day parade, and most of them who have ridiculed Shadrack and Sula are literally torn limb from limb in the strange accident at the tunnel that spans the river. Helen Wright, Nel's mother, and some others did not go to the tunnel; except for Helen those who do not join the parade instinctively understand the ironies and diabolical nature of this strange jubilation over the death of Sula Peace: "the spirits touch, which made them dance, who understood . . . the ecstasy of river baptisms under suns just like this one, did not understand this curious disorder" (p. 137). Their innate African spirituality saved them from death in the tunnel. Those who died there, on this last Suicide Day parade, did not intend to enter the tunnel, the place that had held their hopes and dreams since 1927—hopes and dreams for employment to relieve their abject poverty.

What begins in glee and celebration of Sula's death ends in violent rage intended to kill the memories of deferred dreams in racist America. Sula had been the scapegoat for the long and bitter disappointment of the people in the Bottom. They had damned the wrong person—damned a water-spirit, a priestess, a chosen and select child of traditional African gods:

> A lot of them died there. The earth now warm, shifted. . . . They found themselves in a chamber of *water* [emphasis mine] deprived of the sun that had brought them there. With the first crack and whoosh of the *water,* the clamber to get out was so fierce that others who were trying to help were pulled to their deaths. . . . Tar Baby, Dessie, Ivy, Valentine, the Herrod boys . . . and the Deweys—all died there. (p. 139)

Sula and Shadrack's specialness in reference to African ancestral gods is depicted several times before the death of the townspeople in the tunnel. One might even conjecture that the African gods are angry because the people of the Bottom reject the most African of them all—indeed, the most sacred of them all. Among the Ewe speaking people of West Africa, priests and priestesses are sacred, and they must not be insulted or in some cases even touched, and one must be careful not to jostle a sacred person by accident in the street.[18] Everyone whose life Sula directly touches is adversely affected. Her mother, Hannah, who admits she loves but does not like Sula, burns to death. Her grandmother, Eva, whom Sula fears because she cannot fathom why she chooses to burn her son, Plum, alive, spends her last years discarded in a newly integrated old folk's home. Nel, Sula's girlhood friend, despairs of loneliness and abandonment when her husband Jude leaves her, after Nel finds Sula and him naked on her bedroom floor. When Sula attempts to befriend Teapot, a sad little boy whose mother despises Sula, he falls and fractures his leg. Mr. Finley, who had eaten chicken bones for thirteen years, looks up one day, sees Sula, chokes to death on a bone, and dies instantly. A sty appears over Dessie's eye when she sees Shadrack tip a hat that he is not wearing to Sula. Moreover, unlike other human beings it is rumored that Sula "had no childhood diseases, was never known to have chicken pox, croup, or even a runny nose. She had played rough as a child—where were the scars? . . . she was free of any normal signs of vulnerability . . . neither gnats nor mosquitoes would settle on her" and "when Sula drank beer she never belched" (p. 100).

The fall and winter of 1941, following Sula's death, are especially hard on the people of the Bottom. Rain falls and freezes, fowl die of chill and rain, ice cold winds blow, and the people in general suffer heavily. Ice falls for days on end, the consequences of which are a miserable Thanksgiving. By the time the ice melts "everybody under fifteen had croup or scarlet fever" (p. 131), and everybody over fifteen has a plethora of illnesses.

As Richard Wright observed in "Blueprint for Negro Writing": "No theory of life can take the place of life."[19] Certainly, no theory of life can take the place of life for displaced African people in America. Research indicates that the cosmology and world-view of African-Americans is distinctly African,[20] albeit we are not always consciously aware of this. It is to Toni Morrison's credit that she recognizes African tradition in African-American culture and chooses deliberately to write from an African point of view. In doing so, she removes much of the mystery of Black life and answers, to some degree, the ubiquitous question: What makes Black folk act that way? Perhaps, more important, Morrison offers to both reader and artist her vision of a uniquely complex and multifaceted culture rooted in an African past.

## Notes

1      Sterling D. Plumpp, "Sula," *Black Books Bulletin* 2, nos. 2 and 3 (Winter 1974), 62–64.

2      Ibid.

3      Hellen, Murray, ed., *Newbill Nile Puckett, Collection, Black Names in America Origins and Usage* (Boston: G. K. Hall and Co., 1975), pp. 449–450.

4      Geoffrey Parrinder, *Western African Psychology* (rpt., New York: AMS Press Inc., 1976), p. 181; For credibility of Parrinder's treatment of African Culture see E. Bolaji Idoww, *Olodumare': God in Yoruba Belief* (London: William Clowes and Sons Limited, 1962), p. 26.

5      Morrison's *Song of Solomon* was released after this essay was submitted for publication.

6      Toni Morrison, *Sula* (New York: Alfred A. Knopf, Inc., 1973; rpt 1975), p. 53. All further page references to this work are cited in the text and are taken from this edition.

7      For synonymous use of these terms see Geoffrey Parrinder, *West African Religion: A Study of the Beliefs and Practices of Akan, Ewe, Yoruba, Ibo, and Kindred Peoples* (London: Epworth Press, 1949; rpt., 1967), pp. 39–51.

8      Parrinder, *Western African Psychology*, p. 181.

9      Parrinder, *West African Religion*, p. 45.

10     Ibid., p. 177.

11     Ibid.

12     Personal conversation with overseer of Shrine of river god at Oshogbo, Nigeria, December 21, 1985.

13     P. Amaury Talbot, *Tribes of the Niger Delta* (London: Frank and Company Limited, 1932; rpt., 1967), p. 33.

14     A. B. Ellis, *The Ewe-Speaking Peoples of the Slave Coast of West Africa* (Chicago: Benin Press, Ltd., 1965), p. 146.

15     Talbot, *Tribes of the Niger Delta*, p. 45.

16     John S. Mbiti, *African Religions and Philosophy* (New York: Doubleday, 1969), p. 104.

17     The Holy Bible, Old Testament, Daniel (Revised Standard Version: Thomas Nelson and Sons, 1952), pp. 921–922.

18      Ellis, *Ewe-Speaking Peoples,* p. 147.

19      Richard Wright, "Blueprint for Negro Literature," in *Amistad* 2. ed. John A. Williams and Charles F. Harris (New York: Random House, 1972), p. 12.

20      See Melville K. Herskovitz, *The Myth of the Negro Past* (Boston: Beacon Press, 1941; rpt. 1965). Leroi Jones, *Blues People* (New York: William Morrow and Company, 1963). Lawrence W. Levine, *Black Culture and Black Consciousness* (London: Oxford University Press, 1978). Geneva Smitherman, *Talkin and Testifyin: The Language of Black America* (Boston: Houghton Mifflin, 1977).

# Barbara Christian

---

# "Somebody Forgot to Tell Somebody Something" African-American Women's Historical Novels

T he title of my essay is taken from a radio interview Ntozake Shange did with Toni Morrison in 1978, just after she had published *Song of Solomon*.[1] Morrison's comment referred to a generation of Afro-Americans of the post–World War II era who had seen the new possibilities that period seemed to promise for their children and who thought that knowledge of their history—one of enslavement, disenfranchisement, and racism—might deter the younger generations' hopes for the future. As Morrison put it, the older generation of that era sometimes X'd out the southern grandfather who had been a sharecropper and tried to forget the brutality of the African-American past. In *How I Wrote Jubilee* (1972) Margaret Walker tells a similar story of how her mother resented the stories about slavery her grandmother told the young Margaret, and how she admonished the older woman not to tell the child those "horrifying lies."[2] Alice Walker tells us in a "BBC documentary on '*The Color Purple*'" (1986) that her family spoke "in whispers" about certain parts of their history, whispers which she said fascinated her.[3] These African-American writers, as well as many others, comment on the ambivalence their families felt toward the African-American past.

In the eighties, Morrison, Alice Walker, as well as Sherley Anne Williams, previously a poet and playwright, have written African-

American historical novels, a sign of these writers' desire to re-vision African-American history from their imaginative and informed point of view. This trend, I think, indicates the fascination not only of novelists and scholars but also of many other women who share the experiences of African-American women in the nineteenth and early twentieth century, the very periods that Morrison characterized as being X'd out by upwardly mobile African-Americans of the forties and fifties.

This is not to say that as a group, contemporary African-American women writers had not previously recalled the past. However, generally speaking, they had reached back to the period of their mothers' lives, from the 1920s to the 1960s, to a past that often involved shifts of values in African-American communities, sometimes migration from the rural South or West Indies to the small-town or urban North. So, for example, Morrison's first three novels, *The Bluest Eye* (1970), *Sula* (1974), *Song of Solomon* (1977), much of Walker's short fiction as well as her novels, Paule Marshall's *Brown Girl, Brownstones* (1959), Gloria Naylor's "Mattie Michaels" section of *The Women of Brewster Place* (1982) explore the twenties, thirties, and forties from the African-American women's perspective. As Marshall, Morrison, and Walker have told us, in the process of consciously imagining their novels, they were propelled by the stories their mothers told them about their lives.

During the last decade, these writers have also probed their own contemporary context. Toni Cade Bambara's *Gorilla, My Love* (1971) and Alice Walker's *Meridian* (1976) ask pivotal questions about girls and women who were living in the decade of the intense "black consciousness," the 1960s. Morrison, in *Tar Baby* (1981), Bambara in *The Sea Birds Are Still Alive* (1974), and Shange in *Sassafrass, Cypress, and Indigo* (1982) explore the relationships of women and men as affected by the second wave of feminism, although from very different points of view. Marshall in *Praisesong for the Widow* (1982), Morrison in *Tar Baby*, Naylor in *Linden Hills* (1985) examine the effects of middle-class mobility among some blacks during the 1960s and 1970s, while in *The Women of Brewster Place* (1982), Naylor tells the story of underclass contemporary African-American women. African-American women have even extended the present into the future, as Susan Willis pointed out in her study, *Specifying* (1982), the most overt work being Bambara's *The Salt Eaters* (1980). As a group then, contemporary African-American women have written about every decade of the twentieth century, and about every region of this country—the North, the Midwest, the South, and the West, the country, small town and inner city—as well as the underclass and the middle class. And they have even traveled in their fiction beyond the geographical borders of this country to the Caribbean, to Europe, and to Africa.

Yet, even as many of these writers have, in their earlier novels, focussed on the twentieth century, they have, in these same novels, taken us back in time—perhaps because, as Alice Walker has pointed out, "anything of the immediate present is too artificial, one needs historical perspectives to give resonance and depth to a work of art."[4] So Morrison's Pilate tells us the story of her father, an ex-slave—a story which his grandson Milkman must discover through his travels in time and space to be a part of his own being. The Bottom, the land in which *Sula* is situated, is payment to a slave from his master, while Linden Hills in Naylor's novel of that name is Luther Nedeed's legacy from his ex-slave ancestor. Meridian, in Walker's second novel (1976), must look back to her ancestors of the nineteenth century to understand the meaning of black motherhood, while the mud mothers of Bambara's *Salt Eaters* continually remind us of the mythic past. Even when major characters resist the past, as Macon and Milkman Dead do in *Song of Solomon,* or Avey Johnson does in *Praisesong for the Widow,* it intrudes itself upon their consciousness through dream and/or song and especially the sense of dis-ease they feel in the present. The use of history in the novels of contemporary African-American women writers, then, is constant and consistent.

Although previous novels have used history within the context of the present and the future, however, most of them would not have been properly called historical novels. In the last few years, novels by African-American women have explored those very periods that some post–World-War II African-Americans had attempted to erase. So, *The Color Purple* (1982) is set in Reconstruction Georgia, *Beloved* (1987) in the post-slavery years, and *Dessa Rose* (1986) in the 1840s at the height of American slavery. These three novels are historical in that they recall a life which no longer exists and recreate societies that are apparently past. In examining this trend in African-American women's writing, I am not only interested in the novels themselves but also in why they are appearing at this particular time.

In order to understand the ways these contemporary novels re-vision history, first it is necessary, I think, to emphasize that histori-cal novels by African-American women have appeared before and that there are pieces written by African-American women during the periods about which these three contemporary novels are written.

There is a small but important body of female slave narratives in which successful runaway slaves record aspects of their experience. Perhaps the most notable of these is *Incidents in the Life of a Slave Girl* (1861) written by Harriet Jacobs under the pseudonym, Linda Brent. For much of this century, questions of authorship camou-flaged the significance of this narrative. It is only recently that Jean Yellen has proven beyond a shadow of doubt that Harriet Jacobs did exist, that she was a slave, that she did escape slavery only by hiding out in an attic for seven years, and that she did write her own story. Yet, despite the fantastic incidents she tells us about her experiences in slavery, Jacobs codes her narrative and often tells the reader that because of modesty, a specifically female term, and her desire not to offend her audience, a specifically African-American consideration, she had to omit certain details of her life story.

In the introductory remarks to her reading of *Beloved* at the Uni-versity of California at Berkeley in October 1987, Toni Morrison em-phasized the consistency with which the slave narrators made such statements.[5] Morrison pointed out that their omissions were partly due to the fact that these ex-slaves addressed a white audience. Even more important, she suggested, they omitted events too horrible and too dangerous for them to recall. Morrison went on to state that these consistent comments made by nineteenth-century ex-slaves about the deliberate omissions in their narratives intrigued her and that this was the initial impulse for her writing the novel that would become *Beloved*. Clearly one of the major themes of this masterpiece is the paradox of "re-memory." Morrison emphasizes this theme throughout the novel and reiterates it in the last words of *Beloved*: "This was not a story to pass on."[6] In a different way Sherley Anne Williams, in her preface to *Dessa Rose*, echoes Morrison's idea about her impulse to write *Beloved*. Williams tells us: "I loved history as a child, until some clear-eyed young Negro pointed out, quite rightly, that there was no place in the American past I could go and be free. I now know that slavery eliminated neither heroism nor love; it pro-vided occasions for their expressions."[7]

Not only were the slave narrators restrained by "modesty" and by "audience" from not passing on some stories, so were African-American nineteenth-century novelists. In *Clotel* (1851), the first novel published by an African-American writer in this country, William Wells Brown made palatable the experience of his quadroon slave heroine by fashioning her character according to the acceptable ideal image of woman at that time. Thus, Clotel is beautiful/fair, thoroughly Christian and European upper-class in her demeanor and language. African-American women writers also used this construct, most notably Frances Harper in *Iola LeRoy* (1892), which was thought, until the rediscovery of *Our Nig* (1858), to be the first novel to be published by an African-American woman.

What is *not* focused on in these novels is as important as the images these writers emphasized. For in these novels, little light is shed on the experiences and cultures of "ordinary" slaves like Sethe or Paul D., Dessa Rose or Kaine, or on their relationships or communities. Clotel grows up with her mother who, because she is the "natural wife" of her master, lives in a fairy-tale-like cottage completely apart from other slaves. Nor is she subjected to the hard labor usually exacted from slaves. Iola LeRoy is a slave, but only for a short time and had, as a "white" woman, been educated in fine schools. While Brown and Harper give us hints through some minor characters of the physically and psychologically harsh conditions under which most slaves lived, they reserved privileged positions for their heroines, thus exhibiting even more modesty than the slave narrators. For the sentimental romance form demanded not only a beautiful refined heroine but also that the story be entertaining and edifying.

An idea such as the one which generates *Beloved*, the existence of a "haint," a visitor from the past in which the major characters naturally believe, though an important belief in African-American culture, could not possibly have been seriously considered by these nineteenth-century novelists. They would have been fully cognizant of the detrimental effects that such a "superstitious," or non-Christian concept would have had on their own people. Nor could nineteenth-century audiences react favorably to a contrary slave like Dessa Rose who attacks her master and leads a slave rebellion which results in the death of many whites. Such audiences would have been even more alarmed by the presentation of a "crazy" slave like Sethe who would kill her own child rather than have her returned to slavery.

Clearly Brown and Harper, leading activists of their day would have heard about such events—certainly, the story of Margaret Garner, on which *Beloved* is based, was sensational enough to be known by Harper.[8] But she, as well as other African-American writers, could not muddy the already murky waters of sentiment toward the Negro by presenting characters who might terrify their readers.

That these nineteenth-century writers were constrained by the socio-political biases of their time is graphically demonstrated by the disappearance of Harriet Wilson's *Our Nig* (1858). Although Mrs. Wilson wrote a fluent, strong-voiced novel which is obviously auto-biographical, although she employed a form which fused elements of the slave narrative and sentimental romance that readers expected in works written by Blacks and by women, *Our Nig* did not cater to the accepted mores of the time. By emphasizing the racism of Mrs. Bellmont, her northern white mistress, by exposing racism in the North, as well as by ending her story with her desertion by her fugitive-slave husband, Frado, the protagonist of *Our Nig,* questioned the progressive platform of her time—that white northern women were the natural allies of blacks, that the North was not racist, that all Black men were devoted to the women of their race.

Equally important, Frado herself is the result of an interracial marriage between a white woman and a Black man, a type of union that was simply not supposed to have existed. Readers could cope with Clotel and Iola's ancestry—that their father was white, their mother Black. But acknowledging that white women would willingly be sexually involved with Black men was opposed to white women's sacred position—that they were a treasure to be possessed only by white men. The reception of *Dessa Rose* in this decade illustrates the longevity of this taboo. For many readers, Black and white, are stunned, sometimes offended by the sexual relationship between Mis Rufel, a white mistress, and Nathan, a runaway slave, despite the historical evidence that such relationships existed.

The disappearance of *Our Nig* for some one hundred years was also due to doubts raised about its authorship. Like *Incidents in the Life of a Slave Girl, Our Nig* was thought to have been written by a white woman because of its point of view and its excellent style. So, in his 1983 introduction to this newly discovered classic, Henry Louis Gates had to spend many pages establishing Mrs. Wilson's existence, that she was a free Black woman, and that the incidents in

*Our Nig* are based on her life. When nineteenth-century African-Americans wrote in a manner that did not correspond to deeply held opinions of their time, their very authorship was put in question. Such a restriction, the ultimate one for writers in that it obliterates their very existence, would certainly have affected the way they wrote about African-Americans.

One critical area in which these writers were restricted is their very medium, that of language. Since slaves were hardly conceived of as human beings who had a culture, their language was emphatically discredited. Such a devaluation is central to what experiences could be passed on, for language is the repository of anyone's point of view on experience, whether it is that of oppression, resistence to it, or a value system. Yet African-American language could not be seriously fashioned by nineteenth-century writers to dramatize their characters' essence; for that language was considered at best to be comic, at worse, a symbol of ignorance. Nineteenth-century writers like Brown and Harper imbued their heroines and heroes with a language that indicated their superiority, a language that in no way was distinguished from the language of well-bred white Americans. When these writers do use "dialect," minor characters employ it for comic effect. If one compares Celie, Dessa Rose, or Sethe's language to the language of Clotel or Iola, one immediately feels what is missing. For it is difficult to communicate the authenticity of a character without investing her language with value. If there is any one false sounding note in nineteenth-century novels about slavery and reconstruction it is the language of the characters, the way the imagination of the authors is constrained by the language their characters use.

Language is not only an expression of one's everyday experience but also of those deeper labyrinths of dream and memory, dimensions to which nineteenth-century slave characters had little access. If memory were central to Clotel or Iola, it would take them back to the past, beyond their personal history to stories their mothers told them, possibly back to the Middle Passage, so horrendous a memory that Morrison dedicated *Beloved* to those anonymous "60 million or more." Memory might take them even further back to an African man, like the one who taught Kaine, in *Dessa Rose,* to play the banjo. To acknowledge that slaves had memory would threaten the very ground of slavery, for such memory would take them back to a culture in Africa where they existed, as June Jordan invoked in her essay on Phillis Wheatley, "in terms other than the ones" imposed upon them in America.[9] Specifically, for Black abolitionists like William Wells Brown, allusions to Africa were politically diverting and provided support for the Resettlement Movement which sought to correct the moral problem of American slavery by sending the enslaved and displaced Blacks back to Africa.[10]

So, memory when it does exist in nineteenth-century African-American novels about slavery goes back but one generation, to one's mother, but certainly not much further back than that. Slave-owners were aware of the power of memory, for they disrupted generational lines of slaves in such a way that many slaves did not *know* even their own parents or children. Nineteenth-century writers like Brown and Harper, too, were certainly aware of the power of memory, for their protagonists, above all else, cling to the memory of parent, child, loved one. In Brown's first version of *Clotel,* he has his heroine give up her freedom to search for her child, only to have her drown herself rather than be re-enslaved. Her story is the other side of Sethe's action in the shed, in that one mother kills herself for her child, while the other mother "saves the best part of herself" by freeing her child through death. Brown does not linger long on the personal and emotional aspects of Clotel's suicide for his purpose is to illustrate the evils of the *institution* of slavery. Morrison, on the other hand, is riveted on the use of memory in all her characters' search for self-understanding. Nineteenth-century novelists could not be as much concerned with the individual slave as a subject as they were with the institution itself. They therefore had to sacrifice the subjectivity and, therefore, the memory of their characters to an emphasis on the slaveholders and their system.

Re-memory is a critical determinant in how we value the past, what we remember, what we select to emphasize, what we forget, as Morrison has so beautifully demonstrated in *Beloved.* But that concept could not be at the center of a narrative's revisioning of history until the obvious fact that African-Americans did have a history and culture was firmly established in American society, for writers would be constrained not only by their readers' points of view but also by the dearth of available information about the past that might give their work authenticity.

In her essay on how she wrote her historical novel, *Jubilee* (1966),

Margaret Walker pointed to these difficulties. On the one hand, she made it clear that memory was the impetus for her novel, since it grew out of her promise to her grandmother to write *her* mother's story. On the other hand, as an African-American in the 1940s who wanted to write a historical novel about her past, she knew that few people, black or white, were informed about slavery and early Reconstruction, the contexts in which Vyry, her great-grandmother, lived. She tells us that she found in her research at least three historical versions of slavery: the southern white version in which the institution was benevolent, necessary, and paternalistic; the northern white version, which often emphasized the horrors of slavery but was not particularly interested in the lives of the slaves; and the African-American version, of which there were few accounts, and which tended to focus on the lives of extraordinary slaves, almost always men.[11] In each version, the institution of slavery, meaning the slaveholders themselves, was pivotal, while the slaves were reduced to a voiceless mass. How, then, was Walker to write a novel which gave sufficient information about slaves to the reader who was either ignorant about the period or believed in false myths such as the ones featured in *Gone With the Wind?* How was she to do that *and* focus on Vyry, an ordinary slave woman who knew little about the larger political struggles that determined her life—a woman who could not read or write, and who had not been more than twenty miles from the place where she was born?

Margaret Walker decided that her historical novel would take the form of a folk novel. It would emphasize the fact that African-American slaves had a culture and a community, even as it sketched the outline of more specifically historical data, like the Fugitive Slave Law, or the legal conditions that determined a free Black's status in early nineteenth-century Georgia. She would have to give readers history lessons; she would have to invest with meaning the apparently mundane everyday experiences of her protagonist; and she would have to convince her reader that a viable culture and community existed among slaves.

Confronted with needing to cover so much territory to render Vyry's story, Walker, not surprisingly, created characters, Black and white, who are not subjects so much as they are the means by which we learn about the culture of slaves and slave holders and the historical period. Vyry, for example, hardly speaks in the first half of the novel, although she becomes more vocal in the Reconstruction section. Despite the many historical details about which she informs her readers, her characters have little internal life, perhaps because Walker, who is writing her historical novel in the forties and fifties before the rise of the black culture movements of the sixties, could not give slaves the right to claim those events they do not want to remember—not only what was done to them but what they might have had to do, given their precarious context. So Vyry is not complex in the way that Sethe and Dessa Rose are, for we are seldom privy to her internal conflicts and to the doubts she might have about her relations to others. Interestingly, one of the few times when we do feel her ambivalence about what she should do is when she must choose between escape for herself and leaving her children behind in slavery. As in *Beloved* and *Dessa Rose,* motherhood is the context for the slave woman's most deeply felt conflicts.

What Walker accomplished so effectively in *Jubilee* is the establishment of an African-American culture which enabled the ordinary slave to survive. In building her novel around Vyry, a hard-working mulatto slave, she revised the image of the beautiful, refined mulatto heroine of the nineteenth century, an image that her grandmother's stories refuted.

That image is further revised in Barbara Chase-Riboud's *Sally Hemings* (1979), a fictional biography of the African-American woman reputed to be Jefferson's mistress for some forty years.[12] Brown's first version of *Clotel,* which was sensationally subtitled "The President's Daughter" was based in part on the fact that Hemings was Jefferson's mistress. But Brown used this slave mulatta's existence to cast shadows on the great Jefferson who, at once, had a black mistress and children he would not free and who nonetheless championed freedom and democracy. In contrast to Brown, Chase-Riboud uses a romantic frame to dig into the myth of Sally Hemings and to reveal this complex woman's bond to her master both as a slave and as a lover. Because Chase-Riboud is interested not only in the contradiction between Jefferson's personal and political life, and in the institution of slavery, but also in the way the nineteenth-century definition of love is related to the definition of enslavement—she revisions Brown's sentimental romance. Still, Chase-Riboud has her protagonist tell her story to a white man who is trying to rationalize slavery so that at times Sally's narrative seems as censored as the slave narratives of the nineteenth century.

Because of the historical information available to her, not only about Jefferson himself but also because of the work done in the sixties about African-American slave communities, Chase-Riboud could free her narrative from some of the history lessons that Walker was obliged to give her reader. However, in a telling moment in the novel, Chase-Riboud has Sally Hemings burn all her records—her diaries that proclaim her existence and her life with Jefferson which she no longer wants to remember. Chase-Riboud is faced with a dilemma: Hemings, the main character, is encased in myth; yet she lingers in the margins of historical records. Because Chase-Riboud must rescue her heroine from myth, she cannot completely free herself from the conventional trappings of the historical novel, trappings which constrain her imaginative use of historical data.

Not so with Morrison's *Beloved* and Williams's *Dessa Rose,* both of which are based on historical notes yet are not controlled by them. Although *Beloved* is based on the sensational story of Margaret Garner, a runaway slave woman who attempted to kill herself and her children rather than be returned to slavery, Morrison leaves the historical facts behind to probe a not easily resolvable paradox— how the natural and personal emotion, mother love, is traumatically affected by the political institution of slavery. Morrison has said that she did not inquire further into Garner's life other than to note the event for which this slave woman became famous.[13] And indeed Margaret Garner did not achieve freedom as Morrison's Sethe does. Instead she was tried, not for attempting to kill her child, but for the "real crime," of attempting to escape, of stealing property, herself, from her master. For that crime, she was tried, convicted, and sent back to slavery, thus restoring his property. But Morrison takes us beyond the world of the slave holders into the world of slaves as complex human beings. In creating Sethe, who must remember her killing of her own child and must reflect upon whether she had a right to commit so destructive an act against her child which also, paradoxically, is for her an expression of her love for her child, Morrison raises disturbing questions about mother love. And in giving Sethe her legal freedom Morrison is able to explore the nature of freedom—for "freeing yourself was one thing; claiming ownership of that freed self was another" (*Beloved,* p. 95).

Sherley Anne Williams also based her novel on historical notes. As often happens in historical research, the discovery of one source leads us to another. *Dessa Rose* originates with two brief notes about a southern woman, one a Black slave, the other a free white woman who lived in the first half of the nineteenth century. Williams discovered in Angela Davis's "Reflections on a Black Woman's Role in the Community of Slaves," a pregnant slave woman who helped to lead an uprising and whose death sentence was delayed until after the birth of her child. That note led Williams to another source, Herbert Aptheker's *American Slave Revolts,* in which Williams learned about a white woman living on an isolated farm who was reported to have given sanctuary to runaway slaves. In response to these two women, whose actions appeared to refute what we have been told about both African-American and white southern women of the nineteenth century, Williams refined her point of view. Like *Beloved, Dessa Rose* is based on recorded historical facts but is not determined by them. "How sad," Williams comments in her introduction to the novel "that these two women never met" (*Dessa Rose,* p. 5).

As important to the structure of the novel as the discovery of these two historical sources is Williams's rage at the credibility given to William Styron's *The Confessions of Nat Turner,* which she points out is an indication of how "African-Americans remain at the mercy of literature and writing" (*Dessa Rose,* p. 5). In emphasizing her rage, she highlights another aspect of the slave narrative tradition—one on which Morrison also commented—a tradition which continues unto this day in the form of novels like Styron's. For these narratives were often told to whites, who did not necessarily understand or sympathize with the slave's experience but who, because they were the writers of the narrative, passed on in history the slave experience. To use a title from Valerie Babb's essay on *The Color Purple, Dessa Rose* is a novel which attempts "to undo what writing has done." [14] For in her novel, Williams demonstrates the substantive difference between Dessa Rose's memory of her experience, her telling of it to a white man, and Nehemiah's interpretation of her story, which is of course affected by his desire to write a sensational bestseller.

In *Beloved,* Morrison underlines the way that literary tradition is buttressed by an intellectual one. Schoolteacher not only exploits slaves, he is fascinated by the intellectual arguments he constructs to rationalize that exploitation. Throughout the nineteenth century, American intellectuals performed this function—that of providing intellectual arguments for a profitable legal *and* dehumanizing institution. Nehemiah and Schoolteacher's curiosity about the slave was indeed "scientific"; their historical counterparts did measure the various parts of the slaves' bodies, did observe their "characteristics," did interpret their behavior and did write serious treatises on them. Morrison stresses these activities—the apparently neutral ways in which intellectuals and "scientists" were fascinated with slaves—by having the most terrible act done to Sethe, the milking of her body for Schoolteacher's scientific observation, be a bleeding wound in her memory.

Williams and Morrison then indict the American literary and intellectual tradition. And clearly, neither of their novels would be what they are if it were not for previous historical fiction by African-American women. Nor, paradoxically, would their novels be as vivid as they are if during the last decade there had not been an intense interest, among scholars, in the history of African-American women from their point of view. In recent years we have seen the publication of works—from the heretofore forgotten female slave narratives to analyses by women historians with different perspectives, such as Gerda Lerner, Paula Giddings, Angela Davis, Deborah White, Rosalyn Terborg Penn, Jacqueline Jones, and Dorothy Sterling— reclaiming that neglected past. Such publications have grown out of our increased awareness that women's experiences are integral to African-American history. Paradoxically, such an awareness not only restores historical data, it frees the novelist from that data, to remember that which could not be precisely recorded but which continues to exist in storytelling, in cultural patterns, and in the imagination.

In both these novels, such remembering, such re-imagining centers on motherhood, on mothering and being mothered. On the one hand for slave women, motherhood was denied, devalued, obliterated by slavery since it was considered to be breeding, while on the other hand, it was critical to the concept of self and to the very survival of one's self. It is through the memory of *their* mothers, their reflections on that precarious role, and whether they themselves were able to be mothered, that Sethe and Dessa Rosa delve into themselves as subjects. In *Beloved,* this is true of all the major women characters: Baby Suggs, Sethe, Denver, Beloved, even Amy Denver the white girl, who helps Sethe give birth to Denver. Sethe knows "what it is to be without the milk that belongs to you; to have to holler and fight for it" (*Beloved,* p. 200). Denver knows what it is to see her mother in a terrible place, for she drinks her mother's milk with her sister's blood. Beloved yearns for complete union with her mother, the mother who kills her and saves her in one stroke. For her, her mother's face is her face and without her mother's face "she has no face" (*Beloved,* p. 216).

While Morrison moves us into the chaotic space of mother-love/ mother-pain, daughter-love/daughter-pain, a space that can barely be sketched in terms of historical data, Williams takes us in another direction: she explores the concept of that double-edged term 'mammy,' which slaveowners used for African-American mothering. By reversing the usual image, that of the black mammy nursing the white baby, Williams creates a different context for that term. Rufel, the white mistress and the only nursing woman on her neglected farm feels obliged, because of her own womanhood, to nurse the baby of the ailing darky, Dessa Rose. But the white woman would not have felt she had permission to do such a thing if she were under her husband's control and not isolated from other whites. As she nurses that Black baby, she dreams aloud about what she considers to be the source of her own mother-love, her mammy, who is not her mother but her darky slave. In an exchange that emphasizes the way these two women interpret that love, Williams shows us how power relations affect mothering. When Rufel claims that *her* mammy loved her, Dessa Rose retorts, "You ain't got no mammy . . . What her name then? . . . Child don't know its own mammy's name?" (*Dessa Rose,* p. 119).

In listing the names of *her* mammy's children, names she can remember, Dessa Rose also establishes the existence of a slave community with relationships that provided occasions for the heroism and love that Williams reminds us about in her preface. Her novel opens up the spaces in which that heroism and love can be explored. So Dessa Rose attacks her master because he has killed her lover Kaine. She and the men on the coffle are able to plan an uprising together and that action binds them forever in friendship. Later they are able, in an adventure as exciting as any in American lore, to free themselves and go West. Nevertheless, when she tells her story, many years later to one of her grandchildren, the freed Dessa Rose recalls her mother braiding her hair and her love for Kaine, events that precede the escape adventure. Williams ends the novel with this focus on rememory, for Dessa Rose insists on having her story written down: "'Oh,' she says, 'we have paid for our children's place in the world again, and again. . . .'" (*Dessa Rose,* p. 236).

But while Dessa Rose may remember her mother's name, Sethe, Paul D., and Baby Suggs cannot. For Sethe, her mother is a mark, since she knows her only by the circle with a cross branded into her skin, a sign Sethe cannot even find when her mother's rotting body is cut down from the hanging rope. Morrison's novel, then, moves us into those spaces that we do not want to remember, into the spaces where there are no names *but* Beloved—those forgotten ones of the past even to the sixty million anonymous ones of the Middle Passage, those terrible spaces, those existing spaces which for slave women, men, and children can divide them as much as they can bring them together. So in her novel, the adventure is not an exterior one, but the more dangerous internal one of the self remembering and even understanding its past—of Paul D. who lives through the terror of a chain gang which almost distorts his manhood, of Sethe who kills her own child which almost distorts her womanhood. Of Baby Suggs who cannot remember her own children, of Denver who does not want to remember her mother's act, of Beloved who *is* that part of their past that they all attempt to forget.

In the last pages of the novel Morrison leaves us with that Beloved, "a loneliness that roams" . . . "that is alive on its own," but "by and by is gone," for "remembering seems unwise." "The story of Beloved, of all the beloveds, was not a story to pass on," or one that could be passed on in the records of historians or the slave narrators. And yet it remains in dream, in the "folk tale," "in the wind," in the imagination, in fiction. Paradoxically, only when history is explored and evaluated is memory free to flow. Then, although "somebody forgot to tell somebody something," the past finds its way back into our memory lest, like Beloved, we risk erupting into separate parts. Perhaps that is one reason why African-American women writers are now writing African-American historical novels. As we move into another century when Memory threatens to become abstract history, they remind us that if we want to be whole, we must recall the past, those parts that we want to remember, those parts that we want to forget.

## Notes

1    Toni Morrison interviewed by Ntozake Shange on Steve Cannon's show "It's Magic," WBAI, New York, 1978.

2    Margaret Walker, *How I Wrote Jubilee* (Chicago: Third World Press, 1972).

3    "Alice Walker and *The Color Purple*," BBC TV Documentary, 1986.

4    Alice Walker, interviewed by John O'Brien, *Interviews with Black Writers* (New York: Liveright, 1973), pp. 186–221.

5    Toni Morrison, "Distinguished University of California Regent's Lecture," University of California, Berkeley, Oct. 13, 1987.

6    Toni Morrison, *Beloved* (New York: Alfred A. Knopf, Inc., 1987), p. 275. (All subsequent quotations from novel will be cited in the text.)

7    Sherley Anne Williams, "Author's Note," *Dessa Rose* (New York: William Morrow and Company, Inc., 1986).

8    See Gerda Lerner, ed., *Black Women in White America: A Documentary History* (New York: Vintage, 1973), pp. 60–63, for the Margaret Garner story.

9    See June Jordan, "The Difficult Miracle of Black Poetry in America or Something Like a Sonnet for Phillis Wheatley," *On Call: Essays* (Boston: South End Press, 1985). Also reprinted in this volume.

10    See Barbara Christian's "Shadows Uplifted," in *Black Women Novelists: The Development of a Tradition* (Westport, Conn.: Greenwood Press, 1980), for a discussion of this question.

11    Walker, *How I Wrote Jubilee*.

12    Barbara Chase-Riboud, *Sally Hemings* (New York: Avon Books, 1979).

13    Morrison, "Regent's Lecture."

14    Valerie Babb, "The Color Purple: Writing to Undo What Writing Has Done," *Phylon: The Atlanta University Review of Race and Culture* 47, no. 2 (Summer 1986), 107–116.

# Zala Chandler

## Voices Beyond the Veil: An Interview with Toni Cade Bambara and Sonia Sanchez

W hile interviewing Sonia Sanchez and Toni Cade Bambara, one can easily "feel" the spirit—the spirit of sisterhood, the spirit of peoplehood, the spirit of tradition, and the spirit of change. African spirit. And, somehow, you recognize that theirs are not simply spirits of the moment. They are of yesterday and tomorrow, as well. They are sprung from childhoods laced with hand-made perfection, the traditions of their "Mamas" (grandmothers) who were responsible for helping them to see and be the continuing connections of all the days of Black people—yesterday, today, and tomorrow. And they were both "touched" by the communities of women who surrounded them, embracing and molding their souls. Sonia, a young child of brilliance writing ditties and child poems, would be referred to as "the strange one." Toni, writing on any piece of paper that she could find as a child, would be "read" by the community of elders in her life who "knew" that she held an important role in life.

Toni Cade Bambara and Sonia Sanchez both speak of the "forces" in their lives, in the lives of Black people. They use terminology of the positive and the negative, good and evil, the spiritual and the material. And they both speak of the need for African people to rely upon the spirit and the bones and the knowledge of those who came before us, ancestors. Toni is often very specific in her presentation of this. Amongst other things, she talks about the need for African people in the Americas to erect a meaningful memorial to those African bones in the Atlantic Ocean, the bones of one hundred million

African people who died in the Middle Passage. According to her, this act of acknowledgment would in turn allow Black people to "call upon these forces" in our current struggle for justice. Sonia speaks of the many women made visible in her dreams, unsung women, name-less women who hold her up, who propel her to want to be "correct," "righteous." She projects the belief that any movement for change, if it is to be a successful movement, must embrace *both* the spiritual and the political, must rely upon the people of ancient and current yesterdays who remain spiritually in Black people's lives as they move forward. But they are more than simply two women providing statements about "forces." For they are themselves a force. Their cosmology is both spiritual and earthbound, a sense of "being." They have the ability to "see" the world and all of its complexities. Their descriptions and analyses of events of recent history—of movements and nonmovements of Black life—give testimony to this ability. Their writing, then, becomes the vehicle through which they share their spirit and knowledge with others, and touch the world.

Toni Cade Bambara was born in Harlem, New York. In her current lifetime, she has been mother; healer; social worker; writer of books, articles, and reviews; scriptwriter; teacher in universities, including prestigious Rutgers and Duke universities; community organizer; cultural worker; and an agent for change . . . a conveyer belt of history. She acknowledges Mama, women of the Chitlin' Circuit, sanctified church women, Harriet Tubman, Ida B. Wells, and Zora Neale Hurston as some of her sources of inspiration. She believes in "tomorrow" only as it is connected with what has been done yesterday and what must be done today. She insists that Black people are living in critical times, times which demand that we see and acknowledge connections to the past and develop a comprehensive program for dealing with today, for laying claim to power, and determining world reality.

Sonia Sanchez was born in Birmingham, Alabama. In her current lifetime she has been mother; teacher; writer of many volumes of poetry, short stories, children's books, and plays; world traveler; world speaker; professor at several major institutions of higher learning, including Temple University, City University of New York, and Amherst College; developer of Black and Women's Studies programs; healer of souls and bodies; image maker; and activist for justice, for change. She acknowledges Mama, the church women, Zora Neale

Hurston, Fannie Lou Hamer, and Malcolm X as some of the people who have inspired her the most. She insists that she will never look at herself, her people with "secondary consciousness"—that is, through the eyes of the oppressor. She greets the world as an equal.

The following is a two-part interview with these significant women writers. I visited both artists in the privacy of their Philadelphia, Pennsylvania, homes on January 31, 1987. I interviewed Toni Cade Bambara first, followed by an interview with Sonia Sanchez. Both women freely share information about their development as writers and their analysis of the times in which we live. They are certain that they are but a continuation in a long chain of determined people who keep moving forward in spite of the greatest obstacles and atrocities known to the entire human race. Toni and Sonia both speak of "connections" with the world beyond the veil. Connections between generations. Spiritual connections. Connections with those people who have come before us and left a legacy. These two women, Sonia Sanchez and Toni Cade Bambara, talk and work in the path created by that legacy. Through their voices, in their spirit, we can again hear the voices, feel the spirit of those people who walked this earth before us and passed on the baton for justice.

## Interview with Toni Cade Bambara

CHANDLER: Who are some of the women who have most influenced and inspired your work?

BAMBARA: First, you must consider that I grew up in Harlem in the late thirties, forties, and fifties, at a time when the McCarthy period very much determined political style. It was a period of tremendous fear and paranoia, where people were surrendering up each other without even the threat of torture—in many ways comparable to this current period in which people comply with insanity and surrender up integrity without, again, even the threat of torture.

This period was also characterized by people's consciousness that Harlem was, indeed, a wealthy community, a community where African genius was very much in evidence in individuals, organizations, and forums. One such forum that was very much in place was Speakers Corner, a street corner where at any point in time, on any given day, we could hear women from the sanctified churches, women from the Ida B. Wells clubs, the Temple People (which is what we used to call the Muslims), the Abyssinians (which is what we used to call the Rastas), trade unionists, Party members, and members of the National Negro Congress. We also had the Apollo, lots of clubs, Black bookstores, auditoriums such as that in the Harlem Y.M.C.A., and, of course, the Schomburg Library. Additionally, we had a number of theaters which would open up every now and then as community meeting places, for example, the Lafayette Theater.

When I think of women who have influenced me, several groups of women come to mind immediately. The tap dancers and the b-bop musicians of the forties, the Chitlin' Circuit women, the black slip mamas, the sanctified church women, the women of the Ida B. Wells clubs, and my mother.

The tap dancers and the b-bop musicians influenced the pitch and pace of my work. And along with the Chitlin' Circuit women, including women like Jackie "Moms" Mabley, they made me very curious about the national and international Black community. You see, these were women who traveled a lot, and they would bring back information from all over the country and all over the world.

The black slip mamas were the women who had any number of kinds of jobs; however, they never defined themselves in terms of the work they did. They defined themselves, rather, in terms of what kinds of friends they were to each other. They would gather in various people's kitchens or bedrooms, pulling out the old hatbox and going over old dance programs, talking with each other and playing cards together. And they were always, somehow, walking around in black slips and smoking Lucky Strikes, Old Gold, Pall Mall, or some other filterless cigarette. They were concerned very much with race issues. They were race women in the sense that, like the Chitlin' Circuit and the b-bop women, they did a lot of traveling and they made use of their homes as hostels—a place where other women on the road were always free to stop for a hot meal, a warm bath, and a bed.

There were the beauty parlor women. These women were my first conscious heroines in the sense that not only did they do your hair—they did your head! We young girls would often hang around and eavesdrop on their conversations, not realizing that they were really conversing for our benefit. It is through these women that we learned standards of sexual behavior, sexual politics, and, most important, race issues. Besides being race women, these women also tended to be analysts of various neighborhood situations. If something was going on in the neighborhood, one could stop by the beauty parlor (or barber shop) to hear it laid out.

Another group of women who moved me were the sanctified

church women, members of the Women's Departments of the various sanctified churches. These women frequently spoke on Speakers Corner. They were significant because they were the historians of the church, and, as such, they always insured that the contributions of women in the church were "lifted up." They taught women how to be speakers, to be historians, to be researchers, to be bibliophiles, and they trained women to travel, to balance budgets, and to monitor each other's development.

The members of the Ida B. Wells Club were very important to me because they were historians and they were investigative journalists. They tended to be women with professional privilege who were very clear that their skills were important only when they were put forth in service for mass-class women.

Finally, in terms of individuals, I think that the most important inspiration was, of course, my mother, who was a combination of things beyond the usual "mothering." One, she kept sparkling bookcases and an interesting collection of books for us to read. Two, she had a tremendous respect for the mind—the activity of the mind and the privacy of imagination. My mother never interrupted either my brother or me if we were daydreaming. She recognized that as important work to do. Three, she became very interested and curious about what was going on in the museums and in the music and concert halls; she would drag us everywhere—not only for our benefit but for her benefit as well. And fourth, she had a tremendous sense of justice and injustice. I don't think that she would describe herself as a very fierce or courageous person, but she would always stand up on issues. She reminds me of Ms. Rosa Parks in that way. I think of my mother as very much like that—a very quiet person, not inclined to jump up about issues—certainly not inclined to consider herself a leader. Nonetheless, for a great many people my mother was certainly the first, the paramount, and the ultimate, inspirational woman.

CHANDLER: What about women in the literary tradition?

BAMBARA: Well, ignoring the barrier that we usually erect between 'literature' and other kinds of writing, I would say Ida B. Wells and Harriet Tubman. I am drawn temperamentally toward 'pistol packing mamas,' so from a very early age right up until this moment, they have always been models for me. Their courage, their absolute unwillingness to engage in the politics of silence and the politics of invisibility and amnesia has always inspired me.

Harriet Tubman, as we all know, defied all obstacles, including the threat of death, to make a difference. Ida B. Wells, as a journalist, an organizer, and as a gadfly, was a person who would needle people into correct positions. She would browbeat people, embarrass people into taking radical positions. To me, she is and always has been a model of what a writer is supposed to be about—namely to take very bold positions and not hide behind camouflaged language. In essence, Ida B. Wells recognized that writing is simply one way to get the work done, but organizing is really what it is about.

CHANDLER: Can you discuss some of the spiritual and political forces at work in your life, your writings?

BAMBARA: Through time, I've come to realize that, for many people, there is a division between the religious or the sacred and the secular. For me it is all sacred. I've become recently aware, however, that there need to be statements made about the spiritual and the political . . . the need for the two to join hands.

One of the concerns that led me into the novel *The Salt Eaters* was pretense. I had a 'grandmother' (not blood kin but spirit kin) who had a little statement that would just knock me out. I would come bustling over to her place with all kinds of questions and issues and so forth and so on. And grandma would just look at me and ask, "What are we *pretending* not to know today?" The premise being that colored people on the planet earth really know everything there is to know. And if one is not coming to grips with the knowledge, it must mean that one is either scared or pretending to be stupid.

One of the ways that we pretend (and it is easy to do so because we are rewarded for pretense) is to act as though we live in a logical, rational, "two plus two equals four" setup. Yet reality is also psychic. That is to say, in addition to all the other things, for example, the political, we live in a system that is guided by a spiritual order. Now, there is a Western bias against this kind of thinking that goes back in this country to the Pilgrims. Those astringent Pilgrims who arrived in the New World with what they considered a more perfect way to worship, took one look at the 'unruly' bunch that met them at the shore, the hospitality committee, and called them savages. (This was the beginning of 'disconnectedness' as an American disease.) And they proceeded to ban the drum, ban smoke signals, and ban what they called fetish religions. In its place, they would impose a system of logic on the American psyche, the American sensibility, the American political reality, and, indeed, American life and literature that was aimed all the while at a total control of society by a few.

The unwillingness of the cultural brokers and powerbrokers of this society to acknowledge smoke signals, the drum, or the existence of intelligence channels other than their rationality and logic results in a language, namely English, that does not accommodate discussion of those phenomena outside of the Western logic. English is a wonderful mercantile language. You can get a lot of trade done with English. But you would find it very difficult to validate the psychic and spiritual existence of your life. Consequently, we pretend. We pretend that we're not clairvoyant, and we buy glasses instead. We pretend that we're not telepathic, and we lean on the telephone and post office system instead, etc. As a result, those of us who are adept, who have dormant powers, have to expend a great deal of time and energy denying it and suppressing it—to the detriment of the individual and the entire community.

What compelled me to tackle all of that in *Salt* was the amount of psychic and spiritual damage that is being done to us, and the fact that we're encouraged to either ignore or laugh at the damage. The novel opens with what seems to be a very simple question, "Do we want to be well?" The answer tends to be "no!" To be *whole*—politically, psychically, spiritually, culturally, intellectually, aesthetically, physically, and economically whole—is of profound significance. It is significant because there is a correlative to this. There is a responsibility to self and to history that is developed once you are 'whole,' once you are well, once you acknowledge your powers.

Additionally, I know that we must reclaim those bones in the Atlantic Ocean. Do you know that there is not a plaque, a memorial, a day, a ritual, or an hour that is erected in memorial to those one hundred million bodies in the Atlantic Ocean? All those African bones in the briny deep. All those people who said "no" and jumped ship. All those people who tried to figure out a way to steer, to navigate amongst the sharks. We don't call upon that power. We don't call upon those spirits. We don't celebrate those ancestors. We don't have a marker, an expression, a song that we all use to acknowledge them. We have nothing to indicate that those are our people and they matter! We willingly embrace amnesia and willingly self-administer knockout drops. More horrendous is the fact that we have all that power that we don't tap; we don't tap into the ancestral presence in those waters.

CHANDLER: Does spirituality actually play a role in compelling you to work?

BAMBARA: I work every day, all the time, because it is a compulsion. It is also because there is much for us to consider—there's so much unhealth and just rampant bullshit to counter that every day I know of yet another reason to set the alarm clock one hour earlier. And like most writers I know, most cultural workers I know, and most especially, most Black women I know, I always have ten or fifteen projects cooking because I never know which one is going to fly first or which one is going to get past that bend in the tunnel where the light is stuck.

In terms of that psychic engine that frequently drives a work, there are times when I put my work aside. That is to say that I just don't feel fit to work on it. I'll go and do something else. But spirit will call me back. For example, I have been working for the past six years on a novel based on the missing and murdered children's case in Atlanta. There were times while I was living in Atlanta when the work was simply too horrendous, when the amount of treachery . . . and betrayal . . . and viciousness . . . and lack of heart was simply too dispiriting for me to pick myself up and return to the work table. And I would take what I call a 'vacation.' I would go to the local bar, only to find that the conversation next to me was something about the case. I would hear something that either confirmed what I was thinking or reconstructing regarding the children, or I gained some brand new information. One time I went to the airport to take a plane to do a gig in Houston, and I found the police commissioner on line trying to sneak out of Atlanta to go and take a new job. Or, I would go to the library, attempting to do some research on yet another project, and I would find myself sitting next to a sister who worked in the SAFE office downtown. She would be talking to the person sitting next to her and telling her all that she had experienced with the safety education projects. Or I would take time off and simply try to take a walk in the woods, and I would run into a command unit of "Survivalists" who would be talking about how to capture control of Civilian Search Teams that had been put together by the United Youth and Adult Conference. Or I would be driving with plans to totally get away from the killing ground, and I would go to a restaurant in another county, only to hear at the table behind me a journalist interviewing someone from the Task Force—in spite of the gag order. And I would again be confronted with information that either confirmed the version that I had constructed in my head as a result of my research, my instinct, and my knowledge of our history, or I would receive new information. Do you see the pattern? I was not allowed to leave that case alone.

My "grandmother" used to say that if you're doing what you're supposed to be doing, then the whole universe will accommodate itself to you. That is to say, if you are on the right track, and you are committed, and your intentions are clear, then you can be passive because the information you need, the teachers you need, the people you need, the resources you need are going to come towards you. And all you have to do is be receptive.

While working on that novel, there was a period of approximately nine months in which I never left the house. I would get up in the morning, go straight downstairs, hop in the big leather chair, and begin shuffling the index note cards while trying to decide if the version I had in my head could possibly be correct. The phone would ring, and it might be somone from one of the major television networks or a movie production company that had come to town in search of the story. They called me, I guess, because I'm a Black woman, a writer, a community worker, and I happened to be in the phone book. And when they asked me for an angle, I would look at one of my index cards and send them in search of a particular clue. They would call me back, giving me the information, information they would say that they couldn't use because it had nothing to do with the 'official' version. So for nine months, I had a squad of researchers who I did not have to pay and who were working diligently on my behalf without knowing it. I never had to leave my chair. "Grandma" was right! Once you understand what your work is and you do not try to avert your eyes from it, but attempt to invest energy in getting that work done, the universe will send you what you need. You simply have to know how to be still and receive it.

I think that even if I were not a writer, I would have been compelled to become a writer in order to document what was going on in Atlanta. I felt an obligation to provide a forum for the version that was so different from the official one.

CHANDLER: Can you please talk a little about what you see as the role and responsibility of Black women writers today.

BAMBARA: At this stage in life, I try not to comment on what people ought to be doing. It is enough that I can get clear about what I'm supposed to be doing! But I will tell you what my main thrust has been as an educator, and I will comment on what I think *is being done* by Black women writers today.

As a teacher, my main thrust in the classroom has always been to encourage and equip people to respect their rage and their power. To not back off from what you know to be the case. To understand that your own experiences and knowledge of history make you an expert in regard to certain questions, namely the Black agenda. By the Black agenda, of course, I mean answering questions like: what are our prospects, what are the realities of our condition, and where are our arenas of power?

One of the greatest afflictions in American society for both the teacher/student and the writer is the affliction of disconnectedness. The separation between the world of academia and the world of knowledge that exists beyond the campus gates, the seeming dichotomy between politics and ethics, the division between politics and art, the division between dead authors and live authors, etc., etc. It is extremely difficult to arrive at the formula for living or for defining what the Black agenda should be, once you fall victim to this disconnectedness. In this society, forgetfulness is a virtue, amnesia is a virtue. We are always asked to celebrate the new and improved laundry detergent as though that which came out yesterday is already obsolete. And we carry this habit, this outlook, into our daily lives. This is extremely dangerous. So I teach about the necessity of being connected, and about the necessity of resurrecting the truth about our experiences (and revising the texts) in this place called America.

Three things seem to be going on with the writings of Black women today. One, there is a kind of book and film that is coming out which deals with the experiences of African-Americans in Africa. Most of these books and documents tend to look back at the sixties and seventies at African-Americans in places like Tanzania, Kenya, Ghana, and Nigeria, especially. They tend to be about the collision of two African cultures—New World and Old World. Martina Golden's *Migrations of the Heart* is but one of about fifteen books that I can think of that attempts to look at, to put its finger on, moments of collision between the African-American set of assumptions and the African set of assumptions in the twentieth century.

The second type of book that Black women tend to be producing has to do with our sense of community. Unlike the protest writers of the forties and fifties, the new writers see oppression as a temporary reality. They see the community as the paramount reality, the permanent, eternally valid reality. Consequently, we get books about relationships, about supportive networks. We get books that investigate cultural mores and habits that speak to health, that speak to friendship, and that speak to mutual support. Of course, there is a tradition for this; we have Zora Neale Hurston who provided us with novels of cultural maintenance. Zora Neale was attempting to acknowledge, document, and celebrate the folk tradition—and also to look at ways in which it is useful. (And she caught hell for this.) I think that the women writers who are coming along now—especially the younger sisters out of the South—are tending to take that a step further, namely to look at our culture with a critical eye, determining what is useful and what is reactionary. That which is found to be reactionary is then critiqued, and that which is found to be progressive is celebrated. This is the healthiest strain of writing today.

The third kind of writing tends to be very personal, but in my mind the writers are still part of the collective because connections are made. Many people get impatient with that kind of work because it is so "I," "I," "I" or "me," "me," "me." But I think that the works that come after this will be more consciously collective. When I look at the seeming personal autobiographies written in novel form in 1986, they tend to hark back to that Linda Brent kind of slave narrative, where there is tremendous concern for an individual Black woman with a particular set of experiences. But I think that in the long run they are leading toward presenting an understanding that many of these experiences are not peculiar to the individual, are not symptomatic of some type of personal deficit, but rather are part and parcel of a whole oppressive machinery, engineered against people because they are Black, because they are women, because they are working class, etc. So I think that the novels that come after this will be more intentionally, willfully collective in spirit and, like Zora's, communal in perspective.

CHANDLER: Can you comment on the various movements of Black people in recent history, for example, the Civil Rights Movement, the Black Power Movement; and can you attempt to define the period in which we currently exist?

BAMBARA: We're in the twelfth year of the last quarter of the twentieth century. And the two major issues domestically and internationally are one, the development of an independent Black political party with a sound agenda for our survival and development as a people, and two, the South Africa question. Surrounding the question of South Africa, the reality is that campus and youth forces—particularly Black people—have not skipped a beat. Students are still adamant on the divestment question. There are still demonstrations, rallies, teach-ins, and sit-ins.

One of the things that continues to set us back is this huge land mass in the United States. Unless we're traveling around a lot, we do not make certain kinds of connections. We can get disillusioned and think that nothing is going on. The media 'white out' makes an activist group in one area, unaware of other concerted actions, feel isolated and singular.

One of the reasons that I guess I do not have a 'job' is because there is a lot of traveling that has to be done, and somebody has to do it. I move from campus to campus, community center to community center, and organization to organization in the Southwest, the North-east, and on the West Coast in search of patterns. The patterns show me that we are organizing—cell by cell, block by block, city by city. Clearly, one of the patterns is a move against South Africa and support for the freedom-fighting forces there. Another is a growing coalition amongst homeless people making demands upon cities and states. And still another is an increased move against state violence, i.e., police brutality.

But all of this speaks to the fact that we need an independent Black political party that would have the ability to coordinate these efforts and be able to fashion both domestic and foreign policies, not to mention establish a comprehensive information network of the independent video makers, film makers, radio stations, and press. It is important that we give enough support to our cultural workers so that certain kinds of information can be packaged in different kinds of ways and spread from East Coast to West Coast, from North to South. If we have learned anything from the fifties and sixties, it is that we need an organized, collective response to our oppression.

CHANDLER: Are you optimistic about our future?

BAMBARA: I am always optimistic. Sometimes angry. Concerned. Questioning. Eager for us to resurrect the fighters and the builders who have come before us. Eager for us to see all the connections, the ties that bind us to one another. Eternally optimistic.

# Interview with Sonia Sanchez

CHANDLER: Who are some of the women in your early life who have influenced and inspired your work?

SANCHEZ: I was born in Birmingham, Alabama. And there are a couple of relevant things that happened to me in the South. My mother died when I was one year old. And my grandmother came and got my sister and me because she had decided to raise us "correctly"! (My grandmother was a deaconess in the A.M.E. Zion Church.) She meant so much to me as a child. That is why I offer her a letter in my new book, *Under a Soprano Sky.* I end that letter with, '. . . and I BE, Mama!' You see, my grandmother was a woman who spoiled us outrageously, who dared to just let me "be." I played hard as a child— usually with boys. I would come in the house real ragged from my hard playing, and people would cluck their tongues, shake their heads, and say, "You know, this girl just ain't gon' be!" But Mama would always respond, "Just let her be! Just let her be!"

The realization of who you are, I believe, is necessary for any artist—or anyone else for that matter—who is concerned and involved with liberation. You must be able to understand what it means to "be." And you cannot "be" unless you understand your history . . . the history of all the "Mamas" of the world, who always wanted something better for you . . . who would always stand up for you, risk dangers for you. My grandmother was tough and spiritual enough to never let white people touch me. If they attempted to touch my sister or me, she would always respond, "Don't touch them! These are mine. Don't take the power from them at all!"

Of that period in my life, I also remember that Mama used to have the "Sisters" (church women) over to her house each Saturday to talk, to cook for the Sunday dinners, to heal each other, etc. And these sessions were really important to me. I knew that those women were transmitting knowledge to me . . . wisdom to me that I would keep all my life. And I can remember looking at them and thinking that I want to be just like them. I wanted to be like them because I saw and heard power there. I heard an awareness there. I heard a people very much assured.

These were very important days for me. And I didn't really realize how important until I was asked by an editor of a magazine to write about my empowerment as a Black woman. The editor wanted me to write about my empowerment in terms of my professional life and my success as a writer. But, to their dismay, I could not do this. Many years ago I might have been able to make a statement about empowerment in those terms. But that would have been before I understood the connections. You see, I don't see myself as being empowered because of a certain job or status. I see myself as being empowered because of my grandmother, and people like her. It has really been that kind of transmitting that has given us the power. My power may have gotten manifested in a different kind of politic than that of my grandmother. But nonetheless, it was the same power . . . the same energy that had been infused in me, that had been given to me by my grandmother.

What this means, simply, is that I don't speak alone anymore. I don't speak singularly—for myself. I speak for the many, many women who, though physically dead, remain spiritually alive through me. And I speak for those women here on earth with me, like me. And I speak for the women yet to be born.

My grandmother died when I was six years old, and, after that, I had a lot of other experiences with people in the South—extended families—that were not necessarily good. But that foundation that I had with Mama proved to be so important because it kept me sane, actually. I think it's significant to mention that after Mama's death, I had started to write poetry, these little ditties, because I had started to stutter and found it difficult to communicate with people. I used to be tongue-tied and a stutterer, which was fascinating. Because I couldn't communicate well I retreated to books and to writing. And I spent a lot of time in solitary.

CHANDLER: Who have been some of the Black women who have really inspired you in the literary tradition?

SANCHEZ: I have been inspired by most of the women writers who have come before me, because I recognize that they have accomplished under the greatest of odds. I remember stumbling upon Zora Neale Hurston in the sixties, and I would end up talking endlessly about her. I thought that *Their Eyes Were Watching God* was one of the most beautiful books that I had ever read. I also stumbled upon Nella Larsen's and Jessie Fauset's books, and admired them. And I was very impressed with the Black women poets of the Harlem Renaissance, though I was always disturbed that their only work that seemed to be printed in anthologies were love poems. But I knew that there had to be something beyond that. It wasn't until years later that I found out that, of course, they had other works—works that were not put into these anthologies. For example, Georgia Douglas Johnson wrote a lot about the killings of Black people in the South, and what it meant for that to be happening. I always knew that there had to be writings like hers, but sometimes one has to stumble upon them while doing research. Like I'd stumble across early plays written by Black women that dealt with (what were then) controversial subjects like a woman having a child though she wasn't married. The play would show how there would be a community of women supporting her. There were several works about women supporting women or about the plight of the Black woman. Often you'd look up and wonder why you were never exposed to these works before—works like those written by Frances Ellen Watkins Harper, an abolitionist Black woman who began to write about what it was like for a Black woman in slavery. And of course when I started to teach, I went back into some even earlier literature like that of Linda Brent, who also discussed the slave woman's condition.

Often these works would be very painful, but they inspired me, nonetheless. Because I have developed a very basic understanding about the treatment of Black women and the view that America holds of Black women, I could read these works with compassion, and be inspired by them. I could see the connections between them and me. I can understand what it means to be a Black woman trying to be strong, trying to be woman, trying to be holy, pure, trying to just be "self" in the midst of a society that says that Black women are whores, in the midst of a country that would have a president—Jefferson—who in his notes would make a statement that Black women are stretched out with orangutans. And as a result of this understanding, I know why the forces that have propelled me through the years have always made me feel the necessity to be correct . . . to be righteous. If I did something that was a violation of my people, I would have dreams. I would dream about Black women crying—crying because I had done wrong. I don't walk "correct" because I want to be super righteous. I simply want to say to the world—through my actions—that Black women, having endured, are certainly women who should be revered . . . respected on the stage of history. And that is why I cannot produce a work or walk on a stage as if I am a whore, a harlot. I can't slide on a stage like "Here I am, baby." I must walk on stage saying, "Yes! This is me." I am coming with a whole host of women, unsung heroines, unsung women we will never know. I see them in my dreams. I hear them in my dreams. I walk with them everyday. If I want to do something dumb and stupid, they hold me and say, "Look! You can't do that!" That's why I can answer your questions with names like Phillis Wheatley, Frances Ellen Watkins Harper, Jessie Fauset, Nella Larsen, Zora Hurston, Ann Petry, Margaret Walker, and Gwendolyn Brooks. I can say them because I can truly *feel* history.

One of the things that I've attempted to do in my lifetime via these women and via the women whose dreams I cherish—whose screams I cherish also—is that I will never again involve myself with what I call secondary consciousness. I will never again see myself, see other Black women, see Black men, and Black children secondarily, through the eyes of the oppressor . . . the slave master. I will never again see my kinky hair, my big nose, or my big lips as something horrible. I don't want the bluest eyes. I don't want the long, straight blonde hair. I maintain that I will never in my life walk secondarily again—or even appear to have any secondary views. If you approach me, you must approach me on an equal level. If I see your stuff is incorrect, is racist, then I will tell you. And when I hit the stage, I know that I am just as tough as anyone there. People aren't accustomed to that kind of behavior. That is a legacy that we've gotten from Malcolm, from Fannie Lou, from Du Bois, and from Ida B. I am aggressive; I will not deny myself. I will not be one of those people talking about they need to get some training on how to be aggressive. To them, I say, all you have to do is come into a sense of yourself, announce that you are an African and intend to "be." That is some automatic aggression. And you will see that in order to defend yourself, you will have to move in an aggressive fashion. Because the moment you say that you're not sure of who you are, people will slap you down, will attempt to slap you to the right and the left, tear you up! So yes, it's the Gwendolyn Brooks and the Margaret Walkers and the Ann Petrys and all the others that kept me very much rooted. And that's important.

CHANDLER: Can you talk about some of the recent movements of Black people during the sixties, the seventies, the eighties and tell us what impact these movements had on you, and what messages you were giving during this time.

SANCHEZ: To have discovered oneself in the 1960s—probably the late fifties but definitely manifesting itself in the early 1960s—was almost like being reborn, I would say. It was like waking up each morning and discovering a new part of yourself. For the first time in your life, you did not have to be concerned about your nose, or your lips, or your hair. You could just get up in the morning and comb your hair and be pleased. You did not have to get involved in a whole lot of makeup and eye shadow and you name it. You did not have to be concerned about the right shade of makeup, ensuring that you didn't come out too light, or too dark, or too black, etc. You could be your natural self. What a relief from a peculiar kind of bondage that was there, that we were involved in. It means that we now had more time to do some things with our heads, with our brains.

One of the first things that some of us said in some of our work in the sixties was that we were Black. And that in itself was a hard word for many of us to say because in our history, the word Black meant something negative. I can remember that when I first got on the stage and proclaimed that I am a Black woman, it was very difficult for me. And it was also difficult for the people to respond to that. I mean, sometimes people would ask what do you mean by all of this "Black" stuff? This Black woman stuff? And, again, it was Malcolm and the Muslims who brought that terminology to the forefront. (I'm not a revisionist, you see. I can't revise history. I can't revise that. I'm not saying that people have to then go and like Muslims or dislike Muslims. I just want to be correct and give credit where credit is due.) Yes, Malcolm kept saying that we're Black men, we're Black women, we're Black people. And that really stirred the imagination in the same fashion that Marcus Garvey did when he asserted that Black people are Black, are African. Malcolm made the same impact on writers in the sixties that Garvey made on writers in the Harlem Renaissance period. Garvey made poets say, "What is Africa to me?" He made people begin to talk about "my Black self." People really began to respond to him—many people who might never have responded before. All the way from Countée Cullen, to Claude McKay, to Langston Hughes, writers responded. Well, in the same fashion, the climate of the sixties was all aglow with the words of Malcolm and other people who were saying positive Black things and being very much the activists. The poets of that day could not just stay introspective. This was a period when we called white people a lot of names and cussed them out a lot. But it was also a period when we began to say that we had to move beyond cussing out white folk, and start to do the work that we needed to do for our survival. It was a period when we felt the necessity to write about our internal contradictions, and we often juxtaposed the public image and the private image. For example, I'd often write about the Black woman as woman, as mother, as activist. We also wrote about the problems that existed between Black men and Black women. And we were forced to say sometimes that we were tired . . . just plain old simple tired! Tired, you see, because there were some really depressing things happening sometimes. In addition to the intense attack by the state apparatus, there were a number of internal contradictions. Things like the whole drug scene, where people were on the stage talking about being Black and then walking off the stage to get high. Yes, there were things that could make for great depression. But, on the other hand, there were also things that were happening that would make you feel good—seeing people opening up before your eyes, almost like flowers, and coming to the realization that, indeed, they were Black, and indeed, they were political. It was beautiful to see people recognize that they *had* to be political if they were to survive, to live, to "be."

Those were the kinds of things that one saw happening in the sixties. There was anger, there was love, there was confrontation, and there was us saying to America, "You're racist! You're racist!" We were informing people about racism. And the people took up the call because they were able to personalize the message.

Our work in the seventies was about empowerment. We couldn't just keep on saying that America is racist, America is racist. We had to start talking about what we were going to do about it. We were saying that if this country is racist, then what do you do? Do you just sit down and cry? Do you go home and lower the shade and drink your wine? Do you shoot skag? What do you do? The message was that you must begin to take over schools. You must begin to make the churches be responsive to new times. You must go to school and get more of an education so that you can then go into our community public schools and teach or go into the universities and teach. You must continue to struggle and make sure that African-American history is taught, that African-American culture is taught, that Black Studies is taught, that Black Women's Studies is taught—so that we don't have another generation of Black students coming through life thinking that their people have contributed nothing to the world.

The poetry of the seventies is poetry that talks about work and also about memory. I wrote the book *A Blues Book for Blue Black Magical Women* in 1973, and I realized that the book was really about the use of "memories." I believe that's very important to us. We can find lessons in the memories. Through writing that book, I began to go back and look at some of the things that had happened to me. And I offered that book as something to be informative for Black women. The book says, simply, let me tell you, show you a picture of a woman who came from the South as a little girl, and grew up knowing nothing about herself. She came to a place named New York City, and thought it was just hip to be a carbon copy of a white person. It's about a woman who moved to the Village, ate brie cheese and drank white wine, etc., imitating people. And then all of a sudden this woman hears Black people begin to talk a certain new kind of new way, a way that gave her a sense of self, a way that touched her and put her on the wings of history. It is about male and female relationships, and what it means to be put on the earth—having had your tradition of initiation stolen from you, leaving you with no idea of how you're suppose to choose the "proper" man or define the "proper" relationship. Yet you attempt to do so anyway, only to find out that there is hurt in store for you. The man you choose to love cannot even love himself. So how is he going to love you? And then I talk about this woman finally moving on to the realization that she has got to love herself before she can even think about getting anybody who could love her. And maybe she would end up by herself. As long as you have love of your people, the love of your children, you are not alone. As long as you have your activism, your memories of people who have gone before you—who have propelled you—you are not alone.

That book was a blues book. I attempted to speak about both the political part of us and the personal. I wanted to show that they are so intertwined. I wanted us to know that in order for us to be effective political people, we must be in control of the personal.

The seventies also was a period when many of us were fighting with the forces that would rewrite the history of the sixties. We had to come up against people who said that the sixties were wild, unimportant days. Folk who said that "Black thing" was just a fad. We were up against forces that said that we should stop being angry. After all, they would say, You people have got everything now. You have made it. We gave you affirmative action, and you have more Black people in college now than ever before. You have more people in medical school, dental school, and law school than ever before. And we even let you be "beautiful" they would say. We figured out some better formulas for you to be able to have hair that slings once again. So you can cut loose all that "natural" stuff. We started to hear slogans like "We've come a long way, baby." Yes, we had to fight all of that nonsense in the seventies. There had to be some of us who said that we would not be moved. We would not be tempted by the glitter. There were some of us who sincerely never saw the sixties as a fashion. It was a new-found understanding, a new-found spirit. A spirit that was to be worn proudly. Black spirit. Beautiful Black spirit. You see, there were those of us who would continue to deal with the world politically. Nothing would change that.

One of the pitiful things that happened during the late seventies was that you had an emergence of a group of Black people who got so carried away with themselves that they started to act as if there is no history to their work, their development. They started patting themselves on the head and back saying simply that, "I'm here without anybody." You had young writers not even saying anything about the people who had come before them, people who had helped to produce some of them. That was amazing—and amusing too. Such violation of the African tradition. Such violation of the connections! You must always show the connection. You must always be responsible. Certainly, you can say that we've done some terrible things to each other. But in the end, you must show us as products of this imperialist, racist, oppressive place.

The seventies also was a period for many of us to say, "So now that we have the consciousness, let's implement some of the skills that we had learned in the sixties." Some people want to put down the seventies. But I don't think that we should do that. It was a time of some real learning, some real organizing. Some people want to say that what happened in the sixties became disintegrated in the seventies. But that's not true. Nothing disintegrates fully. There were people who learned what they learned in the sixties and went on to implement it. They continued to be political, and they joined or started organizations that in a very real sense began to speak to what is going on in this country. For example, many Black women's organizations were started. New welfare rights organizations were started. Black mothers organizations were started. New student organizations were started on various campuses, etc. Remember, we had learned how to organize in the sixties. We had held organizing seminars, and now a lot of that has come to fruition. There are people out there who have some serious skills, and they are organizing.

Another important thing that happened during the seventies was that we began to develop a world view—a view that allowed us to see ourselves and see the connections beyond America. And as a result of a lot of mistakes, it was also a time when we began to be more critical of this thing called "Blackness." It wasn't enough to just have Black skin anymore. We began to see the necessity of asking some hard questions about what a person's "Blackness" meant in terms of how they saw America. We learned, for example, that we needed to have been asking questions like: Where do you stand on the issue of racism and sexism in America? How do you view imperialism? Do you like capitalism? How do you view change, revolution, etc.? These are critical questions now. We need to know who are our friends and who are our enemies.

The eighties caught us in a peculiar dilemma. You see, America had a tremendous campaign to counter our energy that was exhibited in the sixties and seventies. So we arrived in the eighties with people saying things like: "We've arrived!" or "There's no need for people to say anything about racism or sexism any more" or "The only thing that we really need to do is make money." There was a belief that if we could only achieve economic power, then we would be all right. These views, of course, fly in the face of history that teaches us that in America, even Black men and women with money get lynched, get beaten. There is a growing mood at all levels of America that says that they can treat us any old kind of way again. It's a time when there is increased racist terror and violence, e.g., police brutality. It is a time when we are no longer walking around with a posture that says, "Don't touch me! I may be dangerous." It is a time when we don't have the organizations needed to say that there will be an equally violent response to the murder of our people. Therefore, we have a lot of work to be done in the eighties to counter all of this. To young people who tell me that they want to be rich and famous, I say, "You'd better have a militia." Because that's what it's about—real power! Being rich without real power means nothing.

CHANDLER: Where do we go from here?

SANCHEZ: I am very optimistic. I am optimistic because I can see a win. You see, I understand the dialectics of people's movements. I understand that there are progressions and regressions. What are four years, eight years, twenty years in terms of a whole lifetime? In terms of the lifetime of the universe? It is but a tiny speck in history. I can see beyond the year 2000. I can see a period when you won't have oppression. You won't have people exploiting people. Granted, there will be a lot of people dying before we get to that point. Some will die because they don't have the strength or the ambition to stay alive. They really don't understand that there can be a better day. Their vision is too limited. And there will be people who die because they will come up against the activities of the oppressors. But you see, these oppressive monsters are carrying out their activities because they are a dying breed. During the end of this century, they will try to murder a lot of people in order to stay in power. But when you see that there are more people who have begun to understand history and who refuse to be exploited, then you understand that the time of the oppressor is numbered. Yes, they are killing many, many people in Africa—via germ warfare (AIDS), via starvation and famine created by the oppressor's violation of the earth, via military violence, etc.— but that's a part of it! That's the pain before the victory. We will be victorious! Their days are numbered. This belief comes from my political understanding.

At the same time that I offer this political understanding, I must offer a sincere belief that in addition to the necessity for us to be political, we must be spiritual. We must have spiritual sources that we rely upon. We must call upon our residual memories. We must call upon our ancestors. And they will propel us through all the crap we currently face on a daily basis. Our spirituality will keep us from becoming cynical, from becoming bitter, from becoming harsh. Our politics combined with our spirituality will keep us from becoming like the people that we are now trying to replace.

Yes! We must hear the voices and have the dreams of those who came before us, and we must keep them with us in a very real sense. This will keep us centered. This will help us to maintain our understanding of the job we must do. And if we do the job we must do, then we will win.

# Rudolph P. Byrd

# Spirituality in the Novels of Alice Walker: Models, Healing, and Transformation, or When the Spirit Moves So Do We

A symbol is as useful to the soul, as a tool is to the hand.

Jean Toomer, *Essentials*

I am preoccupied with the *spiritual* [emphasis mine] survival, the survival *whole* of my people."[1] This statement, which in point of fact is a fierce, unambiguous declaration of purpose, frames and informs each text in Alice Walker's growing canon. It is a statement that is consistent with her mission not only as a writer but as a womanist.[2] For Walker these terms are not in opposition to one another, but are different sides of the same coin that supports a struggle for human rights much broader and deeper than the one now faced by white feminism. Although Walker states that she is immersed in the spiritual trials of "my people," that is to say, of all Americans—male and female—of African descent, Afro-Americans are plainly not the only group that has responded to and benefited from the healing effects of her probing, knowing voice, nor are they the only group for which she, as writer, as womanist, as *artist* speaks. Since Walker's material is the stuff of human experience each situation is, in its essentials, universal. This fact explains her broad appeal and immense popularity. But this rare ability to conjure several faces with one, to invest the soloist with the attitude and feeling of the chorus, is ordinary work for the womanist writer who is, so Walker tells us, "traditionally universalist."

As a womanist, as a writer, Walker not only loves the catholic truth that glitters at the very core of the most specific circumstance, but she also loves music, dance, the moon, love, food, roundness, struggle, the folk, and herself—regardless (here she is, hands squarely on her hips, *truly* womanish!). But she also loves, perhaps most of all, the Spirit. If it can be satisfactorily defined, the Spirit for Walker is that ubiquitous, pansophic Incorporeality that creates and sustains all life and in Whose benevolence all life discovers its meaning, its purpose. As a writer, and as suggested in the essay "Writing *The Color Purple,*" as a medium, Walker is principally interested in charting the presence, the path, and the power of the Spirit in the doings of her fictional creations, and in the process gives us, always with intelligence, humor, and a great sense of urgency, models for living, models for our spirit that function as talismans against any evil sworn to our physical or spiritual annihilation.

Perhaps more than any writer of her generation, Walker is concerned with the spiritual well-being, the spiritual *health* if you will, of all people. Here her precursor and example, more than the amazing Zora Neale Hurston, is plainly Jean Toomer: poet, philosopher, psychologist, and lifelong disciple of George I. Gurdjieff. Thankfully, Walker has avoided the devotion to a single cosmology that destroyed Toomer's impressive talents. If Walker has discovered a codified system of belief that she regards as central to her work and being it has not maimed or diminished the many gifts of her large, generous spirit.

The context for Walker's meditations on the spirit is principally female and Afro-American: these are the chief elements in her cosmology, the chief sources of her inspiration. Although this interest in the particular doings of a particular group may strike some as insular, those who perceive this as a fault would do well to remember that it is Walker's intention to tell all of our stories, or some part of them, by recounting the adventures, mistakes, and triumphs of Afro-American women. We see our faces in the faces of Mem and Ruth Brownfield; we hear our voices in the voices of Meridian Hill and Celie. As indicated by my examples, I am principally interested in Walker's novels—*The Third Life of Grange Copeland* (1970), *Meridian*

(1976), *The Color Purple* (1982)—for it is in this narrative form that her commitment to spirituality, to our spiritual survival, is most apparent. It is here that she gives us her most instructive and most potent models.

*The Third Life of Grange Copeland* is, for many of us, an extremely difficult novel to read. The difficulty does not stem from Walker's selection and manipulation of language for she has consistently proven herself at least equal to the trials of the word. Nor does the difficulty stem from a young writer's—*The Third Life of Grange Copeland* is her first novel—mishandling of a deceptively facile, extremely complex form. The difficulty, and even the pain that we as readers initially avoid and then, perforce, face stems from Walker's capacity to make us, in the spirit of Joseph Conrad, see the good and the evil in ourselves. Plainly, Walker believes that truth is the best medicine for an ailing spirit, but the truth is sometimes, since confabulations are often more appealing than facts, hard to bear.

We despair at the dissolution of Grange's marriage to Margaret and the double suicide that is its coda. Walker tells us that what Margaret and Grange forgot "was that in the drama of their lives . . . they were not alone."[3] Needless to say, their self-absorption had terrible consequences for Brownfield whose capacity for brutality in his marriage to Mem is unrivaled in fiction. "You goddam wrankly faced black nigger slut" (p. 91). Bereft of tenderness, a sense of hope and, as Ralph Waldo Emerson would say, a belief in his own possibilities, Brownfield, whose name suggests something of the depth and completeness of his barrenness and desolation, sought to destroy in Mem the very qualities—resourcefulness, diligence, a sense of responsibility, of self-worth, of beauty—that could have saved him, his children, and his marriage. But Mem is no match for Brownfield's evil. Her ten-point resolution, delivered at gunpoint, fails because, as Walker writes, her "weakness was forgiveness, a stupid belief that kindness can convert the enemy" (p. 162). Poor Mem. She should have shot Brownfield when she had the opportunity because a decision to take a life, when a refusal to do so is a promise of annihilation, is not murder but self-defense. But as Mem lacked the necessary courage to end her suffering, Brownfield showed her the way out of hell. Plainly, the logical conclusion to Brownfield's sadistic, calculated "come down" is Mem's murder, for he could not endure another attempt on her part to invest their lives with dignity and value since each attempt, or so it seemed to him, was made at the expense of his much imperiled manhood.

Against this very violent, very bleak landscape moves the grizzled figure of Grange Copeland. Grange shares in the misery of Brownfield's marriage because on one level he has, by his flawed example and negligence, contributed to it. But it is not this secret knowledge of things painful and true that brings Grange back to the Dew Drop Inn. Grange has not returned to face Brownfield, but to build, through the pattern of life on the farm purchased with the money from the sale of Josie's only real accomplishment, a fortress against the world's fury and violence, a fortress which stands as a strange monument not only to his own pride and stubbornness, but also to a futile attempt to preserve his granddaughter's innocence.

To his credit, Grange enlarges his agenda to include Brownfield who, in his great bitterness and confusion, is very much in need of love and guidance. Coincidentally, the conflict between Grange and Brownfield is as old as the *Odyssey* and as new as *In My Father's House*. Like Homer and Ernest J. Gaines, Walker has taken this classic situation in literature—the search of the son for the father—and woven it into the fabric of a novel that is seemingly about the extraordinary difficulty of being Black and female. Plainly, the point Walker wishes to make by these manipulations is that many of the problems between the sexes have their beginnings in different currents and that nothing less than the health and survival of the clan depends upon their swift and peaceful resolution. Grange understands this. This is why, as Walker writes, "he spent so much time with [Mem] and his grandchildren, and bought them meat and vegetables, and gave them money on the sly, and reaped in the full anger of his wife and the unflagging bitterness of his son" (p. 73).

When Grange returns to Georgia he is, as revealed in his anecdotes and sermons to Ruth, a changed man. He is, as Walker describes him, a "reborn man." What is the basis of Grange's spiritual rebirth but the acceptance of his own evil and a belief in his goodness. Grange has learned that the anger that once threatened to destroy him was misdirected, that it hit upon the wrong target. The path of his rage should have extended outward, not inward; the target should have been Shipley and other men and women of the same regrettable sensibility and not his wife and children. Grange helps

Mem not only out of a sense of guilt—in her face he sees and remembers the dead Margaret—but also out of a growing sense of responsibility. Through his kindnesses Grange hopes to redeem himself and his son, but this, as we know, does not happen.

Grange dies trying to teach Brownfield what life has taught him and defending his cherished, fantastic dream of innocence. Although we may question the objective (the intent is unassailable) of Grange's intentions for Ruth—John Callahan has pointed out that Walker's fiction reveals the futility of innocence in the face of life's complexities—we admire the new, strong, and redeemed self out of which these intentions emerge. In Grange's three lives—the first with Margaret, the second with Josie, and the third with Ruth—we witness the near extinguishment of the great flame that is the human spirit. We see the smoke, the slow kindling, and the blaze that warms and protects itself as well as all those drawn to its brilliance. In Grange's mistakes are traced the outline of our own beleaguered spirit and in his release we apprehend our redemption.

The Civil Rights Movement of the 1960s is the subject of Walker's second novel *Meridian* (1976). Here in a work that deserves a larger audience, Walker travels much farther than other novelists who have aided us in our reexamination of this important period in American history. Although Gaines's *The Autobiography of Miss Jane Pittman* and *In My Father's House,* powerful works in their own right, bring us to a point where we are able to engage the spirit of that volatile time, we do so only for a moment. In these novels Gaines's concerns are not defined by the Civil Rights Movement—this is not a flaw—but more by events that precede it, or by developments that occur alongside it. *Armies of the Night,* by Norman Mailer—another work of the imagination, although there is some debate about whether it is a novel—also treats the Civil Rights Movement. But Mailer seems more interested in documenting his own role in the events of history than in analyzing the events themselves. What sets *Meridian* apart from these texts is that the Civil Rights Movement is the subject, not an episode, backdrop, or mirror. The events of the time and the people who are caught in their pull are the poles between which an imagined, symbolic conflict achieves its resolution.

Of Walker's three novels, *Meridian* is the most highly symbolic. William Carlos Williams insists that an "artist should always speak in symbols even [especially!] when he speaks most passionately."[4]

Plainly, Walker has followed Williams's prescription. It would not be an exaggeration to describe her use of symbolism as aggressively self-conscious, for in her attempt to evoke the spirit of a particular time, she creates symbolic situations that reveal meaning without surrendering ambiguity.

Walker instructs us in the correct reading of her novel by creating a symbolic framework. This framework assumes the form of the definition of the word that serves as the novel's title and the name of its heroine—"meridian." This definition appears, like a guidepost at a fork in the road, before the first chapter. As we examine some of the meanings of "meridian" (we shall only concern ourselves with the noun, for the adjectival meanings are largely repetitious) we discover clues to more than just Walker's attitude toward her subject, but also something of its fascination, locale, and possible effects. The first two definitions are:

1. the highest apparent point reached by a heavenly body in its course.
2. (a) the highest point of power, prosperity, splendor, etc.; zenith; apex; culmination;
    (b) the middle period of one's life, regarded as the highest point of health, vigor, etc.; prime.[5]

If definitions one and two a were rephrased, rewritten to form a complete, unified set of sentences they might read: "The Civil Rights Movement was the highest point reached by our society in its course through history. During this period we reached—morally speaking—our highest point of power, prosperity, and splendor. It was our zenith, our apex, the culmination of years of effort and suffering." Forgive my manipulations, but isn't this the thought upon which the action of the novel turns? Isn't this also our perception of the Civil Rights Movement, or rather, in our despair at the direction of the present epoch, the construction we place upon it? Of course, it is. *Meridian* is a tribute to and a criticism of that great period of revolution and national introspection, that period in history "that forced the trivial to fall away." It was, to make explicit the meaning in "b" of the second definition, the period during which we, again morally speaking, were at the highest point of national health, of national vigor. It was our prime, that is to say, we—the nation—were at our best.

But there is more that Walker wishes us to consider in definitions four through six:

4. in astronomy, an imaginary great circle of the celestial sphere passing through the poles of the heavens and the zenith and nadir of any given point, and cutting the equator at right angles.
5. in geography, (a) a great circle of the earth passing through the geographical poles and any given point on the earth's surface; . . .
6. (a) a place or situation with its own distinctive character;
    (b) distinctive character.

Here Walker pulls off something quite extraordinary and in the process gives us, if we read carefully between the lines, something quite profound. For Walker the Civil Rights Movement was, if we take our cue from "meridian's" meaning in astronomy and geography, an event of both cosmic ("passing through the poles of heaven") and global ("passing through the geographical poles") proportions. Further, this social and political event occurred, as Walker intimates, in a "place with its own distinctive character." Here she is speaking generally of the United States and the "distinctive character" that led to its creation and formation. But the meanings of "distinctive character" are many for they are not only topographical, but regional, political, and human. At the risk of belaboring an obvious point, Walker seems to be implying that the South possesses and has produced a "distinctive character" in those who proudly call it home (nothing could be more true), and also that the Civil Rights Movement, like the South, not only possessed its own "distinctive character," but produced it in all its participants.

Since we have been so careful in deciphering some of the subtleties in Walker's highly symbolic stance, the message of the last definition is plainly a prophecy based on something that appears to be optimism: "first meridian: a carefully located meridian from which secondary or guide meridians may be constructed." What is the "first meridian"? It is at least three things: a) the Civil Rights Movement itself after which other social and political movements—"secondary or guide meridians"—may follow; b) Walker's novel, a "carefully located [or crafted] text from which others of similar force by her and other authors may one day come; c) Meridian Hill herself, whose example serves as a "guide" or model to the reader.

In *Meridian* Walker wishes to evoke not only the spirit of a particular time and place, but also the spirit and spiritual place of a particular writer—Jean Toomer. An awareness of this fact deepens our appreciation of the mystery of Walker's novel, a mystery that gathers its peculiar elements and proportions from places and texts dear to Toomer.

As we know, Meridian Hill is the name of the heroine in Walker's novel, but there is also a beautiful spot in northwest Washington, D.C., called Meridian Hill Park, a park often visited by a young Jean Toomer. Built in 1910 from a design by Horace C. Peaslee, Meridian Hill Park is an approximation of a formal Italian garden. Toomer, who as a boy lived within walking distance of the park, was doubtless drawn there by its splendid vista. On this bluff he could see, with one glance, the White House, the Washington Monument, the Potomac River, and the hills of Virginia. Meridian Hill Park was a special place for Toomer because it was here that he—inspired by the vista, the scowl worn by the towering monument to Dante, and the romantic representation of Joan of Arc—dreamed of becoming a poet. But Meridian Hill Park, as Walker surely knows, is not without geographic and astronomical significance. It was here in 1816 that the "meridian was surveyed in the vain hope of establishing a new prime meridian to free American navigators from dependence on that of Greenwich."[6] Interestingly, by resolution of the District government Meridian Hill Park was renamed Malcolm X Park—a fact very much in keeping with the spirit of Walker's novel—a park where other young men, attracted by the formal garden and the view, pause to dream but not, so rumor has it, exclusively of poetry.

The name of Walker's heroine not only calls to mind a place known to Toomer but a major text by him—"The Blue Meridian." In this long Whitmanesque poem, which first appeared in a truncated version as "Brown River Smile," Toomer describes not only the settlement of North America, but the metamorphosis of the White and Black Meridians into the Blue Meridian. For Toomer the Blue Meridian not only represented the new American race of which he considered himself a member, but also the highest point in our spiritual and psychological development. Based upon Toomer's lifelong study of Gurdjieff's psychological system, the poem functions as a challenge to our complacency as well as a model for our real spiritual possibilities. Not surprisingly, Walker's novel and its heroine function in precisely the same manner.

Terms like "political activist" and "revolutionary" do not adequately describe the depth of commitment to civil rights we observe in Meridian Hill. She is, of course, a "revolutionary" and a "political activist," but she is plainly more than the combined meaning of these terms. Those who once used these terms to describe themselves—Anne-Marion and Truman Held—later proved to be inadequate to the great work to which they were called. The difference between Meridian and many of her contemporaries is revealed in several places, but perhaps most clearly in the following conversation between Truman and herself:

> I grieve in a different way, he said.
> I know, Meridian panted.
> What do you know? [T]
> I know you grieve by running away. By pretending you were never there. [M]
> When things are finished it is best to leave. [T]
> And pretend they were never started? [M]
> Yes. [T]
> But that's not possible. [M] (p. 27)

Meridian neither possesses the charisma and the physical beauty of Truman, nor the bravado and stridency of the exploitive Anne-Marion. What she does possess, as suggested by the above passage, is a memory in which is recorded every transgression against the collective body and spirit of her people, along with the discipline to create and implement new strategies to prevent other such transgressions. In her great and necessary work for the people (I use "work" in the same spirit as Walker does in her uplifting essay "The Unglamorous But Worthwhile Duties of the Black Revolutionary Artist"), Meridian has demonstrated that she is incapable of the cruelty practiced by Truman and Anne-Marion, that is to say, of withdrawing her support from a struggle simply because others have lost interest in it, or because the rewards do not appear when expected, or because others are discouraged by what really needs to be done. She is not a captive, as Truman sometimes appears to be, of convenient, specious reasoning. The ideas of King and Malcolm, which Meridian "allowed . . . to penetrate her life," are not for her, as they are for the pompous Truman, the symptoms of a "fad." Meridian's belief in the vitalness of the ideas of Malcolm and King is revealed in several ways: her involvement in the Atlanta Movement; her devotion to Wild Child; her grief at the razing of the Sojourner; her success at voter registration; her work in the freedom schools and so on.

Although Meridian appears to be in a constant state of creation, she is not a caricature of an ideal. Far from it. As stated, Meridian is no beauty, but is frail, partially bald, and the victim of a bizarre falling sickness. These handicaps, however, do not slow her down. What we admire most in Meridian is her spirit of self-sacrifice and her knowledge of what is essential for others and for herself. It is this special knowledge, the knowledge of her condition (for Walker this is the supreme accomplishment of the Civil Rights Movement), that sustains her and separates her from others who have not achieved this kind of maturity, this kind of authority. As a consequence of this knowledge, Meridian discovers that she could kill, a possibility she could not face earlier, for the revolution. But she also discovers, as her cynical, temporizing critic Anne-Marion does not, that "even the contemplation of murder required incredible delicacy as it required incredible spiritual work, and the historical background and the present setting must be right" (p. 200). In other words, the taking of a life could not be arbitrary and even when merited the cost to herself would be great and lasting.

But Meridian's special knowledge has helped her to make another, indeed, the most important discovery of her life: her part in the revolution. Over time, Meridian realizes that she cannot be the banner-bearer, the rhetorician, or the assassin because she does not possess the temperament for the kind of work these roles require. Instead, with characteristic modesty and perhaps even unconscious irony, she describes her part in the revolution in the following manner:

> to walk behind the real revolutionaries—those who know they must spill blood in order to help the poor and the black and therefore go right ahead—and when they stop to wash off the blood and find their throats too choked with the smell of murdered flesh to sing, I will come forward and sing from memory songs they will need once more to hear. For it is the song of the people, transformed by experiences of

each generation, that holds them together, and if any part of it is lost the people suffer and are without soul. If I can only do that, my role will not have been a useless one after all. (p. 201)

The role of witness, of tradition bearer, is far from "useless." It is plainly a role that Walker and such poets as Michael S. Harper, Sterling A. Brown, Margaret Walker, and Robert Hayden have assumed, much to the grateful satisfaction of their readers.

Meridian's example of self-knowledge through self-sacrifice, of clarity through involvement in a righteous cause is plainly worthy of emulation, as Truman and perhaps even Anne-Marion have always known. Meridian's example is a powerful one, so much so that Truman, having put the fragments of his very complicated life in some kind of order, returns to the work—the work of the people— that before was only a kind of male ornament. Truman now understands the high seriousness of Meridian's great call and responds in the mode of one who apprehends its full significance. What is its significance? The answer to this question is revealed in the novel's last sentence: "[Truman] wondered if Meridian knew that the sentence of bearing the conflict in her own soul which she had imposed on herself—and lived through—must now be born in terror by all of the rest of them" (p. 220). To approach life in a manner which permits one to pretend that evil does not exist, or that it can be forgotten is not only irresponsible, but a sure promise of destruction. This is the thought Meridian attempts to communicate to Truman earlier in the novel when he foolishly insists, over her objections, that it is possible to "pretend" that things "never started." Of course, we know, and Meridian is our example, our model, that that kind of thinking—if we care anything at all about the manner in which we live—is not possible.

In *The Third Life of Grange Copeland* the context for Walker's meditations on the spirit—on our spiritual survival and possibilities—is the home and the family. In *Meridian* her context is chiefly political and we are asked to consider the various ways in which we can assure the survival of that larger, greater family of which we are all members. In *The Color Purple,* her most controversial and most highly acclaimed novel, Walker returns to the home and to the family for it is here that our first spiritual battles are fought. It is here that the spirit is most under siege. It is here that the spirit, when not respected and nurtured, is most in danger of being weakened and trivialized.

"You better not never tell nobody but God. It'd kill your mammy."[7] This is an utterance from the bewildered, frightened place that is Celie's spirit. The "it" that must "not never" be told to anyone except God is Celie's rape by her stepfather Fonso. These rapes, which are regular and violent, begin when Celie is fourteen and continue until she is married off, some years later, to the equally depraved and hateful Albert. The children produced by these rapes are quickly and indifferently disposed of. Fonso's abuse of Celie is horrible to us for many reasons but chiefly because he has violated the sacred code of fatherhood. Since Celie is his stepdaughter, Fonso feels that he is under no obligation to treat her with more respect than he would a farm animal or a tool.

During most of the years of his marriage to Celie, Albert is as mean and as contemptible as Fonso. As we may recall, Albert preferred Celie's sister Nettie over Celie, but Fonso, holding Nettie in reserve as a replacement for Celie, insisted that she would make an unsuitable wife. Because Celie is Albert's second choice, his treatment of her is worse than second-rate. We discover later that Albert loves only one woman, Shug Avery, but that his inability to ignore the prohibitions of his father and the town deprived him of real happiness. This cowardice in love helps to explain Albert's harsh treatment of Celie, but much of it cannot be explained. Like Fonso's, Albert's sins against Celie's spirit are frequently arbitrary and unfathomable. And this—the sins against the spirit—is Walker's principal preoccupation in *The Color Purple*. These transgressions are the framework for the ninety letters, exchanged over a thirty-year period, that are her novel. Walker's accomplishment, however, is more than just an index of the violence Black men have committed against Black women. She attempts to give us more than that, and succeeds. While we are keenly aware of Fonso's and Albert's inhumanity to Celie, we rejoice at her capacity to endure and then, for herein lies the beauty and power of Walker's masterpiece, to prevail.

Celie's talisman is Shug Avery who, in her boldness, humor, and talent, is the incarnation of such blues giants as Bessie Smith and Billie Holiday. Both women meet one another at perhaps the lowest point in their lives. Celie is trapped in the grueling routine of an un-rewarding marriage and Shug it seems has just returned from a not-very-successful singing tour. In their exchange of sympathies, which is initially awkward and for Celie sometimes menacing, they give to one another a special kind of nurturing that restores health to the body and to the spirit. Both women benefit enormously from the contact that over time develops into a life-giving intimacy, but Celie, being more in need, plainly benefits more from the discoveries that follow Shug's ministrations.

These discoveries are various and meaningful and the first has to do with the complexities of female sexuality. Although Celie was raped by Fonso, bore two children and nightly endures the selfish fumbling of Albert, she is, at the time she first meets Shug, sexually innocent. Celie is sexually innocent because she has not learned, through no fault of her own, that sex is more than just the indifferent co-mingling of flesh. Sadly ignorant of her own anatomy, she is un-aware of her capacity to give and to receive pleasure. Thankfully, Shug provides Celie with some insight into her sexual possibilities. But as Shug initiates Celie into the ancient and true properties of the "button," she imparts a knowledge to her that is greater than sex. Although we do not witness the effects until much later, Celie's sex-ual experiences with Shug give her a very real and very keen sense of herself as a complex and developing woman. As a consequence of Shug's patient and loving attention, Celie discovers not only the pleasures of intimacy, but that such intimacy must be based upon a respect for another's body, needs, and spirit. Over time, this discov-ery makes Celie more critical of Albert because she begins to see the deficiencies in their marriage. Over time, this discovery helps Celie to find her own voice, a voice that expresses the ache and anger of that secret true self held captive by years of abuse and violence.

We see the outline of this new self when Celie discovers that Albert has been hiding Nettie's letters. Celie is amazed and appalled by Albert's pettiness. Her mind is an execution chamber riddled with blood and the memory of painful deaths: "All day long I act just like Sofia. I stutter. I mutter to myself. I stumble bout the house crazy for Mr.'s blood. In my mind, he falling dead every which a way. By time night come, I can't speak. Every time I open my mouth nothing come out but a little burp" (p. 115). Celie's comparison of herself to Sophia is significant because it is evidence of her emerging, true, secret self—long oppressed by Albert's tyranny. Celie is beginning to reject the passive stance of the victim and to assume the aggressive, defiant stance of the warrior. Soon after the discovery of Albert's treachery, Celie finds the courage to use against a very startled and blathering Albert, her best weapon and strongest defence—the righteousness of her voice. The lifting of her voice to express the fury of a deeply wronged spirit signals not only a radical change in Celie's life and circumstances, but subtle changes within the fabric of the text as well. When Celie announces to an amazed Albert that it is time for her to leave him and "enter into creation" and that his "dead body [is] just the welcome mat" she needs, her departure from the land of the dead into the land of the living is commemorated within the text by a change in salutation. The letter from which the preceding quotations are taken and all other letters by Celie that follow it are not addressed to God but to Nettie. This textual change underscores Celie's transformation and Walker's belief that the discovery of voice is linked to the discovery of our own true, secret selves. Until we can speak in our own voices the doors leading to the self, the world, and the spirit remain bolted forever.

Celie's last letter, the letter which ends Walker's magnificent novel, begins with a salutation that is a message from a spirit that is expansive and unencumbered, a spirit that is gratefully at peace with itself and with creation: "Dear God. Dear Stars, dear trees, dear sky, dear peoples. Dear Everything. Dear God" (p. 249). Celie no longer lives in fear of Albert, whom religion has made innocuous and penitent, because she is part of a large, expanding circle of love and kinship that includes the universe and all of nature. The early life experiences that threatened to disfigure her physically and spiritually have made her strong, resilient, and wise. Thanks to the very vital support of Shug, Celie has come through her ordeal of family and marriage without bitterness, without cynicism, without despair. We are thankful for this promising, optimistic denouement, one which seemed unlikely at the novel's beginning, and as we celebrate Celie's triumph over adversity we celebrate that very same potential in ourselves.

The novels of Alice Walker contain the things of this world: pain and consolation, betrayal and reconciliation, love and transformation. They also contain the very thing we need to live in this world:

models. It seems that Walker has always known what is essential for our survival because as a writer, as a womanist, and as an *artist* she has never failed to provide us with this vital resource. For Walker, models are essential spiritual aids with revelatory properties. Models reveal many things about ourselves and the world, but most importantly they reveal truth. This is why Walker shares with us situations in literature that are grounded in truth. Although we may sometimes wish to reject these situations, to dismiss them, as does George Stade,[8] as womanist propaganda, the force and purity of these situations as well as our own knowledge of history and of human behavior make such dismissals and rejections—if we love the truth—the greatest self-deception. But Walker's models reveal more than truth; they also reveal direction. Truth without direction is an oppression of the spirit. Without direction we flounder and agonize, but with it we apprehend not just a means of escape, but relief from spiritual suffering and an awareness not only of our fallibility but of our potentiality as well. In *The Third Life of Grange Copeland, Meridian,* and *The Color Purple,* Walker forces us, through her artful use of models, to face the truth, but she also, through these same models, provides direction. We celebrate Grange's transformation, Meridian's commitment, and Celie's triumph because each reveals what is true and possible.

In the essay "Saving The Life That Is Your Own: The Importance of Models in the Artist's Life," Walker writes with great sensitivity of the necessity of models for artists. According to Walker: "the absence of models, in literature as in life, to say nothing of painting, is an occupational hazard for the artist, simply because models in art, in behavior, in growth of spirit and intellect—even if rejected—enrich and enlarge one's view of existence" (p. 4). Plainly, we all share in the artist's need for models. Just as Walker benefits from the example of such models as Jean Toomer and Zora Neale Hurston, we benefit from the example of such models as Grange Copeland, Meridian Hill, and Celie. Again, these characters, complex, fascinating, and realistic, are more than just literary inventions for our amusement, but models that not only "enrich and enlarge [our] view of existence," but models that also enrich, enlarge, and bolster our spirits. They are models for the spirit as well as, and here I have an image of Walker as a medium surrounded by spiritual helpers, gifts from the Spirit.

## Notes

1    Alice Walker, "From an Interview," *In Search of Our Mothers' Gardens* (New York: Harcourt Brace Jovanovich, 1983), p. 250. All further references to Walker's essays are from this edition.

2    For Walker's definition of womanist see p. xi of *In Search of Our Mothers' Garden.*

3    Alice Walker, *The Third Life of Grange Copeland* (New York: Harcourt Brace Jovanovich, 1970), p. 20. All further references to this edition will appear in parentheses.

4    Louis Simpson, *Three on the Tower: The Lives and Works of Ezra Pound, T. S. Eliot and William Carlos Williams* (New York: William Morrow, 1975), p. 293.

5    Alice Walker, *Meridian* (New York: Washington Square Press, 1976). All further references to this edition will appear in parentheses.

6    E. J. Applewhite, *Washington Itself* (New York: Alfred A. Knopf, 1981), p. 99.

7    Alice Walker, *The Color Purple* (New York: Washington Square Press, 1982), p. 11. All further references to this edition will appear in parentheses.

8    George Stade, "Men in Women's Fiction," *Partisan Review* 3 (1985).

# Chinosole

## Audre Lorde and Matrilineal Diaspora: "moving history beyond nightmare into structures for the future . . ."

The fullest vision and deepest wisdom that Audre Lorde shares with us as Black women is what I call matrilineal diaspora: the capacity to survive and aspire, to be contrary and self-affirming across continents and generations. It names the strength and beauty we pass on as friends and lovers from foremothers to mothers and daughters allowing us to survive radical cultural changes and be empowered through differences. Matrilineal diaspora defines the links among Black women worldwide enabling us to experience distinct but related cultures while retaining a special sense of home as the locus of self-definition and power. Through matrilineal diaspora, Audre Lorde realizes her journey to "the house of self." I will trace, explore, and celebrate this vision as voiced in the childhood section of *Zami: A New Spelling of My Name* (1982) and as echoed in her poetry, particularly in part one of *The Black Unicorn* (1978) and in "Sisters in Arms" (1985). While my main purpose is to look directly at Lorde's writing, I will begin by placing the theme of matrilineal diaspora in the context of the overall Black diaspora as exemplified in a slave narrative, and I will end by suggesting how this theme fits into the larger body of contemporary Aframerican literature.

The meaning of matrilineal diaspora is rooted in African and Afro-American cultures. As a working historical definition, "diaspora," or dispersal, means the forced displacement of Africans that was initiated by the European slave trade, perpetuated through colonial governments, and continued through global economic and military control by the United States and other Western powers. For purposes of literary criticism, diaspora is less important as an outcome of oppression than as the proliferation of cultures of people of African descent, especially in the Caribbean and South, Central, and North America, but also in Africa today. Put quite plainly, distinct African-related cultures have flowered in spite of, and even because of, the simultaneous dispersal of Africans among kindred European masters. The cultures of people of African descent are dialectically linked in origin and destination. Most Blacks in the diaspora have West African ancestry, and now they resist in similar ways Western political systems that have colonized, segregated, marginalized, and continue to discriminate against them.

The slave narrative is the earliest Black literary form in the diaspora.[1] While widespread and recurrent, almost everywhere it has the same social and literary function of protesting slavery. Because narrators like Olaudah Equiano, Samuel Ringgold Ward, Linda Brent, and Esteban Montejo fled from city to city and continent to continent escaping their plight as Blacks, it is not surprising that their stories have similar themes and motifs. For example, in narratives from the United States and Cuba the motif of home and displacement recurs.

The Cuban slave narrator, Esteban Montejo, gives a brief but pointed example of the theme of diaspora applicable to Audre Lorde. Still alive in 1973 and, according to Richard Price, probably the last surviving maroon,[2] this former runaway slave expresses an important insight:

> Some people say that when [Blacks] died [they] went back to Africa, but this is a lie. How could a dead [person] go to Africa? It was [the living] who flew there, from a [nation] the Spanish stopped importing as slaves because so many of them flew away that it was bad for business. [Good grief, the dead] don't fly! The Chinese who died here, so they said, came to life again in Canton. But with [Blacks], what happened was their spirits left their bodies and wandered about over the

sea and through space, like when a snail leaves its shell and goes into another and then another and another. That's why there are so many shells. The dead don't appear as corpses but as spirit shapes.[3]

The passage moves like an oblique zig-zag. At first, with a kind of backhanded humoring, Montejo masks his own belief to disarm those who would dismiss as superstition the idea of flying to Africa. With tongue in cheek, he exclaims, "How could a dead [person] go to Africa?" Then he responds with the equally fantastic notion that the living, not corpses, wander over the earth in changing shapes. Using the widespread folk belief and literary image of flying, Montejo enunciates the diasporic motif of home and displacement. Then with a comparison, he creates a metonym for Black cultures and literatures when he says: "like when a snail leaves its shell and goes into another and then another," and establishes the paradox that survival and change are inseparable. He concludes that "the dead don't appear as [shells]" empty and fixed "but as spirit shapes," and so equates home or Africa or cultural identity with cultural improvisation.

How does Montejo help us to enunciate the principle of cultural improvisation? In addition to improvisation being essential to the survival of any culture, in African-based cultures, it functions both as a cultural principle and a highly privileged skill. Privileging improvisation by African-based cultures makes it the most markedly persistent cultural mode. The persistence of improvisational skills in music, dance, and language carries and gives evidence of African cultural origins. In literature, then, we investigate the improvising strategies that ensure survival through change of cultures and peoples of the African diaspora.

Seemingly a remote example, Montejo's slave narrative helps situate Lorde's use of matrilineal diaspora in the context of the motif of home and displacement. After all, Lorde characterizes herself as a kind of maroon, a "sister outsider" and "journeywoman," like the runaway Cuban slave. True, her parents were dispossessed workers and not ex-slaves, and they came to the United States from the Caribbean, not directly from Africa. Yet she is part of the same historical continuum as the runaway slave, a recent by-product of the Atlantic slave trade. Like the slave narrator she, too, through her mother in *Zami,* voices the motif of home and displacement by recalling:

Once *home* was a far way off, a place I had never been to but knew well out of my mother's mouth. She breathed exuded hummed the fruit smell of Noel's Hill morning fresh and noon hot, and I spun visions of sapadilla and mango as a net over my Harlem tenement cot in the snoring darkness rank with nightmare sweat. Made bearable because it was not all. This now, here, was a space, some temporary abode, never to be considered forever nor totally binding nor defining, no matter how much it commanded in energy and attention. (*Zami,* p. 13)[4]

And with equal defiance of Western linear logic reminiscent of the Cuban slave narrator, she dedicates *Between Our Selves* (1978) to: "the embattled! / there is no place that cannot be / home / nor is." Both quotations exemplify a way in which Lorde affirms cultural adaptation and difference through language and the defiance of logic. So the romantic and nostalgic images of "fruit smell [and] sapadilla and mango" contrast with a "snoring darkness rank with nightmare sweat." Rural Caribbean culture as remembered is set alongside the Harlem one lived. The juxtaposition of imagery and sound is not simple word play but an expression of a cultural imperative, that of the Black diaspora. Through imagery, word choice, and the defiance of logic, cultural differences are enhanced.

Affirming cultural differences that are oppositional and even antagonistic is a critical part of Lorde's matrilineal diaspora. I use the terms nonpolarized duality or creative irreconcilability to express the principle and mode of Lorde's affirmation of difference. In the face of an oppressive culture bent on your obliteration, affirming difference as nonthreatening, a difference charged by change like the house of winds—a survival-oriented, self-defining change—is a current in slave narratives tapped and magnified in Lorde's own special vision of matrilineal diaspora. What binds Lorde and other Aframerican writers to the slave narrative, then, is the theme of survival through adaptation or cultural improvisation. What Barbara Christian calls "contrariness," to describe women characters in novels by Toni Morrison and Alice Walker, is rooted in this larger cultural dynamic of survival and change, a connection I will develop in my conclusion.[5]

On the book cover of *Sister Outsider* appears a familiar photograph of Audre Lorde, a black-and-white portrait. In it she wears her usual natural hairstyle. Three tiny earrings, perhaps of gold or crystal, stud one visible ear lobe. Bespectacled, she looks like the English professor she is, in finely wired rectangular glasses perched low on the bridge of her nose. Her head bent slightly, her thumb and index finger touch the side of her glasses. At the lower left-hand corner of the photo, we can glimpse on her wrist several West Indian bracelets. They are probably silver, the ones that curve around and meet as two snake heads or flower buds depending on your mood, and are known to ward off illness. Only the top of a dark tailored suit and a white turtleneck sweater are visible. Tucked just under the suit collar, a delicately draped strip of West African kente cloth accents the entire portrait.

As a cultural icon, this portrait serves as an inset for the essay to introduce the autobiographical work, *Zami.* The photograph is a study in contrasts, symbolic of the cultural oppositions expressed in her life, her work, and in her very person. Drawing from a varied cultural background, she has re-created a self-image. Her mother came from Carriacou, Grenada, and her father came from Barbados. Lorde grew up in Black Harlem and after attending a Catholic grammar school that was Black and Puerto Rican, began attending predominantly white schools in the sixth grade. As a young woman she studied to be a librarian during the day, and at night she would write or join in the gay-bar scene of Greenwich Village. Beneath everything she sees herself as a poet. In a most compellingly personal way, then, the photo anticipates the creative irreconcilability found in her writing.

Looking directly at *Zami,* it is clear that just as Lorde defies conformity in life style, she defies it in literary genre. Some of her finest poems, such as "Litany for Survival," began as journal entries and are autobiographical in subject matter, as is the autobiographical prose work, *Zami,* explicitly mythical and fictional.[6] And while many of her poems are shaped around a narrative skeleton, much of *Zami's* prose reads like poetry. Her meshing of history and myth, prose and poetry, makes studying Lorde's autobiography alongside her poetry appropriate and necessary.

"I am writing a book about the unfolding of my life and loves" is the way Lorde describes the purpose of *Zami* (p. 190). It is also *her* unfolding in a journey to her selves as a Black lesbian feminist poet beginning with her foremothers and the relationship with her mother, and proceeding to her loss in adolescence of the first person she was conscious of loving, Gennie, who committed suicide. Then her lesbian love relationships with Ginger, Bea, and Eudora usher in the central and long-term relationship with Muriel, until the journey ends with the brief and intense semi-mythical romance with Kitty or Afrekete. Afrekete, an African *orisha,* is the "mischievous linguist, trickster . . . whom we must all become" (p. 255). Key to the self which emerges is Lorde's need to mesh a collective racial identity and an individual sexual one. Through Afrekete/Kitty, Lorde circles back to a racial and sexual identity begun with her foremothers of Carriacou.

On the simplest story level, the narrative is roughly divided into three major parts. The first section focuses on her ancestry and early childhood; the second recounts her school years and growing separation from her family up to the start of menses; the third section treats her rebellion against her family and her love relationships with women. The overall movement of the text is cyclical in roughly seven-year intervals; each seven-year cycle ends at a higher "plateau" of self-awareness. I will focus on the first two sections that depict her relationship to her mother most clearly.

The opening pages of *Zami* contain a succinct definition of matrilineal diaspora as "the elegantly strong triad of grandmother mother daughter, with the 'I' moving back and forth flowing in either or both directions as needed" (p. 67). Such a complex and fluid self-definition requires an intricate structure. To accommodate the multiplicity of identities, the narrative moves modally in dyads, triads, and continual unfoldings. Basically, there are two voices in *Zami*: the evocative poetic voice in which dreams, legends, and myths are told, and the simpler prose voice that tells most of the story. Matrilineal diaspora is expressed mainly in poetic voices in the opening sections and at the very end. In addition, there are three basic modes of consciousness: collective memory rendered through myth and legend that recaptures the past; the memory of personal experience that records the personal narrative, and a mythical fantasy dream state that projects into the future through desire. This is why *Zami* is not simply autobiography but biomythography. Myth binds the remotest past to the most distant future, and this is why the semi-mythical Afrekete is so important as self-projection. Myth is the fictional construct that frames past, present, and future selves in *Zami,* and it is the construct that will project a collective and revolutionary self in "Sisters in Arms."

While rooted in the historical experience of the Black diaspora, Lorde's diaspora is matrilineal or woman-centered. But at the same time, what distinguishes her matrilineal diaspora from the Euro-American radical feminist matriarchal tradition is the emphasis on Black women. Black women form the critical link of her diasporic chain. For Lorde, "matrilineal" means that mythical and legendary connection to African women, the legendary and historical connection to the women in the Caribbean, and her autobiographical connection to her mother and the Black women she grew up with in her community. Therefore, she develops matrilineal diaspora on over-lapping historical, biographical, and figurative levels. "Matrilineal" also means that woman-centered power traced through her mother, sustained by loving women, and key to her survival.

The meaning of "matrilineal" that is groundbreaking in *Zami,* however, connects it to a tradition of Black dykes, including her mother: "To this day I believe that there have always been Black dykes around—in the sense of powerful and women-oriented women—who would rather have died than use that name for themselves. And that includes my momma" (p. 615). Her connection to a tradition of Black dykes does not stop with the strong emotional ties characteris-tic of many Black communities, but extends to physical loving: "*Zami. A Carriacou name for women who work together as friends and lovers*" (p. 255). And it is not simply legendary but historical: "There it is said that the desire to lie with other women is a drive from the mother's blood" (p. 256). Lorde's connection of her lesbian identity to matrilineage is based on oral history and supported by anthropology.

In St. Lucia, an island in the Caribbean, "zami" is *patois* for "les-bian," based on the French expression, *les amies.*[7] In Carriacou where the male population is small because they must leave this spice-growing island to find work, lesbianism is a known social phe-nomenon. Also, strong, emotional ties among women are supported by a matrifocal family structure throughout the Caribbean, but most especially in Carriacou. Matrifocality means "a type of family or household grouping in which the woman is dominant and plays the leading role psychologically."[8] Clearly this accounts for her mother's strength.[9] By tracing her lesbian identity to her family origin and history Lorde has cleared an important path in Aframerican literature: freeing the idea of lesbianism from the closet of "white decadence."

What are the paths toward self-definition that link Audre Lorde to the past and point toward the future? How does she "move history"—slave history and the continuing history of dispossessed workers and migrant laborers—"beyond nightmare into structures for the future?" She develops a configuration of selves based on matrilineal diaspora. Her mother, her Caribbean foremothers, and African *orishas* (or spiritual forces) are all cultural pathways in the journey to her selves.

Taking a closer look at *Zami,* then, matrilineal diaspora is a theme that pivots around her relationship to her mother—her mother's ancestry, home, and survival training. Her rebellion against her mother to find her own identity is equally important to this theme. She describes her mother as "a very powerful woman," and continues:

> This was so in a time when the word-combination of *woman* and *powerful* was almost inexpressible in the white american common tongue, except or unless it was accompanied by some aberrant explaining adjective like blind, or hunchback, or crazy, or Black. Therefore when I was growing up, *powerful woman* equaled something else quite different from ordinary woman, from simply 'woman.' (p. 15)

"*I am a reflection of my mother's secret poetry as well as of her hidden angers*" (p. 32). Her mother's poetry came through language and her stories about home, a source of self-gratification; her angers fed her drive to survive in a hostile culture and reflected her suppression of personal desires. The tension between Lorde and her mother reflects a fundamental one in Aframerican culture: women are driven to survive, a collective responsibility, and to experience personal gratification, an individual need. Her mother's training was to survive in a concrete, social sense; Lorde had to break from her mother's house to find personal gratification. And yet it was her mother's secret poetry which introduced Lorde to sensual and aesthetic forms of self-gratification.

Home or house is a dominant image in Aframerican literature. *Home Girls, In Search of Our Mothers' Gardens,* and *The Women of Brewster Place* are titles of Black women's fiction in which matrilineage, home, and identity are linked. For Lorde, home as an image means primarily the place of her most private self, but it alludes to the sacred place of worship of the *orishas* when she speaks of the house of self. House is also linked to her Caribbean heritage. In Carriacou, one is not identified by a church name but by the name of the household, most often female-headed, in which one lives.[10] "Once *home* was a long way off, a place I had never been to but knew out of my mother's mouth. I only discovered its latitude when Carriacou was no longer my home" (p. 256). These lines echo the theme of displacement and home, survival and change discussed earlier.

The break from her mother's home is most decisive in the highly symbolic mortar-and-pestle scene. It takes place at the end of the childhood section, when she begins menses at age fifteen. It demonstrates the conflict in her mother's household between group survival and self-gratification:

> The whole rhythm of my movements softened and elongated, until dreamlike, I stood, one hand tightly curved around the carved mortar, steadying it against the middle of my body; while my other hand, around the pestle, rubbed and pressed the moistening spice into readiness with a sweeping circular movement. I hummed tunelessly to myself as I worked in the warm kitchen, thinking with relief about how simple life would be now that I had become a woman. The catalogue of dire menstruation-warnings from my mother passed out of my head. My body felt strong and full and open, yet captivated by the gentle motions of the pestle, and the rich smells filling the kitchen, and the fullness of the young summer heat.
>
> I heard my mother's key in the lock.
>
> She swept into the kitchen briskly, like a ship under full sail. There were tiny beads of sweat over her upper lip, and vertical creases between her brows. "You mean to tell me no meat is ready?" (p. 79)

The scene ends with her conclusion that "in my mother's kitchen there was only one right way to do anything" (p. 80), and what follows is open rebellion against her mother's rigidity.

Food is a major motif throughout, and here it is a perfect symbol for survival and gratification. This passage also uses the mortar and pestle as a central symbol. It is a woman's tool, traceable to the Caribbean and Africa, in which a traditional Caribbean dish is being prepared. West African legends make the mortar and pestle a symbol of the male/female principle as well.[11] So this scene represents a culmination of matrilineal diaspora as a theme in relation to her mother.

*Zami* uses myth as the major fictional frame connecting Ma-Mariah of Carriacou to Afrekete/Kitty of Africa and Harlem. Myth is also a source of invocation toward self-definition: "I grew Black as my need for life, for affirmation, for love, for sharing—copying from my mother what was in her, unfulfilled. I grew Black as Seboulisa, who I was to find in the cool mud halls of Abomey several lifetimes later—and as alone" (p. 58). Because *Zami* is autobiographical, myth serves a more static and personal function than in "Sisters in Arms." This later poem (1984) pushes toward a more political and collective aspiration of freedom. There is a progression in the use of matrilineal diaspora from a past-oriented, mythical referent to a future-oriented vision.

Matrilineal diaspora is a mainstay of Audre Lorde's prose and poetry. Before examining the culmination of this theme in "Sisters in Arms," I will trace its expression in the use of myth and language in some of the poems in *Black Unicorn* (1978). Especially in part one, African *orishas* are woven into the poems as a way of heightening contrast in language and culture differences and as a way of realizing self-definition.

Because on one level of reading "From the House of Yemenjá" implies a narrative about her relationship to her mother elaborated on in *Zami,* it can serve as a major example of how her poetry uses myth in the overall theme of matrilineal diaspora.

> My mother had two faces and a frying pot
> where she cooked up her daughters
> into girls
> before she fixed our dinner.
> My mother had two faces
> and a broken pot
> where she hid out a perfect daughter
> who was not me
> I am the sun and moon and forever hungry
> for her eyes.

I bear two women upon my back
one dark and rich and hidden
in the ivory hungers of the other
mother
pale as a witch
yet steady and familiar
brings me bread and terror
in my sleep
her breasts are huge exciting anchors
in the midnight storm.

All this has been
before
in my mother's bed
time has no sense
I have no brothers
and my sisters are cruel.

Mother I need
mother I need
mother I need your blackness now
as the august earth needs rain.

I am
the sun and moon and forever hungry
the sharpened edge
where day and night shall meet
and not be
one.[12]

In the above poem, juxtaposition of voice, tone, and diction not only dominate the expressive mode of language, but is transformed into the structural and thematic principle of nonpolarized dualities. Ordinary life situations are adjacent to West African deities. Not simply a mythical allusion, Yemenjá, a primary *orisha* of creation, the spiritual force of the oceans, rivers, and lakes, is compared to a mother's life force as necessary but bitter. The speaker emerges in the end as the principle of difference, and Mawulisa is the implied *orisha* of the sun and moon or nonpolar duality. The first and last stanzas, then, do not simply encapsulate duality, but are structured to represent progression from a tension-ridden difference to a non-threatening one. The power of unity is in that very separateness. Difference as a source of dread in the beginning, becomes the basis of self-acceptance still chanting its need and "ever hungry."

The difference between Lorde and her mother, alluded to in *Zami* but clearer here, is around the conflict of color. Her mother being "pale as a witch" is contrasted with "one dark and hidden." The irreconcilability of a fair mother and a dark daughter is a major source of the mother's rejection in this poem. Difference is not simply a matter of contrasting cultures but the internalization of one culture against another and the conflicts or self-acceptance this generates. As a Black woman, the speaker must accept both aspects of herself and recognize the conflict that cannot be resolved; that is creative irreconcilability.

Other poems that utilize myth as a way of identifying and clarifying the self also are found in the first section. One that refines language juxtaposition and tone is entitled "Letter to Jan." In it Mawulisa surfaces "bent on destruction" in a context where the voice of song and flat conversation measure each other in the same stanza. Beginning with the direct and colloquial line, "No, I don't think you were chicken not to speak," the poem advances to simple lyricism in the statement: "When all the time / I would have loved you / speaking / being a woman full of loving."[13] Language juxtaposition, then, is a literary vehicle that complements and accentuates cultural difference resulting from the Black diaspora.

"Sisters in Arms" is based on a triple rather than a double layer of difference. It contains three implicit lines of narrative: two Black women, one from South Africa, the other from the United States in bed as lovers; the police violence meted out to Blacks in South African townships; and the speaker stationary in her garden. The poem opens: "The edge of our bed was a wide grid / where your 15 year old daughter was hanging / gut sprung on police wheels." The second stanza is in a garden: "Now clearing the roughage from my autumn garden / cow-sorrel, over-grown rocket gone to seed."[14] All reinforce the relative safety of the speaker and the horror of the

South Africa her sister came from and must return to—the violent contrast between loving and war.

Loving is temporary. War continues. To express this Lorde invokes and incorporates a legendary African queen, Mmanthatisi, in a new way. Her earlier poems used mostly West African *orishas,* mythical and timeless. Here we get a concrete reference to a historical figure. Interestingly, when Lorde recited this poem in November 1984, she used Yaa Asantewa from West Africa.[15] The South African legendary figure makes the use of matrilineage more accurately historical. The African figure here is not timeless like Afrekete but breaks the time frame through the need for action to advance the future.

> Mmanthatisi turns away from the cloth
> her daughters-in-law are dying
> the baby drools milk from her breast
> she hands him half-asleep to his sister
> dresses again for war
> knowing the men will follow.
> In the intricate Maseru twilight
> quick sad vital
> she maps the next day's battle
> dreams of Durban sometimes
> visions the deep wry song of beach pebbles
> running after the sea.

"Sisters in Arms" advances matrilineal diaspora to an explicitly collective and functionally revolutionary level. Lorde often reads this poem as part of a concerted effort to raise the political consciousness of Americans about South African apartheid. The poem does battle. This is its function. And in this way Lorde actualizes her intent to "move history beyond nightmare into structures for the future." (*Zami,* p. 3)

Collective survival and self-gratification are two threads that braid their way through Aframerican literature registering a cultural imperative at odds with itself. Matrilineal diaspora as envisioned by Audre Lorde is just one way of responding to these tendencies. She heightens and celebrates difference.

I can only suggest ways in which this theme is incorporated in works of other Aframericans. In a general way, forced displacement of Blacks resulted in a sense of self that often was culturally contradictory and fragmented in a hostile, dominant society. The Black diaspora experience required an acceptance of fragmentation and adaptation as critical to survival. Slave narratives and Aframerican literature are wedded around the motif of difference and adaptation. Based on the historical continuum of survival through change, a premium is placed on the emotional immediacy of creative irreconcilability, which is a nonstatic, and nonthreatening affirmation of difference. That difference may mean how a person is at odds with herself or her environment or the norms of femininity set up by the dominant culture. Slave narratives have affirmed this and so have Black women writers, except that writers like Lorde place difference in a woman-centered sphere, flaunt it, and celebrate it. The portraits of DeLois and Louise Briscoe in *Zami* demonstrate this clearly. The idea of differing, being different, and changing is validated as part of Black women's identity.

Walker borrows the term "contrary instincts" from Virginia Woolf, and Barbara Christian uses the term "contrariness" to describe how different and intractable Aframericans must be to survive emotionally and physically.[16] Zora Neale Hurston's Janie Crawford, Toni Morrison's Sula, and Alice Walker's Shug are characters typifying how contrary Black women can be to the established feminine norms. With matrilineal diaspora this contrariness is projected on a global scale. It maps out internalized conflict created by being caught between cultures inside and outside the United States. In addition to Lorde, Paule Marshall develops the diaspora theme in *Praisesong for the Widow* and *The Chosen Place, The Timeless People*. Morrison in *Tar Baby* has her protagonist, Jadine, moving from the Caribbean to the United States and Europe trying to grapple with internal cultural contradictions. With Audre Lorde's theme of matrilineal diaspora, we have more than a mapping out of cultural differences. She projects a futuristic vision. Few have approached the completeness of vision and expression of matrilineal diaspora found in *Zami, The Black Unicorn,* and "Sisters in Arms."

## Notes

1     See *The Slave's Narrative,* edited by Charles T. Davis and Henry Louis Gates, Jr. (New York: Oxford University Press, 1985), as an example of the growing international importance of these narratives as a literary form.

2     Richard Price, ed., *Maroon Societies: Rebel Slave Communities in the Americas* (Garden City, N.Y.: Anchor Books, 1973), p. 1.

3     Translation altered to make it more contemporary and nonsexist. English version taken from Esteban Montejo, *The Autobiography of a Runaway Slave* as told to Miguel Barnet and translated by Jocasta Innes. (New York: Pantheon Books, 1968, first American edition), p. 1. Originally, *Biografía de un cimarrón* (p. 117):

Hay gente que dice que cuando un negro moría se iba para Africa. Eso es mentira. ¡Cómo iba a irse un muerto para Africa! Los que es iban eran los vivos, que volaban muchísimo. Una raza brava que los españoles no quisieron traer más, porque no era negocio. Pero los muertos, ¡qué va! Los Chinos, sí; ellos morían aquí, por lo menos eso contaban, y resucitaban en Cantón. Lo que les pasaba a los negros, que es lo mismo ayer que hoy, es que el espíritu se iba del cuerpo y se ponía a vagar por el mar o por el espacio. Igual que cuando una babosa suelta el caracol. Ese caracol encarna en otro y otro y otro. Por eso hay tantos. Los muertos so salen, así como muertos. Salen como figuras de espíritus.

4     All textual quotations cited from *Zami: A New Spelling of My Name* (Watertown, Mass.: Persephone Press, 1982).

5     Barbara Christian, *Black Feminist Criticism* (New York: Pergamon Press, 1985), p. 82.

6     As remembered based on a conversation with Lorde, November 13, 1984.

7     Based on a conversation with Garth St. Omer. St. Omer, born in St. Lucia, is a novelist, and one of several Caribbean authors to confirm the oral history of the existence of lesbian relationships in the Caribbean.

8     Nancie L. Solien de Gonzalez, "The Consanguineal Household and Matrifocality," *American Anthropologist* (December 1955), 1541.

9     The guidance and insights of the anthropologist Dr. Alfrieta Monagan on diaspora and matrifocality were used in this section.

10     Peter J. Wilson, "Reputation and Respectability: A Suggestion for Caribbean Ethnology," *Man* 4, no. 1 (1969), 84.

11     Gertrude Jobes, *Dictionary of Mythology and Folklore and Symbols* (New York: Scarecrow Press, 1962), 2:1126.

12     Audre Lorde, *The Black Unicorn* (New York: W. W. Norton, 1978), pp. 6–7.

13     Ibid., p. 88.

14     In *Our Dead Behind Us* (New York: Norton, 1986).

15     This comparison draws upon an earlier version of the poem which Lorde read in Eugene, Oregon, November 12, 1984.

16     Christian, *Black Feminist Criticism,* p. 82.

# Gale P. Jackson

# A Selected Bibliography of English-Language Works by Black Women of the Americas, 1970–1988

## Naming Ourselves: Bibliographer's Statement

The following is a selected listing. A portion. A beginning or a middle of the inventory of what is clearly a dynamic body of writing in English by Black women of the Americas. The citations here compiled are primarily humanities titles. Beyond that, I have attempted to bring together a representative sampling of what is a larger body of writing by Black women on this side of the world. Also listed are a number of documentary works by others which bring together Black women's works, Black women's words.

Bibliographic work, collecting and listing of materials for public access, continues to be hampered by issues of identification, cataloging, and the classification of Black women's writings. These difficulties are an obstacle, in addition to the struggles to write, to publish, to distribute, to access our necessary culture and thought. While progress has been made in the politics of gaining access to information on Black women, this progress has been absolutely contingent upon the growing strength of Black women's voices, collectively, in the world. That we produce a growing body of literature while we wage the cultural political battle to name ourselves creates the conditions for our visibility where visibility has been systematically denied us. This work stands in the spirit of that visibility and that naming. This work is created by virtue and in affirmation of the work which has gone before.

## Studies in History and Literature

Bell, Roseann Pope; Bettye J. Parker; and Beverly Sheftall, eds. *Sturdy Black Bridges: Visions of Black Women in Literature.* New York: Anchor Press, 1979.

Bethune, Mary Jane (McLeod). *Papers, 1923–1942.* New Orleans: Amistad Research Center, 1976.

Bowles, Juliet, ed. *In the Memory and Spirit of Frances, Zora and Lorraine: Essays and Interviews Relating to Black Women and Writing.* Washington, D.C.: Howard University Institute for the Arts and Humanities, 1975.

Braxton, Joanne M. *Black Women Writing Autobiography: A Tradition Within a Tradition.* Philadelphia: Temple University Press, 1989.

Brodber, Erna. *Perceptions of Caribbean Women: Towards a Documentation of Stereotypes.* Women in the Caribbean Project no. 4. Cave Hill, Barbados: UWI, ISER, 1982.

Christian, Barbara. *Black Feminist Criticism: Perspectives on Black Women Writers.* New York and Oxford: Pergamon, 1985.

———. *Black Women Novelists: The Development of a Tradition, 1892–1976.* Westport, Conn. and London: Greenwood Press, 1980.

Clark, Bori S., comp. *Trinidad Women Speak.* Redlands, Calif.: Libros Latinos, 1981.

Cole, Johnetta. *All American Women: Lines That Divide Ties That Bind.* New York: Free Press, 1985.

Collier-Thomas, Bettye. *Black Women in America: Contributors to Our Heritage.* Washington, D.C.: Bethune Museum Archives, 1983.

———. *Black Women: Organizing for Social Change 1800–1920.* Washington, D.C.: Bethune Museum Archives, 1984.

———. *National Council of Negro Women, 1935–1980.* Washington, D.C.: Bethune Museum Archives, 1981.

Evans, Mari, ed. *Black Women Writers (1950–1980): A Critical Evaluation.* New York: Anchor Press; London: Pluto, 1984.

Exum, Pat. *Contemporary Black Women Writers.* Deland, Fla.: Everett/Edwards, 1976.

Gabel, Leona C. *From Slavery to the Sorbonne and Beyond: The Life and Writings of Anna J. Cooper.* Northampton, Mass.: Smith College Publications, 1982.

Giddings, Paula. *In Search of Sisterhood: Delta Sigma Theta and the Challenge of the Black Sorority Movement.* New York: William Morrow, 1988.

———. *When and Where I Enter: The Impact of Black Women on Race and Sex in America.* New York: William Morrow, 1984.

Giovanni, Nikki, and James Baldwin. *A Dialogue: James Baldwin and Nikki Giovanni*. Philadelphia: Lippincott, 1973.

————, and Margaret Walker. *A Poetic Equation: Conversations between Nikki Giovanni and Margaret Walker*. Washington, D.C.: Howard University Press, 1974.

Hamilton, Jill. *Women of Barbados: Amerindian Era to Mid-20th Century*. Bridgetown, Barbados: The Author, 1981.

Harley, Sharon, and Rosalyn Terborg-Penn, eds. *Afro-American Women: Struggles and Images*. New York: Kennikat Press, 1978.

Hine, Darlene Clarke. *When the Truth Is Told: A History of Black Women's Culture and Community in Indiana, 1875–1958*. Indianapolis: National Council of Negro Women Indiana Section, 1981.

Hooks, Bell. *Ain't I a Woman?: Black Women and Feminism*. Boston: South End, 1981; London: Pluto, 1983.

————. *Feminist Theory from Margin to Center*. Boston: South End, 1984.

Hull, Gloria T. *Color, Sex, and Poetry: Three Women Writers of the Harlem Renaissance*. Bloomington: Indiana University Press, 1987.

————. *Give Us Each Day: The Diary of Alice Dunbar-Nelson*. New York: W. W. Norton, 1985.

Hull, Gloria et al., eds. *All the Women Are White All the Blacks Are Men but Some of Us Are Brave: Black Women's Studies*. New York: Feminist Press, 1981.

Jackson, Jaquelyne J. *Black Women: Their Problems and Power*. New York: Barrons, 1974.

Joseph, Gloria, and Jill Lewis. *The Blues Politics of Women's Liberation: Black and White Conflicts in Feminist Perspective*. N.p., n.d.

————. *Common Differences: Conflicts in Black and White Feminism*. New York: Anchor, 1981.

Kincaid, Jamaica. *A Small Place*. New York: Farrar, Straus & Giroux; London: Virago, 1988.

Lader, Joyce. *Tomorrow's Tomorrow: The Black Woman*. New York: Doubleday, 1971.

Lerner, Gerda, ed. *Black Women in White America: A Documentary History*. New York: Pantheon, 1972.

Mair, Lucille M. *Women in the World: The Challenge of the Nineties*. Pinelands, St. Michael: Women and Development Unit, University of the West Indies, April 1987.

Montas, Michelle. *Haiti*. New York: Two Continents Publishing Group, 1976.

Noble, Jeanne. *Beautiful Also Are the Souls of My Black Sisters: A History of the Black Women in America*. Englewood Cliffs, N.J.: Prentice-Hall, 1978.

Osei, G. K. *Caribbean Women: Their History and Habits*. New York: University Place Bookstore, 1979.

Pryse, Marjorie, and Hortense J. Spillers, eds. *Conjuring: Black Women, Fiction, and Literary Tradition*. Bloomington: Indiana University Press, 1985.

Reid, Inez Smith. *Together Black Women*. New York: Emerson, 1971.

Rodgers-Rose, La Frances, ed. *The Black Women*. Beverly Hills, Calif.: Sage, 1980.

Sanchez, Sonia. *Crisis in Culture: Two Speeches by Sonia Sanchez*. New York: Black Liberation Press, 1983.

Sims, Rudine. *Shadow and Substance: Afro-American Experience in Contemporary Children's Fiction*. Urbana, Ill.: National Council of Teachers of English, 1982.

Smith, Barbara. *Towards a Black Feminist Criticism*. New York: Out & Out Books, n.d.

Steady, Filomina Chioma. *The Black Woman Cross-Culturally*. Cambridge, Mass.: Schenkman, 1981.

Sterling, Dorthy, ed. *We Are Your Sisters: Black Women in the Nineteenth Century*. New York: W. W. Norton, 1985.

Tate, Claudia, ed. *Black Women Writers at Work*. New York: Continuum, 1983.

Wade-Gayles, Gloria. *No Crystal Stair: Visions of Race and Sex in Black Women's Fiction*. New York: Pilgram, 1984.

Walker, Margaret. *How I Wrote Jubilee*. Detroit: Broadside Press, 1971.

Watson, Carole M. *Prologue: The Novels of Black American Women 1891–1965*. Westport, Conn. and London: Greenwood Press, 1985.

Willis, Susan. *Specifying: Black Women Writing the American Experience*. Madison: University of Wisconsin Press, 1986.

Wynter, Sylvia. *Jamaica's National Heroes*. Kingston, Jamaica: Jamaica National Commission, 1971.

## Anthologies/Collections

Anzaldúa, Gloria, and Cherrie Moraga, eds. *This Bridge Called My Back: Writings by Radical Women of Color*. Latham, N.Y.: Kitchen Table Press, 1981, 1983.

Bambara, Toni, ed. *The Black Woman*. New York: New American Library, 1970.

Baraka, Amina, and Amiri Baraka, eds. *Confirmations: An Anthology of African-American Women*. New York: William Morrow, 1983.

Center for Black Students Portland State University, eds. *An Anthology of Black Women Poets of Oregon.* Portland, Ore.: Portland State University, 1980.

Cobham, Rhonda, and Merle Collins. *Watchers and Seekers: Creative Writing by Black Women in Britain.* London: The Women Press, 1987.

Dunbar-Nelson, Alice Moore. *The Works of Alice Dunbar-Nelson.* New York: Oxford University Press, 1988.

Exum, Pat, ed. *Keeping the Faith: Writings by Contemporary Black Women.* Greenwich, Conn.: Fawcett Publications, 1974.

Gaptooth Girlfriends, eds. *Gaptooth Girlfriends: An Anthology.* Brooklyn, N.Y.: Gaptooth Girlfriends Publications, 1981.

————. *Gaptooth Girlfriends: The Third Act.* New York: Third Act Press, 1985.

Giovanni, Nikki, ed. *Night Comes Softly: An Anthology of Black Female Voices.* Newark, N.J.: Medic Press, 1970.

Gomez, Alma; Cherrie Moraga; and Mariana Romo-Carmona, eds. *Cuentos: Stories by Latinas.* Latham, N.Y.: Kitchen Table Press, 1987.

Harper, Frances Ellen Watkins. *Complete Poems of Frances E. W. Harper.* New York: Oxford University Press, 1988.

Lotus Press, ed. *Blacksong Series I: Four Poetry Broadsides by Black Women.* Detroit: Lotus Press, 1977.

Randall, Margaret, ed. *Breaking the Silences: Twentieth-Century Poetry by Cuban Women.* Vancouver, B.C.: Pope Press, 1981.

Smith, Barbara, ed. *Home Girls: A Black Feminist Anthology.* Latham, N.Y.: Kitchen Table Press, 1983.

Stetson, Erlene, ed. *Black Sister: Poetry by Black American Women, 1746–1980.* Bloomington: Indiana University Press, 1981.

Walker, Alice, ed. *I Love Myself When I Am Laughing . . . and Then Again When I Am Looking Mean and Impressive: A Zora Neale Hurston Reader.* New York: Feminist Press, 1979.

Washington, Mary Helen, ed. *Black-Eyed Susans: Classic Stories by and about Black Women.* New York: Anchor/Doubleday, 1975.

————. *Invented Lives: Narratives of Black Women 1860–1960.* New York: Anchor Press, 1987; London: Virago, 1989.

————. *Midnight Birds: Stories of Contemporary Black Women Writers.* New York: Anchor/Doubleday, 1980.

Wheatley, Phillis. *The Collected Works of Phillis Wheatley.* New York: Oxford University Press, 1988.

Wilkerson, Margaret B., ed. *9 Plays by Black Women.* New York: Mentor, 1986.

## Poetry

Ai (Florence Ai Ogawa). *Cruelty.* Boston: Houghton Mifflin, 1973.

————. *Killing Floor.* Boston: Houghton Mifflin, 1979.

————. *Sin.* Boston: Houghton Mifflin, 1986.

Angelou, Maya. *And Still I Rise.* New York: Random House, 1978; London: Virago, 1986.

————. *Just Give Me a Cool Drink of Water 'fore I Diiie.* New York: Random House, 1971; London, Virago, 1988.

————. *Oh Pray My Wings Are Gonna Fit Me Well.* New York: Random House, 1975.

————. *Poems.* New York: Bantam, 1986.

————. *Shaker Why Don't You Sing.* New York: Random House, 1983.

Baraka, Amina, and Amiri Baraka. *The Music: Reflections on Jazz and Blues.* New York: William Morrow, 1987.

Bennett, Louise. *Anancy and Miss Lou.* Kingston, Jamaica: Sangster's Book Stores, 1979.

————. *Selected Poems.* Kingston, Jamaica: Sangster's Book Stores, 1982.

Bernadine. *Seeds of Ourselves.* New York: Women for Racial and Economic Equality, 1984.

Bogus, S. Diane. *Woman in the Moon.* San Francisco: Soap Box Publishing, 1977.

————. *I'm Off to See the Goddam Wizard Alright.* San Francisco: The Author, 1976.

Brand, Dionne. *Chronicles of the Hostile Sun.* Toronto: Williams-Wallace Int'l., 1984.

————. *Earth Magic.* Toronto: Kids Can Press, 1980.

————. *'Fore Day Morning.* Toronto: Khoisan Artists, 1978.

————. *Primitive Offensive.* Toronto: Williams-Wallace Int'l, 1982.

————. *Rivers Have Sources, Trees Have Roots.* Toronto: Cross-Cultural Communication Centre, 1986.

————. *Winter Epigrams.* Toronto: Williams-Wallace Int'l., 1983.

Braxton, Jodi. *Sometimes I Think of Maryland.* New York: Sunbury Press, 1977.

Brooks, Gwendolyn. *Aloneness.* Detroit: Broadside Press, 1971.

————. *Beckonings.* Detroit: Broadside Press, 1975.

————. *Family Pictures.* Detroit: Broadside Press, 1970.

————. *The Tiger Who Wore White Gloves, or, What You Really Are You Are.* Chicago: Third World Press, 1974.

————. *The World of Gwendolyn Brooks.* New York: Harper & Row, 1971.

Chase-Riboud, Barbara. *From Memphis and Peking: Poems.* New York: Random House, 1974.

———. *Portraits of a Nude Woman as Cleopatra.* New York: William Morrow, 1987.

Clarke, Cheryl. *Living as a Lesbian.* Ithaca, N.Y.: Firebrand, 1986.

———. *Narratives: Poems in the Tradition of Black Women.* Latham, N.Y.: Kitchen Table Press, 1982.

Clifton, Lucille. *Good News About the Earth: New Poems.* New York: Random House, 1972.

———. *Good Times.* New York: Random House, 1970.

———. *An Ordinary Woman.* New York: Random House, 1974.

———. *Two-Headed Woman.* Amherst, Mass.: University of Massachusetts Press, 1980.

Collins, Merle. *Because the Dawn Breaks! Poems Dedicated to the Grenadian People.* London: Karia Press, 1985.

Cortez, Jane. *Coagulations: New and Selected Poems.* New York: Thunder's Mouth Press, 1984; London: Pluto, 1986.

———. *Festivals and Funerals.* New York: Bola Press, 1971.

———. *Firespitter.* New York: Bola Press, 1982.

———. *Merveilleux Coup de Foudre: Poetry of Jayne Cortez and Ted Joans.* Paris: Handshake Editions, 1982.

———. *Mouth on Paper.* New York: Bola Press, 1977.

———. *Scarifications.* New York: Bola Press, 1973.

Das, Mahadai. *Bones.* Leeds, Yorkshire, U.K.: Peepal Tree Press, 1988.

Davis, Thulani. *All the Renegade Ghosts Rise.* Washington, D.C.: Anemone Press, n.d.

———. *Playing the Changes.* Middletown, Conn.: Wesleyan University Press, 1985.

Dee, Ruby. *My One Good Nerve.* Chicago: Third World Press, 1986.

Derricotte, Toi. *The Empress of the Death House.* Detroit: Lotus Press, 1978.

———. *Natural Birth: Poems.* Trumanburg, N.Y.: Crossing Press, 1983.

DeVeaux, Alexis. *Blue Heat: a Portfolio of Poems and Drawings.* New York: Diva Publishing Associates, 1985.

Dove, Rita. *Museum.* Pittsburgh: Carnegie-Mellon University Press, 1983.

———. *Thomas and Beulah.* Pittsburgh: Carnegie-Mellon University Press, 1986.

———. *The Yellow House on the Corner.* Pittsburgh: Carnegie-Mellon University Press, 1980.

Esteves, Sandra Maria. *Tropical Rains: A Bilingual Downpour.* New York: AfroCaribbean Poetry Theater, 1984.

Esteves, Sandra Maria. *Yerba Buena*. Southport, Conn.: Greenfield Review, 1980.

Giovanni, Nikki. *Black Feeling Black Talk Black Judgement*. New York: William Morrow, 1970.

———. *Cotton Candy on a Rainy Day*. New York: William Morrow, 1978.

———. *Ego Tripping and Other Poems for Young Readers*. New York: Lawrence Hill, 1973.

———. *My House: Poems*. New York: William Morrow, 1972.

———. *Poems for Angela Yvonne Davis*. Newark, N.J.: Nikton, 1970.

———. *ReCreation*. Detroit: Broadside Press, 1970.

———. *Spin a Soft Black Song*. New York: Hill and Wang, 1971.

———. *Those Who Ride the Night Winds*. New York: William Morrow, 1983.

———. *Vacation Times: Poems for Children*. New York: William Morrow, 1980.

———. *The Women and the Men*. New York: William Morrow, 1975.

Gomez, Jewel. *Flamingoes and Bears*. New Brunswick, N.J.: Grace Publications, 1986.

Goodison, Lorna. *Heartease*. London: New Beacon, 1988.

———. *I Am Becoming My Mother*. London: New Beacon, 1986.

Gossett, Hattie. *Presenting . . . Sister Noblues*. Ithaca, N.Y.: Firebrand Press, 1988.

Greenfield, Elouise. *Honey I Love You and Other Poems*. New York: Harper & Row, 1978.

Jackson, Angela. *The Greenville Club, in Four Black Poets*. St. Louis: BK MK, 1977.

———. *Solo in the Boxcar Third Floor E*. Chicago: Obahouse, 1986.

———. *Voo Doo/Love Magic*. Chicago: Third World Press, 1974.

Jones, Gayl. *The Hermit Woman*. Detroit: Lotus Press, 1983.

———. *Song for Anninho*. Detroit: Lotus Press, 1981.

———. *Xarque and Other Poems*. Detroit: Lotus Press, 1985.

Jones, Patricia. *Mythologizing Always: 7 Sonnets*. Guilford, Conn.: Telephone Books, 1981.

Jordan, June. *Living Room*. New York: Thunder's Mouth Press, 1985.

———. *New Days: Poems of Exile and Return*. New York: Emerson Hall, 1973.

———. *Passion: New Poems 1977–1980*. Boston: Beacon Press, 1981.

———. *Some Changes*. New York: E. P. Dutton, 1971.

———. *Things That I Do in the Dark: Selected Poems*. New York: Random House, 1977.

Kim, Willyce. *Eating Artichokes*. San Francisco: Women's Press Collective, 1972.

Lane, Pinkie Gordon. *I Never Scream: New and Selected Poems*. Detroit: Lotus Press, 1985.

———. *The Mystic Female.* Little Rock, Ark.: South & West, 1978.

———. *Wind Thoughts.* Little Rock, Ark.: South & West, 1972.

Loftin, Elouise (Hanna Ecrit). *Barefoot Necklace: Poems.* New York: Jafmina, 1975.

Lorde, Audre. *Between Ourselves.* San Francisco: Eidolon Editions, 1976.

———. *The Black Unicorn.* New York: W. W. Norton, 1978.

———. *Cables to Rage.* London: Breman, 1970.

———. *Chosen Poems: Old and New.* New York: W. W. Norton, 1982.

———. *Coal.* New York: W. W. Norton, 1978.

———. *From a Land Where Other People Live.* Detroit: Broadside Press, 1973.

———. *New York Head Shop and Museum.* Detroit: Broadside Press, 1974.

———. *Our Dead Behind Us.* New York: W. W. Norton, 1986; London: Sheba, 1987.

Madgett, Naomi Long. *Exits and Entrances.* Detroit: Lotus Press, 1978.

———. *Pink Ladies in the Afternoon.* Detroit: Lotus Press, 1972.

———. *Star by Star.* Detroit: Lotus Press, 1970.

Miller, May. *The Clearing and Beyond.* Washington, D.C.: Charioteer Press, 1974.

———. *Dust of an Uncertain Journey.* Detroit: Lotus Press, 1975.

———. *Halfway to the Sun.* Washington, D.C.: Writers Pub. House, 1980.

———. *Not That Far.* Washington, D.C.: Charioteer Press, 1973.

———. *The Ransomed Wait.* Detroit: Lotus Press, 1983.

Morejon, Nancy. *Where the Island Sleeps Like a Wing: Selected Poetry.* San Francisco: Black Scholar Press, 1985.

Nicholas, Grace. *The Far Black Woman's Poems.* London: Virago Poets, 1985.

Parker, Pat. *Child of Myself.* San Francisco: Diana Press, 1972.

———. *Jonestown and Other Madness: Poetry.* Ithaca, N.Y.: Firebrand, 1985.

———. *Movement in Black: The Collected Poetry of Pat Parker.* San Francisco: Diana Press, 1978.

———. *Pit Stop.* San Francisco: Diana Press, 1973.

———. *Womanslaughter.* San Francisco: Diana Press, 1978.

Parkerson, Michelle. *Waiting Rooms.* Washington, D.C.: Common Ground Press, 1983.

Penn, Verna. *The Essence of Life.* Tortola, BWI: Caribbean Printing, 1976.

Pollard, Velma. *Crown Point and Other Poems.* Leeds, Yorkshire, U.K.: Peepal Tree Press, 1988.

Richards, Novella. *Tropic Gems.* New York: Vantage Press, 1971.

Rodgers, Carolyn. *For Flip Wilson.* Detroit: Broadside Press, 1971.

———. *The Heart as Evergreen.* New York: Doubleday, 1978.

———. *How I Got Ovah.* New York: Doubleday, 1976.

———. *Now Ain't That Love.* Detroit: Broadside Press, 1970.

Sanchez, Sonia. *The Adventures of Fathead, Smallhead, and Squarehead.* Chicago: Third World Press, 1973.
———. *A Blue Book for a Magical Woman.* Detroit: Broadside Press, 1974.
———. *Homecoming.* Detroit: Broadside Press, 1970.
———. *Homegirls and Handgrenades.* New York: Thunder's Mouth Press, 1984.
———. *Ima Talkin Bout the Nation of Islam.* New York: TruthDel, 1972.
———. *It's a New Day: Poems for Young Brothas and Sistuhs.* Detroit: Broadside Press, 1971.
———. *I've Been a Woman.* San Francisco: Black Scholar Press, 1978.
———. *Love Poems.* Chicago: Third World Press, 1973.
———. *A Sound Investment.* Chicago: Third World Press, 1980.
———. *Under a Soprano Sky.* New Brunswick, N.J.: Africa World Press, 1987.
———. *We a BaddDDD People.* Detroit: Broadside Press, 1971.
Schwarz-Bart, Simone. *Between Two Worlds.* New York: Harper & Row, 1981.
Shange, Ntozake. *A Daughter's Geography.* New York: St. Martin's Press, 1983; London: Methuen, 1984.
———. *for colored girls who have considered suicide when the rainbow is enuf.* New York: Macmillan, 1975; London: Methuen, 1978.
———. *From Okra to Greens: Poems.* St. Paul, Minn.: Coffeehouse Press, 1984.
———. *Nappy Edges.* New York: St. Martin's Press, 1978; London: Methuen, 1987.
———. *Riding the Moon in Texas: Word Paintings.* New York: St. Martin's Press, 1987.
———. *Some Men.* N.p., n.d.
Simmons, Judy. *Indecent Intentions.* New York: Blind Beggar Press, 1984.
Thomas, Elean. *Word Rhythms from the Life of a Woman.* London: Karia Press, 1986.
Thomas, Joyce Carol. *Bittersweet.* Berkeley, Calif.: Firesign, 1973.
———. *Black Child.* New York: Zamani, 1981.
———. *Blessing.* Berkeley, Calif.: Jocato, 1975.
———. *Crystal Breezes.* Berkeley, Calif.: Firesign, 1974.
———. *Inside the Rainbow.* Palo Alto, Calif.: Zikawuna, 1982.
Turner, Sherile. *Jamaica Chat.* London: Akira Press, 1986.
Walker, Alice. *Five Poems.* Detroit: Broadside Press, 1972.
———. *Goodnight Willie Lee, I'll See You in the Morning.* New York: Dial, 1979; London: Women's Press, 1987.
———. *Horses Make a Landscape Look More Beautiful.* New York: Harcourt Brace Jovanovich, 1984; London: Women's Press, 1985.

————. *Revolutionary Petunias and Other Poems*. New York: Harcourt Brace Jovanovich, 1973; London: Women's Press, 1985.
Walker, Margaret. *October Journey*. Detroit: Broadside Press, 1973.
————. *Prophets for a New Day*. Detroit: Broadside Press, 1970.
Wallace, Susan. *Bahamian Scene*. Philadelphia: Dorrance and Company, 1975.
White, Paulette Childress. *Love Poem to a Black Junkie*. Detroit: Lotus Press, 1975.
————. *The Watermelon Dress: Portrait of a Woman*. Detroit: Lotus Press, 1984.
Williams, Sherley Anne. *One Sweet Angel Child*. New York: William Morrow, 1982.
————. *The Peacock Poems*. Middletown, Conn.: Wesleyan University Press, 1975.
Yvonne. *Iwilla-Scourge: Vol II*. New York: Chameleon, 1986.

## Drama

Carroll, Vinnette, and Micki Grant. *Don't Bother Me, I Can't Cope*. New York: Samuel French, 1972.
Childress, Alice. *Let's Hear It for the Queen*. New York: Coward McCann & Geoghegan, 1976.
————. *Mojo: A Black Love Story*. New York: Dramatist Play Service, 1971.
————. *String & Mojo: A Black Love Story*. New York: Dramatist Play Service, 1971.
————. *Wedding Band: A Love/Hate Story in Black and White*. New York: Samuel French, 1973.
————. *When the Rattlesnake Sounds*. New York: Coward McCann & Geoghegan, 1975.
————. *Wine in the Wilderness*. New York: Dramatist Play Service, 1973.
Franklin, J. E. *Black Girl*. New York: Dramatist Play Service, 1971.
Gibson, P. J. *Long Time Since Yesterday*. New York: Samuel French, 1984.
Hansberry, Lorraine. *Les Blancs: The Collected Last Plays*. Edited by Robert Nemiroff. New York: Random House, 1972.
Kennedy, Adrienne. *Cities in Bezique: Two One-Act Plays*. New York: Samuel French, 1970.
————. *Play: In His Own Write*. New York: Simon and Schuster, 1972.
King, Ramona. *Steal Away*. New York: Samuel French, 1981.
Lee, Leslie. *Between Now and Then*. New York: Samuel French, 1984.

Lee, Leslie. *Colored People's Time*. New York: Samuel French, 1983.
————. *The First Breeze of Summer*. New York: Samuel French, 1975.
Mason, Judi Ann. *Livin' Fat*. New York: Samuel French, 1974.
Molette, Barbara, and Carlton Molette. *Rosalee Pritchett*. New York: Dramatist Play Service, 1973.
Shange, Ntozake. *for colored girls who have considered suicide when the rainbow is enuf*. New York: Macmillan, 1977; London: Methuen, 1978.
————. *From Okra to Greens/a Different Kinda Love Story*. New York: Samuel French, 1983.
————. *A Photograph: Lovers in Motion*. New York: Samuel French, 1981.
————. *Spell #7*. New York: St. Martin's Press, 1981.
————. *Three Pieces*. New York: St. Martin's Press, 1981.

## Fiction

Adisa, Opal Palmer. *Bake-Face and Other Guava Stories*. Berkeley, Calif.: Kelsey Street Press, 1986.
Allfrey, Phyllis S. *The Orchid House*. Washington, D.C.: Three Continents Press, 1985.
Austin, Doris Jean. *After the Garden*. New York: NAL, 1987.
Bambara, Toni Cade. *Gorilla My Love*. New York: Random House, 1972; London: Women's Press, 1984.
————. *The Salt Eaters*. New York: Random House, 1980; London: Women's Press, 1982.
————. *The Sea Birds Are Still Alive*. New York: Random House, 1977; London: Women's Press, 1984.
Birtha, Becky. *For Nights Like This One: Stories of Love and Women*. San Francisco: Frog in the Well, 1983.
————. *Lover's Choice*. Seattle: Seal Press, 1987; London: Women's Press, 1988.
Brodber, Erna. *Jane and Louisa Will Soon Come Home*. London: New Beacon Press, 1980.
————. *Myal—a Novel*. London: New Beacon Press, 1988.
Brown, Linda Jean. *Jazz Dancin wif Mama*. New York: Iridian Press, 1982.
————. *KIWI*. New York: Iridian Press, 1977.
————. *Rainbow River*. New York: Iridian Press, 1980.
Buford, Barbara. *The Threshing Floor*. London: Sheba Feminist Publishers, 1986.
Butler, Octavia E. *Adulthood Rites*. New York: Warner Books; London: Gollancz, 1988.

———. *Clay's Ark.* New York: St. Martin's Press, 1984.

———. *Dawn.* New York: Warner Books; London: Gollancz, 1987.

———. *Kindred.* Garden City, N.Y.: Doubleday, 1979; London: Women's Press, 1988.

———. *Mind of My Mind.* Garden City, N.Y.: Doubleday, 1977.

———. *Patternmaster.* Garden City, N.Y.: Doubleday, 1976.

———. *Survivor.* Garden City, N.Y.: Doubleday, 1978.

———. *Wild Seed.* Garden City, N.Y.: Doubleday, 1980.

Cambridge, Joan. *Clarise Cumberbach Wants to Go Home.* New York: Ticknor & Fields, 1987.

Campbell, Hazel D. *The Rag Doll and Other Stories.* Mona, Jamaica, B.W.I.: Savacou Cooperative, 1978.

———. *Woman's Tongue.* Mona, Jamaica, B.W.I.: Savacou Publications, 1985.

Cancryn, Addelitu. *Man of Vision.* St. Thomas, V.I.: Val Hill Enterprises, 1975.

Chase-Riboud, Barbara. *Sally Hemings.* New York: Viking, 1979.

———. *Valide.* New York: William Morrow, 1986.

Childress, Alice. *A Hero Ain't Nothin but a Sandwich.* New York: Coward McCann & Geoghegan, 1973.

———. *Rainbow Jordan.* New York: Coward McCann & Geoghegan, 1981.

———. *A Short Walk.* New York: Coward McCann & Geoghegan, 1979.

Cliff, Michelle. *ABENG: A Novel.* Trumansberg, N.Y.: Crossing Press, 1984.

———. *Claiming an Identity They Taught Me to Despise.* Boston: Persephone, 1980.

———. *The Land of Look Behind.* Ithaca, N.Y.: Firebrand, 1985.

———. *No Telephone to Heaven.* New York: E. P. Dutton, 1987; London: Methuen, 1988.

Conde, Maryse. *Moi, Tituba, Sorciere, Noire de Salem/I, Tituba, Sorceress, Black Woman of Salem.* Paris: Mercure de France, 1986.

Cooper, California. *Homemade Love.* New York: St. Martin's Press, 1986.

———. *A Piece of Mind.* Navarro, Calif.: Wild Trees Press, 1984.

———. *Some Soul to Keep.* New York: St. Martin's Press, 1987.

DeVeaux, Alexis. *The Adventures of the Dred Sisters.* New York: The Author, n.d.

———. *Spirits in the Streets.* New York: Anchor/Doubleday, 1973.

Dove, Rita. *Fifth Sunday.* Charlottesville: University of Virginia Press, 1985.

Edgell, Zee. *Beka Lamb.* London: Heinemann, 1982.

Gilroy, Beryl. *Frangipani House.* London: Heinemann Caribbean Writers Series, 1986.

Golden, Marita. *Migrations of the Heart.* New York: Anchor, 1983.

———. *A Woman's Place.* New York: Doubleday, 1986; London: Methuen, 1988.

Guy, Rosa. *The Disappearance.* New York: Delacorte, 1979; London: Gollancz, 1980.

————. *Edith Jackson.* New York: Viking, 1978; London: Gollancz, 1979.

————. *The Friends.* New York: Holt, Rinehart & Winston, 1973; London: Gollancz, 1974.

————. *A Measure of Time.* New York: Holt, Rinehart & Winston, 1983; London: Virago, 1984.

————. *My Love, My Love, or, the Peasant Girl.* New York: Holt, Rinehart & Winston, 1985; London: Virago, 1987.

————. *New Guys Around the Block.* London: Gollancz, 1983.

————. *Paris, Pee Wee, and Big Dog.* New York: Delacorte; London: Gollancz, 1984.

————. *Ruby: A Novel.* New York: Viking, 1976; London: Gollancz, 1981.

Hamilton, Virginia. *Avilla Sun Down.* New York: Greenwillow, 1976.

————. *Dustland.* New York: Avon, 1981.

————. *The Gathering.* New York: Avon, 1981.

————. *Jahdu.* New York: Greenwillow, 1980.

————. *Junius Over Far.* New York: Harper & Row, 1985.

————. *Justice and Her Brothers.* New York: Avon, 1981.

————. *Little Love.* New York: Philomel Boones, 1984; London: Gollancz, 1985.

————. *MC Higgins the Great.* New York: Macmillan, 1974.

————. *The Magical Adventures of Pretty Pearl.* New York: Harper & Row, 1983.

————. *The People Could Fly: Afro-American Folktales.* New York: Alfred Knopf, 1985; London: Walker Books, 1986.

————. *Sweet Whispers Brother Rush.* New York: Philomel Boones, 1982; London: Walker Books, 1987.

————. *Time Ago Lost Tales of Jahdu.* New York: Macmillan, 1973.

————. *Willie Bea and the Time the Martians Landed.* New York: Greenwillow, 1983.

Hanson, Joyce. *The Gift Giver.* Boston: Houghton Mifflin, 1980.

————. *Homeboy.* Boston: Houghton Mifflin, 1982.

————. *Which Way Freedom.* New York: Walker, 1986.

————. *Yellowbird and Me.* New York: Ticknor & Fields, 1986.

Hodge, Merle. *Crick Crack, Monkey.* London: Heinemann, 1981.

Hunter, Kristin. *Boss Cat.* New York: Avon, 1981.

————. *God Bless the Child.* Washington, D.C.: Howard University Press, 1987.

————. *The Laketown Rebellion.* New York: Charles Scribners' Sons, 1978.

————. *The Landlord.* New York: Avon, 1977.

————. *Lou in the Limelight.* New York: Charles Scribners' Sons, 1981.

Jones, Gayl. *Corregidora.* New York: Bantam Books, 1975; London: Camden Press, 1988.

————. *Eva's Man.* New York: Random House, 1976.

————. *White Rat.* New York: Random House, 1977.

Jones, Marion Patrick. *J'Ouvert Morning.* Port of Spain, Trinidad: Columbus, 1976.

————. *Pan Beat.* Port of Spain, Trinidad: Columbus, 1973.

Kincaid, Jamaica. *Annie John.* New York: Farrar Straus & Giroux; London: Picador, 1985.

————. *At the Bottom of the River.* New York: Farrar Straus & Giroux, 1983; London: Picador, 1984.

Lee, Andrea. *Russian Journal.* New York: Random House, 1981.

————. *Sarah Phillips.* New York: Random House, 1984; London: Faber, 1986.

Lewis, Enid Kirton. *Voices of Earth: Ten Short Stories of Raw Life in Trinidad in the Forties.* Gasparillo, Trinidad: Rillsprint, 1972.

McMillian, Terry. *Mama.* Boston: Houghton Mifflin, 1987.

Marshall, Paule. *Praisesong for the Widow.* New York: Putnam; London: Virago, 1983.

————. *Reena and Other Stories.* New York: Feminist Press, 1983.

Mathis, Sharon Bell. *Listen for the Fig Tree.* New York: Viking, 1974.

————. *Teacup Full of Roses.* New York: Viking, 1972.

Meriwether, Louise. *Daddy Was a Numbers Runner.* Englewood Cliffs, N.J.: Prentice Hall, 1970.

Mohr, Nicholasa. *El Bronx Remembered.* New York: Harper & Row, 1975.

————. *Felita.* New York: Dial, 1977.

————. *Going Home.* New York: Dial, 1986.

————. *In Nueva York.* New York: Dial, 1977.

————. *Nilda.* New York: Harper & Row, 1973.

————. *Rituals of Survival: A Woman's Portfolio.* Houston, Tex.: Arte Publico Press, 1985.

Morrison, Toni. *Beloved.* New York: Alfred A. Knopf; London: Chatto, 1987.

————. *The Bluest Eye.* New York: Holt, Rinehart & Winston, 1970; London: Chatto, 1980.

————. *Song of Solomon.* New York: Alfred A. Knopf, 1977; London: Chatto, 1978.

————. *Sula.* New York: Alfred A. Knopf, 1974; London: Chatto, 1980.

————. *Tar Baby.* New York: Alfred A. Knopf; London: Chatto, 1981.

Naylor, Gloria. *Linden Hills.* New York: Ticknor & Fields, 1985; London: Methuen, 1986.

Naylor, Gloria. *Mama Day.* New York: Ticknor & Fields; London: Hutchinson, 1988.

———. *The Women of Brewster Place.* New York: Viking, 1982; London: Methuen, 1987.

Nicholas, Grace. *Whole of a Morning Sky.* London: Virago Poets, 1986.

Nuñez-Harrell, Elizabeth. *When Rocks Dance.* New York: G. P. Putnam's Sons, 1986.

Petry, Ann. *Miss Muriel and Other Stories.* Boston: Houghton Mifflin, 1971.

Riley, Joan. *The Unbelonging.* London: The Women's Press.

———. *Waiting in the Twilight.* London: The Women's Press, 1986.

Senior, Olive. *A Summer Lightning and Other Stories.* London: Longman Caribbean Writers, 1986.

Shange, Ntozake. *Betsey Brown: A Novel.* New York: St. Martin's Press; London: Methuen, 1985.

———. *Sassafrass, Cypress, and Indigo.* New York: St. Martin's Press, 1982; London: Methuen, 1984.

Shinebourne, Janice. *The Last English Plantation.* Leeds, Yorkshire, U.K.: Peepal Tree Press, 1988.

———. *Timepiece.* Leeds, Yorkshire, U.K.: Peepal Tree Press, 1986.

Shockley, Ann Allen. *The Black and White of It.* Tallahassee, Fla.: Naiad Press, 1980.

———. *Loving Her.* New York: Bobbs-Merrill, 1974.

———. *Say Jesus and Come to Me.* New York: Avon, 1982.

Southerland, Ellease. *Let the Lion Eat Straw.* New York: Charles Scribners' Sons, 1979; London: Dent, 1980.

———. *The Magic Sun Spins.* London: Paul Breman, 1975.

Taylor, Mildred. *The Friendship.* New York: Dial, 1987.

———. *Gold Cadillac.* New York: Dial, 1987.

———. *Let the Circle Be Unbroken.* New York: Bantam Publishing Group, 1981; London: Gollancz, 1982.

———. *Roll of Thunder Hear My Cry.* New York: Bantam Publishing Group, 1976; London: Gollancz, 1977.

———. *Song of the Trees.* New York: Dial, 1975.

Tennant, Emma Blake. *Marina.* London: Taber, 1985.

Thomas, Joyce Carol. *Bright Shadow.* New York: Avon, 1983.

———. *Journey.* New York: Scholastic, 1988.

———. *Marked by Fire.* New York: Avon, 1982.

Umpierre, Luz Maria. *En el Pais de las Maravillas.* Bloomington, Ind.: Third Woman Press, 1982.

———. *The Margarit.* Bloomington, Ind.: Third Woman Press, 1987.

———. *Y Otras Desgracias/and Other Misfortunes.* Bloomington, Ind.: Third Woman Press, 1985.

Walker, Alice. *The Color Purple.* New York: Harcourt Brace Jovanovich, 1982; London: Women's Press, 1983.

———. *In Love & Trouble: Stories of Black Women.* New York: Harcourt Brace Jovanovich, 1973; London: Women's Press, 1982.

———. *Meridian.* New York: Harcourt Brace Jovanovich, 1976; London: Women's Press, 1982.

———. *The Third Life of Grange Copeland.* New York: Harcourt Brace Jovanovich, 1970.

———. *You Can't Keep a Good Woman Down.* New York: Harcourt Brace Jovanovich, 1981; London: Women's Press, 1982.

Walker, Mildred Pitts. *Because We Are.* New York: Lothrop Lee & Shepard, 1983.

———. *Brother to the Wind.* New York: Lothrop Lee & Shepard, 1985.

Warner-Vieyra, Myriam. *As the Sorcerer Said.* London: Longman, 1982.

———. *Juletane.* Paris: Presence Africaine, 1982.

Williams, Sherley Anne. *Dessa Rose.* New York: William Morrow, 1986; London: Macmillan, 1987.

Wilson-Cartier, Xam. *Bebop Rebop.* New York: Ballantine Books, 1987.

# Essays

Davis, Angela. *Violence Against Women and the Ongoing Challenge to Racism.* Latham, N.Y.: Kitchen Table Press, 1987.

———. *Women, Race, and Class.* New York: Random House; London: Women's Press, 1982.

Giovanni, Nikki. *Sacred Cows and Other Edibles.* New York: William Morrow, 1988.

Jordan, June. *Civil Wars.* Boston: Beacon Press, 1981.

———. *On Call: Political Essays.* Boston: South End, 1985.

Lorde, Audre. *A Burst of Light.* Ithaca, N.Y.: Firebrand; London: Sheba, 1988.

———. *The Cancer Journals.* San Francisco, Calif.: Spinster Aunt Lute, 1980; London: Sheba, 1985.

———. *Sister Outsider: Essays and Speeches.* Trumansberg, N.Y.: Crossing Press, 1984.

———. *Uses of the Erotic: The Erotic as Power.* New York: Out and Out, 1978.

Omolade, Barbara. *It's a Family Affair: The Real Lives of Black Single Mothers.* Latham, N.Y.: Kitchen Table Press, 1987.

Shange, Ntozake. *See No Evil: Prefaces, Essays, and Accounts.* San Francisco: Momo's Press, 1984.

Walker, Alice. *In Search of Our Mothers' Gardens: Womanist Prose.* New York: Harcourt Brace Jovanovich, 1983; London: Women's Press, 1984.

Wallace, Michele. *Black Macho and the Myth of the Superwoman.* New York: Dial; London: John Calder, 1979.

## Biography/Autobiography/Memoir

Andrews, William L., ed. *Sisters of the Spirit: Three Black Women's Autobiographies of the Nineteenth Century.* Bloomington: Indiana University Press, 1986.

Angelou, Maya. *All God's Children Need Traveling Shoes.* New York: Random House, 1986; London: Virago, 1987.

———. *Gather Together in My Name.* New York: Random House, 1974; London: Virago, 1985.

———. *Heart of a Woman.* New York: Random House, 1981; London: Virago, 1986.

———. *I Know Why the Caged Bird Sings.* New York: Random House, 1970; London: Virago, 1984.

———. *Singin' and Swingin' and Gettin' Merry Like Christmas.* New York: Random House, 1976; London: Virago, 1985.

Ashbaugh, Carolyn. *Lucy Parsons: American Revolutionary.* Chicago: Kerr, 1976.

Bailey, Pearl. *Talking to Myself.* New York: Harcourt Brace Jovanovich, 1971.

Baker, Josephine, and Jo Bouillon. *Josephine.* New York: Harper & Row, 1977.

Beckles, Frances N. *20 Black Women: A Profile of Contemporary Black Maryland Women.* Baltimore: Gateway Press, 1978.

Brooks, Gwendolyn. *Report from Part One.* Detroit: Broadside Press, 1972.

Chisholm, Shirley. *The Good Fight.* New York: Harper & Row, 1973.

———. *Unbought and Unbossed.* Boston: Houghton Mifflin, 1970.

Clark, Septima. *Ready from Within: Septima Clark and the Civil Rights Movement.* Navarro, Calif.: Wild Trees Press, 1986.

Clifton, Lucille. *Generations.* New York: Random House, 1970.

Cornwell, Anita. *Black Lesbian in White America.* Tallahassee, Fla.: Naiad Press, 1983.

Darden, Norma Jean, and Carole Darden. *Spoonbread and Strawberry Wine: Recipes and Reminiscences of a Family.* New York: Fawcett Book Group, 1980.

Davis, Angela. *Angela Davis: An Autobiography.* New York: Random House, 1974.

DeVeaux, Alexis. *Don't Explain: A Song of Billie Holiday.* New York: Harper & Row, 1980.

Dunnigan, Alice. *A Black Woman's Experience from Schoolhouse to White House.* Philadelphia, 1974.

Giovanni, Nikki. *Gemini: An Extended Autobiographical Statement.* New York: Bobbs-Merrill, 1971.

Golden Marita. *Migrations of the Heart: A Personal Odyssey.* New York: Anchor Press, 1983.

Green, Mildred Denby. *Black Women Composers: A Genesis.* Boston: Twayne Publishers, 1983.

Guffy, Ossie. *The Autobiography of a Black Woman.* New York: Bantam Books, 1972.

Humez, Jean M., ed. *Gifts of Power: The Writings of Rebecca Jackson, Black Visionary, Shaker Eldress.* Amherst, Mass.: University of Massachusetts Press, 1981.

Hunt, Annie Mae. *I Am Annie Mae: An Extraordinary Woman in Her Own Words: The Personal Story of a Black Texas Woman.* Austin, Tex.: Rosegarden Press, 1983.

Kennedy, Adrienne. *People Who Led to My Plays.* New York: Alfred A. Knopf, 1987.

Kitt, Eartha. *Alone with Me.* Chicago: Henry Regnery Co., 1976.

Lawson, Ellen McKenzie, and Marlene D. Merrill, comps. *The Three Sarahs: Documents of Antebellum Black College Women.* New York: Mellen & Co., 1984.

Loewenberg, B., and Ruth Bogin, eds. *Black Women in Nineteenth-Century American Life: Their Words, Their Thoughts, Their Feelings.* University Park: Pennsylvania State University Press, 1976.

Lorde, Audre. *Zami: A New Spelling of My Name.* Trumansberg, N.Y.: Crossing Press, 1982; London: Sheba, 1984.

Marteena, Constance. *The Lengthening Shadow of a Woman: A Biography of Charlotte Hawkins Brown.* New York: Exposition Press, 1977.

Mebane, Mary. *Mary.* New York: Fawcett, 1982.

———. *Mary, Wayfarer.* New York: Viking, 1983.

Moutoussamy-Ashe, Jeanne. *Viewfinders: Black Women Photographers 1839–1985.* New York: Dodd, Mead, 1986.

Murray, Pauli. *Song in a Weary Throat: An American Pilgrimage.* New York: Harper & Row, 1982.

Ortiz, Victoria. *Sojourner Truth: A Self-Made Woman.* New York: Lippincott, 1974.

Robinson, Jo Ann. *The Montgomery Bus Boycott and the Women Who Started It: The Memoir of Jo Ann Gibson Robinson.* Knoxville: University of Tennessee Press, 1987.

Shakur, Assata. *Assata: An Autobiography.* Westport, Conn.: Lawrence Hill, 1987.

Simonsen, Thordis, ed. *You May Plow Here: The Narrative of Sara Brooks.* New York: W. W. Norton, 1986.

Sistren, with Honor Ford-Smith, ed. *Lionheart Gal: Life Stories of Jamaican Women.* London: The Women's Press, 1986.

Sterling, Dorthy. *Black Foremothers: Three Lives.* New York: Feminist Press, 1979.

Waters, Ethel. *To Me It's Wonderful.* New York: Harper & Row, 1972.

Wilson, Emily. *Hope and Dignity: Older Black Women of the South.* Philadelphia: Temple University Press, 1983.

# Notes on Contributors

*Joanne M. Braxton* is Frances L. and Edwin L. Cummings Professor of American Studies and English at the College of William and Mary. She is the author of many articles, a collection of poetry, *Sometimes I Think of Maryland* (1977), and *Black Women Writing Autobiography: A Tradition Within a Tradition* (1989).

*Rudolph P. Byrd* is Assistant Professor of English and Director of the Program of African/African-American Studies at Carleton College. His essays appear in various literary journals, and he is currently at work on a collection of essays on contemporary African-American women writers.

*Zala Chandler* is Professor of Humanities at Medgar Evers College of the City University of New York where she teaches English and Women's Studies. Her recent articles on women in struggle in Central America and the Caribbean are outgrowths of her work with MADRE, an organization whose board she co-chairs. An exhibition graphic artist, she is presently writing a novel.

*Chinosole,* a founding member of Black Studies and first Acting Dean of the School of Third World/Ethnic Studies at San Francisco State University, is currently Coordinator of Women Studies at SFSU. With a grant from Spelman College, she is preparing a book, *Skeins of Self and Skin in Autobiographical Writing of the African Diaspora,* for the University of California Press.

*Barbara Christian* is author of *Black Women Novelists: The Development of a Tradition* (1980) and *Black Feminist Criticism: Perspectives on Black Women Writers* (1985). Her recent essays on African-American literature include "The Race for Theory" and an extensive Monarch Note on Alice Walker. She is Professor of Afro-American Studies and chair of the Ethnic Studies doctoral program at the University of California at Berkeley.

*David Ames Curtis* is an American community and labor activist (with Carolina Action/ACORN and Yale's feminist clerical worker's union, Local 34, respectively) as well as a writer, translator, and editor, currently living in Paris. He is translator and editor of two volumes of Cornelius Castoriadis's *Political and Social Writings* (1988). A third volume of these translated writings as well as *The Collected Works of John Jea* (the first published black male poet), co-edited with Henry Louis Gates, Jr., and David Dabydeen, are forthcoming.

*Angela Y. Davis* lives in California where she teaches philosophy, aesthetics, and Women's Studies at San Francisco State University and the San Francisco Art Institute. She is author of four books, *If They Come in the Morning: Voices of Resistance; Angela Y. Davis: An Autobiography; Women, Race & Class;* and *Women, Culture & Politics.*

*Robert J. Fehrenbach* is Professor of English at the College of William and Mary. He is editor of James Shirley's *The Politician* for the Garland Renaissance Series (1980) and compiler, with L. A. Boone and M. A. Di Cesare, of *A Concordance to the Plays, Poems, and Translations of Christopher Marlowe* (1982), one of the Cornell Concordances. He is General Editor of *Private Libraries in Renaissance England,* a series published by *Medieval and Renaissance Texts and Studies.*

*Joanne V. Gabbin* is Associate Professor of English and director of the Honors Program at James Madison University in Harrisonburg, Virginia. She is author of *Sterling A. Brown: Building the Black Aesthetic Tradition* (1985).

*Henry Louis Gates, Jr.* is John Spencer Bassett Professor of English and Literature at Duke University. He is the author of *Figures in Black: Words, Signs, and the Racial Self* (Oxford, 1987), the editor of *The Slave's Narrative* and *In the House of Osubgo: Critical Essays on Wole Soyinka* (both by Oxford), the General Editor of the *Norton Anthology of Afro-American Literature,* and editor of Oxford's thirty-volume series The Schomburg Library of Nineteenth-Century Black Women Writers.

*Daphne Duval Harrison* is chairperson and Professor of African American Studies at the University of Maryland Baltimore County. She is author of *Black Pearls: Blues Queens of the 1920s* (Rutgers, 1988) and is currently completing a monograph on the aesthetics of blues women's lyrics and performances.

*Calvin Hernton* is author of eight books, including *Sex and Racism in America,* which has been in print for twenty years and translated into six languages. Poet, novelist, essayist, social scientist, and, for over fifteen years, a professor at Oberlin College, he teaches Black and African literature and creative writing. He is Technical Consultant for the ABC Television Series, "A Man Called Hawk," and his most recent book is *The Sexual Mountain and Black Women Writers: Adventures in Sex, Literature, and Real Life.*

*Gale P. Jackson* is a poet, writer, and a librarian at Medgar Evers College of the City University of New York. She is co-author of *We Stand Our Ground: Three Women Their Vision Their Poems* (1988) and is currently working on her novel of short stories, *The Precision of the Embrace.* She lives and works in Brooklyn, New York.

*June Jordan,* poet, is author of eighteen books of poetry, political essays, and fiction, to date. Her most current book publications are *Lyrical Campaigns* and *Moving Towards Home* (both Virago, 1989). She is a regular political columnist for *The Progressive* magazine, and Professor of English at the State University of New York (SUNY) at Stony Brook. Currently devoted to the theater, she is author of *All These Blessings,* her most recent drama.

*Gloria I. Joseph,* social scientist and essayist, is co-author with Jill Lewis of *Common Differences: Conflicts in Black and White Feminist Perspectives,* which has inspired many U.S. academic women's conferences so named. Professor of Social Science at Hampshire College for the last twelve years, she is now fully devoted to independent studies on Malcolm X and Sojourner Truth, and pioneering work on twentieth-century Black feminists. Her current research on South African women's self-help groups is an outgrowth of her work with Sisterhood in Support of Sisters in South Africa (SISA), an organization of which she is founder.

*Régine Altagrâce Latortue* is Associate Professor of comparative literature and chair of the Africana Studies Department at Brooklyn College. She is co-author, with Gleason Rex Adams, of *Les Cenelles: A Collection of Poems by Creole Writers of the Early Nineteenth Century*

(1979) and is currently at work on a cross-cultural study of African, African-American, and Caribbean novelists.

*Vashti Crutcher Lewis* is Assistant Director of The Center for Black Studies and Assistant Professor of English at Northern Illinois University. Her manuscripts on the use of the near-white female in novels by Black women appear in leading literary journals, and she is presently completing *Worldview in the Fiction of Pauline Hopkins: A Monograph.*

*Audre Lorde,* poet, is Thomas Hunter Professor of English at Hunter College of the City University of New York. The author of thirteen books, she is the recipient of the American Library Association Gay Caucus Book Award for her first book of prose, *The Cancer Journals,* and a National Book Award nomination (1975) for her third book of poetry. She is a founding mother of Kitchen Table: Women of Color Press and of Sisterhood in Support of Sisters in South Africa (SISA), and serves on the Advisory Board of *The Black Scholar.* An international reader and lecturer, she is currently on leave of absence completing a novel.

*Nellie Y. McKay,* Professor of American and Afro-American Literature at the University of Wisconsin at Madison, is the author of *Jean Toomer, Artist: A Study of His Literary Life and Work* (1984) and the editor of *Critical Essays on Toni Morrison* (1988). She serves on the editorial boards of many journals and is active in the Modern Language Association and the American Studies Association.

*Andrée Nicola McLaughlin* is Professor of Humanities at Medgar Evers College of the City University of New York and, currently, Jane Watson Irwin Professor of Women's Studies at Hamilton College. She chairs the editorial board of *NETWORK: A Pan-African Women's Forum,* an international scholarly journal published in Harare, Zimbabwe, and coordinates the International Cross-Cultural Black Women's Studies Summer Institute headquartered in London and New York. She is also author of *Through the Barrel of Her Consciousness: Contemporary Black Women's Literature and Activism in*

*Cross-Cultural Perspective* and a forthcoming collection of selected poems entitled *Double Dutch!*

**Barbara Omolade** is senior counselor and instructor at the City College Center for Worker Education of the City University of New York, and coordinates faculty development seminars on curriculum balancing. She is author of *It's A Family Affair: Black Single Mothers* (1987) and is currently at work on a study of the sex-gender system in the Black community.

**Barbara Smith** is a Black feminist writer, activist, and co-founder of Kitchen Table Press. She is editor and co-editor of three major collections of writing by Black women: *Conditions: Five, The Black Women's Issue* (1979); *All the Women Are White, All the Blacks Are Men, But Some of Us Are Brave: Black Women's Studies* (1982); and *Home Girls: A Black Feminist Anthology* (1983). She is also co-author, with Elly Bulkin and Minnie Bruce Pratt, of *Yours in Struggle: Three Feminist Perspectives on Anti-Semitism and Racism* (1984), and is currently completing a collection of her own short stories.

**Billie Jean Young** teaches speech and drama part-time at Jackson State University and is director of the Southern Rural Women's Network. Between teaching, she performs her one-woman show, *Fannie Lou Hamer: This Little Light . . .* for audiences around the country. She is author of *The Child of Too* (1982) and is currently editing a second book of poems. In her spare time, she regularly speaks to high school and university audiences.

# Index